THE ENCYCLOPEDIA OF UNSOLVED MYSTERIES

THE
ENCYCLOPEDIA
OF
UNSOLVED
MYSTERIES

COLIN WILSON

WITH DAMON WILSON

CB
CONTEMPORARY
BOOKS
CHICAGO · NEW YORK

Library of Congress Cataloging-in-Publication Data

Wilson, Colin, 1931–
    The encyclopedia of unsolved mysteries / Colin Wilson with Damon
Wilson.
       p.   cm.
    Reprint. Originally published: London : Harrap, 1987.
    Includes index.
    ISBN 0-8092-4524-8 : $15.95
    1. Curiosities and wonders.   I. Wilson, Damon.   II. Title.
[AG243.W53   1988]
032′.02—dc19
                                                88-17700
                                                     CIP

Published by Contemporary Books, Inc.
180 North Michigan Avenue, Chicago, Illinois 60601
Manufactured in the United States of America
Library of Congress Catalog Card Number: 88-17700
International Standard Book Number: 0-8092-4524-8

Published simultaneously in Canada by Beaverbooks, Ltd.
195 Allstate Parkway, Valleywood Business Park
Markham, Ontario L3R 4T8 Canada

Illustrations

Acknowledgments

The idea of this book originated with my friend John Kennedy Melling, who is also the author of the articles on Dillinger and the Mona Lisa. I also owe thanks to the late F. W. Holiday, whose final book *The Goblin Universe* (recently published by Llewelyn Publications in America) provided many stimulating ideas. The book is also heavily indebted to Eddie Campbell, Ian Wilson, Henry Lincoln and John Michell, while I would have been unable to complete it without the aid of the Society for Psychical Research and its librarian Nick Clark-Lowes, the College of Psychic Studies, and the London Library. No attempt has been made to distinguish my own articles from those of my son Damon, but our general principle was that he should deal with 'historical mysteries' – like the Money Pit or the Tunguska explosion – while I should concentrate on subjects with some bearing on the paranormal: synchronicity, time-slips, etc.

CW
Cornwall 1986

Contents

1 Introduction

In 1957 the science writer Jacques Bergier made a broadcast on French television that caused a sensation. He was discussing one of the great unsolved mysteries of prehistory, the sudden disappearance of the dinosaurs about sixty-five million years ago. He suggested that the dinosaurs had been wiped out by the explosion of a star fairly close to our solar system – a 'supernova'. He then went on to make the even more startling suggestion that the explosion may have been deliberately caused by superbeings who *wanted* to wipe out the dinosaurs and to give intelligent mammals a chance.

Even the first part of his theory was dismissed by scientists as the fantasy of a crank, and the reaction was no better when in 1970 Bergier repeated it in a book called *Extra-Terrestrials in History*, which began with a chapter called 'The Star that Killed the Dinosaurs'. But five years later an American geologist named Walter Alvarez was studying a thin layer of clay on a hillside in Italy – the clay that divides the age of the dinosaurs (Mesozoic) from our own age of mammals – and brooding on this question of what had wiped out whole classes of animal. He took a chunk from the hillside back to California, and showed it to his father, the physicist Luis Alvarez, with the comment: 'Dad, that half-inch layer of clay represents the period when the dinosaurs went out and about 75 per cent of the other creatures on the earth.' His father was so intrigued that he subjected the clay to laboratory tests, and found it contained a high proportion of a rare element called iridium, a heavy element that usually sinks to the middle of planets, but which is thrown out by explosions. Alvarez also gave serious consideration to the idea of an exploding star, and only dismissed it when further tests showed an absence of a certain radioactive platinum that would also be present in a supernova explosion. The only other alternative was that the earth had been struck by a giant meteorite, which had filled the atmosphere with steam and produced a 'greenhouse effect' that had raised the temperature by several degrees. Modern crocodiles and alligators can survive a temperature of about 100°C; but two or three degrees higher is too much for them, and they die. This is almost certainly what happened to the dinosaurs, about sixty-five million years ago. And that is why this present book contains no entry headed: 'What became of the dinosaurs?' We know the answer. And we also know that Bergier's 'lunatic fringe' theory was remarkably close to the truth.

This is the basic justification for a volume like this. It underlines the point that it is always dangerous to draw a sharp, clear line between 'lunacy' and orthodox science. In the article on spontaneous human combustion, I have quoted a modern medical textbook which states that spontaneous combustion is impossible, and that there is no point in discussing it. But the evidence is now overwhelming that spontaneous combustion not only occurs, but occurs fairly frequently. In 1768 the French Academy of Sciences asked the great chemist Lavoisier to investigate a report of a huge stone that had hurtled from the sky and buried itself in the earth not far from where some peasants were working. Lavoisier was absolutely certain that great stones do not fall from the sky, and reported that the witnesses were either mistaken or lying; it was another half-century before the existence of meteorites was accepted by science.

The 'poltergeist', or noisy ghost, is even more commonplace than spontaneous human combustion; at any given moment there are hundreds of cases going on all over the world. Yet in America scientists have formed a kind of defensive league called CSICOP (Committee for the Scientific Investigation of Claims of the Paranormal) whose basic aim is to argue that the 'paranormal' simply does not exist, and is an invention of cranks and 'pseudos'. Anyone who has taken even the most superficial interest in the paranormal knows that such a view is not merely untenable, but that it represents a kind of wilful blindness.

Let us be quite clear about this. I am not arguing that scepticism is fundamentally harmful. Reason is the highest faculty possessed by human beings, and every moment of our lives demands a continuous assessment of probabilities. Our lives depend upon this assessment every time we cross a busy street – I have to judge the likelihood of that car or bus reaching me before I can step onto the opposite pavement. And when a scientist is confronted by the question of whether, let us say, an Israeli 'psychic' can bend keys by merely stroking them, he can only appeal to his general experience of keys and try to assess the probabilities. Yet I think every scientist would agree that it would be wrong to make an *a priori* judgment and decide that the question is not worth investigating because keys cannot be bent by merely stroking them. If he is honest, then he must at least be willing to be prepared to study the matter more closely.

Most scientists would reply that this is precisely how they operate, and *in principle* this is perfectly true. In fact, they are human beings, and are subject to boredom, impatience and touchiness like the rest of us, which means that they can easily drift over the borderline that separates scientific detachment from emotional commitment.

One of CSICOP's less dogmatic members is the mathematician Martin Gardner, whose book *Fads and Fallacies in the Name of Science* is an amusing and delightful study in 'cults of unreason'. We can read of the prophet Voliva, who believed that the earth is flat, of Captain Symmes, who believed it is hollow, of Cyrus Teed, who believed it is shaped like an egg and that we are living on its inner surface. He is wickedly amusing on the Jehovah's Witnesses and the cranks who believe that the Great Pyramid contains information about the second coming of Christ. But after half a dozen chapters the reader begins to find this attitude of constant superiority rather cloying. Is the author some kind of super-intellect who has discovered the secret of eternal truth? Is he *quite* sure that dowsing for water is a laughable superstition, that everyone who has seen a UFO is deluded or mistaken, that the continent of Atlantis was a figment of Plato's imagination, that Wilhelm Reich's later ideas were pure lunacy? It is surely a question of where one decides to draw the line. I am inclined to agree that Immanuel Velikovsky was, in the last analysis, a crank – that is, that his theories about the connection between Venus and Biblical catastrophes are the result of inspiration rather than careful scientific reasoning. But many of his inspired guesses were amazingly accurate – for example, his belief that earth is surrounded by powerful magnetic fields. And there are influential philosophers of science like Sir Karl Popper, Michael Polanyi and Abraham Maslow who believe that all scientific thinking is based on 'inspiration' rather than on careful scientific reasoning. In short – Gardner seems to me to be drawing his line in the wrong place.

I have written a biography of Wilhelm Reich, and I agree that Reich was dogmatic and paranoid, as well as being a thoroughly disagreeable character. But then, the trouble with Reich was that he had, like so many other psychoanalysts, borrowed from Freud a mantle of papal infallibility. All neurosis is sexual in origin, and a neurotic person is incapable of facing up to the sexual nature of his problems. You disagree? It only proves that you have sexual problems that you are afraid to acknowledge . . . . In this respect Reich is like Dr Johnson; if his pistol misfires he will knock you down with the butt. Anyone who disagrees with him must be 'mentally sick'. But Gardner's own book is full of this same tone of brutal dogmatism. There is an underlying assumption that he is infallible. And while the reader is willing to entertain this as a possibility, he would like to know more of the methods by which Gardner arrives at his unshakeable certainties.

In fact, it would be disastrous if Gardner's attitude became widely accepted as part of the 'conventional wisdom'. The progress of human knowledge depends on maintaining that touch of scepticism even about the most 'unquestionable' truths. A century ago, Darwin's theory of evolution by natural selection was regarded as scientifically unshakeable; today, most biologists have their reservations about it. Fifty years ago, Freud's sexual theory of neurosis was accepted by most psychiatrists; today, it is widely recognized that his methods were highly questionable. At the turn of this century, a scientist who questioned Newton's theory of gravity would have been regarded as insane; twenty years later, it had been supplanted by Einstein's theory although, significantly, few people actually understood this. It seems perfectly conceivable that our descendants of the twenty-first century will wonder how any of us could have been stupid enough to be taken in by Darwin, Freud or Einstein.

Gardner devotes a chapter to attacking the ideas of Charles Fort, the New Yorker who spent his life insisting that scientists are too dogmatic, and ought to be more willing to question their basic assumptions. He objects that, since Fort is merely a destructive critic, with no theories of his own to offer, he is basically barren. There is an element of truth in this. But Gardner fails to grasp that what Fort is really objecting to is the rigid, commissar-like attitude that characterizes his own book. Fort is arguing that scientific discovery has its roots in a sense of wonder, and that a sense of wonder – even with a touch of gullibility – is preferable to a kind of humourless Marxian dogmatism. Newton himself was fascinated by alchemy, and regarded his greatest work as his commentary on the Book of Samuel. Does this qualify Newton as a crank? Obviously not. The inference is surely that it is more fruitful to be intrigued by the possibility of some prehistoric monster in the depths of Loch Ness than to dismiss it as a childish absurdity. It is more fruitful to concede that UFOs may be real than to dismiss them as hallucinations. It may even be more fruitful to admit that the evidence suggests that Shakespeare may not have written his own plays, or that Andrew Crosse created life in his laboratory, or that Orffyreus may have discovered the secret of perpetual motion, than to take the attitude that such extravagances are not even worth discussing.

The truth is that the expansion of human knowledge depends on asking questions. A cow learns nothing because it cannot ask questions; the cow's world is exactly what it looks like, nothing more and nothing less, and there is nothing to ask questions about. But when Thales saw an eclipse he wanted to know what caused it. Newton asked the apparently absurd question: why does an apple fall to the ground instead of staying where it is? And Einstein asked the ultimately absurd question: what would it be like to sit astride a beam of light? All these questions led to fruitful results. If Mr Gardner had been standing behind them with folded arms, they would probably have decided to keep quiet.

Consider a question raised by the zoologist Ivan Sanderson. On a moonlit night, on a dust-covered road in Haiti, he and his wife both experienced a curious hallucination of being back in Paris in the fifteenth century. (The story is told in full in Chapter 37, 'Time in Disarray.') Gardner would declare that this is a question that should simply not be asked unless the answer is that Sanderson was either drunk or lying. But it is obvious that he was neither. Those who knew him (and I have a letter on my desk from one of them at the moment) agree that he was an honest man who was not remotely interested in the 'supernatural'. It is also worth asking how Sanderson's servants knew he had been involved in an accident – although it occurred in a remote and deserted spot – and that he would be home at dawn. And so is another question that Sanderson's experience leads him to discuss: whether the mind is identical with the brain. He mentions a case of a man who died in a New York hospital, and who an autopsy revealed to have no brain, only 'half a cupful of dirty water'. This sounds, admittedly, like another of those absurd stories that are not worth discussing. But in the early 1980s Professor John Lourber of Sheffield University discovered a student with an IQ of 126 whose head was entirely filled with 'water'. A brain scan showed that the student's brain was merely an outer layer, only one millimetre thick. How can a person function with virtually no brain? Lourber, who specializes in hydrocephalis ('water on the brain') replies that he has come across many cases of perfectly normal people whose heads are filled with 95 per cent of fluid, and that 70 to 90 per cent is actually quite common. This does not prove – as Sanderson suspects – that the mind is quite separate from the brain; but it certainly fuels speculation in that direction.

The real problem posed by experiences such as that of the Sandersons is one concerning the nature of time. All scientific reasoning, even the least dogmatic, tells us that it is totally impossible to slip back into the past or foretell the future. Where the past is concerned, we can admittedly speculate that the 'time slip' is some kind of 'tape recording'. But a vision of the future should be a total impossibility, since the future has not yet happened. In spite of which, there are many well-authenticated cases of 'glimpses' into the future. (I once presented a television programme about one of these – an Irish peer named Lord Kilbracken who dreamed repeatedly about the winners of horse races, and won money by backing them.[1]) It seems to follow that there is something fundamentally wrong with the vision of the world presented to us by our senses – in fact, we have only to think for a moment to see that there *must* be something wrong with a logic that tells us that everything has a beginning and an end, and then presents us with the paradox of a universe that apparently has neither.

This is why the views of CSICOP deserve to be treated with suspicion. It is not simply a question of whether ESP or telepathy deserve to be taken seriously, but whether – as Martin Gardner would like to believe – the universe is ultimately as rational and 'normal' as a novel by Jane Austen or Anthony Trollope. This is an easy belief to maintain, because the universe that confronts us when we open our eyes in the morning looks perfectly 'normal', and it is unlikely that we shall encounter any event during the day that contradicts this assumption. But then the universe looks 'unquestionable' to a cow for the same kind of reason. We know that the moment we begin to use our intelligence to ask questions, the universe becomes a far more strange and mysterious place. Most scientists would – in fact – agree wholeheartedly with this sentiment, for science begins with a sense of mystery. But a certain type of scientist – and they are, unfortunately, in the majority – would also like to believe that the mysteries can all be solved by the kind of simple deductive logic employed by Sherlock Holmes. And the problems presented by 'time slips' or precognitions or synchronicities, or by poltergeists and out-of-the-body experiences, make it clear that this is wishful thinking. We can only keep science within comfortable logical boundaries by refusing to acknowledge the existence of anything that lies outside those boundaries.

It may seem reasonable to ask: Where is the harm in that? No one blames a policeman for not being interested in mysticism or philosophy – that is not his job. Why blame a physicist for taking no interest in poltergeists and ESP?

The answer is that his preconceptions about the universe also involve *preconceptions about the human mind*. In the nineteenth century it made no difference whatever whether a scientist was interested in psychical research or regarded it as a delusion. But in the second half of the twentieth century, science is speculating whether the universe might contain eleven dimensions and whether black holes might be an entrance into a dimensionless 'hyperspace' – even whether we might be able to use black holes to travel across the universe. Russian and American scientists have been

[1] See my book *Mysteries*, Part 1, Chap. 4.

experimenting with ESP as a means of communicating with submarines under the polar ice. Suddenly the question of the limits of the human mind has become a question of major scientific importance. If we are merely chance products of a material universe, then our position is basically that of *spectators*, and the extent to which we can 'intervene' is limited. But if – to take just one example – Sanderson's vision of fifteenth-century Paris was not an hallucination, but was some kind of glimpse of *a hidden power of his own mind*, then it would challenge the whole Darwinian picture of evolution.

Consider the strange case of the calculating twins discussed in the article on identical twins. A prime number is a number that cannot be divided exactly by any other number, like 3, 7 and 13. But there is no easy, quick way to tell whether a number is a prime or not: you just have to patiently divide all the smaller numbers into it and see if any of them 'goes' precisely. If a number is very large – say, five figures – then the only quick way to find out if it is a prime is to look it up in a table of prime numbers. Yet these twins can do it instantaneously, and that is absurd. Quite apart from the mystery of *how* they can do it, there is the even more baffling mystery of how such a power could have developed. According to Darwin, the basic mechanism of evolution is 'survival of the fittest'. The cheetah can run faster than a man and the kangaroo jump higher because they *had* to in order to survive. Most animals cannot count beyond a few figures. Man had to learn to count as his social life became more complex. But most people are 'bad at figures'. So how could *any* human being have developed this amazing ability to recognize five-figure primes instantaneously, when even a computer would be unable to do it? There can only be one answer: that we are wrong to think that human intelligence *has* to operate like a computer. It seems to have some 'alternative method'. And presumably it was the same alternative method that accidentally allowed Sanderson his curious glimpse of the past. That statement sounds reasonable enough, for we all agree that 'intuition' seems to operate in mysterious ways. But then we come upon a case in which someone has clearly foreseen the future, and we know this is not simply a question of intuition. The notion that time has a one-way flow is the very foundation of western science; *everything* depends on it. If precognition is possible, then our basic assumptions need revising.

For the scientists of the nineteenth century, such an idea was deeply disquieting; *that* is why so many of them were so hostile to 'psychical research'. It seemed the opposite of all science stood for, a return to superstitions and old wives' tales instead of analysis and experiment. In 1848 this reaction of science had swung so far that a novelist named Catherine Crowe decided it was time to protest. So she went to a great deal of trouble to gather together some of the best-authenticated cases of the 'supernatural' she could find – the kind of cases that would later be carefully examined by the Society for Psychical Research – and published them in a book called *The Night Side of Nature*. It had a considerable impact on thoughtful people. But Mrs Crowe was unfortunate. The year of its publication also happened to be the year when strange poltergeist disturbances took place in the home of the Fox family in New York State – curious rappings and bangings that occurred in the presence of the two children, Kate and Margaret. In a code of raps, the 'entity' claimed to be a murdered peddler who had been buried in the basement. Whether this was true or not is beside the point. What matters is that these manifestations caused a sensation, and soon 'Spiritualism' had spread across America and Europe. Scientists were outraged at this fashionable tide of 'superstition' – particularly when a number of 'mediums' proved to be frauds – and Mrs Crowe's highly reasonable arguments were forgotten. In fact she encountered so much hostility that a little over a decade after the publication of *The Night Side of Nature* she had a nervous breakdown and spent some time in a mental home; during the last sixteen years of her life, she wrote no more.

Now, more than a century later, Spiritualism has ceased to be a challenge to science, and has become little more than a harmless minority religion; in fact, it is perfectly obvious that it never *was* a challenge to science. We can also see that there was never any question of science being supplanted by superstition and old wives' tales, and that CSICOP is quite wrong to imagine that the success of Uri Geller heralds a return to the Middle Ages.

What it *would* involve is a recognition that the history of life on earth may be a little more complex than Darwin thought. If paranormal powers, such as telepathy and 'second sight', actually exist, then it also seems fairly certain that they were possessed in a far greater degree by our primitive ancestors, just as they are now possessed in a greater degree by many primitive peoples. Sanderson makes it clear, for example, that he believes that some of the Haitians he encountered possessed powers of 'second sight'. One of these remarked to him after his 'time-slip' experience: 'You saw things, didn't you? You don't believe it, but you could *always* see things if you wanted to.' In short, Sanderson himself could have developed – or perhaps simply rediscovered – his paranormal faculties.

In my book *The Occult* I have cited many cases that seem to illustrate the same point. For example, the famous tiger-hunter Jim Corbett describes in *Man Eaters of Kumaon* how he came to develop what he calls 'jungle sensitiveness', so he knew when a wild animal was lying in wait for him. Obviously, such a faculty would be very useful to a tiger-hunter in India, but virtually useless to a stockbroker in New York. So it would seem that civilized man has *deliberately got rid of it*. Or rather, the development of another faculty – the ability to deal with the complications of civilized life – has suppressed the 'paranormal' faculty, because we no longer need it.

But is this actually true? Is it even true that a New York stockbroker does not need 'jungle sensitiveness'? After all, he lives in other kinds of jungle – not only the commercial jungle, but the concrete jungle where muggers lurk in pedestrian subways and public parks. His real problem is more likely to be the problem that caused Catherine Crowe's nervous breakdown, that he has allowed civilized life to 'get on top of him'. We have all to some extent lost that primitive vital force that can still be found in most 'savage' peoples. But what has really been lost is a certain sense of wonder, a certain basic optimism. The child thinks that this world of adults is a magical place, full of endless adventures: going into bars, driving motor-cars, catching aeroplanes . . . . He would find it very hard to believe that as he grows up the world will turn into a hard and ruthless and rather nasty place, where the basic rule is 'Nobody gets anything for nothing'. The adult's problem is that his *attitudes* have become negative.

I have described elsewhere how in 1967 I went to lecture at a university in Los Angeles, then went to meet my family in Disneyland. I had forgotten just how big Disneyland is, and when I walked in through the turnstile and saw the crowds my heart sank. But I was feeling cheerful and optimistic, having given a good lecture. So I relaxed, placed myself in a mood of confidence and then simply allowed my feet to take me to them. I strolled at random for about fifty yards, turned left, and found them standing at a Mexican food stall.

Forty-eight hours ago I was looking for a book on the Habsburg empire, and I searched through three bookcases without success. The next morning I made another search, and this time found the book on a shelf I had searched several times. Why had I missed it? Because I was in a state of *tension* as I searched (as if I was in a hurry) and sheer 'haste' made me look at it without seeing it. Conversely, I have noticed again and again that when I am in a mood of relaxed confidence I can find things by some kind of 'sixth sense'.

But I have noticed something even more interesting: that when I am in these moods of relaxed confidence, things just somehow seem to 'go right'. And this obviously has nothing to do with me or with any 'sixth sense'. I just happen to 'stumble upon' an important piece of information the day before I am due to write about it, or avoid some unpleasant experience by sheer 'serendipity'.

Our basic civilized problem is that our attitudes have become quite unjustifiably negative. Everyone is familiar with the experience of how relief can place us in an optimistic frame of mind. The plumbing goes wrong and you have to flush the lavatory with buckets of water for a couple of days. When the plumber finally arrives you feel immense relief, and for the next twenty-four hours feel how delightful it is to have a lavatory that flushes at the touch of a button. And whenever we experience this relief we also recognize that we are surrounded by reasons for delight: with bath taps and light switches and electric toasters that actually work, and doors that open without squeaking, and televisions that provide us with news as often as we want it. It has taken man about fifty thousand years to move out of caves and achieve this felicity. Yet we have become so accustomed to our civilization that we take it for granted, and spend most of our time worrying about trivialities.

Yet whenever some minor inconvenience is followed by relief, we recognize that we have allowed ourselves to discount our blessings, and fall into a narrow and joyless state of mind. Civilization was designed to give us leisure and freedom; instead, we waste our days concentrating obsessively on minor problems that will appear totally unimportant in a week's time. And this anxiety-ridden short-sightedness is due to certain left-brain qualities that we have developed over the past few thousand years. (The left brain deals with logic and language, the right with meaning and intuition.) The only way to regain our birthright of leisure and freedom is to recognize that everyday consciousness left-brain awareness somehow *tells us lies*, and that we have to learn to relax into a wider type of awareness.

Consider the following example from a book called *The States of Human Consciousness* by C. Daly King; he is speaking of states that he calls 'Awakeness'.

The first of them took place upon the platform of a commuters' railway station in New Jersey as the writer walked along it to take a coming train to New York late one sunny morning. On the platform there were several small housings for freight elevators, news-stands and so on, constructed of dun-coloured bricks. He was emotionally at ease, planning unhurriedly the schedule of his various calls in the city and simultaneously attempting to be aware, actively and impartially, of the movements of his body's walking . . .

Suddenly the entire aspects of his surroundings changed. The whole atmosphere seemed strangely vitalized and abruptly the few other persons on the platform took on an appearance hardly more important or significant than that of the doorknobs at the entrance of the passengers' waiting room. But the most extraordinary alternation was that of the dun-coloured bricks, for there was no concomitant sensory illusion in the experience. But all at once they appeared to be tremendously alive; without manifesting any exterior motion they seemed to be seething almost joyously inside and gave the distinct impression that in their own degree they were living actively and liking it. This impression so struck the writer that he remained staring at them for some minutes, until the train arrived . . . .

The first thing to note about this is his comment that 'he was emotionally at ease, planning unhurriedly the schedule of his various calls . . .' That is, he was in a 'right brain' state, free of tension. Then some curious effort, some slight movement of the mind, so to speak, propelled him in the right direction, and made him aware that the bricks he would normally have taken for granted were somehow glowing with inner life. It is also significant that the human beings who would normally have occupied the centre of his field of attention now ceased to seem important. Long habit has made us select human beings as the centre of our field of attention, for we are social animals whose peace of mind depends upon 'fitting into' society.

There is no need to assume that his perception of the bricks was a 'mystical' experience. We can all induce something of the sort by simply staring intently at a perfectly ordinary wall in the sunlight. Our problem is that we do not normally *concentrate* on anything; we 'scan' things automatically. If anything attracts our interest and we focus our full attention on it, we instantly experience this sense of heightened meaning.

I am only trying to point out that the chief reason our experience usually seems so unmemorable is that we have become accustomed to responding 'robotically' to our surroundings, leaving the automatic pilot to do the driving for us.

And what *difference* would such an experience make? Basically this: it would make Daly King aware that the normal assumption he shares with the rest of us, that the world 'out there' is a rather ordinary place, is mistaken. His senses are telling him lies. Or rather, his senses are doing their best; it is his attitudes, his assumptions, that reduce their testimony to 'ordinariness'. His 'glimpse' would have told him that he is surrounded by an unutterably strange universe. And it would help to free him from the vicious circle in which most of us are trapped. This consists in the assumption that the world out there is rather ordinary and dull. And when we are bored our energies sink. And when our energies sink it is rather like a cloud coming over the sun, making the world seem dimmer and less interesting. This feeling that the world is uninteresting prevents us from making any kind of effort. The normal human tendency – unaided by external stimulus – is to sink into a state of lethargy, rather like Samuel Beckett characters sitting in dustbins.

Every glimpse of 'reality', every 'moment of vision' – even setting out on holiday – tells us the opposite. This tells us that when a cloud seems to obscure the sun, what has actually happened is that we have allowed our senses to become dimmer, like the device in a cinema that lowers the lights. Perception is 'intentional'. You see things by a beam of light generated by a dynamo inside your head. When you are bored the dynamo works at half-speed, and everything you look at seems dull. But if you can persuade your subconscious mind that the world out there is fascinating – as holidays persuade it – the dynamo will accelerate, and you will *see* that this is true.

Wordsworth talked about the time of childhood, when everything seems 'apparelled in celestial light'. This is because the child *knows* that there is an infinitely marvellous world out there, and automatically makes that effort that keeps the dynamo working at top speed. Human beings begin to die when they become trapped in the 'vicious circle', and become convinced that they have 'seen it all'. And unless circumstances force them to continue to make an effort they sink gently into a kind of swamp of boredom, of 'taken-for-grantedness', that finally engulfs them. (This is why so many people die after they retire from work.)

Now, obviously, we are on the point of an extremely interesting evolutionary development. The first step towards escape from this vicious circle is to *recognize* that the apparent 'ordinariness' of the world is a delusion. If we could become deeply and permanently convinced that the world 'out there' is endlessly exciting, we would never again allow ourselves to become trapped in the swamp of 'taken-for-grantedness'. And we would become practically unkillable. Shaw says of his 'Ancients' in *Back to Methuselah*: 'Even in the moment of death, their life does not fail them.' 'Life failure' is that feeling that there is nothing new under the sun, and that we all have to accept defeat in the end. If we could learn the mental trick of causing the dynamo to accelerate, this illusion would never again be able to exert its power over us.

Let me state my own fundamental belief about human existence. Man consists of a highly complex body, a 'computer' that has taken millions of years to evolve, controlled by an entity which we call the soul, spirit or whatever. But to place the 'spirit' in charge of such a complicated piece of machinery is like asking a baby to drive a Rolls-Royce. We fail to understand about 90 per cent of its potentialities. Besides, it is simply too 'heavy' for us to handle comfortably. As we drag this massively heavy body around, we are in the position of a space traveller who has been cast away on a planet where gravity is several times greater than on earth, so he cannot even stand upright;

it takes him all his strength just to crawl on his hands and knees. When he is galvanized by some emergency he can summon far more strength, and even stagger briefly on to his feet. Then he can catch a glimpse of the real answer: that he has to develop far more powerful muscles – mental as well as physical muscles. Whenever I am faced by some exciting challenge or crisis I can *see* the answer. I can then see that if I could be 'galvanized' like this all the time, I could rise up to a far higher level of purpose and vitality. Our trouble is that after crisis we quickly lose that sense of emergency, and sink back into the old dull, sleepy state in which every molehill becomes a mountain, and the mind falls into a curious apathy in which it loses all sense of purpose. In fact we are so accustomed to this state that we accept it as normal. We only tend to glimpse our true potentialities when we set out on voyages – either physical or mental.

The answer lies in generating (through the use of determination) a far more powerful imagination, a *sense of reality*, that will make us continually aware of the potential challenges and problems, and *keep* us in the 'galvanized' state. It is a total absurdity that a man sitting on a train should stare dully out of the window, when his mind contains a vast library of past experiences that could keep him entertained for years.

All this explains, of course, why we spend so much of our time seeking out challenges and stimulants – travel, adventure, sport, sex, alcohol; it is a pathetic and misguided attempt to hurl ourselves beyond these stupid limitations. If we could learn to identify and face the basic problem, we would have taken the most decisive step towards solving it. We would become incapable of boredom, and 'discouragement' would lose its power over us. We would begin to see the way out of the trap that has been killing us off prematurely for thousands of generations.

Now it should be clear why I feel such impatience with those people who want to convince us that the universe is a perfectly rational and logical place, and that any attempt to suggest the opposite is a return to medieval superstition. I am prepared to admit that poltergeists are not particularly important – the scientist's instinct is perfectly sound on that point – and neither are 'time slips' or precognitions or out-of-the-body experiences; I myself feel that people who are too obsessed with the paranormal are as boring as people who are too obsessed with football or television soap operas. But these experiences are only a small part of the vast panorama of strangeness that will confront us when we learn that mental trick of slipping out of the bonds of habit, and making a powerful and continuous effort to tear aside the 'curtains of everydayness' that surround us.

If this book needs any justification, it is that it is a modest attempt to catch a few glimpses of the strangeness that lies on the other side of the curtain.

1 Atlantis

The Submerged Continent

Atlantis has been described as the greatest of all historical mysteries. Plato, writing about 350 BC, was the first to speak of the great island in the Atlantic Ocean which had vanished 'in a day and a night', and been submerged beneath the waves of the Atlantic.

Plato's account in the two late dialogues of *Timaeus* and *Critias* has the absorbing quality of good science fiction. The story is put into the mouth of the poet and historian Critias, who tells how Solon, the famous Athenian lawgiver, went to Saïs in Egypt about 590 BC, and heard the story of Atlantis from an Egyptian priest. According to the priest, Atlantis was already a great civilization when Athens had been founded about 9600 BC. It was then 'a mighty power that was aggressing wantonly against the whole of Europe and Asia, and to which your city [Athens] put an end'. Atlantis, said the priest, was 'beyond the pillars of Hercules' (the Straits of Gibraltar), and was larger than Libya and Asia put together. It was 'a great and wonderful empire' which had conquered Libya and Europe as far as Tyrrhenia (Etruria in central Italy). Deserted by their allies, the Athenians fought alone against Atlantis, and finally conquered them. But at this point violent floods and earthquakes destroyed both the Athenians and the Atlantians, and Atlantis sank beneath the waves in a single day and night.

In the second dialogue, the *Critias*, Plato goes into far more detail about the history and geography of the lost continent. He tells how Poseidon (Neptune), the sea god, founded the Atlantian race by fathering ten children on a mortal maiden, Cleito, whom he kept on a hill surrounded by canals. The Atlantians were great engineers and architects, building palaces, harbours, temples and docks; their capital city was built on the hill, which was surrounded by concentric bands of land and water, joined by immense tunnels, large enough for a ship to sail through. The city was about eleven miles in diameter. A huge canal, 300 feet wide and 100 feet deep, connected the outermost of these rings of water to the sea. Behind the city there was a plain 230 by 340 miles, and on this farmers grew the city's food supply. Behind the plain there were mountains with many wealthy villages and with fertile meadows and all kinds of livestock. Plato goes into great detail about the city, suggesting either that he had been told the story at length or that he had the gifts of a novelist. The long account of magnificent buildings with hot and cold fountains, communal dining halls and stone walls plated with precious metals has fascinated generations of readers for more than two thousand years.

But eventually, says Critias, the Atlantians began to lose the wisdom and virtue they inherited from the god, and became greedy, corrupt and domineering. Then Zeus decided to teach them a lesson. So he called all the gods together . . .

And there, frustratingly, Plato's story breaks off. He never completed the *Critias*, or wrote the third dialogue that would complete the trilogy, the *Hermocrates*. But we may probably assume that the final punishment of the Atlantians was the destruction of their continent.

Many later scholars and commentators assumed that Atlantis was a myth, or that Plato intended it as a political allegory: even Plato's pupil Aristotle is on record as disbelieving it. Yet this seems unlikely. The *Timaeus*, the dialogue in which he first tells the story, is one of his most ambitious works; his translator Jowett called it 'the greatest effort of the human mind to conceive the world as a whole which the genius of antiquity has bequeathed to us'. So it seems unlikely that Plato decided to insert a fairy tale into the middle of it; it seems more likely that he wanted to preserve the story for future generations.

For more than two thousand years the story of Atlantis remained a mere interesting curiosity. But in the late nineteenth century an American congressman named Ignatius Donnelly became fascinated by it, and the result was a book called *Atlantis, the Antediluvian World* (1882), which became a bestseller and has been in print ever since. Even a century later, the book remains surprisingly readable and up to date. Donnelly asks whether it is possible that Plato was recording a real catastrophe, and concludes that it was. He points out that modern earthquakes and volcanic eruptions have caused tremendous damage, and that there is evidence that the continent of Australia is the only visible part of a continent that stretched from Africa to the Pacific, and which scientists have named Lemuria. (Lemuria was named by the zoologist L.P.Sclater, who noted that lemurs existed from Africa to Madagascar, and suggested that a single land-mass had once connected the two.) He also studied flood legends from Egypt to Mexico, pointing out their similarities, and indicated all kinds of affinities connecting artifacts from both sides of the Atlantic. He notes that there is a mid-Atlantic ridge, and that the Azores seem to be the mountain-tops of some large submerged island. Donnelly's knowledge of geology, geography, cultural history and linguistics appears encyclopedic. The British prime minister Gladstone was so impressed by the book that he tried to persuade the cabinet to allot funds to sending a ship to trace the outlines of Atlantis. (He failed.)

Writing seventy years later in his book *Lost Continents*, the American writer L.Sprague de Camp commented on this impressive theory: 'Most of Donnelly's statements of facts, to tell the truth, either were wrong when he made them, or have been disproved by subsequent discoveries.' And he goes on to say: 'It is not true, as he stated, that the Peruvian Indians had a system of writing, that the cotton plants native to the New and Old Worlds belong to the same species, that Egyptian civilisation sprang suddenly into being, or that Hannibal used gunpowder in his military operations . . .' De Camp demonstrates that Donnelly's scholarship is not as reliable as it looks; but there is still a great deal in the 490-page book that he leaves unchallenged.

Five years before the publication of Donnelly's book, the subject of Atlantis had been raised in an immense two-volume work called *Isis Unveiled* by the Russian 'occultist' Helena Blavatsky, who had dashed off its fifteen hundred pages at a speed that suggests automatic writing. But her comments on Atlantis occupy only one single page of Volume One (593), in which she explains that the inhabitants of Atlantis were the fourth race on earth, and that they were all natural 'mediums'. Having acquired their knowledge without effort, this people was an easy prey for 'the great and invisible dragon' King Thevetat, who corrupted them so that they became 'a nation of wicked magicians'. They started a war which ended in the submersion of Atlantis . . . .

Isis Unveiled astonished its publisher by becoming a best-seller; it made its author a celebrity, and she went on to leave New York for India and to found the Theosophical Society. After a shattering exposé in which she was declared a fraud, she returned to London and died of Bright's disease at the age of sixty in 1891. But she left behind her the manuscript of a book that was even larger and more confusing than *Isis Unveiled*, a book called *The Secret Doctrine*. This is a commentary on a mystical work called *The Book of Dzyan*, allegedly written in Atlantis in the Senzar language, and it explains that man is not the first intelligent race on earth. The first 'root race' consisted of invisible beings made of fire mist, the second lived in northern Asia, the third lived on the lost island continent of Lemuria or Mu in the Indian Ocean, and consisted of ape-like giants who lacked reason. The fourth root race were the Atlantians, who achieved a high degree of civilization, but were destroyed when the island sank after a battle between selfish magicians. The present human species is the fifth root race, and we are the most 'solid' so far; the sixth and seventh that succeed us will be more ethereal. According to Madame Blavatsky, all knowledge of the past is imprinted on a kind of psychic ether called Akasa, and this knowledge is called the Akasic records. She also claims that the survivors of Atlantis peopled Egypt and built the pyramids about a hundred thousand years ago. (Modern scholarship dates the earliest about 2500 BC.)

By the time *The Secret Doctrine* appeared, Donnelly's book had popularized the subject of Atlantis. A leading member of the Theosophical Society in London, W.Scott-Elliot, now produced a work called *The Story of Atlantis* (1896), which achieved immense popularity; Scott-Elliot claimed to possess the ability to read the Akasic records. He made the astonishing claim that Atlantian civilization was flourishing a million years ago. There were seven sub-races, one of which, the Toltecs, conquered the whole continent and built a magnificent city, which is described by Plato. When some of the Atlantians practised black magic, a great lodge of initiates moved to Egypt and founded a dynasty; others built Stonehenge in England.

Scott-Elliot later used his insight into the Akasic records to write an equally startling book about Lemuria. Both books are regarded together with *Isis*

Unveiled and *The Secret Doctrine* as basic scriptures of the Theosophical Society.

After Madame Blavatsky, the most influential of all Theosophists was the Austrian Rudolf Steiner, who quarrelled with the British Theosophists and developed his own system of 'occult philosophy' known as Anthroposophy. In 1904, before the break, Steiner produced a work called *From the Akashic Records* (Akashic being an alternative spelling), which deals with Atlantis and Lemuria. It would be easy to dismiss this as yet another production of the lunatic fringe; yet, like most of Steiner's work, it has a solid core of intellectual understanding that rings true. Steiner thinks in terms of the evolution of worlds, and according to his scheme, higher beings called hierarchies are in charge of the process. The basic aim of evolution is for spirit to conquer the realm of matter. Man began as a completely etherialized being, and has become steadily more solid with each step in his evolution. But the increase in solidity has meant that he has become a slave to matter. When, after evolving through three earlier 'worlds', man was reborn on our present earth, his body was little more than a cloud of vapour. By the time he had developed to the 'third root race' (the Lemurians) he had learned the secret of telepathy, and of direct use of his will-power. Fear, illness and death entered human history during this period. In the next epoch of Atlantis man was able to control the vegetable life forces and use these as an energy source; he was unable to reason but possessed an abnormally powerful memory. But hostile forces which Steiner called Ahriman pushed man into mere scientific achievement; he became increasingly corrupt and egotistic, and his attempt to use destructive forces finally caused the catastrophe that overwhelmed Atlantis . . . Unlike Madame Blavatsky, Steiner dates this catastrophe around 8000 BC, which places it within the realm of reasonable possibility. (It is true that, according to archaeological research, the first mesolithic farmers had only just made their appearance on earth at this time. However, one American professor of history, Charles Hapgood, has argued seriously that certain 'maps of the ancient sea kings' suggest that there was an advanced civilization covering the globe in 8000 BC.)

Just as it began to look as if Atlantis had fallen into the hands of occultists and the purveyors of science fiction, a new and more serious advocate appeared on the scene. Lewis Spence was a Scottish newspaper editor who also wrote scholarly studies of the mythologies of Babylonia, Egypt, Mexico and Central America. His *Problem of Atlantis* appeared in 1924, and, like Donnelly's book, reached a wide audience. What Spence proposed was that there is geological evidence for the existence of a great continent in the Atlantic region in late Miocene times (25 to 10 million years ago). It disintegrated into smaller island masses, the two largest of which were in the Atlantic close to the Mediterranean. Another large island existed in the region of the West Indies. Further disintegration of the eastern continent began about 25,000 years ago, and it finally vanished about 10,000 years ago, as Plato said. The other continent to the west – Antillia – survived until more recently. Spence argued that man was not a seafarer ten thousand years ago (Hapgood would probably disagree) so there should be evidence of the inhabitants of Atlantis taking refuge in nearby lands. Studying the coast of south-western France, northern Spain and the Bay of Biscay, Spence adduces evidence that three primitive races, the Cro-Magnon, the Caspian and the Azilian, all migrated from the west. He believes that Cro-Magnon man arrived about 25,000 years ago and wiped out Neanderthal man. (Modern students of prehistory would place the date of the disappearance of Neanderthal at least ten thousand years earlier than this.)

The Caspian and Azilian people came 15,000 years later; the Azilians are known to have used boats for deep-sea fishing, and Spence reasons that the land bridge that had joined Atlantis and Europe had now ceased to exist. Spence believed that the Azilians founded the civilizations of Egypt and Crete. Other 'Atlantians' fled westward to Antillia, and remained there until it was also partly submerged some time before the Christian era; its inhabitants became the Mayans. (This identification of the Mayans with Atlantians is one of the usual features of Atlantis speculation.) One of Spence's odder theories is that lemmings – the small rodents who often drown themselves in large numbers – are attempting to migrate back to Atlantis. In fact, we now know that lemmings are simply responding to overcrowding, like so many other animals, and that mass suicide is not one of their usual habits – they simply tend to disperse randomly from areas where the birth rate has risen too steeply.

There are other objections to Spence's theory. He argues that the cultures of Egypt, Crete and South America appeared suddenly; archaeology has since established that this is untrue; they evolved slowly from primitive beginnings. Nevertheless, there is a great deal in Spence's first three Atlantis books – *The problem of Atlantis* was followed by *Atlantis in America* and *The History of Atlantis* – that deserves to be taken seriously. The same cannot be said of the two later books: *Will Europe Follow Atlantis?*, in which he speculates whether the modern world is plunging into the same wicked excesses that destroyed Atlantis (this was in the Hitler period) and *The Occult Sciences in Atlantis*, in which he is inclined to build bricks without straw ('the reader must bear in mind that here we are dealing with the question of Alchemy in Atlantis only . . .') But altogether, Spence is probably the most interesting and reliable writer on Atlantis, and his *Problem of Lemuria* shows the same sober, scholarly approach, even though he is forced to rely too heavily on speculation and guesswork.

Spence advised Conan Doyle on his Atlantis novel *The Maracot Deep*, and also corresponded with the explorer Colonel Percy H.Fawcett, who was convinced that Brazil was part of ancient Atlantis – a theory Doyle utilized in *The Lost World*. The novelist Rider Haggard presented Fawcett with a basalt image inscribed with characters, and when the British Museum was unable to identify it, Fawcett took it to a psychometrist (psychometry is the ability to 'read' the history of an object by holding it in the hands).[1] Although the psychometrist had no clue to Fawcett's identity, he told him: 'I see a large irregularly shaped continent stretching from the north coast of Africa across

[1] For the history of psychometry, see my book *The Psychic Detectives*.

to South America. Numerous mountains are spread over its surface, and here and there a volcano looks as though about to erupt . . .. On the African side of the continent the population is sparse. The people are well-formed, but of a varied nondescript class, very dark complexioned though not negroid. Their most striking feature are high cheek bones and eyes of piercing brilliance. I should say their morals leave much to be desired, and their worship borders on demonology . . .'

On the western side, the inhabitants are 'far superior to the others. The country is hilly and elaborate temples are partly hewn from the faces of the cliffs, their projecting facades supported by beautifully carved columns . . . . Within the temples it is dark, but over the altars is the representation of a large eye. The priests are making invocations to this eye and the whole ritual seems to be of an occult nature, coupled with a sacrificial . . . . Placed at various parts of the temple are a few effigies like the one in my hand – and this one was evidently the portrait of a priest of very high rank.'

The psychometrist went on to say that this image would eventually come into the possession of a reincarnation of the priest 'when numerous forgotten things will through its influence be elucidated'. 'The teeming population of the western cities seems to consist of three classes; the hierarchy and the ruling party under an hereditary monarch, a middle class, and the poor or slaves. These people are absolute masters of the world, and by a great many of them the black arts are practised to an alarming extent.' The psychometrist went on to describe how, as punishment for presumption, the land is destroyed by volcanic eruptions, and sinks beneath the sea. 'I can get no definite date of the catastrophe, but it was long prior to the rise of Egypt, and has been forgotten except, perhaps, in myth.'

So Fawcett became a firm believer in the reality of Atlantis, and considered that he would find further evidence for it in certain lost jungle cities of Brazil and Bolivia. He had another reason for wishing to go to the Mato Grosso of south-western Brazil. In Rio de Janeiro he had found an old document in Portuguese written by a man called Francisco Raposo, who had gone into the jungle in 1743 in search of the lost mines of Muribeca – Muribeca being the son of a Portuguese adventurer and an Indian woman. According to Raposo's manuscript (which is cited in Fawcett's posthumous book *Exploration Fawcett*), he found a remarkable ruined city that had obviously been destroyed by earthquakes, 'tumbled columns and blocks weighing perhaps fifty tons and more'. After spending some time in this ruined city, Raposo and his party made their way back to Bahía, where he wrote his account for the viceroy, who pigeonholed it.

So when Fawcett finally set off in 1924, after endless frustrations and delays, he had a threefold objective: the search for the mines of Muribeca, for the lost city of Raposo, and for Atlantian remains like his basalt idol. With his son Jack and a friend named Raleigh Rimell, he made his way finally to Dead Horse Camp in the Xingu Basin, where he took a final photograph of Jack and Rimell. On 29 May 1924 he wrote a final note to his wife. Then all three men vanished. In 1932 a Swiss trapper named Rattin reported that Fawcett was a prisoner of an Indian tribe. Rattin himself went in search of the 'white colonel', but never returned. Various other rumours about Fawcett were carried back by explorers and missionaries, and in 1951 the chief of the Kalapalos tribe, Izarari, made a deathbed confession to killing Fawcett and his companions. He had refused Fawcett carriers and canoes, 'on grounds of intertribal strife', and Fawcett slapped his face, whereupon the chief had clubbed him to death, then killed the other two men when they attacked him. He also alleged that Jack Fawcett had been consorting with one of his wives, and the Brazilian who reported this story mentioned that the chief's eldest son seemed to have white blood. However, a team of experts announced that bones found in a jungle grave were not those of Colonel Fawcett; so the mystery of his disappearance remains unsolved. It has even been suggested that Fawcett found his lost city and preferred to stay there rather than return to civilization . . ..

Other students of the Atlantis myth preferred to believe that it was to be found on the other side of the Atlantic ocean. A group of German archaeologists named Schulten, Herman, Jessen and Hennig began searching for another lost city, Tartessos, in 1905; it was supposed to be on the Atlantic coast of Spain near the mouth of the Guadalquivir, and had been captured by the Carthaginians in 533 BC. They believed that the lost Tartessos had been Plato's Atlantis – it was certainly on the right side of the Straits of Gibraltar. Another archaeologist, Elena Maria Whishaw, also spent twenty-five years studying the same area – around the ancient fortress of Niebla – and was led by evidence of masonry and skilled hydraulic engineering in the Rio Tinto mines to the conclusion that Andalusia had once been colonized by people from North Africa who had fled from Atlantis. This explains the title of her book, *Atlantis in Andalusia* (1930).

By the 1930s another interesting theory of the destruction of Atlantis had gained millions of followers; it was the work of a Viennese mining engineer named Hans Hoerbiger (1860-1931). As a child Hoerbiger had been an amateur astronomer, and while he was looking at the moon and the planets through a telescope he was suddenly struck by the certainty that the way they reflect the sunlight indicates that they are covered in ice. Later he saw waterlogged soil exploding with puffs of steam, as molten iron ran over it, and thought he saw the answer to the explosive energies of the universe. Space, according to Hoerbiger, is full of hydrogen and oxygen, although in an extremely rarified state. (This is certainly true of hydrogen!) This condenses around small stars as ice, and when these balls of ice fall into a hot star there is a tremendous explosion – the same kind of explosion that formed our solar system. Most of the planets, Hoerbiger insisted, are covered with a layer of ice hundreds of miles thick, while our present moon has an ice-covering 125 miles thick. It is necessary to speak of our *present* moon (Luna) because it is only the latest of a considerable number, perhaps as many as six. The natural movement of all planetary bodies, says Hoerbiger, is a spiral, and the planets are spiralling in towards the sun like the needle on a gramaphone record. Small objects move faster than large ones, so as they spiral past larger planets they are likely to be captured and become 'moons'. A quarter of a million years ago our earth had another moon – a captured comet. When this approached close to the earth it was moving so fast that it caused the seas to bunch together into a ridge of water that had not time to retreat. The rest of the earth became covered with ice; human beings were forced to move to the tops of mountains, like those of Ethiopia and Peru. (Colonel Fawcett also believed that Tiahuanaco, in the Peruvian Andes, contained evidence of some mysterious lost civilization.) The lighter gravity at these heights turned men into giants – hence the comment in the Bible that there were 'giants in the earth' in those days. When the moon finally exploded the result was a great flood, like the one recorded in the Bible and in many other sacred books. When the earth captured our present moon (about twelve thousand years ago) the result was again a tremendous flood, together with earthquakes and volcanic eruptions, and this destroyed Atlantis and Lemuria.

Hoerbiger died in 1931, but his work was continued by one of his foremost disciples, Hans Schindler Bellamy. Bellamy was an Austrian, whose book *Moon, Myths and Man* – published in the year of Hoerbiger's death – made thousands of converts in England and America. Hoerbiger's German converts included Hitler, who proposed to build an observatory dedicated to the three greatest astronomers of all time, Ptolemy, Copernicus and Hoerbiger. Hitler's belief in Hoerbiger may have cost him the war. A weather bureau based on Hoerbiger's principles forecast a mild winter for 1941–2, and Hitler sent his troops into Russia in light summer uniforms . . . . Hoerbiger continued to have hosts of disciples until the 1960s, when space exploration finally made it clear that his belief that the moon and planets were covered in thick ice was erroneous.

The chief problem with 'crank' books like Hoerbiger's *Glacial Cosmogony* (1913) is that they often contain more than a grain of truth. This is certainly the case with that astonishing bestseller of the 1950s, *Worlds in Collision*, by Immanuel Velikovsky. Velikovsky, a Russian Jew born in 1895, was startled and impressed by Freud's book *Moses and Monotheism*, which suggested that Moses was not a Jew but an Egyptian, and that he was a follower of the 'sun-worshipping' pharaoh Akhnaton. Velikovsky reached the even more startling conclusion that Akhnaton was the Greek king Oedipus. In 1939, the year he moved from Palestine to the United States, Velikovsky was much preoccupied with Hoerbiger's theory, but finally decided against it. But he was impressed by the theory of W. Whiston, Newton's successor at Cambridge, that the comet of 1680 had caused the Biblical deluge on an earlier encounter. He also encountered Donnelly's *Ragnarok, The Age of Fire and Ice* (1883), successor to *Atlantis*, in which Donnelly concludes that the 'drift', the vast deposit of sand, gravel and clay which lies in irregular patches over much of the earth's surface, was the result of a tremendous explosion that occurred when a comet struck the earth. Whiston and Donnelly were seminal influences on the book Velikovsky now went on to write, *Worlds in Collision* (see Chapter 40), in which a close brush with a comet is blamed for the destruction of Atlantis, as well as for various Biblical catastrophes.

A rather more credible theory of Atlantis was propounded in the late 1960s by a Greek archaeologist, Professor Angelos Galanopoulos, based on the discoveries of Professor Spyridon Marinatos on the island of Santorini or Thera, in the Mediterranean. Around the year 1500 BC a tremendous volcanic explosion ripped apart Santorini, and probably destroyed most of the civilization of the Greek islands, the coastal regions of eastern Greece, and of northern Crete. This, Galanopoulos suggests, was the catastrophe that destroyed Atlantis. But surely the date is wrong? – the destruction of Santorini took place a mere nine hundred years before Solon, not nine thousand. This is the essence of Galanopoulos's argument – he believes that a scribe accidentally multiplied all the figures by ten. He points out that all Plato's figures seem far too large. The 10,000 stadia (1,150 mile) ditch around the plain would stretch around modern London twenty times. The width and depth of the canal 300 feet wide and 100 feet deep seems absurd; surely 30 feet wide by 10 feet would be more likely? As to the plain behind the city, 23 by 34 miles would be a more reasonable size than 230 by 340 miles. If all Plato's figures are reduced in this way, then Santorini begins to sound altogether more like Atlantis although Galanopoulos suggests that the Atlantian civilization stretched all over the Mediterranean, and that Crete itself was probably the Royal City. And how could such a mistake come about? Galanopoulos suggests that the Greek copyist mistook the Egyptian symbol for 100 – a coiled rope – for the symbol for 1,000 – a lotus flower.

There is only one major objection to all this: Plato states clearly that Atlantis was beyond the Pillars of Hercules. Galanopoulos argues that Hercules performed most of his labours in the Peloponnese, and that the Pillars of Hercules could well refer to the two extreme southern promontories of Greece, Cape Matapan and Cape Maleas. But Plato says clearly: 'They [the Atlantians] held sway . . . over the country within the pillars as far as Egypt and Tyrrhenia.' And no amount of revisionary geography can place Egypt and Etruria within the promontories of Greece. So another fascinating theory must be reluctantly abandoned. But the notion that Santorini was the legendary Atlantis has brought thousands of tourists to the island and greatly improved its economy . . . .

In 1975 a symposium held at the University of Indiana discussed the question: Atlantis, fact or fiction? Various experts stated their views, and reached the predictable conclusion that Atlantis was a myth. And it must be admitted that, apart from the kind of 'cultural' evidence adduced by Donnelly, Spence and Whishaw, there is not one grain of solid proof of the existence of the sunken continent. And the kind of 'proof' that convinced Colonel Fawcett – the evidence of a psychometrist – is understandably dismissed by geologists, archaeologists and classical scholars alike. Yet anyone who has studied such evidence will agree that, while it is far from convincing, it still leaves a great deal to explain. How did Fawcett's psychometrist come to think of Atlantis? For the evidence to be of any value, we would need to know a great deal more about the psychometrist – whether, for example, he had read Donnelly or Spence. And if he could convince us that his unconscious mind was not playing him tricks, there would still remain the possibility that he was somehow reading Fawcett's mind. Yet anyone who is willing to study the evidence for psychometry with an open mind will end by agreeing that there are many cases that cannot be explained as unconscious self-deception or telepathy.

Similar questions are raised by the detailed descriptions of Atlantian civilization produced by the 'psychic healer' Edgar Cayce (pronounced Casey). When Cayce was twenty-two (in 1899) he suffered from psychosomatic paralysis of the vocal cords, which was cured by hypnosis. The hypnotist then asked Cayce some questions about his own medical problems, and Cayce's replies revealed a medical knowledge that consciously he did not possess. Cayce's ability to produce 'trance diagnosis' soon made him a minor celebrity. In 1923 Cayce was questioned as to whether there is life after death; when he woke from his trance he was shocked to learn that he had been preaching the doctrine of reincarnation – as an orthodox Christian, he rejected the idea. Eventually he came to accept it. In 1927, giving a 'life reading' on a fourteen-year-old boy, Cayce described his previous lives under Louis XIV, Alexander the Great, in ancient Egypt, and in Atlantis. For the remainder of his life Cayce continued to add fragments to his account of Atlantis.

According to Cayce, Atlantis extended from the Sargasso Sea to the Azores, and was about the size of Europe. It had experienced two periods of destruction, in the first of which the mainland had divided into islands. The final break-up occurred, as Plato said, about 10,000 BC, and the last place to sink was near the Bahamas. What he says echoes Steiner to a remarkable extent: '. . . man brought in the destructive forces that combined with the natural resources of the gases, of the electrical forces, that made the first of the eruptions that awoke from the depth of the slow-cooling earth . . .' He claimed that archives dealing with Atlantis now exist in three places in the world, one of these in Egypt. In June 1940 Cayce predicted that the island called Poseidia would rise again, 'expect it in '68 or '69'. It would happen in the area of the Bahamas.

Early in 1968 a fishing guide called Bonefish Sam took the archaeologist Dr J.Manson Valentine to see a line of rectangular stones under twenty feet of water in North Bimini, in the Bahamas. Valentine was startled to find two parallel lines of stones about 2,000 feet long. They became known as the Bimini Road. But scientists disagreed from the beginning. John Hall, a professor of archaeology from Miami, said they were natural formations; John Gifford, a marine biologist, thought that if the stones were produced by 'geological stress', then there would be far more of them over a wider area; he concluded that 'none of the evidence conclusively disproves human intervention'. One of the investigators, Dr David Zink, wrote a book called *The Stones of Atlantis*, and had no doubt whatsoever that some of the stones were hand-made – in fact, one object was a stone head. But even if the Bimini Road could be shown to be part of a temple, this would still not prove that it was built more than ten thousand years ago; it could be the product of a much more recent culture.

Obviously, Cayce's prediction that Atlantis would 'rise again' has not been fulfilled. This in itself does not prove the prediction to have been pure imagination; parapsychologists who have studied precognition have often noted that the time scale is seldom correct. But it *does* mean that for the time being Cayce must be classified with Scott-Elliott, Steiner and Madame Blavatsky as a highly suspect witness.

Of all the theories of the destruction of Atlantis, a recent one by an English geologist, Ralph Franklin Walworth, is in some ways one of the most convincing. Walworth's book *Subdue the Earth* is only incidentally concerned with Atlantis; it is basically an attempt to explain the problem of the ice ages. So far no geologist has produced a convincing theory to account for the tremendous variations in climate that have periodically covered the earth with immense sheets of ice. Robert Ardrey's *African Genesis* contains several fascinating pages in which the various theories are outlined. A 'wandering north pole' could not explain why the ice sheets extended down to Africa. A near-brush with a comet could not explain why there have been so many ice ages, and why they are at irregular intervals (the same comet would return regularly). A Jugoslav, M.Milankovitch, produced a marvellously convincing theory based on the known fact that our planet goes through minor cyclical variations in the weather, and argued that when such variations happen to coincide – like lightning striking twice in the same place – the result is an ice age. Ardrey points out that even Milankovitch's simultaneous variations cannot account for twenty million cubic miles of ice. Sir George Simpson produced a highly convincing theory to the effect that ice ages are due to a rise in solar temperature, which causes more rain to fall on highlands in the form of snow. Eventually, there is so much snow that it cannot melt away during the summers, and an ice age begins. But if Simpson's theory is correct, then the seas should become a great deal warmer during ice ages; in fact, studies of sea-bottom deposits during the Pleistocene – the last great ice age – show that there was a variation in temperature of only a few degrees. Ardrey's own theory is that the earth passes periodically through some vast intergalactic gas cloud, and that the earth's magnetic field sucks murky gas into our atmosphere, thus excluding the sunlight. But he admits that his theory fails to explain why, in that case, ice ages do not occur at regular intervals . . . .

Walworth sets out to explain some of the problems already noted by Donnelly and Velikovsky: the evidence for great upheavals that buried whole forests. Most geologists, he points out, are now 'Uniformitarians'; they propose that the earth has evolved very slowly over vast epochs of time, and that the great catastrophes (floods, earthquakes and so on) that were posited by scientists in the eighteenth century, when the earth was thought to be only a few thousand years old, are unnecessary to explain earth's evolution. Walworth points out that, be that as it may, there is still a great deal of evidence for giant catastrophes. And he asks some simple but very puzzling questions. How, for example, can we account for fossils? The standard explanation is that fossilized fishes, animals, etc, became stuck in mud, which hardened around them and 'preserved' them. But if a fish dies in a river it quickly decays, or is eaten by predators; even if it sinks into a few inches of mud, it still decays. Walworth believes that fossils are best formed in the presence of the 'activated dust which a volcano ejects'.

His theory is that ice ages are caused by tremendous volcanic eruptions, great enough to eject gas, magma and dust far out into space. The air that was hurtled out into space would lose all its heat; when gravity pulled it back to earth it would be 'an icy, lethal gas' that would extinguish life in vast areas, and plunge even large creatures like mammoths into an instantaneous deep-freeze. The volcanic dust would cause an ice age. Snow would fall on high ground, until the oceans were hardly more than puddles. 'The evidence from the sea floors indicates that sea level has, for long periods of time, been three miles lower than it is now.' Human settlements would move to the shores of these seas, since the temperature close to the sea is always slightly higher than inland. The ice sheets would raise soft sediments and magmas to high altitudes, where they would set like concrete, forming mountains and the 'drift' that so puzzled Donnelly. Then, as the ice age gradually ended, the settlements would be forced to retreat higher and higher as their former homes were submerged. Some people would even move to mountain-tops like the civilization of Tiahuanaco. And great civilizations would disappear beneath the waves . . . .

But if this is true, then why do we not have such tremendous explosions nowadays? Krakatoa, which erupted in 1883, and sent a giant tidal wave across the Pacific, devastating whole islands, only hurled its vapours seventeen miles into the atmosphere. Walworth points to the planet Jupiter, which produces tremendous eruptions of energy every ten years, and he suggests that this is basically an electromagnetic phenomenon: 'eddy currents developed by Jupiter's motion through the electrified solar wind cause a buildup of heat under the planet's surface.' Because earth is so much smaller, the same mechanism could cause such eruptions at far longer intervals, accounting for the ice ages.

Perhaps the most controversial aspect of Walworth's theory is his suggestion that the earth's core may not be a mass of molten iron, as geologists believe. If volcanic activity is caused by the 'electrified solar wind' acting upon the earth's magnetic field and setting up tremendous stresses just below the surface, then presumably the centre of the earth is relatively cool and solid. Presumably science should one day be able to develop 'depth sounders' that could prove or disprove this unorthodox notion. As far as the human race is concerned, it would probably be a relief if Walworth proved to be mistaken, since his theory also involves another catastrophic eruption over the next thousand years or so, followed by an ice age that would re-create the conditions that destroyed Atlantis.

2 The Barbados Vault

Mystery of the Moving Coffins

On 9 August 1812 the coffin of the Hon. Thomas Chase, a slave-owner on the Caribbean island of Barbados, was carried down the steps of the family vault. As the heavy slab was moved aside and the lamplight illuminated the interior, it became clear that something strange had happened. One of the three coffins it already contained was lying on its side. Another, that of a baby, was lying, head-downward, in a corner. It seemed obvious that the tomb had been desecrated. The odd thing was that there was no sign of forced entry. The coffins were replaced in their original positions, and the tomb resealed. The local white population had no doubt that Negro labourers were responsible for the violation; Thomas Chase had been a cruel and ruthless man. In fact, the last coffin to be laid in the vault only – a month before Chase's – was that of his daughter, Dorcas Chase, who was rumoured to have starved herself to death because of her father's brutality.

Four years went by. On 25 September 1816 another small coffin – this time of eleven-month-old Samuel Brewster Ames – was carried into the vault; once again, it was found in wild disorder. Someone had tumbled all four coffins about the floor, including the immensely heavy lead-encased coffin of Thomas Chase, which it had taken eight men to lift. Once more the coffins were arranged neatly, and the vault resealed.

It was opened again seven weeks later, this time to receive the body of Samuel Brewster, a man who had been murdered in a slave uprising the previous April, and who had been temporarily buried elsewhere in the meantime. Yet again the vault was in disorder, the coffins tumbled about in confusion. No one doubted that Negro slaves were responsible, and that this was an act of revenge. The mystery was: *how* had it been done? The great marble slab had been cemented into place each time, and there was no sign that it had been broken open and then recemented.

One of the coffins – that of Mrs Thomasina Goddard, the first occupant of the vault – had disintegrated into planks, apparently as a result of its rough treatment. They were tied together roughly with wire, and the coffin was placed against the wall. Since the vault (which was only 12 feet by 6½ feet) was becoming somewhat crowded, the children's coffins were placed on top of those of adults. Then once more the vault was resealed.

The story had now become something of a sensation in the islands. Christ Church, and its rector, the Rev. Thomas Orderson, became the focus of unwelcome curiosity. He showed understandable impatience with some of the sensation-seekers; but to those whose rank demanded politeness he explained that he and a magistrate had made a careful search of the vault after the last desecration, trying to find how the vandals had got in. There was undoubtedly no secret door; the floor, walls and curved ceiling were solid and uncracked. He was also convinced that the problem had not been caused by flooding. Although the vault was two feet below ground-level, it had been excavated out of solid limestone. And floods would have left some mark. Besides, it was unlikely that heavy leaden coffins would float. Orderson naturally dismissed the theory held by the local black population that the tomb had some kind of curse on it, and that supernatural forces were responsible.

By the time the next and last burial took place, there was universal interest and excitement. On 7 July 1819 (other accounts say the 17th), Mrs Thomazina Clarke was carried into the vault in a cedar coffin. The cement took a long time to remove from the door – it had been used in abundance to reseal the vault – and even when it had been chipped away, the door still refused to yield. Considerable effort revealed that the massive leaden coffin of Thomas Chase was now jammed against it, six feet from where it had been placed. All the other coffins were disturbed, with the exception of the wire-bound coffin of Mrs Goddard. This seemed to prove that flooding was not the answer – would leaden coffins float when wooden planks lay unmoved?

The governor, Lord Combermere, had been one of the first into the vault. He now ordered an exhaustive search. But it only verified what Orderson had said earlier; there was no way that vandals could have forced their way into the vault, no hidden trapdoor, no entrance for floodwater. Before he ordered the tomb resealed, the governor ordered that the floor should be sprinkled with sand, which would show footprints. Then once more the door was cemented shut. Combermere even used his private seal on it so that it could not be opened and then recemented without leaving obvious traces.

Eight months later, on 18 April 1820, a party was gathered at Lord Combermere's residence, and conversation turned as it often did on the vault. Finally, the governor decided that they would go and investigate whether their precautions had been effective. There were nine of them in all, including the governor, the rector, and two masons. They verified that the cement was undisturbed and the seals intact. Then the masons opened the door. Once again the place was in chaos. A child's coffin lay on the steps that led down into the chamber, while Thomas Chase's coffin was upside down. Only Mrs Goddard's bundle of planks remained undisturbed. The sand on the floor was still unmarked. Once again the masons struck the walls with their hammers, looking for a secret entrance. And finally, when it seemed obvious that the mystery was insoluble, Lord Combermere ordered that the coffins should be removed and buried elsewhere. After that the tomb remained empty.

None of the many writers on the case have been able to supply a plausible explanation. The obvious 'natural' explanations are flooding and earth tremors. But flooding would have disarranged Mrs Goddard's coffin and moved the sand on the floor; besides, someone would have noticed if rain had been so heavy that it flooded the graveyard. The same applies to earth tremors strong enough to shake coffins around like dice in a wooden cup. Conan Doyle suggested that the explanation was some kind of explosion inside the vault, and to explain this he suggests that the 'effluvia' (sweat?) of the Negro slaves somehow combined with unnamed forces inside the vault to produce a gas explosion. Nothing seems less likely.

Yet a 'supernatural' explanation is just as implausible. It has often been pointed out that the disturbances began after the burial of a woman believed to have committed suicide; the suggestion is that the other 'spirits' refused to rest at ease with a suicide. But the movement of the coffins suggest a poltergeist (qv), and all the investigators are agreed that a poltergeist needs some kind of 'energy source' – often an emotionally disturbed adolescent living on the premises. And an empty tomb can provide no such energy source.

The Negroes obviously believed there was some kind of voodoo at work – some magical force deliberately conjured by a witch or witch doctor, the motive being revenge on the hated slave-owners. It sounds unlikely, but it is the best that can be offered.

3 The Bermuda Triangle

On the afternoon of 5 December 1945 five Avenger torpedo-bombers took off from Fort Lauderdale, Florida, for a routine two-hour patrol over the Atlantic. Flight 19 was commanded by Flight Leader Charles Taylor; the other four pilots were trainees, flying what is known as a 'milk run' that is, a flight whose purpose is simply to increase their number of hours in the air without instructors. By 2.15 the planes were well over the Atlantic, and following their usual patrol route. The weather was warm and clear.

At 3.45 the control tower received a message from Taylor: 'This is an emergency. We seem to be off course. We cannot see land . . . repeat . . . we cannot see land.'

'What is your position?'

'We're not sure of our position. We can't be sure where we are. We seem to be lost.'

'Head due west,' replied the tower.

'We don't know which way is west. Everything is wrong . . . strange. We can't be sure of any direction. Even the ocean doesn't look as it should.'

The tower was perplexed; even if some kind of magnetic interference caused all five compasses to malfunction, the pilot should still be able to see the sun low in the western sky. Radio contact was now getting worse, restricting any messages to short sentences. At one point the tower picked up one pilot speaking to another, saying that all the instruments in his plane were 'going crazy'. At four o'clock the flight leader decided to hand over to someone else. At 4.25 the new leader told the tower: 'We're not certain where we are.'

Unless the planes could find their way back over land during the next four hours, they would run out of fuel and be forced to land in the sea. At 6.27 a rescue mission was launched. A giant Martin Mariner flying-boat, with a crew of thirteen, took off towards the last reported position of the flight. Twenty-three minutes later, the sky to the east was lit briefly by a bright orange flash. Neither the Martin Mariner nor the five Avengers ever returned. They vanished completely, as other planes and ships have vanished in the area that has become known as 'the Devil's Triangle' and 'the Bermuda Triangle'.

What finally happened to the missing aircraft is certainly no mystery. The weather became worse during the course of that afternoon; ships reported 'high winds and tremendous seas'. Flight 19 and its would-be rescuer must have run out of fuel, and landed in the sea. The mystery is *why* they became so completely lost and confused. Even if the navigation instruments had ceased to function, and visibility had become restricted to a few yards, it should have been possible to fly up above the clouds to regain their bearings.

What seems stranger still is that this tragedy should have failed to alert the authorities that there was something frightening and dangerous about the stretch of ocean between Florida and the Bahamas – a chain of islands that begins a mere fifty miles off the coast of Florida. But then the authorities no doubt took the view of many more recent sceptics, that the disappearance was a rather complex accident, due to a number of chance factors: bad weather, electrical interference with the compasses, the inexperience of some of the pilots and the fact that the flight leader, Charles Taylor, had only recently been posted to Fort Lauderdale and was unfamiliar with the area.

Similar explanations were adopted to explain a number of similar tragedies during the next two decades: the disappearance of a Superfortress in 1947, of a four-engined Tudor IV in January 1948, of a DC3 in December 1948, of another Tudor IV in 1949, of a Globemaster in 1950, of a British York transport plane in 1952, of a Navy Super Constellation in 1954, of another Martin seaplane in 1956, of an Air Force tanker in 1962, of two Stratotankers in 1963, of a flying boxcar in 1965, of a civilian cargo plane in 1966, another cargo plane in 1967, and yet another in 1973 . . . . The total number of lives lost in all these disappearances was well in excess of two hundred. Oddly enough, the first person to realize that all this amounted to a frightening mystery was a journalist called Vincent Gaddis; it was in February 1964 that his article 'The Deadly Bermuda Triangle' appeared in the American *Argosy* magazine, and bestowed the now familiar name on that mysterious stretch of ocean. A year later, in a book about sea mysteries called *Invisible Horizons*, Gaddis included his article in a chapter called 'The Triangle of Death'. His chapter also contained a long list of ships which had vanished in the area, beginning with the *Rosalie*, which vanished in 1840, and ending with the yacht *Connemara IV* in 1956. In the final chapter Gaddis entered the realm of science fiction, and speculated on 'space-time continua [that] may exist around us on the earth, interpenetrating our known world', implying that perhaps some of the missing planes and ships had vanished down a kind of fourth-dimensional plughole.

Soon after the publication of his book Gaddis received a letter from a man called Gerald Hawkes, who told of his own experience in the Bermuda Triangle in April 1952. On a flight from Idlewild Airport (now Kennedy) to Bermuda, Hawkes's plane suddenly dropped about two hundred feet. This was not a nose-dive, but felt if he had suddenly fallen down a lift-shaft in the air; then the plane shot back up again. 'It was as if a giant hand was holding the plane and jerking it up and down,' and the wings seemed to flap like the wings of a bird. The captain then told them that he was unable to find Bermuda, and that the operator was unable to make radio contact with either the US or Bermuda. An hour or so later the plane made contact with a radio ship, and was able to get its bearings and fly to Bermuda. As they climbed out of the plane they observed that it was a clear and starry night, with no wind. The writer concluded that he was still wondering whether he was caught in an area 'where time and space seem to disappear'.

Now, all pilots know about air pockets, where a sudden change in pressure causes the plane to lurch and fall, and about air turbulence which causes the wings of a plane to 'flap'. What seems odd about this case is the total radio blackout.

This was an anomaly that had also struck students of UFOs (see Chapter 39), or flying saucers, who had been creating extraordinary theories ever since that day in June 1947 when a pilot named Kenneth Arnold saw nine shining discs moving against the background of Mount Rainier in Washington State. The flying-saucer enthusiasts now produced the interesting notion that the surface of our earth has a number of strange 'vortices', whirlpools where gravity and terrestrial magnetism are inexplicably weaker than usual. And if extra-terrestrial intelligences happened to know about these whirlpools, they might well find them ideal for collecting human specimens to be studied at leisure upon their distant planet . . . .

Ivan Sanderson, a friend of Gaddis's and a student of earth mysteries, felt that this was going too far. His training had been scientific, so he began by taking a map of the world, and marking on it a number of areas where strange disappearances had occurred. There was, for example, another 'Devil's Triangle' south of the Japanese island of Honshu where ships and planes had vanished. A correspondent told Sanderson about a strange experience on a flight to Guam, in the western Pacific, when his ancient propeller-driven plane covered 340 miles in one hour, although there was no wind – about 200 miles more than it should have covered; checks showed that many planes had vanished in this area.

Marking these areas on the map, Sanderson observed that they were shaped like lozenges, and that these lozenges seemed to ring the globe in a neat symmetry, running in two rings, each between 30°C and 40°C north and south of the equator. There were ten of these 'funny places', about 72°C apart. An earthquake specialist named George Rouse had argued that earthquakes originated in a certain layer below the earth's surface, and had speculated that there was a kind of trough running round the central core of the earth, which determined the direction of seismic activities. Rouse's map of these seismic disturbance areas corresponded closely with Sanderson's 'lozenges'. So Sanderson was inclined to believe that if 'whirlpools' really caused the disappearance of ships and planes, then they were perfectly normal physical whirlpools, caused, so to speak, by the earth's tendency to 'burp'.

Sanderson's theory appeared in a book entitled *Invisible Residents* in 1970. Three years later a female journalist, Adi-Kent Thomas Jeffrey, tried to put together all the evidence about the Bermuda Triangle in a book of that name, printed by a small publishing company in Pennsylvania. It was undoubtedly her bad luck that her book failed to reach the general public. For one year later Charles Berlitz, grandson of the man who founded the famous language schools, once again rehashed all the information about the Bermuda Triangle, persuaded a commercial publisher, Doubleday, to issue it, and promptly rocketed to the top of the American best-seller lists. It had been twenty years since the disappearance of Flight 19, and ten years since Vincent Gaddis invented the phrase 'Bermuda Triangle'. But Berlitz was the first man to turn the mystery into a worldwide sensation, and to become rich on the proceeds.

Berlitz's *Bermuda Triangle*, while highly readable, is low on scholarly precision – it does not even have an index. One reason for its popularity was that he launched himself intrepidly into bizarre regions of speculation about UFOs, space-time warps, alien intelligences, chariots of the gods (à la Von Däniken) and other such matters. And among the weirdest of his speculations were those concerning the pioneer 'Ufologist' Morris K. Jessup, who had died in mysterious circumstances after stumbling upon information about a certain mysterious 'Philadelphia experiment'. This experiment was supposed to have taken place in Philadelphia in 1943, when the Navy was testing some new device whose purpose was to surround a ship with a powerful magnetic field. According to Jessup's informant, a hazy green light began to surround the vessel, so that its outlines became blurred; then it vanished – to reappear in the harbour of Norfolk, Virginia, some three hundred miles away. Several members of the crew died; others went insane. According to Jessup, when he began to investigate this story, the Navy asked him whether he would be willing to work on a similar secret project; he declined. In 1959 he was found dead in his car, suffocated by exhaust gas; Berlitz speculates that he was 'silenced' before he could publicize his discoveries about the experiment.

And what has all this to do with the Bermuda Triangle? Simply that the Philadelphia experiment was supposed to be an attempt to create a magnetic vortex, like those suggested by Sanderson, and that (according to Jessup) it had the effect of involving the ship in a space-time warp that transported it hundreds of miles.

Understandably, this kind of thing roused sceptics to a fury, and there were suddenly a large number of articles, books and television programmes all devoted to debunking the Bermuda Triangle. These all adopted the common-sense approach that had characterized the Naval authorities in 1945: that is to say, they assumed that the disappearances were all due to natural causes, particularly to freak storms. In many cases it is difficult not to agree that this is indeed the most plausible explanation. But when we look at the long list of disappearances in the area, most of them never even yielding a body or a trace of wreckage, the explanation begins to sound thin.

Is there, then, an alternative which combines common sense with the boldness necessary to recognize that all the disappearances cannot be conveniently explained away? There is, and it rests on the evidence of some of those who have escaped the Bermuda Triangle. In November 1964 a charter pilot named Chuck Wakely was returning from Nassau to Miami, Florida, and had climbed up to 8,000 feet. He noticed a faint glow round the wings of his plane, which he put down to some optical illusion caused by cockpit lights. But the glow increased steadily, and all his electronic equipment began to go wrong. He was forced to operate the craft manually. The glow became so blinding that he was dazzled; then slowly it faded, and his instruments began to function normally again.

In 1966 Captain Don Henry was steering his tug from Puerto Rico to Fort Lauderdale on a clear afternoon. He heard shouting, and hurried to the bridge. There he saw that the compass was spinning clockwise. A strange darkness came down, and the horizon disappeared. 'The water seemed to be coming from all directions.' And although the electric generators were still running, all electric power faded away. An auxiliary generator refused to start. The boat seemed to be surrounded by a kind of fog. Fortunately the engines were still working, and suddenly the boat emerged from the fog. To Henry's amazement, the fog seemed to be concentrated into a single solid bank, and within this area the sea was turbulent; outside it was calm. Henry remarked that the compass behaved as it did on the St Lawrence River at Kingson, where some large deposit of iron – or a meteorite – affects the needle.

Our earth is, of course, a gigantic magnet (no one quite knows why), and the magnetic lines of force run around its surface in strange patterns. Birds and animals use these lines of force for 'homing', and water-diviners seem able to respond to them with their 'dowsing rods'. But there are areas of the earth's surface where birds lose their way because the lines somehow cancel one another out, forming a magnetic anomaly or vortex. The *Marine Observer* for 1930 warns sailors about a magnetic disturbance in the neighbourhood of the Tambora volcano, near Sumbawa, which deflected a ship's compass by six points, leading it off course. In 1932 Captain Scutt of the *Australia* observed a magnetic disturbance near Freemantle that deflected the compass 12°C either side of the ship's course. Dozens of similar anomalies have been collected and documented by an American investigator, William Corliss, in books with titles like *Unknown Earth* and *Strange Planet*. It was Corliss who pointed out to me the investigations of Dr John de Laurier of Ottawa, who in 1974 went to camp on the ice-floes of northern Canada in search of an enormous magnetic anomaly forty-three miles long, which he believes to originate about eighteen miles below the surface of the earth. De Laurier's theory is that such anomalies are due to the earth's tectonic plates rubbing together – an occurrence that also causes earthquakes.

The central point to emerge from all this is that our earth is not like an ordinary bar magnet, whose field is symmetrical and precise; it is full of magnetic 'pitfalls' and anomalies. Scientists are not sure why the earth has a magnetic field, but one theory suggests that it is due to movements in its molten iron core. Such movements would in fact produce shifting patterns in the earth's field, and bursts of magnetic activity, which might be compared to the bursts of solar energy known as sunspots. If they *are* related to earth-tensions and therefore to earthquakes then we would expect them to occur in certain definite zones, just as earthquakes do. What effects would a sudden 'earthquake' of magnetic activity produce? One would be to cause compasses to spin, for it would be rather as if a huge magnetic meteor was roaring up from the centre of the earth. On the sea it would produce an effect of violent turbulence, for it would affect the water in the same way the moon affects the tides, but in an irregular pattern, so that the water would appear to be coming 'from all directions'. Clouds and mist would be sucked into the vortex, forming a 'bank' in its immediate area. And electronic gadgetry would probably be put out of action . . . .

All this makes us aware why the 'simplistic' explanations of the problem – all those books explaining that the mystery of the Bermuda Triangle is a journalistic invention are not only superficial but dangerous. They discourage the investigation of what could be one of the most interesting scientific enigmas of our time. With satellites circling the earth at a height of 150 miles, it should be possible to observe bursts of magnetic activity with the same accuracy that earth tremors are recorded on seismographs. We should be able to observe their frequency and intensity precisely enough to plot them in advance. The result could not only be the solution of the mystery, but the prevention of future tragedies like that of Flight 19.

4 Bigfoot

Like the gun-fight in OK Corral, the siege of Ape Canyon has become part of American folklore.

It begins in 1924, when a group of miners were working in the Mount St Helen's range in Washington State, seventy-five miles north of Portland, Oregon. One day they saw a big ape-like creature peering out from behind a tree. One of the miners fired at it, and thought the bullet hit its head. The creature ran off into the forest. Then another miner, Fred Beck – who was to tell the story thirty-four years later – met another of the 'apes' at the canyon rim, and shot it in the back three times. It toppled over into the canyon; but when the miners went to look there was no body.

That night the miners found themselves under siege. From dusk until dawn the next day the creatures pounded on the doors, walls and the roof, and rocks were hurled. The miners braced the heavy door from inside, and fired shots through the walls and roof. But the creatures were obviously angry and determined, and the assault ceased only at sunrise. That day the miners decided to abandon the site.

Beck's description of the 'Bigfoot' is of a creature about eight feet tall, and very muscular. It looked not unlike a gorilla, but if it could use rocks as a weapon of assault, then it was clearly humanoid.

Fred Beck's account of the siege, together with other sightings on the West Coast, made Bigfoot something of a national celebrity in the late 1950s. But stories about the creature had been in circulation for centuries. The Salish Indians of British Columbia called the creature 'Sasquatch', meaning 'wild man of the woods'. In northern California the Huppa tribe call them 'Oh-mah-ah'; in the Cascades they are known as 'Seeahtiks'.

The notion of colonies of monsters living quietly in the modern US and Canada admittedly sounds absurd; but this is partly because few people grasp the sheer size of the North American coniferous forests – thousands of square miles of totally uninhabited woodland, some still unexplored, where it would be possible to hide a herd of dinosaurs.

The first recorded story of a Sasquatch footprint dates back to 1811. The well-known explorer and trader David Thompson was crossing the Rockies towards the mouth of the Columbia river when, at the site of modern Jasper, Alberta, he and his companion came upon a footprint fourteen inches by eight inches, with four toes and claw marks. Thompson thought it was probably a grizzly bear, but his companion insisted that it could not have been a bear because bears have five toes. In any case, few bears leave behind fourteen-inch footprints.

The *Daily Colonist* of Victoria, British Columbia, for Friday, 4 July 1884, published an account of the capture of a Bigfoot. Jacko (as his captors called him) seems to have been a fairly small specimen, only 4ft 7in high, and weighing 127 pounds. He was spotted from a train which was winding its way along the Fraser river from Lytton to Yale, in the shadow of the Cascade mountains, and apparently captured without too much difficulty. He was described as having long black, coarse hair and short glossy hairs all over his body. The forearms were much longer than a man's, and were powerful enough to be able to tear a branch in two. Regrettably, Jacko's subsequent fate is unknown, although the naturalist John Napier reports that he may have been exhibited in Barnum and Bailey's Circus.

In 1910 Bigfoot was blamed for a gruesome event that took place in the Nahanni Valley, near Great Slave Lake in the Northwest Territories. Two brothers named MacLeod were found headless in the Valley, which subsequently became known as Headless Valley. It seems far more likely that the prospectors were murdered by Indians or desperados; nevertheless, Bigfoot was blamed, and the legend acquired a touch of horror.

In 1910 the *Seattle Times* contained a report about 'mountain devils' who attacked the shack of a prospector at Mount St Lawrence, near Kelso. The attackers were described as half human and half monster, and between seven and eight feet tall. To the Clallam and Quinault Indians the creatures are known as Seeahtiks. Their legends declare that man was created from animals, and that Seeahtiks were left in a half-finished state.

One of the most remarkable Bigfoot stories dates from 1924, although it was not written down until 1957, when it was uncovered by John Green, author of *On the Track of the Sasquatch*. Albert Ostman, a logger and construction worker, was looking for gold at the head of the Toba Inlet in British Columbia, and was unalarmed when an Indian boatman told him tales of 'big people' living in the mountains. After a week's hiking he settled down in a campsite opposite Vancouver Island. But when he woke up in the morning he found that his supplies had been disturbed. He decided to stay awake that night, so when he climbed into his sleeping-bag he removed only his boots; he also took his rifle into the sleeping-bag with him. Hours later, he reported, 'I was awakened by something picking me up. I was asleep and at first I did not remember where I was. As I began to get my wits together, I remembered I was on this prospecting trip, and in my sleeping-bag.'

Hours later, his captor dumped him down on the ground, and he was able to crawl out of the sleeping-bag. He found himself in the presence of a family of four Sasquatches – a father eight feet tall, a mother and teenage son and immature daughter. Ostman described them in considerable detail – the woman was over seven-feet tall, between forty and seventy years of age, and weighed between 500 and 600 pounds. They apparently made no attempt to hurt him, but seemed determined not to let him go. Possibly they regarded him as a future husband for the girl, who was small and flat-chested. He spent six days in their company until, choosing his moment, he fired off his rifle. While his captors dived for cover, Ostman escaped. Asked by John Green why he had kept silent for so long, Ostman explained that he thought nobody would believe him.

In 1928 an Indian of the Nootka tribe called Muchalat Harry arrived at Nootka, on Vancouver Island, clad only in torn underwear, and still badly shaken. He explained that he had been making his way to the Conuma river to do some hunting and fishing when, like Ostman, he was picked up – complete with sleeping bag – and carried several miles by a Bigfoot. At daybreak he found himself in the midst of a group of about twenty of the creatures, and was at first convinced they intended to eat him. When one of them tugged at his underwear it was obviously astonished that it was loose – assuming it to be his skin. He sat motionless for hours, and by afternoon they had lost interest and went off looking for food. Harry took the opportunity to escape, and ran a dozen or so miles to where he'd hidden his canoe, then paddled another forty-five miles back to Vancouver Island, where he told this story to Father Anthony Terhaar, of the Benedictine Mission. Terhaar says that Harry was in such a state of nervous collapse that he needed to be nursed carefully back to health, and that his hair became white. The experience shook him so much that he never again left the village.

In 1967 a logger called Glenn Thomas from Estacada, Oregon, was walking down a path at Tarzan Springs near the Round Mountain when he saw three big hairy figures pulling rocks out of the ground, then digging down six or seven feet. The male figure took out a nest of rodents and ate them. Investigators looking into his story found thirty or forty holes, from which rocks weighing as much as two hundredweight had been shifted. Chucks and marmots often hibernate under such rocks, and there were many of these animals in the area.

By that time one of the most convincing pieces of evidence for the existence of Bigfoot had emerged. In October 1967 two young men called Roger Patterson and Bob Gimlin were in Bluff Creek in Del Norte county, northern California, when they were thrown from their horses as they rounded the bend in the Creek. About a hundred feet ahead, on the other side of the Creek bed, there was a huge, hairy creature that walked like a man. Roger Patterson grabbed his ciné-camera, and started filming. The creature – which they had by now decided was a female – stopped dead, then looked around at them. 'She wasn't scared a bit. The fact is, I don't think she was scared of *me*, and the only thing I can think of is that the clicking of my camera was new to her.' As Patterson tried to follow her the creature suddenly began to run, and after three and a half miles they lost her tracks on pine needles.

The film – which has become famous – shows a creature about seven feet high, weighing around 350 to 450 pounds, with reddish-brown hair and prominent furry breasts and buttocks. As it strides past it turns its head and looks straight into the camera, revealing a fur-covered face. The top of the head is conical in shape. Both mountain gorillas and Bigfoot's cousin the Yeti or Abominable Snowman (of which more in a moment) display this feature. According to zoologists, its purpose is to give more anchorage to the jaw muscles to aid in breaking tough plants.

Inevitably, there were many scientists who dismissed the film as a hoax, claiming that the creature was a man dressed in a monkey suit. But in his book *More 'Things'* the zoologist Ivan Sanderson quotes three scientists, Dr Osman Hill, Dr John Napier and Dr Joseph Raight, all of whom seem to agree that there is nothing in the film that leads them, on scientific grounds, to suspect a hoax. Casts taken of the footprints in the mud of the Creek indicate a creature roughly seven feet high.

The Asian version of Bigfoot is a Yeti, better known as the Abominable Snowman. When Eric Shipton, the Everest explorer, was crossing the Menlung Glacier on Everest in 1951 he observed a line of huge footprints; Shipton photographed one of them, with an ice axe beside it to provide scale. It was eighteen inches long and thirteen inches wide, and its shape was curious – three small toes and a huge big toe that seemed to be almost circular. The footsteps were those of a two-legged creature, not a wolf or a bear. The only animal with a vaguely similar foot is an orang-utan. But they have a far longer big toe.

Ever since European travellers began to explore Tibet they had reported legends of a huge ape-like creature called the Metoh-kangmi, which translates roughly as the filthy or abominable snowman. The stories cover a huge area, from the Caucasus to the Himalayas, from the Pamirs, through Mongolia, to the far eastern tip of Russia. In central Asia they are called Meh-teh, or Yetis, while tribes of eastern Asia refer to them as Almas. The earliest reference to them in the West seems to be a report in 1832 by B.H.Hodgson, the British Resident at the Court of Nepal, who mentioned that his native hunters were frightened by a 'wild man' covered in long dark hair. More than half a century later, in 1889, Major L.A.Waddell was exploring the Himalayas when he came across huge footprints in the snow at 17,000 feet; his bearers told him that these were the tracks of a Yeti. And the Yeti, according to the bearers, was a ferocious creature which was quite likely to attack human beings and carry them off for food. The best way to escape it was to run downhill, for the Yeti had such long hair that it would fall over its eyes and blind it when it was going downhill.

In 1921 an expedition led by Colonel Howard-Bury, making a first attempt on the north face of Everest, saw in the distance a number of large dark creatures moving against the snow of the Lhapta-la Pass; the Tibetan porters said these were Yetis. And in 1925 N.A.Tombazi, a Fellow of the Royal Geographical Society, almost managed to get a photograph of a naked, upright creature on the Zemu Glacier; but it had vanished by the time he sighted the camera. And so the legends and the sightings continued to leak back to civilization, always with that slight element of doubt which made it possible for scientists to dismiss them as lies or mistakes. Shipton's photograph of 1951 caused such a sensation because it was taken by a member of a scientific expedition who could have no possible motive for stretching the facts. Besides, the photograph spoke for him.

At least, so one might assume. The Natural History Department of the British Museum did not agree, and one of its leading authorities, Dr T.C.S.Morrison-Scott, was soon committing himself to the view that the footprint was made by a creature called the Himalayan langur. His assessment was based on a description of the Yeti by Sherpa Tensing, who said it was about five feet high, walked upright, had a conical skull and reddish-brown fur. This, said Dr Morrison-Scott, sounded quite like a langur. The objection to this was that the langur, like most apes, walks on all fours most of the time; besides, its feet have five very long toes, quite unlike the four rounded toes of the photograph. Morrison-Scott's theory was greeted with hoots of disdain, as it undoubtedly deserved to be. But that brought the identification of the strange creature no closer.

A more imaginative view was taken by the Dutch zoologist Bernard Huevelmans in a series of articles published in Paris in 1952. He pointed out that in 1934 Dr Ralph von Koenigwald had discovered some ancient teeth in the shop of a Chinese apothecary in Hong Kong – the Chinese regard powdered teeth as a medicine. One of these was a human-type molar which was twice as large as the molar of an adult gorilla, suggesting that its owner had stood about twelve feet tall. Evidence suggested that this giant – he became known as Gigantopithecus – lived around half a million years ago. Huevelmans suggested that Shipton's footprints were made by a huge biped related to Gigantopithecus. But few scientists considered his theory seriously.

In 1954 the *Daily Mail* sent out an expedition to try to capture (or at least photograph) a Yeti. It spent fifteen weeks plodding through the Himalayan snows without so much as a glimpse of the filthy snowman. But the expedition gathered one exciting piece of information. Several monasteries, they learned, possessed 'Yeti scalps', which were revered as holy relics. Several of these scalps were tracked down, and proved to be fascinating. They were all long and conical, rather like a bishop's mitre, and covered with hair, including a 'crest' in the middle, made of erect hair. One of these scalps proved to be a fake, sewn together from fragments of animal skin. But others were undoubtedly made of one piece of skin. Hairs from them were sent to experts for analysis, and the experts declared that they came from no known animal. It looked as if the existence of the Yeti had finally been proved. Alas, it was not to be.

Sir Edmund Hillary was allowed to borrow one of the scalps – he was held in very high regard in Tibet – and Bernard Huevelmans had the opportunity to examine it. It reminded him of a creature called the southern serow, a kind of goat, which he had seen in a zoo before the war. And serows exist in Nepal, 'abominable snowman' country. Huevelmans tracked down a serow in the Royal Institute in Brussels. And comparison with the Yeti scalp revealed that it came from the same animal. The skin had been stretched and moulded with steam. It was not, of course, a deliberate fake. It was made to be worn in certain religious rituals in Tibet; over the years its origin had been forgotten, and it had been designated a Yeti scalp.

All this was enough to convince the sceptics that the Yeti was merely a legend. But that conclusion was premature. Europeans who went out searching for the snowman might or might not catch a glimpse of some dark creature moving against the snow. But their tracks were observed, and photographed, in abundance. A Frenchman, the Abbè Bordet, followed three separate lots of tracks in 1955. Squadron Leader Lester Davies filmed huge footprints in the same year. Climber Don Whillans saw an ape-like creature on Annapurna in June 1970, and Lord Hunt photographed more Yeti tracks in 1978.

In Russia more solid evidence began to emerge. In 1958 Lt Col Vargen Karapetyan saw an article on the Yeti – or, as it is known in Russia, Alma – in a Moscow newspaper, and sought out the leading Soviet expert, Professor Boris Porshnev, to tell him his own story. In December 1941 his unit had been fighting the Germans in the Caucasus near Buinakst, and he was approached by a unit of partisans and asked to go and look at a man they had taken prisoner. The partisans explained that Karapetyan would have to go along to a barn to look at the 'man', because as soon as he was taken into a heated room, he stank and dripped sweat; besides, he was covered in lice. The 'man' proved to be more like an ape: naked, filthy and unkempt, he looked dull and vacant, and often blinked. He made no attempt to defend himself when Karapetyan pulled out hairs from his body, but his eyes looked as if he was begging for mercy. It was obvious that he did not understand speech. Finally, Karapetyan left, telling the partisans to make up their own minds about what to do with the creature. He heard a few days later that the 'wild man' had escaped. Obviously this story could have been an invention. But a report from the Ministry of the Interior in Daghestan confirmed its truth. The 'wild man' had been court-martialled and executed as a deserter.

It was in January 1958 that Dr Alexander Pronin, of Leningrad University, reported seeing an Alma. He was in the Pamirs, and saw the creature outlined against a cliff-top. It was man-like, covered with reddish-grey hair, and he watched it for more than five minutes; three days later he saw it again at the same spot. For some reason good Marxists poured scorn on the notion of a 'wild man'; but the evidence went on accumulating, until Boris Porshnev began to make an attempt to co-ordinate the sightings. The considerable body of evidence he has accumulated is described in some detail in Odette Tchernine's impressive book *The Yeti*.

To summarize: the evidence for the existence of the Yeti, or Alma, or Bigfoot, or Sasquatch, is very strong indeed; hundreds of sightings make it unlikely that it is an invention. If, then, we assume for a moment that it really exists, what is it?

Dr Myra Shackley, lecturer in archaeology at Leicester University, believes she knows the answer. She is convinced that the Yeti is a Neanderthal man. And this is also the conclusion reached by Odette Tchernine on the basis of the Soviet evidence.

Neanderthal man was the predecessor of modern man. He first seems to have appeared on earth about a hundred thousand years ago. He was smaller and more ape-like than modern man, with the well-known receding forehead and simian jaw. He lived in caves, and the piles of animal bones discovered in such caves suggest that Neanderthal woman was a sluttish housewife, and that his habitation must have stunk of rotting flesh. He was also a cannibal. But he was by no means a mere animal. Colouring pigments in Neanderthal caves suggest that he loved colour; he certainly wove screens of coloured flowers. And since he buried these with his dead, it seems certain that he believed in an after-life. Mysterious round stones found in his habitations suggest that he was a sun-worshipper.

Our ancestor, Cro-Magnon man, came on earth about fifty thousand years ago; it was he who made all the famous cave paintings. Neanderthal man vanished completely over the next twenty thousand years, and the mystery of his disappearance has never been solved. The general view is that he was exterminated by Cro-Magnon man (William Golding's novel *The Inheritors* is a story of the encounter between the two; so is H.G.Wells's earlier *The Grisly Men*).

The psychologist Stan Gooch advanced a startling thesis in his book *The Neanderthal Question*: that Neanderthals were not entirely exterminated, but that their women occasionally bore children to Cro-Magnon males. The descendants of these products of cross-breeding became the Jews. (It should be noted that Gooch is himself Jewish.) Gooch believes that Neanderthal man was more 'psychic' than Cro-Magnon, and that such psychic faculties as present-day man now possesses are inherited from these Neanderthal ancestors.

Whether or not we can accept Gooch's theory, it seems reasonable to suppose that Neanderthal man may have survived, driven into the wilder and less hospitable places of the earth by his conqueror. Myra Shackley has travelled to the Altai mountains of Mongolia and collected evidence for the existence of Almas. 'They live in caves, hunt for food, use stone tools, and wear animal skins and fur.' And she mentions that in 1972 a Russian doctor met a family of Almas. In fact, Odette Tchernine cites a number of such stories. Professor Porshnev discovered again and again evidence among mountain people that they knew of the existence of 'wild men'; the Abkhazians still have stories of how they drove the wild men out of the district they colonized. Tchernine refers to these wild men as 'pre-hominids'.

Porshnev himself investigated a case of a female Alma who had been caught in the Ochamchir region in the mid-nineteenth century. Hunters captured a 'wild woman' who had ape-like features and was covered in hair; for several years in captivity she was so violent that she could not be approached, and food had to be thrown to her. They called her Zana. Porshnev interviewed many old people – one was a hundred and five – who remembered Zana. They told him how she had become domesticated, and would perform simple tasks like grinding corn. She had a massive bosom, thick muscular arms and legs, and thick fingers; she could not endure warm rooms but preferred the cold. She loved to gorge herself on grapes in the vineyard, and also enjoyed wine – she would drink heavily, then sleep for hours. This may explain how she became a mother on several occasions, to different fathers. Her children usually died because she washed them in the freezing river. (Presumably, having half-human characteristics, they lacked her tremendous inherited endurance of cold.) Finally, her newborn children were taken away from her, and they grew up among the people of the village. Unlike their mother, they could talk and were reasonable human beings. The youngest of these died as recently as 1954 (Zana died about 1890). Porshnev interviewed two of her grandchildren, and noted their dark skin and Negroid looks. Shalikula, the grandson, had such powerful jaws that he could pick up a chair with a man sitting on it. Here, it would seem, is solid, undeniable evidence of the existence of 'wild men'.

5 The Disappearance of Agatha Christie

In 1926 Agatha Christie was involved in a mystery that sounds like the plot of one of her own novels. But unlike the fictional crimes unravelled by Hercule Poirot, this puzzle has never been satisfactorily solved.

At the age of thirty-six, Agatha Christie seemed an enviable figure. She was an attractive redhead, with a touch of grey, and lived with her husband, Colonel Archibald Christie, in a magnificent country house which she once described as 'a sort of millionaire-style Savoy suite transferred to the country'.

She was also the author of seven volumes of detective fiction, of which the latest, *The Murder of Roger Ackroyd*, had caused some controversy because of its 'unfair' ending. Yet the authoress was hardly a celebrity; few of her books achieved sales of more than a few thousand.

Then on the freezing cold night of 3 December 1926 she left her home at Sunningdale, in Berkshire, and disappeared.

At eleven the next morning, a Superintendent in Surrey Police was handed a report on a 'road accident' at Newlands Corner, just outside Guildford. Agatha Christie's Morris two-seater had been found halfway down a grassy bank with its bonnet buried in a clump of bushes. There was no sign of the driver, but she had clearly not intended to go far, because she had left her fur coat in the car.

By mid-afternoon the Press had heard of the disappearance, and were besieging the Christie household. From the start the police hinted that they suspected suicide. Her husband dismissed this theory, sensibly pointing out that most people commit suicide at home, and do not drive off in the middle of the night. But an extensive search of the area around Newlands Corner was organized and the Silent Pool, an allegedly bottomless lake in the vicinity, was investigated by deep-sea divers.

What nobody knew was that Agatha Christie's life was not as enviable as it looked. Her husband had recently fallen in love with a girl who was ten years his junior – Nancy Neele – and had only recently told her that he wanted a divorce. The death of her mother had been another psychological shock. She was sleeping badly, eating erratic meals, and moving furniture around the house in a haphazard manner. She was obviously distraught, possibly on the verge of a nervous breakdown.

The next two or three days produced no clues to her whereabouts. When it was reported that some female clothes had been found in a lonely hut near Newlands Corner, together with a bottle labelled 'opium', there was a stampede of journalists. But it proved to be a false alarm, and the opium turned out to be a harmless stomach remedy. Some newspapers hinted that

Archibald Christie stood to gain much from the death of his wife, but he had a perfect alibi: he was at a weekend party in Surrey. Other journalists began to wonder whether the disappearance was a publicity stunt. Ritchie-Calder suspected that she had disappeared to spite her husband, and bring his affair with Nancy Neele out into the open. He even read through her novels to see whether she had ever used a similar scenario. When the *Daily News* offered a reward reports of sightings poured in. They all proved to be false alarms.

Another interesting touch of mystery was added when her brother-in-law Campbell revealed that he had received a letter from her whose postmark indicated that it had been posted in London at 9.45 on the day after her disappearance, when she was presumably wandering around in the woods of Surrey.

In the *Mail* the following Sunday there was an interview with her husband in which he admitted 'that my wife had discussed the possibility of disappearing at will. Some time ago she told her sister, "I could disappear if I wished and set about it carefully . . . ." ' It began to look as if the disappearance, after all, might not be a matter of suicide or amnesia.

On 14 December, eleven days after her disappearance, the head waiter in the Hydropathic Hotel in Harrogate, North Yorkshire, looked more closely at a female guest and recognized her from newspaper photographs as the missing novelist. He rang the Yorkshire police, who contacted her home. Colonel Christie took an afternoon train from London to Harrogate, and learned that his wife had been staying in the hotel for a week and a half. She had taken a good room on the first floor at seven guineas a week, and had apparently seemed 'normal and happy', and 'sang, danced, played billiards, read the newspaper reports of the disappearance, chatted with her fellow guests, and went for walks'.

Agatha made her way to the dinner table, picked up an evening paper which contained the story of the search for herself, together with a photograph, and was reading it when her husband made his way over to her. 'She only seemed to regard him as an acquaintance whose identity she could not quite fix,' said the hotel's manager. And Archibald Christie told the Press: 'She has suffered from the most complete loss of memory and I do not think she knows who she is.' A doctor later confirmed that she was suffering from loss of memory. But Lord Ritchie-Calder later remembered how little she seemed to correspond with the usual condition of amnesia. When she vanished, she had been wearing a green knitted skirt, a grey cardigan and a velour hat, and carried a few pounds in her purse. When she was found she was stylishly dressed, and had three hundred pounds on her. She had told other guests in the hotel that she was a visitor from South Africa.

There were unpleasant repercussions. A public outcry, orchestrated by the Press, wanted to know who was to pay the £3,000 which the search was estimated to have cost, and Surrey ratepayers blamed the next big increase on her. Her next novel, *The Big Four*, received unfriendly reviews, but nevertheless sold nine thousand copies – more than twice as many as *The Murder of Roger Ackroyd*. And from then on (as Elizabeth Walter has described in an essay called 'The Case of the Escalating Sales') her books sold in increasing quantities. By 1950 all her books were enjoying a regular sale of more than fifty thousand copies, and the final Miss Marple story, *Sleeping Murder*, had a first printing of sixty thousand.

Agatha Christie divorced her husband (who wed Miss Neele) and in 1930 married Professor Sir Max Mallowan. But for the rest of her life she refused to discuss her disappearance, and would only grant interviews on condition that it was not mentioned. Her biographer, Janet Morgan, accepts that it was a case of nervous breakdown, followed by amnesia. Yet this is difficult to accept. Where did she obtain the clothes and the money to go to Harrogate? Why did she register under the surname of her husband's mistress? And is it possible to believe that her amnesia was so complete that, while behaving perfectly normally, she was able to read accounts of her own disappearance, look at photographs of herself, and still not even suspect her identity?

Lord Ritchie-Calder, who got to know her very well in later life, remains convinced that 'her disappearance was calculated in the classic style of her detective stories'. A television play produced after her death even speculated that the disappearance was part of a plot to murder Nancy Neele. The only thing that is certain about 'the case of the disappearing authoress' is that it turned Agatha Christie into a best-seller, and eventually into a millionairess.

6 Andrew Crosse

'The Man Who Created Life'

We are all aware, of course, that to create life in the laboratory is an impossibility. Yet this is precisely what was done in 1837 by an amateur scientist named Andrew Crosse – not once, but repeatedly, under the strictest conditions; moreover, his experiments were repeated successfully by a member of the London Electrical Society who followed Crosse's instructions to the letter. One result was that Crosse became one of the most hated men in England; clergymen denounced him as a blasphemer, local villagers damaged his property, and one vicar started to perform a ceremony of exorcism from a hill overlooking Crosse's house. Crosse became virtually a prisoner in his own home; he died eighteen years later, and his secret – if he had a secret – died with him. And the episode remains one of the strangest and most baffling in the annals of science.

Crosse had inherited wealth from his parents, as well as the beautiful manor house Fyne Court, near Broomfield, in Somerset. He had become fascinated by electricity while still a schoolboy, and spent most of his adult life experimenting with it. In 1814, when Crosse was thirty, he had delivered a lecture on his experiments, and there is a reasonable certainty that it was attended by the poet Shelley and by his future wife Mary – if this is so, then it may have inspired Mary to write her novel *Frankenstein* in 1816, and there would be some justification for describing Crosse – as one modern biographer has – as 'the man who was Frankenstein'.

But it was twenty-one years after Mary Shelley had written *Frankenstein* that Crosse performed those experiments that were to make his name famous (or infamous) throughout Europe, and which earned him his entry in the *Dictionary of National Biography*. He was attempting nothing more ambitious than to create crystals of silica. Thirty years earlier, he had passed an electric current through water that came from a cavern full of stalactites and stalagmites, and been delighted when crystals of calcium carbonate (of which stalagmites are made) formed on one of the electrodes. And now, in 1837, he wanted to make crystals of natural glass. So he made glass out of ground flint and potassium carbonate, and dissolved it in hydrochloric acid. His idea was then to allow this fluid to drip, little by little, through a lump of porous stone which had been 'electrified' by a battery, and to see whether it formed crystals. It did not. However, after two weeks, he observed that something odd was happening to the lump of red-coloured stone (it was, in fact, a piece of iron oxide from the slopes of Mount Vesuvius, chosen merely because it was porous). Little white nipples began to stick out of it. Then the 'nipples' began to grow tiny hairs, or filaments. They looked oddly like tiny insects, but Crosse knew this was impossible. On the twenty-eighth day, he went into his laboratory and examined the rock through a magnifying glass, and was staggered to see that the filaments were moving around. And after a few more days, there could be no possible doubt. The tiny creatures were walking around. Under a microscope, he could see that they were little bugs, and that the small ones had six legs while the larger ones had eight.

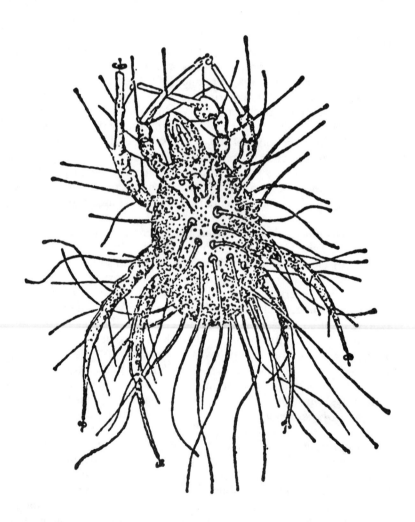

It was very strange. But it could have some natural explanation. Perhaps the original white 'nipples' were eggs laid by some insect that had got into his laboratory. Or perhaps the eggs were already present in the rock from Vesuvius. The alternative explanation – that the electric current had somehow turned crystals of iron oxide into living creatures – seemed preposterous. Still, he could see no signs of insects in his laboratory, and no 'eggs' in the iron oxide from Vesuvius, so the other explanation was worth checking. This time Crosse took a number of glass cylinders and filled them with various solutions – copper nitrate, copper sulphate, iron sulphate, and so on – and connected them all to the poles of a battery. This time, months went by with no result. But then five out of seven chemicals began to show 'certain crystalline matter', and soon after this he saw the tiny bugs swimming around. In a final effort to make sure that no 'eggs' could get into his fluids, he made glass at a temperature that would melt cast iron, and dropped it into boiling distilled water. This mixture was sealed into an air-tight retort, with platinum wires that passed through the glass stopper. The retort was washed in hot alcohol before it was placed in a dark cellar. Crosse had forgotten one thing, to leave some little ledge for the bugs to crawl out on to. But after a hundred and forty days he found just one of the tiny creatures crawling about inside the retort. After taking so many precautions, he had to believe that he had 'created' life.

Further experiments showed that the tiny organisms were able to reproduce themselves, but none of them lived beyond the first autumn frost. Entomologists to whom he showed the creatures identified them unhesitatingly as ticks or mites, of the order *Acari*; it was even proposed to label the new species *Acari Crossii*.

Crosse sent off a paper about his experiments to the London Electrical Society, and an electrician named W.H.Weeks, who lived at Sandwich in Kent, repeated the experiments, and announced his results in *Annals of Electricity* as well as in the *Transactions* of the society: he had also obtained the mites.

Crosse spoke of his results in front of a local newspaper editor, who published a friendly report in *The Western Gazette*. In no time at all Crosse's name was known throughout Europe. And he made the interesting discovery that most people were inclined to believe that he was some kind of magician. He was even blamed for a potato blight that swept the West Country that year. Clergymen denounced him as an atheist and blasphemer, a 'reviler of our holy religion', who had presumptuously set himself up as a rival to the God in whom he disbelieved. Crosse did his best to defend himself, pointing out that he was a 'humble and lowly reverencer of that Great Being', and insisting that his discovery had been made by pure chance. It made no difference. Indignant locals destroyed his fences, and one clergyman, the Rev. Philip Smith, led his congregation to a hilltop above Fyne Court and proceeded to read the ceremony of exorcism; he was interrupted by Crosse's arrival on a horse, and the crowd instantly dispersed, no doubt convinced that Crosse could blight them with his magical powers.

In 1837 Crosse was defended at the Royal Institution by one of the greatest scientists of his day, Michael Faraday. And Faraday also claimed to have duplicated Crosse's experiments and produced the mites. But even this failed to silence the critics. When it dawned on Crosse that it was now practically impossible to make the general public aware of what he had really said and done, he decided that the simplest course was to withdraw in dignified silence.

For the next ten years life was bitter. Both his wife and his brother were ill, and both died in 1846. Crosse was a lonely man; his neighbours shunned him. He was beset by financial worries – not, according to his own account, due to extravagance or excessive spending on scientific apparatus, but to his failure to pay enough attention to household expenditure, which he claimed had led to his being cheated. In a letter to the writer Harriet Martineau in 1849 – she wanted to write about his experiments – he described himself gloomily as 'surrounded by death and disease'. Yet it was in that year, when he was sixty-five years old, that he accepted an invitation to dinner and found himself sitting next to a pretty, dark-haired girl in her twenties who was fascinated by science and by Crosse himself. Cornelia Burns became his second wife. The last six years of his life were relatively happy; he went to visit Faraday in London and received friends at Fyne Court. But a deep streak of pessimism persisted; one day he told his wife that he was convinced that this world was hell, and that we are sent here because of sins committed in a previous existence (a theory Bernard Shaw was to put into the mouth of Father Keegan in *John Bull's Other Island*). At that moment there was a violent flash of electricity in the room. But it was not God rebuking him for his lack of faith, merely the result of falling snow causing a short circuit in some of his electrical equipment. He died of a stroke, at the age of seventy-one, in 1855.

The mystery of the Acari remains, and no explanation can cover all the facts. In *Oddities* Commander Rupert Gould cites Dr A.C.Oudemans, the authority on Acari, who said that he was convinced that Crosse's bugs were the common *Glycophagus domesticus*, which can get into hermetically sealed tins. But why should they crawl into solutions of copper nitrate, iron sulphate, and the rest? In *Unsolved Mysteries* Valentine Dyall suggests that the insects may have been ova transported to earth in a meteorite – a view that nowadays might find a certain amount of support in the theories of Fred Hoyle and Chandra Wickramasinghe, which suggest that life may have been brought to earth by a meteorite. But while this might explain how the lump of iron oxide contained eggs, it would not explain how they got into the other experiments.

One of the great puzzles of science is why some experiments work for some people but not for others. In my biography of Wilhelm Reich I have described how Reich placed dry sterile hay in distilled water, and how after a day or two it was full of tiny living organisms, some even visible to the naked eye. When Reich studied the experiment through a microscope he found that the cells at the edge of the hay disintegrated into 'bladders', and that the bladders would tend to cluster together. He became convinced that the bladders were the basic unit of life, and called them 'bions'. And Reich alleged that he was able to produce bions not only from organic substances like hay and egg white, but from inorganic substances like earth and coke. He seemed to believe that life pervades the whole earth, and that it can, under the right conditions, 'take over' simple cells. To silence sceptics who insisted that his culture had become contaminated by germs or minute living organisms from the air, he took the same precautions that Crosse took in his own experiments. He heated coke to red heat, then immersed it in a solution of potassium chloride; he claimed that the bions began to form immediately. These bions, he demonstrated, had an electrical charge, and were attracted to the anode or cathode of his apparatus. Reich finally concluded that his bions were not living cells but an intermediate form of life between dead and living matter.

I have gone on to cite Jung's theory of synchronicity, and of 'exteriorization phenomena'. We know that coincidences far outside the laws of probability are everyday occurrences. Jung thought that, particularly in people of high vitality, the unconscious mind can in some unknown way engineer coincidences. 'Exteriorization phenomena' are phenomena caused by these unknown powers of the unconscious – in one famous story, Jung and Freud were having a heated argument about the supernatural when Jung experienced a strange feeling of heat in his diaphragm, and there was a loud explosion from the bookcase. Jung said that this was an example of 'exteriorization phenomena' and Freud replied, 'Bosh.' 'It is not bosh', replied Jung, 'as you will realize in a moment when there is another explosion.' And at that moment another explosion occurred. Jung believed that so-called Flying Saucers were a kind of exteriorization phenomena, or 'projections' of the unconscious. It seems possible that Reich's bions – and his sightings of Flying Saucers – may have been in some way dependent upon his abnormally active unconscious mind.

What we know of Crosse suggests that the same explanation could apply to his mites. He was a man of powerful feelings, but always inclined to gloom and depression. According to Valentine Dyall, he had many illnesses during childhood, and finally learned to conquer them by sheer will-power. His biographer Peter Haining tells one amusing story of how Crosse one day tried to throw a cat into a pond (as a practical joke) and was badly bitten; later that day the cat died of hydrophobia. Some weeks later Crosse experienced agonizing pains in the arm that had been attacked, and was convinced that this was the beginning of hydrophobia. After an hour of misery and depression he decided that it would be better to make an effort to throw off the disease by will-power, so he took his gun and went out looking for game. By evening he felt well enough to eat and drink a little, and in a day or two the pain was gone.

He also had at least one semi-mystical experience. He was on his way back home from Plymouth, and stopped overnight in Exeter, feeling tired and very low. Then, according to his second wife's account,

he had scarcely lain down upon his bed, when a sudden train of thought burst upon him with such intensity, that it seemed almost like inspiration; he was not asleep, it was no dream; but yet in imagination he roamed over the universe; and beheld with the eye of fancy the unbounded glories of creation; it appeared to him, he said, as if the soul had quitted its prison of clay, and was free to reach the limits of space, or rather, to annihilate space with the intensity of its perception. Centuries of time were condensed into those moments of ecstatic life, and Nature's laws seemed clear to the omniscience of its glance; a sense of blessedness sustained him – he felt immortal.

Cornelia Crosse's *Memorials* of her husband make it clear that he was not merely a man obsessed by science; he was a poet (albeit not a very good one) and a visionary. The reader feels that he was not the kind of man who was destined for a life of total obscurity; sooner or later, his name would reach the general public . . . .

But this 'Jungian' theory is finally as unacceptable as the other two. If the Acari were the result of an abnormally active unconscious mind, then why were others able to repeat the experiments? Reich would no doubt have replied that they were able to do so because Crosse had stumbled on the secret of manufacturing bions (which, we may recall, have an electrical charge and are attracted to the anode or cathode), and the bions turned into simple life-forms. If so, then Crosse's experiments should be repeatable today. It is worth noting that the various scientists who tried to explain away Crosse's strange results actually stopped short of repeating his experiments.

7 The Curse of the Pharaohs

On 26 November 1922 the archaeologist Howard Carter peered through a small opening above the door of the tomb of Tutankhamon's tomb, holding a candle in front of him. What he saw dazzled him: 'everywhere the glint of gold'. He and his colleague Lord Carnarvon had made the greatest find in the history of archaeology. But a few days later they found a clay tablet with the hieroglyphic inscription: 'Death will slay with his wings whoever disturbs the peace of the pharaoh.' The following April Lord Carnarvon died of some unknown disease. By 1929 – a mere six years later – twenty-two people who had been involved in opening the tomb had died prematurely. Other archaeologists dismissed talk about 'the curse of the pharaohs' as journalistic sensationalism. Yet it is difficult to imagine that this long series of deaths was merely a frightening coincidence.

Tutankhamon was the heir of the 'great heretic' Akhnaton (about 1375 BC to 1360), the first monotheist king in history. He abandoned the capital Thebes, with all its temples, and built himself a new capital, called Akhetaton (Horizon of Aton), at a place now called Tell el Amarna. He worshipped only one god, the sun god Aton. His people, who were more comfortable with the host of old animal gods, disliked this new religion, and were relieved when Akhnaton died young, or perhaps possibly murdered. (So were the priests!) His successor was his son-in-law – possibly his son – Tutankhamon, who was a mere child when he came to the throne, and who died of a blow on the head at the age of eighteen. Historically speaking, therefore, Tutankhamon is a nonentity, whose name hardly deserves to be remembered. His only achievement – if it can be called that – was to restore the old religion, and move his capital back to Thebes. No one knows how he died, whether from a fall, or possibly from the blow of an assassin.

The strangest part of this story is still to come. The high priest (and court chamberlain) was a man called Ay. He seized power, and married Tutankhamon's fifteen-year-old widow, Enhosnamon. He reigned less than four years, and once again the throne was seized by a usurper, a general called Horemheb, who had been a little too slow off the mark when Tutankhamon died. The wait for the throne had apparently filled him with resentment; as soon as he became pharaoh, he behaved like a dictator, and set out to erase the names of Akhnaton and Tutankhamon from history; he had their names chiselled off all hieroglyphic inscriptions, and used the stones of the great temple of the sun at Tell el Amarna to build three pyramids in Thebes. He even destroyed many tombs of the courtiers of Ay and Tutankhamon.

Yet he omitted to do the most obvious thing of all: to destroy the tomb of

Tutankhamon, and to seize its treasures for his own treasury. Why? One possible explanation is that the location of the tomb was kept secret. But that is unlikely; after all, Horemheb came to the throne a mere four years after the death of Tutankhamon; even if the tomb's location *was* a secret, there must have been dozens of priests or workmen who could have been 'persuaded' to reveal it. It is natural to suspect that Horemheb had some other reason for deciding to leave the tomb inviolate . . . .

Howard Carter, the man who finally discovered the tomb, had come out to Egypt as a teenager – he was born in 1873 – and while still in his twenties became Chief Inspector of Monuments for Upper Egypt and Nubia. Acting on his advice, a wealthy American, Theodore Davis, began excavating the Valley of the Kings in 1902. In the previous year grave-robbers had mounted an armed attack on the men guarding the newly discovered tomb of Amonhotep II – a bloodthirsty character who was the great-grandfather of Akhnaton – and made off with all its gold and jewels. Carter had rounded them up and prosecuted them, an action that made him so unpopular with the Egyptians that he found himself without a job. Theodore Davis took him on as a draughtsman, and with Carter's help made some astonishing discoveries, including the tomb of Horemheb, of the great Queen Hatshepsut, and of Akhnaton's grandfather Thutmose IV.

It was during this period that there was a curious curtain-raiser to the story of the curse of the pharaohs. Joe Linden Smith was another skilled draughtsman who worked closely with the excavators; he was married to an attractive 28-year-old American named Corinna. Among their closest friends were Arthur and Hortense Weigel; Weigel was an English archaeologist, while Hortense, like Corinna, was a young American. One day when they were descending the slope into the Valley of the Queens, Smith and Weigel came upon a natural amphitheatre that struck them as the ideal site for the presentation of a play. They decided to present their own 'mystery play', and to invite most of the archaeological community from Luxor. But the purpose was not mere entertainment. Both men had immense admiration for Akhnaton and for the artistic productions of his reign, which were far more lifelike than the stylized works of other periods. Their aim was nothing less than to intercede with the ancient gods to lift the curse that consigned Akhnaton's spirit to wander for all eternity.

According to tradition, Akhnaton died on 26 January 1363 BC. Smith and Weigel decided to present their play on 26 January 1909, and the invitations were sent. On 23 January they held their dress rehearsal. The god Horus appeared and conversed with the wandering spirit of Akhnaton – played by Hortense – offering to grant him a wish; Akhnaton asked to see his mother, Queen Tiy. The Queen was summoned by a magical ceremony; she spoke of her sadness to see her son condemned to eternal misery. Akhnaton replied that even in his misery he still drew comfort from the thought of the god Aton; he asked his mother to recite his hymn to Aton . . . .

As Corinna Smith began to recite the hymn her words were drowned by the rising wind. Suddenly a violent storm was upon them; the gale blew sand and small stones, so the cowering workmen thought the gods were stoning them.

The rehearsal had to be abandoned, and the actors hurried back to their headquarters, the nearby tomb of Amet-Hu, once governor of Thebes. Later that evening Corinna complained of a pain in her eyes, and Hortense of cramps in her stomach. That night both had similar dreams; they were in the nearby temple of Amon, standing before the statue of the god; he came to life and struck them with his flail – Corinna in the eyes, Hortense in the stomach. The next day Corinna was in agony with inflamed eyes, and had to be rushed to a specialist in Cairo, who diagnosed one of the worst cases of trachoma – Egyptian ophthalmia – he had ever seen. Twenty-four hours later, Hortense joined Corinna in the same nursing-home; during the stomach operation that followed she came close to losing her life. The play had to be abandoned.

Howard Carter and Lord Carnarvon had both been invited to the play; at this period Carter was working for Theodore Davis. By 1914 Davis had decided that he had now found all there was to be found in the Valley of the Kings, and decided to abandon his labours. Carnarvon snapped up the concession. He knew that Davis was convinced that he had found the grave of Tutankhamon, a pit grave containing gold plates and other items; but neither Carnarvon nor Carter believed that a pharaoh would be buried so modestly.

The war made it impossible to begin digging until 1917. Then Carter began to dig, slowly and systematically, moving hundreds of tons of rubble left from earlier digs. He found nothing. By 1922 Carnarvon felt he had poured enough money into the Valley of the Kings. Carter begged for one more chance.

On 1 November 1922 he began new excavations, digging a ditch southward from the tomb of Rameses IV. On 4 November the workmen uncovered a step below the foundations of some huts Carter had discovered in an earlier dig. By evening twelve steps had been revealed, then a sealed stone gate. Carter hastened to send a telegram to Carnarvon in England; Carnarvon arrived just over two weeks later. Together Carnarvon and Carter broke their way through the sealed gate, now in a state of increasing excitement as they realized that this tomb was virtually unplundered. Thirty feet below the gate, they came upon a second. With trembling hands, Carter scraped a hole in the debris in its upper corner, and peered through; the candlelight showed him strange animals, statues and gold. There were overturned chariots, lifesize figures, gilded couches, a gold-inlaid throne. But there was no mummy, for this was only the antechamber. However, it was in this antechamber that they found the tablet with the inscription: 'Death will slay with his wings whoever disturbs the peace of the pharaoh.' It was recorded by Carter, then disappeared – they were afraid rumours of the inscription might terrify the workmen. A statue of Horus also carried an inscription stating that it was the protector of the grave. On 17 February 1923 a group of distinguished people was invited to witness the opening of the tomb itself. It took two hours to chisel a hole through into the burial chamber. Then only two sets of folding doors separated them from the magnificent gold sarcophagus that was to become world-famous; they decided to leave that for another day. The wealth that surrounded them made them all feel dazed.

Carnarvon was never to see it. That April he fell ill. At breakfast one morning he had a temperature of 104, and it continued for twelve days; his doctors suspected that he had opened an old wound with his razor while shaving, but the fever suggested a mosquito-bite. Howard Carter was sent for. Carnarvon died just before two in the morning. As the family came to his bedside, summoned by a nurse, all the lights suddenly went out, and they were forced to light candles. Later they went on again. It was a power failure that affected all Cairo. Some accounts of Lord Carnarvon's death state that the failure has never been explained, but none of them mention whether any inquiry was actually addressed to the Cairo Electricity Board.

According to Lord Carnarvon's son, another peculiar event took place that night; back in England, Carnarvon's favourite fox terrier began to howl, then died.

The newspapers quickly began printing stories about the 'curse of the pharaohs'. This was partly Carnarvon's own fault; he had sold exclusive rights in the Tutankhamon story to the London *Times*, and other newspapers had to print any stories they could unearth or concoct. But the curse story hardly needed any journalistic retouching. Arthur Mace, the American archaeologist who had helped unseal the tomb, began to complain of exhaustion soon after Carnarvon's death; he fell into a coma and died in the same hotel – the Continental – not long after Carnarvon. George Jay Gould, son of the famous American financier, came to Egypt when he heard of Carnarvon's death, and Carter took him to see the tomb. The next day he had fever; by evening he was dead. Joel Wool, a British industrialist who visited the grave site, died of fever on his way back to England. Archibald Douglas Reid, a radiologist who X-rayed Tutankhamon's mummy, suffered attacks of feebleness and died on his return to England in 1924. Over the next few years thirteen people who had helped open the grave also died, and by 1929 the figure had risen to twenty-two. In 1929 Lady Carnarvon died of an 'insect bite', and Carter's secretary Richard Bethell was found dead in bed of a circulatory collapse. Professor Douglas Derry, one of two scientists who performed the autopsy on Tutankhamon's mummy, had died of circulatory collapse in 1925; the other scientist, Alfred Lucas, died of a heart attack at about the same time.

In his book *The Curse of the Pharaohs*, Philip Vandenburg not only lists the deaths associated with Tutankhamon, but goes on to mention many other archaeologists associated with Egypt who have died prematurely. He points out how frequently these deaths seem to involve a curious exhaustion – Carter himself suffered from this, as well as from fits of depression – and speculates whether the ancient priests of Egypt knew of poisons or fungoid growths that would retain their power down the centuries. Among the premature deaths he mentions François Champollion, who decoded the Rosetta Stone, the great Egyptologist Belzoni, the Swabian doctor Theodore Bilharz (after whom the disease bilharzia was named), the archaeologist Georg Möller, and Carter's close associate Professor James Henry Breasted. It was James Breasted who reported that Carter became sick and feeble after excavating the tomb, that he seemed at times 'not all there', and that he had difficulty making decisions. Carter died at sixty-six.

Vandenberg begins his book by citing a conversation he had with Dr Gamal Mehrez, director-general of the Antiquities Department of the Cairo Museum. Mehrez, who was fifty-two, expressed disbelief in the idea of a curse. 'Look at me. I've been involved with tombs and mummies of pharaohs all my life. I'm living proof that it was all coincidence.' Four weeks later Mehrez had died of circulatory collapse. . . .

Yet although Vandenberg himself seems to discount the coincidence theory, his attempts to explain the 'curse' scientifically are unconvincing – he even considers the possibility that the shape of the pyramid can cause it to absorb certain cosmic energies capable of affecting human health, and that the Egyptians 'knew how to influence radioactive decay'.

The ancients themselves would have dismissed such theories as absurd. For them a curse was the result of a ritual to evoke a guardian 'demon' or spirit. Such beliefs have survived down to modern times. The psychical researcher Guy Lyon Playfair has described the years he spent in Brazil, and how he investigated 'poltergeist' hauntings which appeared to be the result of a curse – that is to say, of 'black magic'. Most investigators of the paranormal are inclined to believe that the poltergeist – 'noisy ghost' – is some kind of unconscious manifestation of the mind of a 'disturbed' teenager, and that when objects suddenly fly around the room, this is due to 'spontaneous psychokinesis'. Playfair, while accepting this explanation in some cases, nevertheless came to believe that most poltergeists are in fact disembodied 'spirits'. Such spirits can be persuaded, by means of rituals, to 'haunt' certain individuals, or to cause disturbances in houses. When this happens another candomblé specialist (candomblé is an African-influenced cult) is called in to dispel the malign influence. In fact, traditional magic through the ages has been based upon this belief in the use of spirits for magical purposes.

Another modern investigator, Max Freedom Long, studied the Huna religion in Hawaii, and became convinced that the Huna priests – known as kahunas – were able to cause death by means of the 'death prayer'. He writes:

> The truth was that over a period of several years during which time I checked the data through doctors frequenting the Queen's Hospital in Honolulu, not a year passed but one or more victims of the potent magic died, despite all the hospital doctors could offer by way of aid.

The kahunas, Long says, believe that man has three 'selves' or souls, known as the low self, the middle self and the high self. The low self corresponds roughly to what Freud called the unconscious; it controls man's vital forces, and seems to be predominantly emotional. The middle self is man's 'ordinary consciousness', his everyday self. The 'high self' might be called the superconscious mind; it has powers that are unknown to the everyday self. These three selves inhabit the body, and are separated from it after death. But sometimes a 'low self' may become detached from the other two. It becomes an 'earthbound spirit' of the sort that causes poltergeist disturbances. The low self, according to the kahunas, possesses memory, while the middle self does not. So a disembodied 'middle self', separated from the other two, is a wandering wraith without memory – what we would regard as a ghost.

According to Long, the 'death prayer' involves disembodied 'low spirits', who are highly susceptible to suggestion, and can easily be persuaded to obey. The victim of the death prayer experiences an increasing numbness as the spirits drain his vital energies.

Long obtained much of his information about the kahunas (recorded in his book *The Secret Science Behind Miracles*) from a doctor, William Tufts Brigham, who had studied them for many years. Brigham told him a typical story of the death prayer. He had hired a party of Hawaians to climb a mountain, and a fifteen-year-old boy became ill, experiencing a numbness that rose from his feet. He told Brigham that he was a victim of the death prayer. The kahuna in his local village hated the influence of the white men, and declared that any Hawaian who worked for the whites would become a victim of the death prayer. When the boy accepted the job with Brigham the kahuna knew it by clairvoyance, and had invoked the death prayer.

The Hawaians, who also believed that Brigham was a magician, asked him to try to save the boy. Brigham decided to try. Acting upon the assumption that the lad was being attacked by highly suggestible 'lower spirits', he stood over him and addressed the attackers, flattering them and arguing that the boy was an innocent victim, and telling them that it was the witch doctor who sent them who ought to be destroyed. He kept his mind concentrated on this idea for another hour, when suddenly the tension seemed to vanish and he experienced a sense of relief. The boy declared that he could now feel his legs again. When Brigham visited the boy's village he learned that the kahuna had died, after telling the villagers that the 'white magician' had redirected the spirits to attack him. Within hours of this he was dead. Brigham thought he had gone to sleep early, and awoke to find himself under attack, by which time it was too late.

Long believes that the kahunas originated in Africa, possibly in Egypt. 'Their journey commenced at the "Red Sea of Kane", which fits neatly into the idea that they came from Egypt by way of the Red Sea.'

The Egyptians also believed that man is a multiple being, a body animated by several spirits, the main ones being the *ka* or double (corresponding roughly to what is sometimes called the 'astral body'), the *ba*, or heart-soul, and the *khu*, or spiritual soul. There was also the *ab* (heart-soul), *khaibit* (shadow), *sekhem* (or vital force) and the *ren*, the man's name.

Long writes: 'In Egypt, as we might expect . . . there are definite traces of the kahuna system to be found', and he goes on to describe the Egyptian beliefs in some detail. He believes that the kahunas came to Hawaii by way of Egypt, and also left traces of their system in the Hindu religion.

The strange debilitating effects experienced by some of the archaeologists including Carter sound in many ways like the effects of the death prayer as described by Brigham and Long. But it is unnecessary to establish some direct connection between the kahunas of Hawaii and the religion of ancient Egypt. *If* Long and Playfair are correct, and poltergeists or 'low spirits' can be used for magical purposes, then it is logical to believe that they were used by the priests of ancient Egypt as the 'guardians of the tomb'.

In *A Search in Secret Egypt* the English occultist Paul Brunton describes a night spent in the King's Chamber in the Great Pyramid. He speaks of 'a strange feeling that I was not alone', which developed into a feeling of being surrounded by 'antagonistic beings'. 'Monstrous elemental creations, evil horrors of the underworld, forms of grotesque, insane, uncouth and fiendish aspect gathered around me. . . . The end came with startling suddenness. The malevolent ghostly invaders disappeared. . . .' After this Brunton experienced a feeling that a benevolent being was present in the chamber, then thought that he saw two high priests.

Vandenberg, who quotes this, admits that it may all have been Brunton's imagination. But he goes on to describe how when he was visiting the pyramid in 1972 a woman screamed, then collapsed and was unable to move. She said to Vandenberg later: 'It was as if something had suddenly hit me.' The guide told Vandenberg that such attacks were not unusual.

If these odd effects are merely the result of imagination, then it is also arguable that the same applies to the curse of the pharaohs. After all, Carnarvon died of something that resembled a mosquito bite, others of heart attacks, others of circulatory failure – nothing that sounds like the creeping numbness of the death curse. In a BBC programme on the curse of the pharaohs, Henry Lincoln, investigator of the mystery of Rennes-le-Château (*q.v.*), stated emphatically: 'There never was a curse of the pharaohs.' It is certainly more comfortable to think so.

8 The Devil's Footprints

The winter of 1855 was an exceptionally severe one, even in the south-west of England, where winters are usually mild. On the morning of 8 February Albert Brailsford, the principal of the village school in Topsham, Devon, walked out of his front door to find that it had snowed in the night. And he was intrigued to notice a line of footprints – or rather hoofprints – that ran down the village street. At first glance they looked like the ordinary hoofprints of a shod horse; but a closer look showed that this was impossible, for the prints ran in a continuous line, one in front of the other. If it was a horse, then it must have had only one leg, and hopped along the street. And if the unknown creature had two legs, then it must have placed one carefully in front of the other, as if walking along a tightrope. What was odder still was that the prints – each about four inches long – were only about eight inches apart. And each print was very clear, as if it had been branded into the frozen snow with a hot iron.

The villagers of Topsham were soon following the track southward through the snow. And they halted in astonishment when the hoofprints came to a halt at a brick wall. They were more baffled than ever when someone discovered that they continued on the other side of the wall, and that the snow on top of the wall was undisturbed. The tracks approached a haystack, and continued on the other side of it, although the hay showed no sign that a heavy creature had clambered over it. The prints passed under gooseberry bushes, and were even seen on rooftops. It began to look as if some insane practical joker had decided to set the village an insoluble puzzle.

But it was soon clear that this explanation was also out of the question. Excited investigators tracked the prints for mile after mile over the Devon countryside. They seemed to wander erratically through a number of small towns and villages – Lympstone, Exmouth, Teignmouth, Dawlish, as far as Totnes, about halfway to Plymouth. If it was a practical joker, he would have had to cover forty miles, much of it through deep snow. Moreover, such a joker would surely have hurried forward to cover the greatest distance possible; in fact, the steps often approached front doors, then changed their mind and went away again. At some point the creature had crossed the estuary of the river Exe – it looked as if the crossing was between Lympstone and Powderham. Yet there were also footprints in Exmouth, farther south, as if it had turned back on its tracks. There was no logic in its meandering course.

In places it looked as if the 'horseshoe' had a split in it, suggesting a cloven hoof. It was the middle of the Victorian era, and few country people doubted

the existence of the Devil. Men armed with guns and pitchforks followed the trail; when night came people locked their doors and kept loaded shotguns at hand.

It was another week before the story reached the newspapers; on 16 February 1855 the London *Times* told the story, adding that most gardens in Lympstone showed some trace of the strange visitor. The following day the *Plymouth Gazette* carried a report, and mentioned the theory of a clergyman that the creature could have been a kangaroo — apparently unaware that a kangaroo has claws. A report in the Exeter *Flying Post* made the slightly more plausible suggestion that it was a bird. But a correspondent in the *Illustrated*

London News dismissed this idea, pointing out that no bird leaves a horse-shoe-shaped print. He added that he had passed a five-month winter in the backwoods of Canada, and had never seen a more clearly defined track.

In the *Illustrated London News* for 3 March the great naturalist and anatomist Richard Owen announced dogmatically that the footmarks were those of hind foot of a badger, and suggested that many badgers had come out of hibernation that night to seek food. He did not explain why all these badgers hopped along on one hind foot. (Five years later, he was to be equally dogmatic – and equally wrong – on the subject of Charles Darwin and the origin of species.) Another correspondent, a doctor, described how he and another doctor 'bestowed considerable time in endeavouring to discover the peculiarities of this most singular impression' (the Victorians loved this kind of pompous language). He claimed that 'on more minute examination of the tracks, we could distinctly see the impressions of the toes and pad of the foot of an animal'. His own candidate was an otter. Another correspondent, who signed himself 'Ornither', was quite certain that they were the prints of a Great Bustard, whose outer toes, he claimed, were rounded. Another gentleman, from Sudbury, said he had recently seen impressions of rats surrounding a potato patch, and that they looked exactly like the drawings of 'the devil's footprints'. He thought that the rats had been leaping through the snow, landing with their full body weight and producing a roughly horseshoe-shaped impression. A Scottish correspondent thought that the culprit could be a hare or polecat bounding through the snow. These suggestions are less absurd than they sound. They would certainly explain the most baffling feature of the footprints – that they followed one upon another, as if made by a one-legged animal. But they still fail to explain why they continued for forty miles or so.

Perhaps the likeliest hypothesis is one put forward by Geoffrey Household, who edited a small book containing all the major correspondence on the matter.[1] He comments as follows, in a letter to the author:

I think that Devonport dockyard released, by accident, some sort of experimental balloon. It broke free from its moorings, and trailed two shackles on the end of ropes. The impression left in the snow by these shackles went up the sides of houses, over haystacks, etc. . . A Major Carter, a local man, tells me that his grandfather worked at Devonport at the time, and that the whole thing was hushed up because the balloon destroyed a number of conservatories, greenhouses, windows, etc. He says that the balloon finally came down at Honiton.

This information is fascinating, and could well represent the solution of the mystery. But if so there is still one major anomaly to be explained. A glance at the map of the 'footprints' will show that they meandered in a kind of circle between Topsham and Exmouth. Would an escaped balloon drift around so erratically? Surely its route would tend to be a more or less straight line, in the direction of the prevailing wind which, moreover, was blowing from the east.

The fact that it took a week for the first report of the mystery to appear in

[1] *The Devil's Footprints*, edited by G.A.Household, Devon Books 1985.

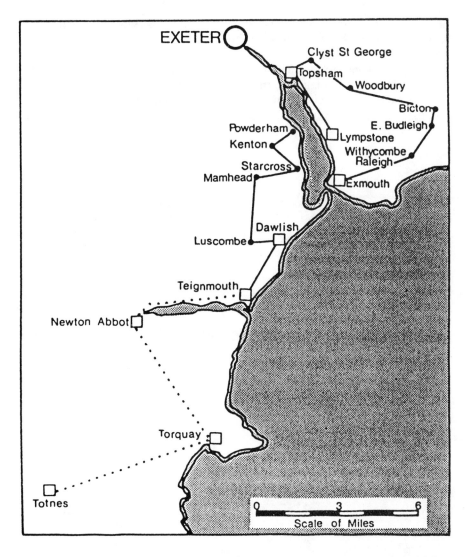

print means that certain vital clues have been lost for ever. It would be interesting to know, for example, whether the snow that fell that night was the first snow of February 1855. It had been a hard winter that year, and many small animals, including rats, rabbits and badgers, must have been half starved by February, and have been out looking for food. The letter to the *Plymouth Gazette* (dated 17 February) begins: 'Thursday night, the 8th of February, was marked by a heavy fall of snow, followed by rain and boisterous wind from the east, and in the morning frost.' Small animals had probably been out every night, but it was not until that Friday morning, with its fresh carpet of snow, that their tracks were noticed for the first time. Such tracks would have sunk deep into the soft snow, and would have been further deepened by the rain before they were frozen solid. This would explain why they seemed to be 'branded' into the snow.

But if the ground was already covered with snow before the night of 8 February, then one more plausible theory would have to be abandoned. And in any case it fails to explain how the tracks managed to wander over rooftops and haystacks. . .. At this distance in time, the only certainty seems to be that the mystery is now insoluble.

9 Was Dillinger Shot?

Towards the end of his short life, John Herbert Dillinger was designated 'public enemy number one', a distinction he shared with hold-up men like Baby Face Nelson, Pretty Boy Floyd and 'Bonnie and Clyde'. According to police records, Dillinger's sudden and violent end occurred outside the Biograph cinema in Chicago on 22 July 1934, when he was shot down by FBI agents. But since then there have been frequent doubts expressed about whether the man who died was actually the famous gangster.

John Herbert Dillinger was born on 22 June 1903, the product of an unhappy home life. When he was in sixth grade at school he was charged with stealing coal from the Pennsylvania Railroad's wagons to sell to residents of his Indianapolis neighbourhood. An angry magistrate shouted at him, 'Your mind is crippled!'

When his father bought a small farm outside Mooresville, Indiana, Dillinger found country life intolerable. When a love affair went wrong he stole a car, drove to Indianapolis, and enlisted in the US Navy. During his four months as a sailor he was AWOL several times, and finally deserted in December. Back in Indiana, he married a sixteen-year-old girl and moved in with her parents. One day, after drinking in a pool hall, Dillinger and a former convict named Edgar Singleton concocted a robbery plan. They attacked a Mooresville grocer with a baseball bat, but the grocer fought back so vigorously that the would-be bandits fled. Dillinger was arrested on suspicion. When his father arrived at the gaol he admitted to the robbery, and the prosecutor promised his father that his son would receive a lenient sentence if he threw himself on the mercy of the court. It was Dillinger's bad luck to be brought before a severe judge, who fined him $200 and sentenced him to from ten to twenty years. Outraged at the broken promise, Dillinger made several unsuccessful attempts to escape from the State Reformatory at Pendleton. He also came under the influence of two determined bank robbers – Harry Pierpont and Homer Van Meter. Dillinger, who had homosexual tendencies, also had a lover in prison.

Released in May 1933, after a petition from the residents of Mooresville, Dillinger set out to organize a mass escape for his former friends, who were then in the state prison in Michigan City. He began committing a series of bank robberies, in one of them netting $10,600. But a girl cashier in a bank at Daleville, Indiana, told the police that she felt that Dillinger – who wore a straw boater to commit the robbery – was anxious not to frighten her. His sense of impudent humour revealed itself when, in the World Fair in Chicago in the summer of 1933, he asked a policeman if he would snap a picture of himself and of his girl-friend Mary Longnaker.

In September 1933 Dillinger tossed three guns wrapped in newspapers into the athletic field at Michigan City prison, but other inmates found them and handed them over to the Warden. Next, Dillinger bribed the foreman of a thread-making company to conceal loaded guns in a barrel that was being sent to the shirt shop in the prison. But by the time his friends broke out of gaol Dillinger was already back in custody again – police keeping a watch on his girl-friend Mary had succeeded in arresting him. Ten men escaped. Shortly after, they rescued Dillinger from the Lima gaol, killing Sheriff Jess Sarber in the process. Eight days later, Dillinger and Pierpont walked into the gaol at Peru, Indiana, explained that they were tourists, and asked the police chief what precautions they had taken against the Dillinger gang. The police showed them their arsenal; Dillinger and Pierpont produced their guns, and left town with a car full of machine guns, shotguns and bullet-proof vests.

Now the 'Dillinger mob' (as the press had already dubbed them) committed a whole series of robberies – the exact number is not certain – which made them notorious. When Dillinger was in a bank in Greencastle, Indiana, he saw a farmer standing at the counter with a pile of money in front of him. He asked, 'Is that your money or the bank's?' 'Mine,' the farmer said. 'Keep it,' said Dillinger, and walked out with his sack full of the bank's cash. This kind of story brought Dillinger a reputation as a modern Robin Hood. The robbery brought the gang over $75,000. That winter they decided to move down to a warmer climate, and drove to Daytona Beach, Florida. But when they moved to Tucson, Arizona, their luck ran out: a fire broke out in their hotel, and a fireman discovered that their cases contained guns and ammunition. They were arrested and sent back to Indiana. Pierpont was charged with killing Sheriff Sarber.

On 3 March 1934 Dillinger made his spectacular escape from Crown Point gaol, Indiana, with a wooden gun that he had carved with a razor. The escape made him famous. (In fact, later investigation showed that Dillinger had somehow managed to get a real gun from somewhere.) Two weeks after the escape, Dillinger's fellow-escapee, Herbert Youngblood, was killed in a battle with police. Dillinger quickly organized another gang, including Homer Van Meter and the short-tempered Baby Face Nelson (real name Lester Gillis). He also sent money for Pierpont's defence, but it did no good – Pierpont and another accomplice died in the electric chair. Soon after this Dillinger himself narrowly escaped death in a gun battle with police in St Paul, Minnesota. A month later police closed in around Dillinger's hideout at Little Bohemia Lodge, near Rhinelander, Wisconsin, but again the gang escaped. Only some innocent bystanders were shot. (The comedian Will Rogers joked that the only way Dillinger would get shot was if he got among some innocent bystanders some time.)

Under a plastic surgery operation to alter his face, Dillinger almost died, but the surgeon managed to pull his tongue out of his throat and got him breathing again.

With his new face, Dillinger had the confidence to go out into the open again. In Chicago he began to date a waitress named Polly Hamilton. Polly's

room-mate was a 42-year-old woman called Anna Sage, who had served time
for running a brothel. Anna was under threat of deportation, and when she
learned Dillinger's identity it struck her that she might persuade the
authorities to lift the deportation order if she betrayed him. Dillinger was
now using the name James Lawrence.

So it came about that on the evening of 22 July 1934 Dillinger took his girl-
friend Polly and Anna Sage to the Biograph cinema to see *Manhattan
Melodrama*, starring Clark Gable. Anna Sage was wearing a bright red dress,
in order to be easily identifiable. As they came out of the cinema FBI agent
Melvin Purvis approached him and challenged him. The gangster pulled a
Colt automatic from his pocket and sprinted for the nearest alleyway. Three
agents fired, and Dillinger fell dead, with a bullet through his left eye; the man
who had fired it was police detective Martin Zarkovich, of East Chicago.
Later that day newsmen were taken to the morgue to see Dillinger's body.
Foreign correspondent Negley Farson tells how the policeman pulled back
the sheet over the naked body, and said grinning: 'Well hung, isn't he?'

But was it Dillinger? The autopsy notes – made by Dr J.J.Kearns, the Cook
County chief pathologist – reveal that the corpse's eyes were brown.
Dillinger's were blue. The dead man possessed a rheumatic heart condition,
chronic since childhood. Dillinger did not – he would not have been allowed
to join the navy if he had. Lawrence was shorter and heavier than Dillinger,
and had none of the scars and wounds or birthmarks that Dillinger was
known to have.

Crime writer Jay Robert Nash has argued that the FBI was duped into
believing that the dead man was Dillinger, and that J.Edgar Hoover was too
embarrassed to admit the mistake afterwards. 'Jimmy Lawrence', according
to Nash, was a small-time hoodlum, who came from Wisconsin to Chicago
about 1930 and was often seen in the neighbourhood of the Biograph cinema.
If Nash is correct, then we may assume that the 'lady in red' deliberately 'set
up' the small-time hoodlum in a plot to provide Dillinger with a permanent
escape. A photograph taken from the handbag of Dillinger's girl-friend Billie
Frechette some time before his 'killing' shows her with a man who bears an
amazing resemblance to the corpse of James Lawrence. It seems possible,
therefore, that she was also involved in the plot to take the heat off her former
lover.

Within months Dillinger's gang was wiped out. Homer Van Meter was
killed in an alley and Baby Face Nelson died in a gun battle, after killing two
FBI agents. Harry Pierpont attempted to escape from the death house in the
Ohio State Prison by carving a gun out of soap, but the ruse failed. He was
electrocuted in October 1934.

What happened to Dillinger? A fellow-gangster, Blackie Audett, who
claims to have been in the Biograph cinema that evening, asserts in his book
Wrapsheet that Dillinger married and fled to Oregon. He 'disappeared' in the
1940s.

10 The Mystery of Eilean More
The Island of Disappearing Men

In the empty Atlantic, seventeen miles to the west of the Hebrides, lie the Flannan Islands, known to seafarers as the Seven Hunters. The largest and most northerly of these is called Eilean More – which means in fact 'big island'. Like the *Mary Celeste*, its name has become synonymous with an apparently insoluble mystery of the sea.

These bleak islands received their name from a seventh-century bishop, St Flannan, who built a small chapel on Eilean More. Hebridean shepherds often ferried their sheep over to the islands to graze on the rich turf; but they themselves would never spend a night there, for the islands are supposed to be haunted by spirits and by 'little folk'. In the last decades of the nineteenth century, as Britain's sea trade increased, many ships sailing north or south from Clydebank were wrecked on the Flannans, and in 1895 the Northern Lighthouse Board announced that a lighthouse would be built on Eilean More. They expected construction to take two years; but rough seas, and the problems of hoisting stones and girders up a 200-foot cliff, made it impossible to stick to the schedule; Eilean More lighthouse was finally opened in December 1899. For the next year its beam could be seen reflected on the rough seas between Lewis and the Flannans. Then, eleven days before Christmas 1900, the light went out.

The weather was too stormy for the Northern Lighthouse Board steamer to go and investigate, even though the lighthouse had been built with two landing-stages, one to the west and one to the east, so one of them would always be sheltered from the prevailing wind. Joseph Moore, waiting on the seafront at Loch Roag, had a sense of helplessness as he stared westward towards the Flannans. It was inconceivable that all three men on Eilean More – James Ducat, Donald McArthur and Thomas Marshall – could have fallen ill simultaneously, and virtually impossible that the lighthouse itself could have been destroyed by the storms.

On Boxing Day, 1900, the dawn was clear and the sea less rough. The *Hesperus* left harbour soon after daylight; Moore was so anxious that he refused to eat breakfast, pacing the deck and staring out towards the islands; the mystery had tormented him, and now he was too excited to take food.

The swell was still heavy, and the *Hesperus* had to make three approaches before she was able to moor by the eastern jetty. No flags had answered their signals, and there was no sign of life.

Moore was the first to reach the entrance gate. It was closed. He cupped his hands and shouted, then hurried up the steep path. The main door was closed, and no one answered his shouts. Like the *Mary Celeste*, the lighthouse was empty. In the main room the clock had stopped, and the ashes in the fireplace were cold. In the sleeping quarters upstairs – Moore waited until he was joined by two seamen before he ventured upstairs, afraid of what he might find there – the beds were neatly made, and the place was tidy.

James Ducat, the chief keeper, had kept records on a slate. The last entry was for 15 December at 9 a.m., the day the light went out. But this had not been for lack of oil; the wicks were trimmed and the lights all ready to be lit. Everything was in order. So it was clear that the men had completed their basic duties for the day before tragedy struck them; when evening came there had been no one on the island to light the lamp. But the 15th of December had been a calm day. . . .

The *Hesperus* returned to Lewis with the men's Christmas presents still on board. Two days later investigators landed on Eilean More, and tried to reconstruct what had happened. At first it looked as if the solution was quite straightforward. On the westward jetty there was evidence of gale damage; a number of ropes were entangled round a crane which was sixty-five feet above sea-level. A tool chest kept in a crevice forty-five feet above this was missing. It looked as if a hundred-foot wave had crashed in from the Atlantic and swept it away, as well as the three men. The fact that the oilskins belonging to Ducat and Marshall were missing seemed to support this theory; they only wore them to visit the jetties. So the investigators had a plausible theory. The two men had feared that the crane was damaged in the storm; they had struggled to the jetty in their oilskins, then been caught by a sudden huge wave. . . . But in that case, what had happened to the third man, Donald McArthur, whose oilskins were still in the lighthouse? Had he perhaps rushed out to try to save them and been swept away himself?

All these theories came crashing when someone pointed out that the 15th had been a calm day; the storms had not started until the following day. Then perhaps Ducat had simply entered the wrong date by mistake? That theory also had to be abandoned when, back at Loch Roag, Captain Holman of the *Archer* told them he had passed close to the islands on the night of the 15th, and that the light was already out. . . .

Then what if the three men had been on the jetty on a calm morning – which would explain why McArthur was not wearing his oilskins – and one of them had slipped into the water? Perhaps the other two had jumped in after him and been drowned. But then there were ropes and lifebelts on the jetty – why should men leap into the water when they only had to throw in a lifebelt?

Suppose the drowning man was unconscious, and could not grab a lifebelt? In that case only one of his companions would have jumped in after him, leaving the other on the jetty with a rope. . . .

Another theory was that one of the three men had gone insane and pushed the others to their deaths, then thrown himself into the sea. It is just possible; but there is not the slightest shred of evidence for it.

The broadcaster Valentine Dyall – the 'Man in Black' – suggested the most plausible explanation in his book *Unsolved Mysteries*. In 1947 a Scottish journalist named Iain Campbell visited Eilean More on a calm day, and was standing near the west landing when the sea suddenly gave a heave, and rose seventy feet over the jetty. Then, after about a minute, it subsided back to normal. It could have been some freak of the tides, or possibly an underwater earthquake. Campbell was convinced that anyone on the jetty at that time would have been sucked into the sea. The lighthouse keeper told him that this curious 'upheaval' occurs periodically, and that several men had almost been dragged into the sea.

But it is still hard to understand how *three* men could be involved in such an accident. Since McArthur was not wearing his oilskins, we can presume he was in the tower when it happened – *if it* happened. Even if his companions were swept away, would he be stupid enough to rush down to the jetty and fling himself into the sea?

Only one thing is clear: that on that calm December day at the turn of the century, some accident snatched three men off Eilean More, and left not even a shred of a clue to the mystery.

11 Fulcanelli and the Mysteries of Alchemy

In the autumn of 1926 there appeared in Paris a limited edition of a book called *The Mystery of the Cathedrals – La Mystère des Cathédrales –* whose author was named on the title page simply as 'Fulcanelli'. It was a book written by a man who claimed to be an alchemist, and was addressed to his fellow-alchemists. Its thesis is that the great Gothic cathedrals are not simply temples of the Christian religion but are also 'stone books' whose pages contain the encoded secrets of alchemy. According to Fulcanelli, the word 'Gothic' is not derived from the Germanic people known as the Goths but from the word *argot*, meaning slang. *Arts gothiques –* Gothic art – should be spelt *argotiques*: for argot is a language used by those who do not wish their meaning to be understood by outsiders. The rest of the book is an elegant exposition of some of the 'stone secrets' of the cathedrals of Notre Dame, Amiens and Bourges.

The preface to the first edition was written by one 'Eugene Canseliet', who declares that the author of the book, his 'Master', has now disappeared. 'Having achieved the pinnacle of knowledge, could he refuse to obey the commands of Destiny?' 'Fulcanelli is no more,' says Canseliet, and then goes on to thank the artist, Julien Champagne, 'to whom my master has entrusted the illustration of his work'.

Although printed only in an edition of three hundred copies – or possibly because of this – the reputation of *Mystery of the Cathedrals* continued to grow, so that another edition was called for in 1957. In his new preface Canseliet admits that 'Fulcanelli' is a pseudonym under which his master has chosen to conceal his identity, and he quotes a long letter from Fulcanelli to *his* master, congratulating him on finally achieving the 'Gift of God' or the 'Great Work', the Philosopher's Stone of the alchemists.

When the book was translated into English in 1971 it contained an additional introduction by the translator's husband, Walter Lang – the pseudonym of Edward Campbell – in which he reveals that he has met Canseliet, and learned that Canseliet *had* seen Fulcanelli after his 'disappearance' in 1922. That meeting occurred thirty years later, yet according to Canseliet, his master appeared to be thirty years younger than when he had last seen him. Fulcanelli had been eighty in 1924; now he looked a mere fifty. What was stranger still was that Fulcanelli was now dressed as a woman. Canseliet's story was that he had received a summons from Fulcanelli, and journeyed to a château in the mountains. There he was greeted by Fulcanelli in his normal male guise, and assigned an alchemical laboratory to work in. A few days later he strolled downstairs early in the morning and stood in his braces. Across the courtyard he saw a group of three women dressed in the style of the sixteenth century. As they passed him one of them turned, and he recognized Fulcanelli. But later Canseliet recollected that one of the basic symbols of alchemy is the androgyne or hermaphrodite, and that this is sometimes used as a symbol of the 'completed work' – the achievement of the philosopher's stone. Was Fulcanelli telling him that he had now achieved the aim of a lifetime?

By the time *Mystery of the Cathedrals* appeared in English, Fulcanelli had achieved a legendary status, rather like that of the Comte de Saint-Germain (see chapter 32). This was largely due to the role he plays in a best-selling work by Louis Pauwels and Jacques Bergier, *The Morning of the Magicians* (1960), which was largely responsible for the 'occult revival' of the 1960s. According to Pauwels, his friend Bergier was studying chemistry in 1933 when he confided to his professor his desire to study alchemy – and was instantly and predictably rebuffed. The student protested that one form of alchemy – nuclear energy – should be possible, but the professor assured him that this was also an impossibility. All the same, Bergier continued to study alchemy. From 1934 to 1940 he worked with André Helbronner, the distinguished physicist who died in Buchenwald. And among Helbronner's acquaintance there were many pseudo-alchemists, and at least one genuine alchemist, whose name Bergier never learned. 'The man of whom we are speaking disappeared some time ago without leaving any visible traces, to lead a clandestine existence, having severed all connection between himself and the century in which he lived.' Bergier can only guess that he may have been the man who, under the pseudonym of Fulcanelli, wrote 'two strange and admirable books, *Les Demeures Philosophales* and *La Mystère des Cathédrales . . .*'

Pauwels goes on to tell how, one afternoon in June 1937, Bergier thought he was in the presence of Fulcanelli. At Helbronner's request Bergier met the 'alchemist' at the laboratory of the Gas Board in Paris. What the man had to tell him was that Helbronner's researches into nuclear energy were very close to success, and that 'the research in which you and your colleagues are engaged is fraught with terrible dangers . . . for the whole human race'. Radioactivity, said the alchemist, could poison the atmosphere of the planet, and a few grams of metal could produce enough energy to destroy a whole city. 'Alchemists have known it for a very long time.' Picking up Soddy's book *The Interpretation of Radium*, he read aloud a paragraph suggesting that earlier civilizations (Atlantis?) had been destroyed by atomic radiation.

But the most interesting part of the account lies in the alchemist's reply to Bergier's question about the nature of his researches.

I can tell you this much: you are aware that in the official science of today the role of the observer becomes more and more important . . . The secret of alchemy is this: there is a way of manipulating matter and energy so as to produce what modern scientists call a 'field of force.' This field acts on the observer and puts him in a privileged position *vis-à-vis* the Universe. From this position he has access to the realities which are ordinarily hidden from us by time and space, matter and energy. This is what we call 'The Great Work'.

'But what about the philosopher's stone? The fabrication of gold?'
'These are only applications, particular cases. The essential thing is not the
transmutation of metals, but that of the experimenter himself. It's an ancient secret
that a few men rediscover once in a century.'

Jacques Sadoul, another modern student of alchemy, makes the same point in
his book *Alchemists and Gold.*

Actually the transmutatory powder was simply *an experiment* carried out at the
end of the Master Work, to make certain that the substance manufactured was
indeed the Philosopher's Stone. . . . Their aim, after having transmuted a metal,
was to transmute themselves by swallowing a homoeopathic dose of the Stone
twice a year.

When he swallows this dose, the alchemist loses all his hair, nails and teeth;
but they grow again, stronger and healthier than before. The adept becomes
younger, and no longer needs food although he may still eat for enjoyment.

    Most modern readers will be understandably sceptical about all this, and
the only full-length book on Canseliet's mysterious Master, *The Fulcanelli
Phenomenon* by Kenneth Raynor Johnson (1980), will do little to undermine
his scepticism. He tells how in the 1930s a student of the occult named Robert
Ambelain became so intrigued by Fulcanelli's books (the second, *The
Dwelling Places of Philosophy*, is an expansion of the ideas of the first) that he
set out to try to track him down. He called on the publisher, Jean Schemit, to
ask permission to quote Fulcanelli's books in a work of his own, *In the
Shadow of the Cathedrals.* Schemit told him how, in the early part of 1926,
he was visited by a shortish man with a long Gallic moustache. The stranger
began talking to Schemit about Gothic architecture, and claimed that it was a
kind of code ('argot'), known as the 'green language'. He went on to argue
that slang contained many plays on words and puns that actually indicated a
profound philosophical depth: in fact, it was the ancient hermetic language,
the 'Language of the Birds' – that is to say, of the initiates. He then left. A few
weeks later Canseliet appeared in Schemit's office, and left with him the
manuscript of *The Mystery of the Cathedrals.* Schemit read it, and
recognized the speech patterns of his previous visitor. He decided to publish
it. Soon after, Canseliet called again, bringing with him the artist who would
illustrate the book, Jean-Julien Champagne. And in Champagne Schemit
recognized his previous visitor. Canseliet showed him 'extraordinary respect
and admiration, addressing him one minute as 'Master', the next as 'my
Master'. Canseliet also referred to Champagne as 'my Master' in his absence.
Schemit consequently reached the conclusion that Fulcanelli *was*
Champagne.

    Canseliet always insisted that his friend Champagne was simply an
illustrator, but this was flatly contradicted by an article in a popular occult
magazine containing a description of an illustration by Champagne; the
illustration was full of alchemical symbols, and the author of the article
admitted that the description was by Champagne himself. The same author,
a man called Jules Boucher, told Ambelain that Champagne possessed a
biscuit tin containing gum resin, and that Champagne would often inhale its

odours deeply, telling Boucher that it possessed some magical quality that enabled him to gain 'intuitive insights into the knowledge he sought'. Boucher also said that Champagne could induce 'OBE's' – 'out-of-the-body experiences' – at will.

Champagne had died in 1932, in his mid-sixties. His former landlady told Ambelain that Canseliet and Champagne had occupied rooms at 59 bis rue de Rochechouart – the attic – and that Canseliet treated Champagne with great respect, addressing him as Master. So it would seem to be a logical conclusion that Champagne *was* Canseliet's 'master' – i.e., Fulcanelli.

Boucher – who was also a 'pupil' of Champagne – had no doubt that Champagne and Fulcanelli were the same person. When Champagne was correcting the proofs of *The Mystery of the Cathedrals* he became extremely indignant at printing errors, and the proofs of the two books 'were redrafted eight times under the watchful eyes of their author'. Moreover, said Jules Boucher, Champagne wrote the introductions to the books, which he asked Canseliet to sign.

Canseliet, predictably, denies all this. He claims that Schemit never met Champagne, and insists that he himself wrote the introductions. He tends to be dismissive of Boucher's claims to have known Champagne intimately. But then if Champagne and Canseliet invented Fulcanelli between them, this would be perfectly understandable. Having gone to the trouble of creating a modern myth – not unlike that of Saint-Germain – why should he admit that the whole thing is a straightforward piece of mystification?

Kenneth Raynor Johnson's arguments against the Champagne-Fulcanelli identification are also unconvincing. He points out that Champagne was a well-known practical joker, as well as an alcoholic. As an example of Champagne's sense of humour, he tells how Champagne advised a gullible student that the first step in alchemy was to fill his room with bags of coal. When the student had heaved sack after sack up several flights of stairs, and had scarcely enough room left to lie down on his bed, Champagne told him that the search for the philosopher's stone was a waste of time, and that he had better forget it. This suggests that Champagne's sense of humour was both puerile and cruel. This, Johnson argues, hardly sounds like the author of *The Mystery of the Cathedrals*, to which the obvious answer is: why not? Immersion in magic and 'occultism' seems to demand a peculiar temperament; it can be seen in a dozen cases, from Paracelsus and Cornelius Agrippa to Macgregor Mathers and Aleister Crowley, all of whom combined the temperament of a genuine 'seeker after truth' with that of a confidence trickster. Contemporary accounts reveal that the 'great adept' Saint-Germain was vain, talkative and boastful, and among 'adepts' this seems to be the rule rather than the exception.

Does this mean then that alchemy should be regarded as a fantasy or a waste of time? The commonsense answer should obviously be yes. But common sense can easily lead us into error, as when it tells us that the sun revolves round the earth or that matter is solid. Jung's studies of alchemy led him to conclude – like Bergier's mysterious alchemist – that the real purpose of alchemy is to transform the alchemist: in other words, that it is, like yoga or mysticism, a spiritual discipline. The main difference between Jung and Freud was that for Freud the world is divided into sick people and 'normal' people, while Jung had always been fascinated by 'supernormal' people – saints and men of genius. Jung wanted to find a connection between 'depth psychology' and supernormal people, and thought that he might have found it in alchemy, which like certain earlier researchers he was inclined to see as a 'mystery religion'. But after studying obscure alchemical texts for many years, and attempting to 'interpret' them as if they were full of dream symbolism, he reached the somewhat disappointing conclusion that the alchemist 'projected' his own basic obsessions into his experiments, much as we might 'see' faces in the clouds, so that alchemy became a kind of mirror in which he saw his own hidden depths. In other words, it was a kind of unconscious self-deception.

Yet in his later work on synchronicity (see Chapter 36) Jung had stumbled on some vital clues to this problem. By synchronicity Jung meant 'meaningful coincidence as, for example, when we hear a name for the first time, then hear it half a dozen times more over the next twenty-four hours, almost as if 'fate' is trying to make sure we learn it by heart. Jung tried hard to find 'scientific' explanations for such coincidences, talking about an 'acausal connecting principle' and about Heisenberg's uncertainty principle. Critics like Arthur Koestler have suggested that Jung was merely trying to dress up 'occult' ideas in acceptable scientific terminology.

But it is generally agreed that the basis of 'occultism' is the statement attributed to Hermes Trismegistos (after whom the 'hermetic art' is named) 'As above, so below', which means that the pattern of the greater universe (macrocosm) is repeated in the smaller universe of the human soul (microcosm). In *Alchemists and Gold* Jacques Sadoul begins by quoting a translation of the so-called Emerald Tablet of Hermes by Fulcanelli: 'As below, so above; and as above, so below. With this knowledge alone you may work miracles.'

What we might call the Jungian interpretation of this is as follows. It is self-evident that external events influence our states of mind (or soul). But perhaps the most fundamental tenet of occultism is that the human soul can influence external events, possibly by some process of induction not unlike that employed in an induction coil. The principle of the latter is as follows. When an electric current is passed through a coil of wire it creates a 'field' around the wire. And if another coil of wire, with more 'circles' of wire, is wound around the first, a far more powerful current is somehow induced in the second coil. A piece of American electrical equipment runs off a current of 120 volts; in England the voltage is twice as high; so if I wish to use an American electric razor in England, or vice versa, I merely have to buy a small transformer which will either 'step up' 120 to 240 volts, or 'step down' 240 volts to 120. The electrical vibrations in one coil communicate themselves to the other, and induce a stronger – or weaker – current.

The law 'As above, so below' may be thus interpreted: the human soul can, under the right circumstances, induce its own 'vibrations' in the material world; one result of this process is coincidence – or rather, synchronicity.

It is also true, of course, that the 'mind-transformer' can be used for the opposite purpose: to 'step down' the vital current to a lower level. This is in fact the problem with most human beings: we use our mind-transformer the wrong way round. More often than not, a vague general sense of 'discouragement' or pessimism causes 'negative induction' in the environment. We are all familiar with the feeling that this is just 'one of those days', and how on such days everything seems to go wrong. Moreover, we all recognize instinctively that this is due to our own negative attitudes; they seem to attract bad luck.

The reverse is the feeling that things are somehow destined to go right, and that in some odd way the optimism induced by this intuition will *induce* 'serendipity'. In such moments we also have a glimpse of an exciting insight: that if we could learn to create this mood of optimism *at will* we could somehow *make* things go right. Everyone recognizes the other side of the same coin: that pessimistic people who 'expect the worst' somehow attract bad luck. Yet the feeling that the right mental attitudes can induce good luck is oddly worrying; it seems to be tempting fate. . . .

All this, I would argue, is implied in the Jungian theory of synchronicity, and in the 'hermetic law', As above, so below. And if this law is also the starting-point of alchemy, then it is obviously a mistake to think of alchemy as a misguided form of chemistry whose aim is the transmutation of lead into gold. Sadoul is obviously right; the transmutation is merely a symbol of something else. But if the transmutation is merely another name for mystical insight, a synonym for satori or enlightenment, then why waste time with retorts and crucibles?

What seems to be implied is that alchemy is *a method*, like yoga or the disciplines of Zen. Ancient alchemists may well have believed that lead can be transmuted into gold by some straightforward chemical process, but their modern counterparts know better. They recognize that, in a basic sense, alchemy is a symbol for the actual process of living. The traditional alchemist begins with the so-called *prima materia* (which some believe to be salt, some mercury, others earth, even water), which must be mixed with 'secret fire' and heated in a sealed vessel; this should first of all become black (the 'nigredo') then white (the 'albedo'). This is mixed with 'mercury' (but not necessarily the mercury of the chemist), and then dissolved in acid; after a process known as 'the green lion' it finally turns red – the philosopher's stone. For all human beings, the *prima materia* is the world of their everyday experience. Pleasant surprises, enjoyable physical stimuli, flashes of 'holiday consciousness' can transmute everyday experience into what J.B.Priestley calls 'delight', and that strange feeling that 'all is well'. When we experience such moments we always find ourselves confronting the same insight: that, as absurd as it sounds, the pleasant experience that triggered the insight *was unnecessary*; we should be able to achieve it *by an act of will*.

The whole chemical process of alchemy may be seen as a parallel to this experience. Canseliet remarks that Fulcanelli would never have attempted 'the great work' unless he started with a conviction that it was possible. And this seems to be the initial step in the process we are discussing: the creation of a state of optimism, a pragmatic state of 'intentionality'. The implication of the classic texts of alchemy is that the alchemist must somehow 'support' the chemical process by a psychological process. It is only when he has achieved the right state of mind, of 'positive induction', that the transformation can be achieved. And the ultimate aim of the process is not the philosopher's stone but the state of mind in which the philosopher's stone can be manufactured. The aim of the alchemical process is to make the 'operator' recognize that he can control his own mental states. The use of sexual symbolism in alchemy may be a hint that the nearest most human beings come to this control is in the mental component of sexual experience.

In a sense, therefore, it is irrelevant whether Fulcanelli really existed or whether he was Jean-Julien Champagne, or even whether Canseliet invented him. The 'adepts' themselves recognize this basic principle when they insist upon anonymity. All the classic texts seem to agree that physical transmutation *is* a genuine possibility; yet even this may be regarded as an irrelevant by-product. Sadoul states that this is why no successful alchemist has ever bothered to make large quantities of gold.

In a *Books and Bookmen* review of Timothy Leary's *Flashbacks* (November 1983) John Walsh remarked: 'Expanded consciousness, Leary maintains, leads to a radically different, wider and more libertarian system of "imprinting" by which the human brain gives itself, in a single blinding moment, an image of the whole world within which it moves, and thereafter draws strength and mental sustenance from such a paradigm.' This could also be taken as a convenient summary of the fundamental purpose of 'alchemy'.

12 The Grey Man of Ben MacDhui

At the 27th Annual General Meeting of the Cairngorm Club in Aberdeen, in December 1925, the eminent mountaineer Professor Norman Collie made a startling disclosure. He told how in 1890 he was climbing alone on Ben MacDhui, 4,000 feet above sea-level, when he had a terrifying experience. As he was returning from the cairn on the plateau there was a heavy mist, and Collie heard crunching noises behind him, 'as if someone was walking after me, but taking steps three or four times the length of my own'. He told himself it was nonsense, but as he walked on, and the footsteps continued to sound behind him, 'I was seized with terror and took to my heels, staggering blindly among the boulders for four or five miles down to Rothiemurchus Forest.'

In fact Collie had told the story twenty-three years earlier, to friends in New Zealand, and the result was a report in a New Zealand newspaper headlined: 'A Professor's Panic.' As a result of this story, another Scottish mountaineer, Dr A.M.Kellas – who was to die during the Mount Everest Reconnaissance expedition of 1921-2 – wrote to Collie telling him of his own curious experience on Ben MacDhui. Kellas and his brother Henry had been chipping the rock for crystals late one afternoon when they saw a giant figure coming down towards them from the cairn. It passed out of sight briefly in a dip, and as the two men fled down the mountainside again in mist both of them were convinced that they were being followed by the 'giant'.

This account makes it sound as if some form of 'Yeti', or Abominable Snowman, lives on the slopes of Ben MacDhui. But accounts by other climbers make it clear that the explanation may not be as simple as this. Peter Densham, who was in charge of aeroplane rescue work in the Cairngorms during the Second World War, described in an interview with a journalist how in May 1945 he had left the village of Aviemore and climbed to the cairn on the summit. Suddenly, as he was looking across at Ben Nevis, the mist closed in. He sat there eating chocolate, conscious of strange noises which he attributed to the expansion and contraction of the rocks, when he had a strong feeling that there was someone near him. Then he felt something cold on the back of his neck, and a sense of pressure. He stood up, and heard crunching noises from the direction of the cairn. He went towards the cairn to investigate, 'not in the least frightened'. Then suddenly he experienced a feeling of apprehension, and found himself running towards Lurcher's Crag, with its sheer drop. 'I tried to stop myself and found this was extremely difficult to do. It was as if someone was pushing me. I managed to deflect my course, but with a great deal of difficulty. . . .' He ran most of the way back down the mountain.

On another occasion Densham was on the mountain with his friend Richard Frere, searching for an aeroplane that was reported to have crashed. They were sitting close to the cairn when Densham was surprised to hear Frere apparently talking to himself on the other side of the cairn. Then he realized that Frere was talking to someone else. 'I went round and found myself joining in the conversation. It was a strange experience which seemed to have a psychic aspect. We talked to someone invisible for some time, and it seemed we had carried on this conversation for some little time when we suddenly realized that there was no one there but ourselves. Afterwards, neither of us, strangely, could recall the purport of this extraordinary conversation.' What seems even stranger is that when Frere himself was tracked down by Affleck Gray, the author of a book called *The Big Grey Man of Ben MacDhui*, he had no recollection of the episode described by Densham. But he had had his own strange experiences on the mountain, and described it to Gray as 'the most mysterious mountain I have ever been on'. He told Gray of a day when he had climbed to the high pass of Lairig Ghru, above Ben MacDhui, and sat gazing down on the cliffs of Lurcher's Crag with its cascade of water. Then he found himself slipping into a 'weird and disagreeable' train of thought, so he stood up and walked. But the gloom turned to a sense of deep depression and apathy. Then suddenly he became certain that he was not alone. 'Very close to me, permeating the air which moved so softly in the summer's wind, there was a Presence, utterly abstract but intensely real.'

Then Frere noticed something else. 'The silence of the mountain was violated by an intensely high singing note, a sound which was just within the aural capacity, which never rose or fell. . . . The sound, it seemed, was coming from the very soil of the mountains.' This sound continued until he was below Lurcher's Crag, when the music became so faint that he was not sure whether it was there at all. But the 'abstract Presence' seemed to cling to him 'with some sort of desperate eagerness as if it passionately desired to leave the mountain which it haunted. . .' Then there was a momentary flash of terror, and it was gone.

The experience of the strange, sustained note is not as unusual as Frere apparently thought. In her autobiography *The Infinite Hive* the eminent psychical investigator Rosalind Heywood calls it 'the Singing'. She describes it as 'a kind of continuous vibrant inner *quasi*-sound, to which the nearest analogy is the noise induced by pressing a seashell against the ear, or perhaps the hum of a distant dynamo'. Rosalind Heywood could hear 'the Singing' fairly constantly – although very faintly – if she switched her full attention to it. She says that 'it is far more evident in some places than in others; particularly so in a quiet wood, for instance, or on a moor or a mountain. . .' She notes that she also hears it in churches and college libraries, 'places where thought or devotion have been intense for years'. She finds that 'mountain Singing conveys a different "atmosphere" from church Singing, as an oboe conveys a different "atmosphere" from a trumpet'. And she says that she has met four other people who have heard it; in one case, she mentioned it to a young engineer, convinced that he was a thorough pragmatist; to her surprise, he replied, 'Oh yes, I hear that too, in places where there have just been strong emotions.' So to some extent the 'Singing' seems to be a kind of 'recording': Rosalind Heywood says that she can also 'feel' it when she goes into a room where intense thought has been going on. Yet it cannot be wholly due to human 'vibrations', since she mentions that the Hampstead tube station – the deepest in London – is the only place where she has not heard it. 'The silence was dead.'

If 'the Singing' can be heard in places where intense thought or worship has taken place, this verifies that it could be regarded as some kind of 'recording'. In the 1840s an American professor of anatomy named Joseph Rodes Buchanan came to the interesting conclusion that every object has its own history somehow 'imprinted' on it, and that 'psychics' can sense this history by holding it in their hands; he called this faculty 'psychometry'. He observed that handwritten letters seem to be particularly good 'recorders' of the writer's state of mind, particularly if the writer was feeling some powerful emotion at the time. In the early twentieth century the scientist and psychical researcher Sir Oliver Lodge advanced the theory that 'ghosts' may be 'recordings' – that the powerful emotions associated with some tragedy may be imprinted on the walls of the room in which it has taken place, so that a 'sensitive' person who walked into the room would have a strange feeling of misery and oppression, or perhaps even see the tragedy re-enacted. A Cambridge don named Tom Lethbridge suggested a very similar 'tape recording' theory half a century later. Lethbridge suggested that these 'recordings' are imprinted on some kind of electrical field, and he believed that mountains, deserts and woodlands each have their own special type of 'field'. (He seemed to feel that the field of water is the best 'recorder', so that ghosts are often associated with damp places.)

It seems conceivable, then, that when Rosalind Heywood heard 'the Singing' she was simply picking up some kind of electrical field – a field which, on account of its properties, we might christen 'the psychic field'. Why Richard Frere should suddenly have become aware of this field on the slopes of Ben MacDhui must remain an open question. But at least it seems to offer some kind of confirmation that his feeling of menace and depression was not merely imagination.

The episode in which Frere and Densham held a conversation with some invisible entity seems even stranger; presumably they were responding to some 'presence' on a subconscious level, almost as if dreaming. This could also explain why Frere could not even remember the episode later.

Frere also told Affleck Gray a curious story about a friend – whose identity he was not at liberty to disclose – who decided to spend the night on Ben MacDhui to win a bet. He set up his tent by the summit cairn on a January night. (This is not a man-made cairn, but a natural formation eroded by the weather.) He also began to experience the familiar sense of unreality, and 'the morbidly analytical directioning of thought'. Frere explained: 'He did not feel in any way mad: the terror which possessed him concerned the imminent impact of knowledge which he knew would always set him aside from his fellows. It was as if he was the unwilling recipient of a vast range of new revolutionary thought impulses built up in some all-powerful mind. And the mind was neither human nor anti-human; it just had nothing to do with him at all.'

He fell asleep and woke up 'to a fear of a more terrifying nature'. Moonlight fell through the crack of the flysheet of his tent, and as he stared at it he saw a brown blur, and 'knew that something lay between himself and the moon'. He lay there in frozen immobility until the shadow went away. He now pulled aside the flysheet of the tent. 'The night was brilliant. About twenty yards away a great brown creature was swaggering down the hill. He used the word "swaggering" because the creature had an air of insolent strength about it.' His impression was that the creature was about twenty feet high, and was covered with shortish brown hair. It was too erect to be a huge ape; it had a tapering waist and very broad shoulders. Affleck Gray's book contains a photograph of footprints in the snow taken on Ben MacDhui, and they look oddly like the famous photograph of the footprints of the 'Abominable Snowman' discovered on the Menlung glacier on Everest by Eric Shipton in 1951.

Frere was inclined to wonder whether the brown-haired creature was real, or whether perhaps it was somehow created by his friend's imagination in that oddly 'unreal' state of mind.

In her book *The Secret of Spey* the writer Wendy Wood describes her own experience on Ben MacDhui. She had reached the entrance to the pass of Lairig Ghru on a snowy day, and was preparing to return when she heard a voice 'of gigantic resonance' close behind her. 'It seemed to speak with the harsh consonants and full vowels of the Gaelic.' She wondered if someone was lying injured in the snow, and tramped around in circles until she was convinced that she was alone. Now feeling afraid, she began to hurry back, and as she descended the mountain, thought she could hear footsteps following her. 'She had a strange feeling that something walked immediately behind her.' At first she thought it might be echoes of her own footsteps, until she realized that the crunching noises did not exactly correspond with her steps. She asks in her book whether perhaps the strange happenings on Ben MacDhui might be 'the concretion of the imaginings of the race, clinging to a particular place, discernable only to those whose racial sensitiveness is open to receive the primal impressions and fears of a bygone day'. In other words, she is suggesting that the 'ghost' of Ben MacDhui is a 'recording'.

This seems to be confirmed, to some extent, by an experience recounted by the novelist Joan Grant in her autobiography *Time Out of Mind*. Her book reveals her to be highly psychic. She and her husband were not even on Ben MacDhui but down below near Aviemore; Gray suggests they were on the Lairig Ghru path near Coylum Bridge. For no apparent reason, she was suddenly overwhelmed with fear. 'Something – utterly malign, four legged, and yet obscenely human, invisible and yet solid enough for me to hear the pounding of its hooves, was trying to reach me. If it did I should die for I was far too frightened to know how to defend myself.' She fled in terror. 'I had run about half a mile when I burst through an invisible barrier behind which I knew I was safe. I knew I was safe now, though a second before I had been in mortal danger; knew it as certainly as though I were a torero who has jumped the barrier in front of a charging bull.'

What seems to be emerging from most of these stories about Ben MacDhui is that the chief manifestation is a sudden feeling of depression followed by panic. Joan Grant's account underlines another important point. Tom Lethbridge, who has already been quoted, had observed repeatedly that these sudden unpleasant sensations of fear or 'nastiness' seem to have a precisely defined area, so that it is possible to step in or out of them in one single stride. He describes for example how one day he and his wife Mina went to Ladram beach in Devon to gather seaweed for the garden. At a point on the beach where a small stream flowed from the cliff both experienced an odd feeling of gloom. 'I passed into a kind of blanket, or fog, of depression, and, I think, of fear.' Mina Lethbridge went off to gather seaweed at the other end of the beach but soon hurried back. 'I can't stand this place any longer. There's something frightful here.' The following week they returned, on another dull, grey day, and were again greeted by the same feeling of depression – Tom compared it to a bad smell. It was at its worst around the stream, making him feel almost giddy. Mina went to the cliff-top to make a sketch, and had a sudden feeling that she was being urged to jump. Later they verified that someone had committed suicide from this precise spot.

Tom noted that it was possible to step in and out of the 'depression' – and he noticed it once again when the old lady next door died under strange circumstances after an attempt to practise black magic. An 'unpleasant' feeling hung around her house, but it was possible to step in and out of it, as if it was some kind of invisible barrier, like Joan Grant's bullring barrier.

Gray recounts many stories that seem to support Lethbridge's 'tape recording' theory. The Scots poet James Hogg, known as the Ettrick Shepherd (because he was a shepherd by profession), once saw a herd of Highland cattle on the far side of the stream, and since they had no right to be there he sent a shepherd to drive them off the land, together with two more farmhands armed with cudgels. But they found no sign of a herd, or even of hoofmarks. No one had seen a herd of cattle in the district that day. It had been some kind of 'mirage', or perhaps a 'recording' of something long past.

Gray also quotes *The Mountain Vision* by the mountaineer Frank S.Smythe. Smythe describes how, crossing the hills from Morvich to Loch Duich, on a bright sunny day, with a wonderful panorama of cloud-dappled hills and the distant sea, he entered a grassy, sun-warmed defile and 'became instantly aware of an aura of evil' in the place. 'It was as if something terrible had once happened there, and time had failed to dissipate the atmosphere created by it.'

On impulse, Smythe decided to eat lunch there. As he smoked his pipe the atmosphere seemed to become increasingly unpleasant. Then, as he strove to be receptive to the strange influence, he seemed to witness a massacre: a score or so of ragged people were straggling wearily through the defile when concealed men rushed down on them with spears and axes, and killed them all. As Smythe hurried on, he seemed to hear screams behind him. He was later able to confirm that a massacre of Highlanders by British troops *had* taken place on the road, but he remained convinced that this is not what he had seen. 'The weapons I saw, or seemed to see, were those of an earlier date.'

Yet the many strange accounts of invisible presences on Ben MacDhui seems to throw doubt on the notion that the 'big grey man' is nothing more than a 'recording'. George Duncan, an Aberdeen lawyer and a mountaineer, was totally convinced he had seen the devil on the slopes of the mountain. He and a fellow-climber, James A. Parker, had descended from Devil's Point, and were driving in a dog cart along the Derry Road. Duncan said: 'All at once, I got the shock of my life by seeing before me a tall figure in a black robe – the conventional figure of the Devil himself, waving his arms, clad in long depending sleeves, coming towards me.' He seemed to see the figure surrounded by smoke. In a few moments it passed from view as the cart went round a corner. James A. Parker verified the story. 'It was only at dinner that evening he told me that when we were about a mile below Derry Lodge he had looked up to the hillside on his right and seen the Devil about a quarter of a mile away waving his arms to him.'

Perhaps the oddest and in some ways the most interesting explanation that Gray encountered was given by Captain Sir Hugh Rankin, Bart, and his wife. Rankin was a Mahayana Buddhist, and his wife was a Zen Buddhist. He and Lady Rankin were cycling from Rothiemurchus to Mar via the Lairig Ghru pass, and although it was July it was bitterly cold in the pass. At the Pools o' Dee they suddenly felt 'the Presence' behind them; they turned and saw a big, olive-complexioned man dressed in a long robe and sandals, with long flowing hair. 'We were not in the least afraid. Being Buddhists we at once knew who it was. We at once knelt and made obeisance.' They had instantly recognized the stranger as a Bodhisattva, 'one of the five "Perfected Men" who control the destinies of this world, and meet once a year in a cave in the Himalayas'. According to Sir Hugh, the Presence addressed them in a language he thought was Sanskrit, and he replied respectfully in Urdu. 'All the time the Bodhisattva was with us [he gave the time as about ten minutes] a heavenly host of musicians was playing high up in the sky. . . . Immediately the Bodhisattva left us the music ceased and we never heard it again.' It sounds as if they had heard some version of 'the Singing'. But his comment that the Presence spoke in Sanskrit raises the question of whether Wendy Wood had not mistaken Sanskrit for Gaelic when she heard it on the mountain.

Shortly before his death, F.W. Holiday, author of a classic book on the Loch Ness monster (see Chapter 18), advanced the startling theory that the Grey Man, like the Loch Ness monster and the Surrey puma, and possibly the Abominable Snowman of the Himalayas, is a member of 'the phantom menagerie', creatures who belong to some other world or dimension. In *The Goblin Universe* (chapter 6) he cites various stories about the *Fear Liath More* (the Celtic name for the Grey Man), and goes on:

Pan, the goat-footed god, is not so funny when you encounter him. . . The chief symptom of being in the presence of Pan is panic, which the Oxford dictionary defines as 'unreasoning and excessive terror, from Greek *panicos*, of god Pan, reputed to cause panic. . . .' The phenomenon is certainly not localised to the Cairngorms. Hamish Corrie, when he was nearing the summit of Sgurr Dearg on Skye, turned back when he was overcome by 'an unaccountable panic'.

The late John Buchan reported the same effect in the Bavarian Alps. He describes how in 1910 he was returning through a pinewood on a sunny morning with a local forester when panic struck them out of the blue. Both of them fled without speaking until they collapsed from exhaustion on the valley highway below. Buchan comments that a friend of his 'ran for dear life' when climbing in Jotunheimen in Norway. The Pan effect may be worldwide.

Holiday connects 'the phantom menagerie' with Unidentified Flying Objects, and cites the authority on UFOs, John Keel, who began by assuming that UFOs are some kind of unknown aircraft, perhaps from other planets, and ended by accepting that they come from 'another dimension', and that they seem to have a distinctly supernatural element. In one of his books, *The Mothman Prophecies*, Keel speaks of a gigantic winged figure sighted again and again in West Virginia, and describes his own feeling of 'panic' on a road close to one of the sightings. Like Lethbridge, Keel found that the area of 'panic' seemed to be sharply defined, so that he could walk in and out of it with one stride. And the area of sightings of 'Mothman' also has many sightings of UFO phenomena.

Oddly enough, Affleck Gray is willing to consider the 'space visitors' theory as an explanation of the Ben MacDhui phenomena. He points out that in 1954 an ex-taxi driver named George King inaugurated the Aetherius Society in Caxton Hall, London. King claimed that he had met the Master Jesus on Holdstone Down, North Devon, and been made aware that he had been chosen as the primary mental channel of certain Space Intelligences. He was told to travel the world, his task being to serve as the channel for 'charging' eighteen mountains with cosmic energy. One of these mountains was Creag an Leth-Choin, three miles north-west of Ben MacDhui, and King asserts that there is a huge dome-shaped auditorium, a retreat of the Great White Brotherhood, in the bowels of Ben MacDhui. Another group of 'seekers', the Active Truth Academy in Edinburgh, also believe that Ben MacDhui 'has become the earth-fall for space beings'. But it is clear from Gray's chapter on Space Beings that he regards this explanation with scepticism.

If we wish for a 'scientific' explanation of the Ben MacDhui phenomena, then the likeliest seems to be that the answer lies in Ben MacDhui itself: that the 'panic' is caused by some natural phenomenon, a kind of 'earth force' which may be connected with the earth's magnetic field. There are areas of the earth's surface where birds lose their way because the lines of earth magnetism somehow cancel one another out, forming a magnetic vortex. 'Ley-hunters' also believe that so-called 'ley lines' – which connect sacred sites such as churches, barrows and standing stones – are basically lines of magnetic force. Many are also convinced that places in which this force is exceptionally powerful are likely to be connected with 'supernatural' occurrences – in fact, that such places 'record' human emotions, producing the effects that are described as 'hauntings'. This explanation would account for Frank Smythe's experience of the 'haunted' valley where the massacre had occurred.

The non-scientific explanation may be sought in the belief of most primitive peoples that the earth is alive, that certain places are holy, and that such places are inhabited by spirits. The Western mind is inclined to dismiss such beliefs as superstition; but many travellers who have been in close contact with them are inclined to be more open-minded. In *The Lost World of the Kalahari* Laurens Van der Post tells how, when he was seeking the vanished Bushmen of South Africa, his guide Samutchoso took him to a place called the Slippery Hills. The guide insisted that there must be no hunting as they approached the hills, or the gods would be angry. Van de Post forgot to tell his advance party, and they shot a warthog. From then on they ran into an endless stream of bad luck. When Samutchoso tried to pray Van der Post saw that he was pulled over backward by some unknown force. All their technical equipment began to malfunction. Then Samutchoso 'consulted' the spirits and began to speak to invisible presences. He told Van der Post that they *were* angry, and would have killed him if he had tried to pray again. Van der Post suggested that they should all write a message of apology, and that this should be buried in a bottle at the foot of a sacred rock. Apparently this worked; the spirits were propitiated, and suddenly the equipment ceased to malfunction. Through the guide, the 'spirits' told Van der Post that he would find bad news waiting for him when he reached the next place on his route. In fact his assistant found a message saying that his father had died and he had to return home immediately. After all this, Van der Post had no doubt of the real existence of the 'earth spirits' worshipped by primitive people.

F.W.Holiday's view was that the explanation of such phenomena as the 'Grey Man' lay somewhere between these two sets of explanations: the scientific and the 'supernatural'. But he believed that the Western mind will be capable of grasping the answer only when it has broadened its conception of science.

13 Kaspar Hauser

The Boy from Nowhere

The case of Kaspar Hauser is perhaps the greatest of nineteenth-century historical mysteries. But it is rather more than that. The unfortunate youth was the subject of a cruel experiment in what would now be called 'sensory deprivation', and the results of this experiment were in some ways more interesting than the admittedly fascinating enigma of Kaspar's identity.

On Whit Monday, 26 May 1828, the Unschlitt Square in Nuremberg was almost deserted, most people being in the surrounding countryside enjoying the *Ausflug* (or holiday excursion). At about five in the afternoon a weary-looking youth dragged himself into the square, and almost fell into the arms of the local cobbler, George Weichmann. He was well built, but poorly dressed, and walked in a curious, stiff-limbed manner. Weichmann took the letter that the youth held out to him, and saw that it was addressed to the captain of the 4th Squadron, 6th Cavalry Regiment. The lad seemed to be unable to answer questions, replying in a curious mumble – Weichmann suspected he was drunk. He led the youth to the nearest guardroom, and the sergeant in charge took him to the captain's home. When Captain Wessenig came home a few hours later he found the place in a state of excitement. The youth seemed to be an idiot. He had tried to touch a candle flame with his fingers, and screamed when he was burned. Offered beer and meat, he had stared at them as if he had no idea what to do with them; yet he had fallen ravenously on a meal of black bread and water. The grandfather clock seemed to terrify him. The only words the boy seemed to know were '*Weiss nicht*' – I don't know.

The envelope proved to contain two letters. The first began: 'Honoured Captain. I send you a lad who wishes to serve his king in the army. He was brought to me on October 7, 1812. I am but a poor labourer with children of my own to rear. His mother asked me to bring up the boy. . ... Since then I have never let him go outside the house.' The letter had no signature. The other note stated: 'This child has been baptised. His name is Kaspar; you must give him a second name yourself. His father was a cavalry soldier. When he is seventeen take him to Nuremberg to the Sixth Cavalry regiment: his father belonged to it. He was born on April 30, 1812. I am a poor girl; I can't take care of him. His father is dead.' This was presumably the letter that had accompanied Kaspar when he had been handed over to the 'poor labourer'.

Taken to the police station, the boy accepted a pencil and wrote 'Kaspar

Hauser'. But to other questions he answered 'Don't know.'

It all seemed straightforward enough – an illegitimate child left on someone's doorstep and brought up by a kind stranger. But in that case why keep him indoors for seventeen years? The boy's feet were so tender – he was bleeding through his shoes – because he was unaccustomed to walking on them. His skin was pale, as if he had been confined in darkness. Moreover, on close examination it became clear that the two letters had been written by the same hand at about the same time, not sixteen years apart. The clothes he was wearing looked as if they had been taken from a scarecrow, and they were obviously not his own. Someone was trying to draw a red herring across the trail.

The boy was locked in a cell, and his gaoler observed that he seemed perfectly contented to sit there for hours without moving. He had no sense of time, and seemed to know nothing about hours and minutes. It soon became clear that he had a small vocabulary. He could say that he wanted to become a Reiter (cavalryman) like his father – a phrase he had obviously been taught like a parrot. To every animal he applied the word 'horse', and he seemed to be fascinated by horses. When a visitor – one of the crowd who flocked to stare at him every day – gave him a toy one he adorned it with ribbons, played with it for hours, and pretended to feed it at every meal. The audience caused him no concern, and he caused amusement by performing his natural functions quite openly, with no sense of shame. He did not even seem to know the difference between men and women – he referred to both as 'boys' (Junge).

One of the most curious things about him was his incredible physical acuteness. He began to vomit if coffee or beer was in the same room; the sight and smell of meat produced nausea. The smell of wine literally made him drunk, and a single drop of brandy in his water made him sick. His hearing and eyesight were abnormally acute – in fact, he could see in the dark, and would later demonstrate his ability by reading from a Bible in a completely black room. He was so sensitive to magnets that he could tell whether the north or south pole was turned towards him. He could distinguish between different metals by passing his hand over them, even when they were covered with a cloth. (A few years later, the American doctor Joseph Rodes Buchanan would stumble upon the faculty he called psychometry (see Chapter 27) when he learned that many of his students could do the same thing.)

At first Kaspar seemed to be an imbecile; he lived in a daze. Like an animal, he was terrified of thunderstorms. But the notion that he was mentally retarded soon had to be abandoned. The attention of his visitors obviously gave him pleasure, and he became visibly more alert day by day – exactly like a baby learning from experience. His vocabulary increased from day to day, and his physical clumsiness vanished – he learned to use scissors, quill pens and matches. And as his intelligence increased, his features altered. He had struck most people as a typical idiot, coarse, lumpish, clumsy and oddly repulsive; now his facial characteristics seemed to change and become more refined. But he continued to walk rather clumsily: in the place at the back of the knees where most of us have a hollow he had protrusions, so that when he sat with outstretched legs, the whole leg was in contact with the ground.

As he learned to speak he was gradually able to tell something of his own story. But it seemed to make the mystery even more baffling. A bulletin issued by Burgomeister Binder and the town council of Nuremberg stated that for as long as Kaspar could remember he had lived in a small room, about seven feet long by four feet wide, and its windows were boarded up. There was no bed, only a bundle of straw on the bare earth. The ceiling was so low that he could not stand upright. He saw no one. When he woke up he would find bread and water in his cell. Sometimes his water had a bitter taste, and he would go into a deep sleep; when he woke his straw would have been changed and his hair and nails cut. The only toys were three wooden horses. One day a man had entered his room and taught him to write his name, Kaspar Hauser, and to repeat phrases like 'I want to be a soldier' and 'Don't know.' One day he woke up to find himself wearing the baggy garments in which he had been found, and the man came and led him into the open air. As they trudged along the man promised him a big, live horse when he was a soldier. Then he was abandoned somewhere near the gates of Nuremberg.

Suddenly Kaspar was famous; his case was discussed all over Germany. This must doubtless have worried whoever was responsible for turning him loose; his captor, or captors, had hoped that he would vanish quietly into the army and be forgotten; now he was a national celebrity, and everyone was asking questions.

The Burgomaster and town council decided to take Kaspar under their protection; he would be fed and clothed at the municipal expense. In the rather dull town of Nuremberg he was an object of endless interest, and everyone wanted to solve the mystery. The town paid for thousands of handbills appealing for clues to his identity, and even offering a reward. The police made a careful search of the local countryside for his place of imprisonment, which was obviously within walking distance; but they found nothing.

The town council also appointed a guardian for its celebrity, a lecturer and scientist named Georg Friedrich Daumer. He was interested in 'animal magnetism', and it was he who conducted the tests that revealed that Kaspar could distinguish the poles of a magnet and read in the dark. Under Daumer's tutelage Kaspar finally developed into a young man of normal intelligence. Like any teenager, he enjoyed being the centre of attention. His appearance became almost foppish, and in the last months of his life he looked not unlike Roman busts of Nero, with his plump face and little curls.

One of the many learned men who examined him was the lawyer and criminologist Anselm Ritter von Feuerbach, distinguished author of the Bavarian penal code; and he reached the interesting conclusion that Kaspar must be of royal blood. There could be no other explanation for the boy's long imprisonment; he must be *somebody*'s heir. Kaspar was obviously not displeased at this notion.

Then, a mere seventeen months after he had been 'found', someone tried to kill him. It happened on the afternoon of 7 October 1829, when Kaspar was found lying on the floor of the cellar of Daumer's house, bleeding from a head-wound, with his shirt torn to the waist. Later he described being attacked by a man wearing a silken mask, who had struck him either with a club or a knife. The police immediately made a search of Nuremberg, but had no success in finding anyone who fitted Kaspar's description of his assailant. There were those in Nuremberg who muttered that there had never been an assailant, and that Kaspar had invented the whole episode to attract attention. Not everyone believed, as Daumer did, that Kaspar was some sort of angel. But most people took the view that his life was in danger. He was moved to a new address, and two policemen were appointed to look after him; Ritter von Feuerbach was appointed his guardian. And for the next two years Kaspar vanished from the public eye. But not from the public mind. Now the novelty had worn off, there were many in Nuremberg who objected to supporting Kaspar on the rates.

Then a solution was proposed that satisfied everyone. A wealthy and eccentric Englishman, Lord Stanhope – nephew of the former prime minister Pitt – became interested in Kaspar and came to interview him. The two seemed to take an instant liking to one another; they began to dine out in restaurants, and Kaspar was often to be seen in Lord Stanhope's carriage. Stanhope was convinced that Kaspar was of royal blood, and was evidently fascinated by the mystery. When he offered to take Kaspar off on a tour of Europe the town council was delighted. And from 1831 until 1833 Kaspar was exhibited at many minor courts of Europe, where he never failed to arouse interest. But various members of the Bavarian royal houses, particularly that of Baden, threatened lawsuits if their names were publicly linked with Kaspar's. . . .

It seems that all this attention and good living was not good for Kaspar's character; predictably, he became vain, difficult and conceited. Stanhope became disillusioned with him. In 1833, back in Nuremberg, Stanhope asked permission to lodge him in the town of Ansbach, twenty-five miles away, where he would be tutored by Stanhope's friend Dr Meyer, and guarded by a certain Captain Hickel, a security officer. Then, feeling that he had done his duty, Stanhope disappeared back to England.

Kaspar was not happy in Ansbach. It was even more of a backwater than Nuremberg – in fact, Nuremberg was a glittering metropolis by comparison. Kaspar resented being made to do lessons, particularly Latin, and longed for the old life of courts and dinner parties. His home-sickness became stronger after a brief visit to Nuremberg. He seems to have felt that Ansbach was hardly better than the cell in which he had spent his early years.

Then, only a few days before Christmas, he died. On 14 December 1833, on a snowy afternoon, he staggered into Mayer's house gasping: 'Man stabbed . . . knife . . . Hofgarten . . . gave purse . . . Go look quickly.' A hastily summoned doctor discovered that Kaspar had been stabbed in the side, just below the ribs. The blow had damaged his lung and liver. Hickel rushed to the park where Kaspar had been walking, and found a silk purse containing a note, written in mirror-writing. It said: 'Hauser will be able to tell you how I look, whence I came and who I am. To spare him from that task

I will tell you myself. I am from . . . on the Bavarian border . . . On the River . . . My name is M.L.O.'

But Kaspar could not tell them anything about the man's identity. He could only explain that he had received a message through a labourer, asking him to go to the Hofgarten. A tall, bewhiskered man wearing a black cloak had asked him, 'Are you Kaspar Hauser?' and when he nodded handed him the purse. As Kaspar took it the man stabbed him, then ran off.

Hickel revealed a fact that threw doubt on this story; there had only been one set of footprints – Kaspar's – in the snow. But when two days later, on 17 December, Kaspar slipped into a coma his last words were: 'I didn't do it myself.'

His death was a signal for a flood of books and pamphlets, each with its own theory about the mystery. Feuerbach published a book called *Example of a Crime Against the Soul of a Man*, arguing that Kaspar must be of royal blood. To avoid libel, he avoided naming any suspects, but his readers had no difficulty supplying their own names. The favourite candidates were the Grand Dukes of Baden. The old Duke Karl Frederick had contracted a morganatic marriage with a pretty eighteen-year-old, Caroline Geyer, who was rumoured to have poisoned his sons by an earlier marriage to make sure her own children became the future Grand Dukes. Kaspar Hauser was supposed to have been one of these children. The story was obviously absurd, for it would have meant stealing him away as a baby and handing him over to a 'minder'. One suggestion was that this 'minder' was a man named Franz Richter, and that Kaspar's childhood home was Castle Pilsach, near Nuremberg. (The castle is in fact merely a large farmhouse.) It was suggested that Richter had decided to send Kaspar Hauser to Nuremberg when his wife died. But there is no conclusive evidence for this view, or for any other theory of Kaspar's origin.

There is of course no evidence whatsoever that Kaspar was of royal blood. If he was the legitimate heir to some throne, or even to some rich estate, it is difficult to understand why he should be kept in a small room all his life; it would have been enough to hand him over to a 'minder' in some distant place. Kaspar's strange and inhuman treatment sounds more typical of ignorant peasants than of guilt-stricken aristocrats. In a Cornish case of the twentieth century, an army deserter of the First World War, William Garfield Rowe, was kept concealed in his family's farmhouse for thirty years. It does not seem to have struck anyone that this was a kind of insanity – far worse than the few months' imprisonment he might have suffered if he had given himself up.[1] The theory that Kaspar was the step-child of some wicked Grand Duke seems on the whole less likely than that he was the illegitimate child of some respectable farmer's daughter who was engaged to a local landowner, and was terrified that her secret would become local gossip.

In that case, who was behind the attacks? It is just possible that they never happened. After the first attack, in Daumer's cellar, Nuremberg gossip

---

[1] Rowe achieved a different kind of notoriety in 1963 when he was murdered by two out-of-work labourers, who were later hanged.

suggested that his wound was self-inflicted, and that Kaspar was trying to draw attention to himself after the failure of his recently published Autobiography. By the time the second attack occurred his fame was in decline, and he was desperately unhappy about his situation.

It is important to try to gain some insight into the psychology of a boy who has spent the first seventeen years of his life in a kind of prison cell. Most boys love being the centre of attention and will go to great lengths to achieve it. (Mark Twain shows how deeply he understands the mentality in the episode where Tom Sawyer pretends to be drowned, and attends his own funeral.) Most boys crave the approval of adults, and will tell lies to get it. In his book about Kaspar, Jacob Wassermann describes how disappointed Daumer felt when he discovered that Kaspar was not as truthful as he seemed. Kaspar emerged quite literally from obscurity, to find himself the centre of sympathetic attention – in fact a European celebrity. But although his chronological age was seventeen, he was in the most basic sense a two-year-old boy. Intellectually speaking, he grew with astonishing rapidity; emotionally speaking, he remained a child. So it *is* perfectly conceivable that he was prepared to go to desperate lengths to retain public sympathy.

In the light of this suspicion, Kaspar's story of both attacks begins to seem implausible. Would a masked man somehow find his way into the basement of Daumer's house, then merely hit Kaspar on the head with a club (or a knife; there seems to be some conflict about the weapon) and rush away without making sure he was dead? As to the second attack, could Hickel have been mistaken when he asserted that there were only one set of footprints in the snow? And why was the mysterious letter written in mirror writing? Was it because Kaspar wrote it with his left hand, looking in a mirror, in order to disguise his writing? (It is a well-known fact that it is easy to train the left hand to write backward, using a mirror.) Why was the message so nonsensical: 'Hauser will be able to tell you how I look, whence I came and who I am...' etc. Why should a paid assassin write a letter at all? Is it not more likely that Kaspar, in a desperate state of unhappiness, decided to inflict a harmless wound, and stabbed himself too deeply?

If so, Kaspar at least achieved what he wanted – universal sympathy and a place in the history books.

14 The Holy Shroud of Turin

The notion that a fourteen-foot oblong of cloth preserved in the Cathedral of Turin could be the shroud in which the founder of Christianity was laid in the tomb seems on the face of it an obvious absurdity, particularly since the Turin shroud had forty-odd rivals in other parts of Europe. Yet if the 'Holy Shroud' is a fake, then the mystery is in a sense greater than ever; for we are then left with the problem of trying to explain away a great many pieces of remarkably convincing evidence.

The known history of the shroud begins in 1353, when Geoffroy de Charny, Lord of Savoisie and Lirey, built a church at Lirey and put on show 'the true burial sheet of Christ'. This was a strip of linen, just over fourteen feet long and three and a half feet wide. On this linen there was the dim brown image of a man – or rather, two images, one of his front and one of his back. Apparently the body had been laid out on the bottom half of the sheet, which had then been folded down over the top of the head. And, in some strange way the image of the man had been imprinted on the shroud like a very poor photographic image.

A 'relic' like this was worth far more than its weight in gold, as pilgrims poured into the church to see it and dropped their coins into the collection box. In 1389 the bishop of Troyes, Peter D'Arcis, declared the shroud to be a fake, painted by an artist, and tried to seize it; but he was unsuccessful. In 1532 the shroud was almost destroyed in a fire in the Sainte Chapelle at Chambéry, France, and when it was recovered it had been badly damaged – many holes had been burnt in it by molten silver. Fortunately, these completely missed the central part which contained the image, and when the nearby nuns of St Clair had patched it it looked almost as good as new.

As far as the modern reader is concerned, the real history of the shroud begins on 28 May 1898. The shroud had been in Turin cathedral since 1578 – it was now the property of the Duke of Savoy – and on 25 May 1898 it was again put on public display. A Turin photographer, Secondo Pia, was commissioned to photograph it. And it was in his apartment, towards midnight, that the photographer removed the first of two large plates from the developing fluid. What he saw almost made him drop the plate. Instead of the dim, blurred image he was looking at a real face, quite plainly recognizable. Yet he was looking at a photographic negative, not the final product. This could only mean one thing: that the image on the shroud was itself a photographic negative, so by 'reversing' it Pia had turned it into a positive – a real photograph. If the relic was genuine, Pia was looking at a photograph of Christ.

The Duke of Savoy – now King Umberto I (he would be assassinated two years later) – was told the news; a procession of distinguished visitors began to arrive at the photographer's house. Most of them, understandably, were convinced that this must be the true Holy Shroud, since no painter would have thought of forging a photographic negative. The only other possibility was that the effect had been achieved accidentally by a forger, but this seemed unlikely. Two weeks later a journalist broke the story, and it spread round the world.

But the shroud's fame was not to last for long. Two years later a detailed report on it by a medieval scholar, Fr. Ulysse Chevalier, defused the excitement. Chevalier studied all the documents he could find, including Peter D'Arcis's assertion that it was a fake (D'Arcis claimed that the artist had confessed), and declared firmly that the image on the shroud was a painting; he quoted a well-known photographer to the effect that the 'negative' aspect of the picture was merely a technical accident. Scholars were convinced; the Holy Shroud was just another false relic, like the thousands of pieces of the 'true cross' in churches all over the world.

But a new defender had already appeared on the scene. Paul Vignon, a painter with an interest in biology, had become the assistant of Professor Yves Delage of the Sorbonne. Vignon was a Catholic, Delage an agnostic. But it was Delage who in 1900 showed Vignon photographs of the shroud, and aroused his interest in the problem. Surely, Vignon reasoned, close examination should prove once and for all if the shroud had been painted by hand? He went to Turin and obtained copies of Secondo Pia's photographs, as well as two snapshots of the shroud taken at the same time by other men.

The first question Vignon asked himself was how the brown stains could have been made. If it *had* been painted by an artist, could he have produced such an impressive negative? It would mean painting without really seeing what he was doing, and as an artist, Vignon knew this was virtually impossible. And since photography did not exist in 1353, the artist would have had no means of checking his work. And why should he have wanted to produce a negative if the intention was to deceive pilgrims? They would prefer a recognizable face . . . .

Vignon tried coating his face in red chalk-dust, then lying down and covering his face with a cloth, which was then pressed gently against his face. The result was not a negative; it was just blotches.

So if the image had been produced by 'contact', it could not have been this kind of crude, direct contact. But in that case, what kind of contact? One mystery was that even the hollows of the face had been 'imprinted'; the image showed the bridge of the nose, yet a cloth laid over someone's face would not touch the bridge of the nose.

Suppose the image had been produced by sweat? The commonest burial ointments were myrrh and aloes at the time of the Crucifixion. Vignon and Delage tried impregnating a cloth with myrrh and aloes, then seeing what effect sweat had on it. Sweat contains a substance called urea, which turns into ammonia (hence the disagreeable smell of people with BO). They found that sweat would produce brown stains on their impregnated cloth.

Oddly enough, the agnostic Delage finally became convinced that the shroud was genuine – although he stopped short of becoming converted to Christianity. This man's 'photograph' showed signs of scourging, and of being pierced in one side with a spear; the forehead had marks that would correspond to a crown of thorns. There were nail-marks in the wrists and the feet. Most paintings of the Crucifixion show nails driven through the hands, but Vignon established that the hands would not support a man on the cross – they would tear. In fact, historical research has shown that crucifixion involved nailing the wrists, not the hands.

The report by Vignon and Delage was read on 21 April 1902 at the Academy of Sciences, and caused a sensation. Vignon and Delage were praised and denounced. Yet, oddly enough, some influential Catholics still regarded the shroud as an imposture; the Jesuit Father Herbert Thurston, of London's Farm Street, contributed a piece to the Catholic Encyclopedia in which he stated his view that the shroud was a mere 'devotional aid', painted by some fourtenth-century monk.

The controversy died down; almost thirty years passed. In May 1931 it was decided to exhibit the shroud again in belated celebration of the marriage of Crown Prince Umberto. More photographs were taken, by Giuseppe Enrie. They were far better in quality than Pia's earlier photographs, and the sense of reality was even stronger. Moreover, close examination of the cloth showed that the paint theory was unlikely; paint would have soaked in, and the brown stain seemed to be on the surface. Even under a microscope, no fragments of paint were visible.

The photographs were shown to an eminent French anatomist, Pierre Barbet, who proceeded to study them in minute detail. The photograph showed that the nail that had penetrated the wrist had emerged in the back of the hand. Could this be a forger's mistake? Barbet tried nailing a severed wrist; when the nail struck the bone it slipped upward, and emerged at exactly the spot shown in the photograph. The wrists showed two streaks of blood, as if the wrist had been in two different positions. Barbet showed that a man hanging by the wrists would soon suffocate; in order to breathe he would have to force himself upright, literally standing on the nails that held his feet; but he would soon become exhausted, and slump again. The bloodstains corresponded precisely to the two positions. Brooding on the apostle John's description of the lance-thrust into the side of the dead Christ, 'and immediately there came out blood and water', Barbet tried to experiment of thrusting a knife into the side of a corpse above the heart; the result was 'blood and water' – a mixture of blood and pericardial fluid.

All these investigations gave Barbet an appalling insight into the sufferings of a man dying on the cross – to such an extent that he admitted he no longer dared to think about them and his book the Corporal Passion of Jesus Christ became the subject of endless Easter sermons. Barbet was himself overcome with emotion when he succeeded in catching a close-up glimpse of the shroud in October 1933, and realized that some of the brown stains were bloodstains – the blood of Christ . . . . He sank to his knees and bowed his head.

One thing was by now obvious: that the information contained in the shroud was so complex that the chances of it being a fake were a thousand to one against. The study of the shroud became something of a science in its own right. It was christened sindonology (the Italian for the shroud being *sindone*), and Paul Vignon became its acknowledged leader. It was Vignon who made the interesting suggestion that the shroud might be responsible for a sudden change in the representations of Jesus in the time of the emperor Constantine (AD 274-337); in the first three centuries after the Crucifixion, Jesus is represented as a beardless youth, but after that as a bearded man with a moustache. Could it have been the discovery of the shroud that caused the change? Vignon studied hundreds of paintings, and concluded that a large number of them seemed to have been influenced by the shroud. For example, there was a small square above the nose, due to an imperfection in the weave of the cloth, and he found this in many of the portraits of Jesus. In the so-called 'holy face of Edessa' a portrait dating from a century after Constantine there is a distinct resemblance to the face on the shroud.

A later scholar, Ian Wilson, has argued convincingly that the shroud is identical with a relic known as the Mandylion, the handkerchief with which St Veronica wiped the face of Jesus when he was on his way to Calvary, and on which Jesus miraculously imprinted his image. The Mandylion (or a relic claiming to be the original handkerchief of St Veronica) was preserved in Byzantium until it was sacked by the Crusaders in 1204; it had come there from Edessa (Urfa, in modern Turkey) in August AD 994 . Wilson argues that the shroud was folded so that only the face was visible, and that this was the Mandylion. In his book *The Turin Shroud*, Wilson devotes more than a hundred pages to studying documentary sources and attempting to trace the history of the shroud-Mandylion before it appeared in Lirey in the mid-fourteenth century. His arguments are too long to detail here, but his tentative reconstruction is as follows.

After the Crucifixion (about AD 30), the shroud was folded and disguised as a portrait, to hide its 'unclean' nature as a burial cloth. It was taken to Edessa, then a thriving Christian community; but when Ma'nu VI reverted to paganism in AD 57 and persecuted the Christians it was hidden in a niche in the wall above Edessa's west gate. Although Christians were once again tolerated about 120 years later, the shroud's existence remained unknown. In 525 severe floods in Edessa cost 30,000 lives and destroyed many public buildings; the shroud was rediscovered when the walls were being rebuilt. (This version, of course, contradicts Vignon's hypothesis that it was rediscovered in the reign of Constantine three centuries earlier.) In the spring of 943 the Byzantine army besieged Edessa and offered to spare the city in exchange for the Mandylion; so the Mandylion was transferred to Constantinople. It was discovered to be a burial shroud in about AD 1045, probably when someone unpinned the Mandylion from its frame to remount it. In 1204, when the Crusaders took Constantinople from the Greek Christians, the shroud vanished again. What happened next is unknown, but one conjecture is that it fell into the hands of the Knights Templars, who were accused of worshipping a man's head with a red beard. In 1291, after the fall of Acre (where the Templars had their treasury), the cloth was brought to Sidon, then to Cyprus.

In 1306 the Treasury of the Templars came to France, brought by Jacques Molay. On 13 October 1307 the Templars were arrested on the orders of King Philip the Fair, who was anxious to lay his hands on their money, and in March 1314 Jacques Molay was burnt at the stake, together with Geoffrey de Charnay, the order's Normandy master. It is not known if this Geoffrey de Charnay was related to the Geoffroy de Charny who built the Lirey church in 1353, and who seems to have exhibited the shroud there about 1355. When Geoffroy was killed at Poitiers in September 1356 the shroud became the property of his infant son, also called Geoffroy; the shroud was exhibited (perhaps to raise money) in 1357, but Bishop Henry of Poitiers ordered the exhibition (or 'exposition') to be stopped. In 1389 another exposition aroused the anger of Peter D'Arcis, Bishop of Troyes, who appealed to the king, then to the pope, to gain possession of the relic; he insisted that the shroud had been forged by an artist around 1355. The pope supported the de Charny family, and the Bishop's attempt was a failure. In 1400, after the death of the younger Geoffroy de Charny, his daughter Margaret married Humbert of Villersexel, and the shroud was handed over to him for safe-keeping. It was kept in the chapel at St Hippolyte-sur-Doubs, and was exhibited yearly in a meadow on the banks of the Doubs (known as the Saviour's Meadow, Pré du Seigneur). The Lirey canons tried hard to recover it from about 1443, and even succeeded in having Margaret excommunicated; but they failed to regain it. When Margaret died in 1460 the shroud already seems to have been in the possession of the Duke of Savoy, who gave Margaret two French castles. In 1502 the shroud was deposited in Chambery castle, where thirty years later it was almost destroyed in a fire. And in 1578 the shroud was taken to Turin, where it has remained ever since, except for the Second World War, when it was taken to the Abbey of Monte Vergine at Avellino for safety.

In 1955 Group Captain Leonard Cheshire took a crippled Scottish girl to Turin, and she was allowed to hold the shroud in her lap; however, no cure took place. Possibly this failure decided Cardinal Pellegrino of Turin to make a determined attempt to establish the shroud's authenticity or otherwise by scientific means. In June 1969 a scientific commission was allowed to examine the shroud, and more photographs (some in colour) were taken by Giovanni-Battista Judica-Cordiglia. For two days the commission examined the shroud, and recommended a series of tests that would involve the 'removal of minimum samples'. In Portugal exiled King Umberto II gave his permission for the tests. On 23 November 1973 the shroud was shown for the first time on television. The next day it was removed to a small room at the rear of Turin cathedral, and a total of seventeen samples were carefully removed. Part of the backing-cloth sewn on by the nuns after the fire was also removed, and this revealed the interesting fact that the image on the cloth had not 'soaked through' to the other side. In fact, closer examination of a thread showed that the brown stain was restricted to the very surface of the cloth. This also seemed to rule out the possibility that there was actual blood on the shroud – we may recall the fact that Pierre Barbet had fallen on his knees when it had struck him that he was looking at a real bloodstain. In fact tests showed that there was no blood on the shroud.

Another scientist, Dr Max Frei of Zurich, had noticed that there was dust on the shroud, and he took samples by pressing adhesive tape to the surface of the linen. Back in his laboratory, a microscope revealed that there were many pollen grains among the dust and mineral particles. Frei, a criminologist, was an expert on pollens. One of his first discoveries was of pollen from a cedar of Lebanon. That looked promising – except that such trees have spread far from Lebanon, especially in public parks. Then he came upon something more revealing: pollens from plants unique to the Jordan valley, adapted to live in a soil with a high salt content. He went on to identify forty-nine varieties of pollen, many from Jerusalem, others from Istanbul (Constantinople), others from Urfa (Edessa), others from France or Italy. This constituted powerful evidence that the shroud had originated in the Holy Land, had travelled to Turkey, then to France and Italy. This was undoubtedly the most exciting discovery to emerge from the 1973 examination.

By the time of this examination, important research was also being carried on in America by a physicist, John Jackson, and his friend Dr Eric Jumper, a USAF captain. They made a 'dummy' shroud by using a transparency and marking all the shroud's main features on a similar piece of cloth. Placing the dummy over a man who was lying down, they then plotted the relative darkness of the brown markings. This revealed the curious fact that the markings were strongest where the cloth would have touched the body, and that they seemed to be in exact proportion to the distance the cloth would have been from the flesh – for example, being faintest below the chin, where the cloth would have been stretched between the chin and the chest.

But it was in 1976 that the two stumbled on their most fascinating piece of information – and perhaps the most exciting discovery since Secondo Pia's original photograph. They decided to subject the shroud to 'image-enhancement'. This is a modern technique whose purpose is to analyse the relative brightness of areas of a photograph – for example, one taken by a space-probe – and to intensify them selectively to 'bring out' underlying images. (It has been used on photographs of the Loch Ness monster.) Since the image-enhancer can also interpret information about distance, it can also turn a flat photograph into a three-dimensional image, the equivalent of turning it into a statue. The 'statue' can then be turned from side to side. From a small transparency of the shroud Jackson and Jumper obtained an amazingly perfect image of the face. It proved that the brown marks on the shroud actually provided enough information for the computer to reconstruct the original and, in doing so virtually ruled out the possibility that the shroud was a painted forgery. In fact, as Jackson and Jumper pointed out, the shroud was in many respects superior to a modern photograph. A photograph may not contain enough 'distance information' to produce an accurate 'statue' – so an attempt to translate a photograph of Pope Pius XI into a three-dimensional image flattened the nose, distorted the mouth and made the eyes too deeply set. The image on the shroud was more accurate than that. It even revealed something never before recognized – that coins had been placed on both eyes, according to the Jewish burial custom of the time.

Other researchers, Donald Lynn and Jean Lorre, were even able tentatively to identify the coins – as 'leptons', the 'widow's mite' of the New Testament.

In 1977 Dr Walter McCrone, a Chicago microanalyst, submitted a request to take samples from the shroud. McCrone had disproved the authenticity of the 'Vinland map', which was supposed to prove that Vikings discovered America, by showing that although the parchment was medieval, the ink contained a component only used after 1920. McCrone stated that with the use of the ion microscope he could identify the nature of the shroud's image. But in 1977 his chances of laying his hands on material from the shroud seemed minimal; Turin had demanded the return of the small samples. Then a new Cardinal of Turin was appointed, Anastasio Ballestrero, former archbishop of Bari. In August 1978 Ballestrero mounted another exposition of the shroud, and it was clear that he was not averse to more scientific tests. Jackson and Jumper, Lynn and Lorre, were able to take more material; Max Frei took more dust and pollen samples. And McCrone got his test samples.

For the believers, McCrone's results were disappointing. He announced that his microscopic examination had revealed traces of iron oxide and of paint fragments on the shroud, and concluded that this proved that it was a forgery. Other scientists pointed out that flax is soaked in water before it is made into linen, and that this could easily be the source of the minute traces of iron oxide. Moreover, the shroud has often come into contact with artists – many copies around Europe bear an inscription certifying that they have been in actual contact with the Holy Shroud of Turin (and have thus, presumably, absorbed some of its virtue). Nothing is more likely than that it has some traces of the pigments used to make such copies.

At the time of writing these questions remain unresolved. The sceptical school has returned to the old assertion, first made by Fr. Ulysse Chevalier, that the shroud is a forgery whose peculiar properties – when subjected to photography and image-enhancement – are due somehow to the 'decay' of the original pigment. This belief seems as absurd now as it seemed at the turn of the twentieth century. Carbon 14 dating could perhaps resolve the question once and for all, if it proved that the linen of the shroud dates from long after the Crucifixion. This had still not been carried out when this book was written, partly because carbon dating techniques would still involve the destruction of a small amount of the cloth of the shroud, but permission for this has apparently now been granted.

But if, as seems likely on the basis of Max Frei's pollen results, the shroud proves to be of the right date, we are still faced with the mystery of *how* the image was 'imprinted' on it. American investigators have pointed out the similarity of the markings to 'radiation burns' produced by atomic explosions, and suggested that the image may have been impressed on the shroud by a very brief and intense burst of radiation – perhaps when the body of Jesus was brought back to life in the tomb. The sceptics counter this by asking why a 'miracle' should involve atomic radiation. Their question seems unanswerable. But then, so does the evidence of the extraordinary amount of 'information' encoded in the shroud. If the shroud proves to be a fourteenth-century forgery, the miracle will be almost as great as if it is proved genuine.

15   The Enigma of Identical Twins
One Mind in Two Bodies

When Jim Lewis was six years old, he learned that he had an identical twin brother. Their unmarried mother had put them up for adoption soon after they were born in August 1939. Jim had been adopted by a couple named Lewis in Lima, Ohio; his brother was adopted by a family named Springer in Dayton, Ohio. Oddly enough, both boys were christened 'Jim' by their new parents.

In 1979, when he was thirty-nine, Jim Lewis decided to try to find his twin brother. The court that had arranged the adoption was exceptionally helpful. Six weeks later, Jim Lewis knocked on the door of Jim Springer in Dayton. The moment they shook hands they felt close, as if they had been together all their lives. But when they began to compare notes they became aware of a staggering series of coincidences. To begin with, they had the same health problems. Both were compulsive nail-biters and suffered from insomnia. Both had started to experience migraines at the age of eighteen, and stopped having them at the same age. Both had heart problems. Both had developed haemorrhoids. They were exactly the same weight, but had both put on ten pounds at exactly the same period of their lives, and then lost it again at the same time.

All this might seem to indicate that genetic programming is far more precise and complex than anyone had suspected. But their coincidences went much further than genetics. Both had married girls named Linda, divorced, then married girls called Betty. Both had named their sons James Allan. Both had owned a dog named Toy. Both had worked as deputy sheriff, petrol-station attendant, and at McDonald's Hamburger restaurants. Both spent their holidays on the same Florida beach. Both chain-smoked the same make of cigarette. Both had basement workshops in which they made furniture . . . .

The twins were fascinated, not only by these similarities in experience but by their mental similarities – one would start to say something and the other· would finish it.

Their reunion received wide press coverage, and they appeared on the Johnny Carson chat show. And in Minnesota a psychologist named Tom Bouchard was so intrigued that he persuaded the University to give him a grant to study the 'Jim twins' scientifically. Then he went on to look for other similar pairs: that is, twins who were separated at a very early age, and who had not seen each other since. In their first few years of research they discovered thirty-four sets of such twins. And again and again they discovered the same extraordinary coincidences – coincidences that cannot be scientifically explained. Two British twins, Margaret Richardson and Terry Connolly, who did not even know they were twins until they were in their mid-thirties, had married on the same day within an hour of each other. Two others, Dorothy Lowe and Bridget Harrison, had decided to keep a diary for just one year, 1962, and had both filled in exactly the same days. The diaries looked identical because they were of the same make and colour. Both played the piano as children but gave it up in the same year. Both like eye-catching jewellery.

Since then work on twins has continued to show that in many cases – particularly of identical twins – there are incredible coincidences. Identical twins are those who are formed by a splitting of the same ovum. They have identical genes, which means they have identical eyes, ears, limbs, even fingerprints. The scientific term for such twins is *monozygotic*, or MZ for short. *Dizygotic* twins (DZ) are formed from two different eggs. The astonishing level of 'coincidence' applies mainly to MZ twins. In fact, the similarities in many cases become almost monotonous. For example, the twins last mentioned, Bridget Harrison and Dorothy Lowe, had sons called respectively Richard Andrew and Andrew Richard. Their daughters were called Katherine Louise and Karen Louise, but Dorothy Lowe had originally intended to call her daughter Katherine, and changed it to Karen to please a relative. Both wear the same perfume. Both leave their bedroom doors ajar. Both had had meningitis. Both collect soft toys and had cats called Tiger. Bouchard's intelligence tests showed they had identical IQs.

Barbara Herbert and Daphne Goodship were the twins of an unmarried Finnish student, and were adopted by different familea at birth. Both their adoptive mothers died when they were children. Both had fallen downstairs when they were fifteen and broken an ankle. Both met their future husbands at town-hall dances when they were sixteen, and married in their early twenties. Both had early miscarriages, then each had two boys followed by a girl. Both have a heart murmur and a slightly enlarged thyroid. Both read the same popular novelists and take the same women's magazine. And when they met for the first time both had tinted their hair the same shade of auburn, and were wearing beige dresses, brown velvet jackets and identical white petticoats.

In 1979 Jeanette Hamilton and Irene Read each discovered they had twin sisters, and hastened to get together. They discovered that both suffered from claustrophobia and dislike of water, both sit with their backs to the sea on beaches, both hated heights, both got a pain in the same spot in the right leg in wet weather, and both are compulsive calculators. As children they had led scout packs, and they had both worked at one time for the same cosmetics firm.

Two male twins studied by Bouchard had been brought up in backgrounds that could scarcely have been more different. Oscar Stohr and Jack Yufe were born in Trinidad in 1933, then their parents went off in opposite directions, each taking a twin. Oscar went to Germany and became a member of the

Nazi youth movement, while Jack was brought up as an orthodox Jew. They met for the first time at the airport in 1979, and found they were both wearing square, wire-rimmed glasses and blue shirts with epaulettes; they had identical moustaches. Closer study showed remarkable similarities in their habits. Both flushed the lavatory before and after using it, stored rubber bands on their wrists, and liked to eat alone in restaurants so they can read. Their speech rhythms were identical, although one spoke only German and the other only English. Both had the same gait and the same way of sitting. Both had the same sense of humour – for example, a tendency to sneeze loudly in lifts to startle the other passengers.

It is obviously very difficult, if not impossible, to explain such a series of 'coincidences' without positing some form of telepathy – that is, some form of hidden connection between the twins – that persisted even when they were separated by long distances. In fact Jung, who invented the word 'synchronicity' (see Chapter 36) for 'meaningful coincidences', would have accepted the telepathic explanation: there are many anecdotes in his work that are designed to illustrate the reality of telepathy. But even telepathy cannot explain how two sisters met their husbands under similar circumstances or worked for the same cosmetic firm; it must be either dismissed as coincidence or explained in terms of some peculiar theory about 'individual destinies', or even what Professor Joad once called 'the undoubted strangeness of time'. If people can have glimpses of the future, or dream of events before they happen, it suggests that, in some odd way these events are already 'programmed', like a film that has already been made. If individual lives are to some extent 'pre-programmed', then perhaps the lives of MZ twins have the same basic programming . . . .

Other cases certainly seem to demonstrate the reality of telepathy. In 1980 two female twins appeared in court in York, and attracted the attention of reporters because they made the same gestures at the same time, smiling simultaneously, raising their hands to their mouths at the same moment, and so on. The Chaplin twins, Freda and Greta, were in court for a peculiar reason: they had both apparently developed a powerful 'crush' on a lorry-driver, Mr Ken Iveson, who used to live next door, and had been pursuing him for fifteen years. They seem to have had rather a curious way of showing affection, shouting abuse and hitting him with their handbags. When this had been going on for fifteen years Mr Iveson decided to ask the court for protection.

The publicity surrounding the court case led to various medical studies of the twins. Their obsession with Mr Iveson was defined medically as erotomania, a condition in which a patient sinks into melancholy or mental disturbance due to romantic love. The twins proved to be mentally subnormal, although this seems to have been a later development. At school they had been slow, but not backward, and teachers described them as neat, clean and quiet. The deputy headmaster placed the blame on their mother. 'It was quite clear that they had a doting mother who never allowed them a seperate identity.' They were apparently dressed identically and allowed no friends.

The twins showed a tendency to the 'mirror imaging' which is often typical of MZ twins. (That is to say, if one is left-handed, the other is right-handed; if the whorls of the hair grow clockwise in one, they grow anti-clockwise in the other, and so on.) One twin wears a bracelet on the left wrist, the other on the right. When one broke a shoelace the other removed her own shoelace on the opposite side.

At some point the twins had been forced to leave home – neither they nor their mother would disclose why. At thirty-seven they were unmarried and jobless; they lived in a local service hostel. They cooked breakfast in their room together, both holding the frying-pan, then went out in identical clothes. When they both had identical grey coats with different-coloured buttons they simply swapped half the buttons so each had both colours. When given different pairs of gloves, they took one of each pair. When given two different bars of soap, they cut both in half and shared them. They told a woman journalist that they had one brain, and were really one person, claiming to know exactly what the other is thinking. Their 'simultaneous behaviour' suggests that some form of telepathy exists between them. They occasionally quarrel, hitting one another lightly with identical handbags, then sulking for hours. But in spite of these disagreements, it seems clear that their common aim is to exclude the external world and to live in their own small private universe.

Two Californian twins, Grace and Virginia Kennedy, even developed a private language in which they conversed; this started when they were seventeen months old. By 1977, when they were seven, a speech therapist in the San Diego children's hospital began to study their private language, and discovered that it seemed to be a mixture of invented words, like 'nunukid' and 'pulana', and a mixture of English and German words mispronounced (their parents were respectively American and German). They called one another Poto and Cabenga, and spoke their unknown language swiftly and fluently. Eventually they were coaxed into speaking English; but they declined to explain their former language – or perhaps they were simply unable to.

One of the strangest cases involving twins was recorded in the *New York Review of Books* (28 Feb 1985) by the psychiatrist Oliver Sacks. Michael and John, known simply as The Twins, have been in state institutions since they were seven (in 1947). They have been diagnosed as autistic, psychotic and severely retarded. Yet they possess one extraordinary ability: the ability to say on what day of the week any date in the past or future will fall; asked, say, about 11 June 55 BC, they would instantly snap 'Wednesday' – and prove correct. They are, says Sacks, a grotesque Tweedledum and Tweedledee, mirror-image twins who are identical in face, personality and body movements, as well as in their brain and tissue damage. They wear glasses so thick that their eyes seem distorted.

They can repeat any number of digits after one hearing – as many as three hundred. Yet they are not 'calculating prodigies', able to multiply huge numbers within seconds or extract tenth roots from twenty digit numbers, as many such prodigies have been able to. But when a box of matches fell on the floor, both murmured '111' before the matches hit the floor – and again, proved to be correct.

One day Sacks found them sitting in a corner, wearing an odd, contented smile and swopping six-digit numbers. He noted down several of these, and when he got home, checked through a book of mathematical tables, and discovered that all the numbers were primes – numbers that cannot be divided by any other number without a 'leftover'. Now, the odd thing is that there is no mathematical method of determining whether some large number is a prime or not – except painstakingly to try dividing all the smaller numbers into it; if it gives a 'remainder' with every smaller number up to half its own size, then it is a prime. Yet the twins were apparently pulling primes out of the air without the slightest effort.

The next day Sacks again sat in on their game, and suddenly interupted it with an eight-figure prime (taken from his book of tables). They looked at him in astonishment; then, after a half-minute pause their faces broke into broad smiles. Then the twins began swopping nine-figure primes. Sacks offered a ten-figure prime; once again there was wonderment. After a long silence John brought out a twelve-figure number. Sacks had no way of checking this, because his book only went up to ten-figure primes; but he had no doubt it *was* a prime. An hour later the twins were swopping twenty-figure numbers.

What were the twins *doing* during their half-minute silence when Sacks introduced the eight-figure prime? The answer can only be that they were making the effort to *see* the number – to see it in some symmetrical way so they could see if there was any 'remainder'. Most of us can visualize, say, nine or sixteen by imagining a group of dots laid out in three rows of three or four rows of four; the twins must have been doing the same thing on a far vaster scale.

This offers us an important clue. We know that the two hemispheres of the brain have different functions: in effect, the left is a scientist, the right an artist. The left is concerned with language and logic; the right with intuitions and insights. The left sees the world from a 'worm's-eye view', the right from a 'bird's-eye view'. In civilized human beings the left is the 'dominant hemisphere', and my *sense of identity* resides there, so that when I use the word 'I' it is the left brain speaking. (See also article on coincidences.) In most of us the powers of the right brain – to visualize patterns, for example – are fairly limited compared to the reasoning powers of the left. It seems clear that in the Twins the powers of the left are extremely limited, but the powers of the right are apparently hundreds of times greater than in the rest of us.

It would seem that the general lesson to be learned from twins is that the non-stop left-brain activity demanded by civilization has suppressed all kinds of 'natural' powers in the right, such as telepathic communication, physical empathy, and the ability to grasp reality with a 'bird's-eye vision' – with a 'telescope' instead of the microscope we habitually use. And cases like those of the Jim twins – in which the same kind of things have happened to twins who have been separated since birth – seem to hint there are laws and patterns of events scientists and philosophers have not even begun to suspect.

16 Did Joan of Arc Return from the Dead?

On 30 May 1431 Joan of Arc was burnt as a heretic by the English; she was only nineteen years old. She regarded herself as a messenger from Heaven, sent to save the French from their enemies the English (who were in league with the Burgundians who captured her). At the age of thirteen Joan began to hear voices, which she later identified as those of St Gabriel, St Michael, St Marguerite and St Catherine. When the news of the encirclement of Orleans reached her little village in Lorraine, Domremy, her voices told her to go to lift the siege. Her military career was brief but spectacular: in a year she won many remarkable victories, and saw Charles VII crowned at Rheims. Then she was captured by the Burgundians, sold to the English for ten thousand francs, tried as a witch, and burnt alive.

But that, oddly enough, was not quite the end of 'the Maid'. 'Now one month after Paris had returned to her allegiance to King Charles', writes Anatole France, 'there appeared in Lorraine a certain damsel. She was about twenty-five years old. Hitherto she had been called Claude; but now she made herself known to divers lord of the town of Metz as being Jeanne the Maid.' This was in May 1436, five years after Joan had died at the stake.

It sounds very obviously as if some imposter had decided to pose as Joan the Maid. But there is some astonishing evidence that suggests that this is not so. Joan's two younger brothers, Petit-Jean and Pierre, were still serving in the army, and they had no doubt whatever that their sister had been burnt at Rouen. So when they heard that a woman claiming to be Joan was at Metz, and that she had expressed a wish to meet them, the brothers hastened to Metz – Petit-Jean was not far away, being the provost of Vaucouleurs. One chronicler describes how the brothers went to the village of La-Grange-aux-Ormes, two and a half miles south of Metz, where a tournament was being held. A knight in armour was galloping around an obstacle course and pulling stakes expertly out of the ground; this was the person who claimed to be their sister. The brothers rode out on to the field, prepared to challenge the impostor. But when Petit-Jean demanded, 'Who are you?', the 'impostor' raised her visor, and both brothers gaped in astonishment as they recognized their sister Joan.

In fact Joan was surrounded by various people who had known her during her spectacular year fighting the English, including Nicole Lowe, the king's chamberlain. If she was in fact an impostor, it seems absurd that she should go to a place where she would be sure to be recognized. (John of Metz was one of her first and most loyal supporters.) And the next day her brothers took her to Vaucouleurs, where she spent a week, apparently accepted by many people who had seen her there seven years earlier, when she had gone to see the local squire Robert de Baudricourt, to ask him to send her to see the Dauphin, the heir to the throne. After this she spent three weeks at a small town called Marville, then went on a pilgrimage to see the Black Virgin called Notre Dame de Liance, between Laon and Rheims. Then she went to stay with Elizabeth, Duchess of Luxembourg, at Arlon. Meanwhile her brother Petit-Jean went to see the king and announced that his sister Joan was still alive. We do not know the king's reaction, but he ordered his treasurer to give Petit-Jean a hundred francs. An entry in the treasury accounts of Orléans for 9 August 1436 states that the council authorized payment of a courier who had brought letters from 'Jeanne la Pucelle' (Joan the Maid).

The records of these events are to be found in the basic standard work on Joan of Arc, Jules Quicherat's five-volume *Trial and Rehabilitation of Joan of Arc* (1841), which contains all the original documents. One of these documents states that on 24 June 1437 Joan's miraculous powers returned to her. By then she had become something of a protégée of Count Ulrich of Württemberg, who took her to Cologne. There she became involved in a clash between two churchmen who were rivals for the diocese; one had been appointed by the chapter, the other by the pope. Count Ulrich favoured one called Udalric, and Joan apparently also pronounced in his favour. But her intervention did no good; the Council of Basle considered Udalric a usurper, and the pope's nominee was appointed. The Inquisitor General of Cologne became curious about the count's guest (remember that this was at the height of the 'witchcraft craze'), and was apparently shocked to learn that she practised magic, and that she danced with men and ate and drank more than she ought. (The magic sounds more like conjuring: she tore a tablecloth and restored it to its original state, and did the same with a glass which she broke against a wall.) He summoned her before him, but she refused to appear; when men were sent to fetch her the count hid her in his house, then smuggled her out of the town. The inquisitor excommunicated her. Back at Arlon, staying with the Duchess of Luxembourg, she met a nobleman named Robert des Armoires and – no doubt to the astonishment of her followers – married him. (The original Joan had sworn a vow of perpetual chastity under a 'fairy tree' at Domremy.) Then they moved to Metz, where Robert had a house, and during the next three years she gave birth to two children.

Two years later, in the summer of 1439, the 'Dame des Armoires' went to Orléans, whose magistrates gave her a banquet and presented her with 210 livres by way of thanking her for her services to the town during the siege. Oddly enough, these same burgesses had paid for Masses in memory of the Maid's death three months earlier; presumably they must have changed their minds in the meantime. After 1439 the Masses ceased.

After two weeks she left Orléans in rather a hurry, according to one chronicler, and went to Tours, where she sent a letter to the king via the Baillie of Touraine, Guillaume Bellier, who had been the Maid's host ten years earlier. Moreover, she soon afterwards went to Poitou, where she seems to have been given the nominal command of a place called Mans – presumably by the king she had enthroned. Then the king transferred this command to Joan's ex-comrade in arms, Gilles de Rais. Since the days when he had fought beside Joan before the walls of Paris, Gilles had begun to practise black magic – in an attempt to repair his fortunes, drained by his excesses – and had become a sadistic killer of children. In the following year, 1440, Gilles would be tried and condemned to be hanged and burned. Meanwhile – assuming he met the Dame des Armoises (which seems practically certain, since she had to hand over her command to him) – he seems to have accepted her as his former comrade-in-arms. He also placed her in authority over the men-at-arms.

In 1440 Joan finally went to Paris and met the king. And for the first time she received a setback; after the meeting the king declared her an impostor. It may be significant that he did so after the interview. Surely if he could see she was a fraud he would have said so at the time? He even attempted to practise on her the same trick he had tried at their first meeting eleven years earlier, concealing himself and asking one of his men to impersonate him. But as on the previous occasion Joan was not to be deceived; she walked straight up to the king and knelt at his feet, whereupon the king said: 'Pucelle, my dear, you are welcome back in the name of God.' It seems, to say the least of it, strange that he should then have decided she was an impostor.

And now, according to the journal 'of a Bourgeois of Paris', Joan was arrested, tried and publicly exhibited as a malefactor. A sermon was preached against her, and she was forced to confess publicly that she was an imposter. Her story, according to the 'Bourgeois of Paris', was that she had gone to Rome about 1433 to seek absolution for striking her mother. She had, she said, engaged as a soldier in war in the service of the Holy Father Eugenius, and worn man's apparel. This, presumably, gave her the idea of pretending to be the Maid . . . .

But the whole of this story is doubtful in the extreme. To begin with, Joan then returned to Metz, and continued to be accepted as 'la Pucelle'. In 1443 her brother Pierre refers to her in a petition as 'Jeanne la Pucelle, my sister', and her cousin Henry de Voulton mentions that Petit-Jean, Pierre and their sister la Pucelle used to visit the village of Sermaise and feast with relations, all of whom accepted her. Fourteen years later she makes an appearance in the town of Saumur, and is again accepted by the officials of the town as the Maid. And after that she vanishes from history, presumably living out the rest of her life quietly with her husband in Metz.

What then are we to make of the story that the king declared her an impostor, and that she admitted it publicly? First of all, its only source is the 'journal of a Bourgeois of Paris'. This in itself is odd, if she was involved in such a public scandal. Moreover, the 'bourgeois' was hostile to the earlier Joan, in the days before her execution. Anatole France mentions that the common people of Paris were in a fever of excitement at the news that the Maid was still alive and was returning to Paris. The University of Paris was still thoroughly hostile to the Maid, who had been condemned as a witch.

Her sentence could only be reversed by the pope, and he showed no sign of doing this, in spite of a movement to rehabilitate Joan. So as far as the clerks and magistrates of Paris were concerned, the return of Joan would have been nothing but an embarrassment. As to those authorities of the Church who were trying to have the Maid declared innocent (they succeeded in 1456, and Joan was finally canonized in 1922), they would have found the return of their heroine – alive, healthy and married – an obstacle to their patriotic campaign. The king must have found himself under intolerable pressure to declare Joan an impostor. After all, if *he* declared her genuine, then it was 'official', and no one in France had a right to doubt her identity. Moreover, there would be some question of public recognition . . . . On the other hand, if he expressed doubts about her, the whole scandal was defused. She could return home and drop out of sight. And everyone would be much happier. And that, it seemed, is precisely what happened.

Anatole France takes it for granted that the Dame des Armoises was an impostor. But then his biography of Joan of Arc is permeated with his famous irony, and takes the view that she was a deluded peasant girl; France was basically a disciple of Voltaire. The notion that she was an impostor is indeed the simplest explanation. But it leaves us facing the problem: why, in that case, did so many people who knew 'the Maid' accept the Dame des Armoises as genuine? It is conceivable that her brothers may have decided that it would be to their advantage to have their famous sister alive, and so condoned the imposture. But why should so many old comrades have agreed to support the story?

The Dame des Armoises never as far as we know explained how she came to escape the flames. But then presumably she would not know the answer to this question. She would only know that she had been rescued, and that someone else had died in her place – perhaps another 'witch'. It is easy to see how this could have come about. We know that Joan was an extraordinarily persuasive young lady, and that dozens of people, from Robert de Baudricourt to the Dauphin, who began by assuming she was mad, ended by believing that she was being guided by divine voices. We know that even in court Joan declared that she could hear St Catherine telling her what to say. Even at her trial she had certain friends; a priest called Loyseleur was her adviser. When Joan complained about the conduct of her two guards the Earl of Warwick was furious, and had them replaced by two other guards – which suggests that the earl held her in high regard. So it would not be at all surprising if there was a successful plot to rescue her. And it is possible that the English themselves may have been involved in such a plot; when Joan was apparently burnt at the stake in Rouen the crowd was kept at a distance by eight hundred English soldiers, which would obviously prevent anyone coming close enough to recognize her. At the trial for her rehabilitation in 1456 the executioner's evidence was entirely second-hand, although three of Joan's comrades who were with her at the 'end' – Ladvenu, Massieu and Isambard – were actually present. *If* Joan was rescued, presumably they also were involved in the plot.

The rehabilitation itself has its farcical aspects. It began in 1450, and

Joan's mother was the person who set it in motion, supported by Joan's brother Pierre. We do not know whether Joan's mother accepted the Dame des Armoires as her daughter, but there can be no doubt that she lent credence to the claim by not denouncing her as an impostor. Yet now she and Pierre joined in the claim that was based on the assertion that Joan was executed by the English in 1431. But then the aim of the rehabilitation was financial; Joan had been a rich woman, thanks to the generosity of the king, and the wealth remained frozen while Joan was excommunicated. So, whether or not Joan's family believed that the Dame des Armoires was the Maid, they now had good reason to try to have her rehabilitated – even if it meant swearing that she was dead.

If the Dame des Armoires was genuine, she must have felt there was a certain irony in the situation. She had been an embarrassment to everyone during her first career as the saintly virgin warrior; now she was just as much an embarrassment as the heroine returned from the dead. It is thankless work being a saint.

17 The Mystery of Lord Kitchener's Death

Accident or Murder?

No death of the twentieth century (except that of President Kennedy) has been surrounded by more sinister rumours than that of Lord Kitchener, the British Secretary for War, in June 1916. Kitchener sailed from Scapa Flow, in southern Orkney, en route for Archangel, on the White Sea. His mission was to see the Tsar of Russia, and try to make plans that would counteract some of the disasters suffered by the Russian armies in the previous year. HMS *Hampshire*, with Kitchener on board, left the safety of Scapa Flow at 4.45 p.m. on 5 June 1916; at 7.45, two miles west of Marwick Head, the *Hampshire* struck a high-explosive mine laid by the German U-75; fifteen minutes later, the *Hampshire* had sunk. One of the survivors, Fred Sims, recalled Kitchener standing impassively on deck, dressed in a greatcoat, awaiting the inevitable end. Kitchener's body was never found, and the Royal Navy immediately placed the whole incident under a wrap of secrecy that was imposed for fifty years.

Kitchener's death was a severe blow to British morale. His face, with its heavy drooping moustache, was perhaps the best known in Great Britain, since it had appeared on recruiting posters ('Your country needs YOU!'). He had been one of the great British heroes ever since he reconquered the Sudan in 1896, and avenged the death of General Gordon at Khartoum; after his conquest of the followers of the Mahdi in 1898 at Omdurman he was raised to the peerage as Baron Kitchener of Khartoum. In the Boer War (1900-2) Kitchener used fortified blockhouses and the systematic denudation of Boer lands to wear down the resistance of the guerrillas. His methods were severely criticized, but he was made a viscount and awarded $50,000 and the Order of Merit. By the beginning of the 1914 war Kitchener had been made an earl for distinguished services in India and Egypt. Appointed head of the War Office, he immediately laid plans to expand the British army from twenty to seventy divisions – hence the famous recruiting posters. Another major task was furnishing munitions for this immense army, and the Ministry of Munitions was set up (rather belatedly) in June 1915.

By June 1916 Russia was in serious trouble. That notorious incompetence and corruption, portrayed so brilliantly by nineteenth-century Russian novelists, had almost cost them the war by the Christmas of 1914; money that should have been spent on munitions went into the pockets of ministers. The war minister, General Sukhomlinov, turned down a French offer of munitions because he thought the war would be over by Christmas; in mid-1915 he was dismissed for incompetence. Great Britain promised arms to the Russians, but its own munitions industry took a long time to get into its stride; meanwhile the Russians fought their battles with bayonets, at a terrifying cost in lives. Lloyd George, then the British minister of munitions, also did his best to create problems; he detested the Tsarist regime, and seemed to think that if he gave arms to Russia they might be used against Britain on some future occasion.

Lloyd George was also involved in a War Office plot to get rid of Kitchener, and just before Kitchener went to Scapa Flow a member of Parliament proposed in the House that his salary should be reduced; other MPs violently attacked his policies. So when Kitchener went to Scapa Flow he was a tired and worried man. He seems to have had presentiments of death; he told his colleague Sir William Robertson: 'If anything happens to me, look after Haig.' But shortly before his departure he seemed to have won his battle against critical MPs, and he left a meeting with his critics 'gay, alert, elastic and sanguine'.

Security seems to have been poor. One Fleet Street journalist said that all Fleet Street knew about the Russian trip a month in advance; it was certainly talked of openly in court circles in St Petersburg. No special precautions seem to have been taken; on the evening of 4 June, the day before he was due to sail, Kitchener stood alone on the platform at King's Cross, and was recognized by a startled porter. The rest of Kitchener's entourage was phoning all over London to try to locate a servant who had been misdirected to the wrong station; this servant was essential since he carried the Foreign Office cipher. The man was finally located at Marylebone station, and it was agreed that he and his Foreign Office master H.J.O'Beirne should follow later by special train.

When Kitchener arrived at Thurso, in Scotland, the following morning, the weather was deteriorating, and it seemed advisable to postpone sailing for twenty-four hours; but Kitchener would not hear of it. He crossed from Thurso to Scapa Flow – where he wanted to pay a visit to the Grand Fleet – in HMS *Oak*, and had lunch with Admiral Sir John Jellicoe; he told Jellicoe he was looking forward to the Russian trip as a welcome holiday.

So the doomed cruiser *Hampshire* set sail that afternoon with Field Marshal the Earl Kitchener in a cheerful mood. He had declined to wait while minesweepers swept the channel, pointing out that the weather looked so bad that they would not be able to start for at least twenty-four hours, and that he could not afford a two-day delay. Soon after they left Scapa Flow the storm struck, and a north-west gale whipped the sea to a fury.

At about 7.45 there was an explosion; it was almost drowned by the noise of the storm, and one survivor later compared it to an electric-light bulb bursting. It was followed by a second explosion, perhaps a boiler bursting. Then the lights failed, and there was a hiss of escaping steam. Men in the engine-room were trapped as water rushed in. Some were scalded to death. Mutilated men staggered up on to the deck.

The loss of electric power was a disaster, since the mechanism for launching the lifeboats was worked by electricity. One boat was launched by hand, and about fifty men leapt into it; a few seconds later it had been splintered to pieces against the *Hampshire*'s side. Captain Savill called to Kitchener to come to a lifeboat, but the noise of the storm made it impossible to hear him. Men were jumping overboard with lifebelts: only twelve would survive out of 665. Carley life-rafts, each of which could hold about four dozen men, were successfully launched, but found it hard to get away from the doomed ship. Only one succeeded in getting far enough away to escape the suction, and most of the fifty men on board were swept off by the waves. Many sailors had decided to sit in the boats and wait until the ship went down, hoping to float away. But splintered rigging fell on them as the ship turned on to its side. By eight o'clock the *Hampshire* had vanished. Five hours later the men on the surviving raft were swept into a gap in the cliffs.

Britain was shocked by the news; houses drew their blinds and shops put up their shutters for the day. All army officers were ordered to wear mourning bands. When the journalist Hannen Swaffer telephoned Lord Northcliffe, owner of the *Daily Mail*, to tell him of Kitchener's death, Northcliffe said: 'Good. Now we can get on with winning the war.' But not many felt as he did. Two days later *The Times*, also under Northcliffe's control, printed the comment that it was possible that 'Lord Kitchener's movements had been conveyed to the enemy by spies . . .' Soon after this Berlin issued a statement that a woman spy had been responsible for Kitchener's death. Before the end of June most members of the British public believed that there was some mystery connected with Lord Kitchener's end.

The most popular supposition was that it was sabotage. In February 1916, five months before the sinking, the *Hampshire* had been refitted in Belfast; one survivor told an odd story of returning to the ship one afternoon and finding it surrounded by soldiers; he was told that someone had been tampering with electric switches in the ammunition passage. Kitchener had refused to allow Irish troops to wear a harp symbol on their uniforms, and it was reported that the IRA had vowed to kill him. But other 'suspects' included Lord Asquith, the Prime Minister, and Lloyd George, who was to succeed Asquith after the latter's downfall at the end of that year. Kitchener was certainly disliked by many politicians; on the evening of his departure for Scapa Flow the American ambassador Walter Page wrote to Washington: 'There is in England a hope and a feeling that he may not come back from Russia.' But neither Lloyd George nor Asquith – nor any of the other rumoured suspects, such as Lord Northcliffe, Lord Haldane and Lady Asquith – had any possible motive for plotting his death. Trebitsch Lincoln, an ex-Member of Parliament who became a German spy, has also been named as the man who organized the 'assassination'; but on the day Kitchener travelled to Scapa Flow, Lincoln was landing at Liverpool under arrest, having been deported from America.

In 1921 there were more shocking allegations. Lord Alfred Douglas – who thirty years earlier had been Oscar Wilde's close friend and lover – owned a small-circulation magazine called *Plain English*, and it was in this that on 2 July 1921 he published his own astonishing account of 'the truth' behind the sinking of the *Hampshire*. Six days before the death of Kitchener, on 31 May

1916, the battle of Jutland had been fought off the coast of Denmark between the British and German fleets; 248 ships had been involved. Britain lost fourteen ships, Germany eleven. Both sides claimed victory. Arthur Balfour, First Lord of the Admiralty, asked Winston Churchill to write a commentary on the battle that would make it sound like an unequivocal victory for England, and Churchill – the author of many books – did so, describing Jutland as 'a definite step towards the attainment of complete victory'. British morale had soared, only to be depressed again by news of Kitchener's death a few days later.

According to Lord Alfred Douglas, this was all part of a disgraceful money-making plan. Balfour's original communiqué was rather gloomy in tone, and had been designed to cause a sharp fall in British stock in Wall Street. Rich Jews, including the publisher Sir Ernest Cassel, had bought the stock at rock-bottom price. Then Churchill's commentary had sent the stock soaring, and the Jews had made a handsome profit. Cassel alone had made $40 million, and had given Churchill a large cheque and some expensive furniture. The same rich Jews had organized the sinking of the *Hampshire* because Kitchener intended to make sure that corrupt Bolshevik Jews were expelled from their key positions in Russia.

This story was printed in *Plain English*, and was brought to the attention of Churchill; Churchill decided to ignore it. But the *Jewish Guardian* accused Douglas of publishing lies. Douglas promptly sued for libel, and was awarded a derisory farthing damages. Douglas then organized a 'Lord Kitchener and Jutland Committee' and advertised a mass meeting in Memorial Hall, Farringdon Street. (Douglas's biographer Rupert Croft-Cooke states that Kitchener was homosexual, and that Douglas had hinted that he and Kitchener had become lovers when they met in Cairo in 1893.) At the meeting in the Memorial Hall Douglas told a packed audience that Churchill was a rogue and a swindler, then presented an extraordinary version of the sinking of the *Hampshire*. The two destroyers that were to have escorted the *Hampshire* were deliberately held back for many hours (this was untrue; the *Unity* and the *Victor* had battled through the storm beside the *Hampshire*, but had been forced to drop further and further behind because of the roughness of the seas); the launch of lifeboats from Orkney had also been held back. (This was partly true, but seems to have been incompetence on the part of the naval authorities, who for reasons of secrecy flatly denied that any cruiser had sailed that day.)

The enthusiastic audience adopted a resolution demanding a public inquiry, but the meeting was ignored by Fleet Street newspapers. Douglas sent his speech to the editor of the *Border Standard*, who not only published it in full but issued it as a pamphlet called *The Murder of Lord Kitchener and the Truth about the Battle of Jutland and the Jews*. Thirty thousand copies were printed, and six thousand had been distributed when Douglas was arrested on 6 November 1923 and charged with libel.

For Douglas the trial was a disaster. The prosecution had no trouble in demonstrating that stocks on Wall Street had slumped before the Balfour announcement, after the Germans had announced their 'victory'. And it was also proved that Sir Ernest Cassel (who was now dead) had not bought or sold any stocks at that time. Douglas's only defence witness was a former editor of *Plain English* – a Captain Harold Spender – who was shown to be a liar who had been certified insane three times. Douglas antagonized the judge, Mr Justice Avory, by objecting that he had not been allowed to put his case, and that it was 'the most abominable piece of unfairness I have ever seen in my life'. Avory sentenced him to six months in prison.

Tales of the 'true story' behind the mystery continued to circulate; there were reports that Kitchener had escaped and had been seen alive in various parts of the world; also that his body had been washed up in Norway and buried near Stavanger. A spirit medium produced a book in which the ghost of Lord Kitchener alleged that he had been locked in his cabin by a cabin boy to whom he had been strongly attracted, and who had subsequently shot himself. (There were no cabin boys on the *Hampshire*.) A book called *The Man Who Killed Kitchener* by Clement Wood (1932) revealed that Kitchener had been hunted down by a German spy named Fritz Duquesne, who had developed his hatred of Kitchener during the Boer War, and who had managed to get on board the *Hampshire* disguised as a Russian liaison officer. He had signalled a German submarine to fire a torpedo, using a flashlight, and had subsequently flung himself overboard and been picked up by the submarine.

Donald McCormick's *Mystery of Lord Kitchener's Death* considers the possibility that Lloyd George might have been behind the 'murder'. McCormick believes that Lloyd George was almost certainly responsible for the 'leaks' that made Kitchener's trip to Archangel an open secret. McCormick says: 'For two years Lloyd George had been intriguing against the War Minister Kitchener. Leakages of Cabinet business aimed at discrediting Kitchener and Asquith had been continually occurring. Mrs Asquith noted in her diary, 'When I point out that someone in the Cabinet is betraying secrets, I am counselled to keep calm . . . .' The news of Kitchener's death had hardly been received before Lloyd George was plotting to succeed him. And soon after this Lloyd George was intriguing how to get rid of Sir William Robertson, who together with Kitchener had been joint head of the War Office.

In his *War Memoirs* Lloyd George claimed that he had intended to travel to Russia with Kitchener, but that when the Rising of Easter 1916 occurred in Dublin he was requested by Asquith to 'try his hand' with Ireland; this, he said, undoubtedly saved his life. Donald McCormick obviously finds this story completely unbelievable, commenting that Lloyd George hated the sea and was in any case a physical coward; besides, he was constantly at loggerheads with Kitchener, and the latter would almost certainly have declined the honour of sailing with the unreliable Welshman. In any case, McCormick points out, Lloyd George's Irish mission was ended by the time Kitchener sailed from Scapa Flow. 'All the evidence seems to suggest that Lloyd George wished to give the impression that he intended going to Russia, though . . . there was never any question of his going.' Why should Lloyd George want to give such an impression? One motive could have been a desire to divert suspicion from himself if he *was* in some way responsible for the sinking of the *Hampshire* . . . .

McCormick's book appeared in 1959, and he was not allowed access to the records of the NID (the Naval Intelligence Department). But in 1985 another biographer, Trevor Royle, finally gained access to these records. What he then discovered seemed to confirm the rumours that Kitchener's death had not been simply a piece of appalling bad luck. McCormick had already revealed that in the spring of 1916, a German listening-post at Neumünster had picked up a naval signal from a British destroyer to the Admiralty declaring that a certain channel west of Orkney had been swept clear of mines; when the same signal was repeated twice more the Germans realized that the Navy must have some important reason for sweeping the channel and then reporting to the Admiralty. The German Admiral von Scheer sent a submarine, U-75, commanded by Oberleutnant Kurt Beitzen, to lay more mines in the recently cleared channel. One of these mines sank the *Hampshire*. This story, if correct, lays the blame firmly at the door of the Admiralty or whoever ordered the destroyer to report direct to the Admiralty. (If the report had been made to the Orkney shore station, no one would have paid any attention.)

What Trevor Royle discovered was that Naval Intelligence had intercepted this signal from von Scheer, and since the British had broken the German secret code, they were able to read it. Then, on the day Kitchener was due to sail, Naval Intelligence learned that the German submarine was still lurking in the area, and three signals to this effect were sent to Admiral Jellicoe. Yet he failed to pass these on to Kitchener. This information was not presented to a court of inquiry in 1916, or mentioned in a government White Paper on the tragedy in 1926. In fact, Jellicoe went on record after the sinking as saying: 'It was practically impossible that this route could have been mined owing to the dark period in northern latitudes being confined to a couple of hours, during which no enemy ship could expect to approach the shore . . . Mine laying by enemy submarines had been confined to waters well to the southward of the Firth of Forth . . .' Royle's researches show that this was a lie, and that Jellicoe knew it was a lie, and allowed Kitchener to sail to almost certain death. It is of course on record that Jellicoe begged Kitchener to delay his departure, but that was on account of the weather, and Kitchener could have been expected to refuse.

There seem to be two possible explanations. One is ordinary incompetence; Jellicoe was hoping for the best. But if he knew that the U-75 had been ordered to lay mines a week before, why had he not already swept the channel? Is it possible that Jellicoe, like Lloyd George, was one of the men whom the American Ambassador reported as hoping that Kitchener would not return from Russia? And was Lloyd George's part in Kitchener's death an accident, due to indiscreet talk, or was it part of a plot to send a rival whose post he coveted to his death? The evidence undoubtedly establishes that Kitchener's death can be laid at the door of Lloyd George and Jellicoe. But it seems unlikely that we shall ever know whether this is what they consciously intended.

18   The Loch Ness Monster

Loch Ness, the largest of British lakes, is twenty-two miles long and about a mile wide; at its greatest depth, it is 950 feet deep. It is part of the Great Glen, which runs like a deep crack right across Scotland, from one coast to the other; it opened up between 300 and 400 million years ago as a result of earthquakes, then was deepened by glaciers. At the southern end of the loch there is the small town of Fort Augustus; at the northern end, Inverness. Until the eighteenth century, the loch was practically inaccessible, except by winding trackways; it was not until 1731 that General Wade began work on the road that runs from Fort Augustus up the south side of the loch (although Fort Augustus was not so christened until 1742). But this steep road, which makes a long detour inland, was obviously not the shortest distance between Fort Augustus and Inverness; the most direct route would run along the northern shore. In the early 1930s a road was finally hacked and blasted out of this northern shore, and vast quantities of rock were dumped down the steep sides of Loch Ness.

The road had only just been completed in April 1933, and it was on the 14th of that month that Mr and Mrs John Mackay, proprietors of the Drumnadrochit Hotel, were returning home from a trip to Inverness. It was about three in the afternoon when Mrs Mackay pointed and said, 'What's that, John?' The water in the middle of the loch was in a state of commotion; at first she thought it was two ducks fighting, then realized that the area of disturbance was too wide. As her husband pulled up they saw some large animal in the middle of the surging water; then as they watched the creature swam towards Aldourie pier on the other side of the loch. For a moment they glimpsed two black humps, which rose and fell in an undulating manner; then the creature made a half-turn and sank from sight.

The Mackays made no attempt to publicize their story, but gossip about the sighting reached a young water bailiff, Alex Campbell, who also happened to be local correspondent for the *Inverness Courier*; he called on the Mackays, and his report went into the *Courier* on 2 May, more than two weeks after the sighting occurred. The editor is said to have remarked: 'If it's as big as they say, it's not a creature it's a monster.' And so the 'Loch Ness Monster' acquired its name.

This was not, strictly speaking, the first account of the monster to appear in print. This distinction belongs to a *Life of St Columba* dating from about AD 565. This tells (in vol. 6, book 11, chap. 27) how the saint arrived at a ferry on the banks of the loch and found some men preparing to bury a comrade who had been bitten to death by a water monster while he was swimming. The saint ordered one of his own followers to swim across the loch. The monster heard the splashing and swam towards him, at which the saint made the sign of the cross and commanded the creature to go away; the terrified monster obeyed. . . .

Other reportings down the centuries are more difficult to pin down; in his book on the monster, Nicholas Witchell mentions a number of references to the 'beast' or 'water kelpie' (fairy) of Loch Ness in old books between 1600 and 1800. And after Commander Rupert Gould published a book on the monster in 1934, a Dr D.Mackenzie of Balnain wrote to Gould claiming to have seen it in 1871 or 1872, looking rather like an upturned boat but moving at great speed, 'wriggling and churning up the water'. Alex Campbell, the water bailiff, reported that a crofter named Alexander MacDonald had seen the monster in 1802 and reported it to one of Campbell's ancestors. But hearsay reports like this inevitably led sceptics to suspect that local people, particularly hoteliers, had a financial interest in promoting the monster, so that by the mid-1930s 'Nessie' (as she was soon christened in the area) had become something of a joke. In fact the first 'modern' report of the monster had occurred in 1930; the *Northern Chronicle* reported that three young men who were out in a boat fishing on 22 July of that year, close to Dores, on the southern shore, saw a loud commotion in the water about 600 yards away, and some large creature swimming towards them just below the surface; it turned away when it was about 300 yards away. The young men commented that it was 'certainly not a basking shark or a seal'.

That summer of 1933 was one of the hottest on record, and by the end of the summer the Loch Ness monster was known to readers all over the British Isles; it was still to become a world-wide sensation.

By now the monster had also been sighted on land. On a peaceful summer afternoon, 22 July 1933, Mr and Mrs George Spicer were on their way back to London after a holiday in the Highlands. At about four o'clock they were driving along the southern road from Inverness to Fort William (the original General Wade road) and were on the mid-portion between Dores and Foyers. About two hundred yards ahead of them they saw a trunk-like object apparently stretching across the road. Then they saw that it was in motion, and that they were looking at a long neck. This was soon followed by a grey body, about five feet high (Mr Spicer said later 'It was horrible – an abomination') which moved across the road in jerks. Because they were on a slope, they could not see whether it had legs or not, and by the time their car had reached the top of the slope it had vanished into the undergrowth opposite. It seemed to be carrying something on its back. They saw no tail, and the drawing that Commander Gould made later under their direction justifies Mr Spicer's description of a 'huge snail with a long neck'. When Gould heard of this sighting he thought it was a hoax; but after he had interviewed the Spicers in London he had no doubt that they were telling the truth. The Spicers still seemed shaken and upset. It was later suggested the object over the monster's shoulder could have been a dead sheep.   In 1971 Nicholas Witchell interviewed Mrs Margaret Cameron, who claimed to have seen the monster on land when she was a teenager, during the First

World War; she said, 'It had a huge body and its movement as it came out of the trees was like a caterpillar.' She also described it as being about twenty feet long, and said that it had two short, round feet at the front, and that it lurched from side to side as it entered the water. She and her friends felt so sick and upset that they were unable to eat their tea afterwards. Witchell also interviewed a man called Jock Forbes, who claimed to have seen the monster in 1919, when he was twelve; it was a stormy night, and he and his father were in a pony and trap when the pony shied, and they saw something large crossing the road ahead of them, then heard a splash as it plunged into the loch.

In November 1933 'Nessie' was photographed for the first time. Hugh Gray, an employee of the British Aluminium Company, was walking on a wooded bluff, fifty feet above the loch, near Foyers. He had seen the monster on a previous occasion, and was now carrying a camera. It was Sunday 12 November 1933, a sunny morning, and Gray sat down for a moment to look out over the loch. As he did so he saw the monster rising up out of the water, about two hundred yards away. He raised his camera and snapped it while it was two or three feet above the surface of the water. It is not the clearest of all photographs – it is easy to focus attention on the dark shadow and to overlook the vague, greyish bulk of the creature rising from the water above it. This was only one of five shots; the others seem to have been even less satisfactory. Gray was so ambivalent about the sighting – afraid of being subjected to derision – that he left the film in his camera for two weeks, when his brother took it to be developed. It appeared in the Scottish *Daily Record* and the London *Daily Sketch* on 6 December 1933, together with a statement from the Kodak film company that the negative had not been retouched. But Professor Graham Kerr, a zoologist at Glasgow University, declared that he found it utterly unconvincing as a photograph of any living thing. It was the beginning of the 'debunking' of the monster, in which major zoologists were to be prominent for many decades to come.

And the sightings continued. The day after Hugh Gray had snapped the monster, Dr J.Kirton and his wife were walking down the hill behind the

Invermoriston Hotel when they saw the monster swimming away from them. They saw a rounded back with a protuberance in the middle, 'like the rear view of a duck in a pond'. Gould lists this as the twenty-sixth sighting of 1933. A week later, on the 20th of November, the monster was seen lying motionless in the water for some ten minutes by a Miss N.Simpson, near Altsigh; she judged its length to be about 30 feet. Then she saw it swim underwater to the centre of the loch 'at about the speed of an outboard motor boat'.

On 12 December 1933 a firm of Scottish film producers, Irvine, Clayton and Hay, managed to film the monster in motion for a few seconds; unfortunately, the film shows little but a long dark shadow moving through the water.

The most famous photograph of the monster was taken in the following April, 1934 – the celebrated 'surgeon's photograph'. On 1 April 1934 Robert Kenneth Wilson, Fellow of the Royal College of Surgeons, was driving northward with a friend; they had leased a wild-fowl shoot near Inverness, and meant to go to it and take some photographs of the birds. Wilson had borrowed a camera with a telephoto lens. It was early in the morning about seven and they stopped the car on a small promontory two miles north of Invermoriston. As they stood watching the surface they noticed the signs of 'considerable commotion' that seem to herald the arrival of the monster, and the friend, Maurice Chambers, shouted, 'My God, it's the monster.' Wilson rushed to the car, came back with the camera, and managed to expose four plates in two minutes in such a hurry that he did not even look at what he was photographing. The serpentine head, not unlike an elephant's trunk, then withdrew gently into the water. Unsure as to whether he had captured anything, Wilson hurried to Inverness and took the plates to a chemist to be developed. They were ready later that day. Two proved to be blank; one showed the head about to vanish into the water. But the fourth was excellent, showing the dinosaur-like neck and tiny head.

Wilson sold the copyright of the photograph to the *Daily Mail* and it appeared on 21 April 1934, creating a sensation. It also aroused the usual roars of derision from the scientific establishment, who branded the photograph a fake, and pointed out that the 'surgeon' (who had withheld his identity) could be an invention of the perpetrator of the fraud. In fact, Wilson soon allowed himself to be identified, and his name appeared in Commander Gould's book *The Loch Ness Monster and Others*, which came out later the same year, with the 'surgeon's photograph' as a frontispiece. (The fact that the photograph was taken on 1 April may have increased the general scepticism.) Many years later another monster-investigator, Tim Dinsdale, held the photograph at arm's length and noticed something that convinced him of its authenticity. When viewed from a distance, a faint concentric circle of rings is visible around the monster, while there is another circle in the background, as if some other part of the body is just below the surface. No one, Dinsdale pointed out, would take the trouble to fake a detail that is almost invisible to the eye. Another piece of evidence in favour of its authenticity emerged in 1972, when the photograph was subjected to the computer-enhancement process at NASA; the improved picture showed signs of whiskers hanging down from the lower jaw.

In July 1934 a team of fourteen men was hired by Sir Edward Mountain, at a wage of £2 per week per man, to spend five weeks standing on the shores of the loch, armed with cameras. Five promising photographs were taken; four of them only showed a dark wake, which could have been caused by a boat; the fifth showed a head disappearing in a splash of spray. After the watchers had been paid off, Captain James Frazer, who had been in charge of the expedition, succeeded in shooting several feet of film from a position just above Castle Urquart. It showed an object like an upturned, flat-bottomed boat, about fifteen feet long; it disappeared in a spume of spray. Zoologists who viewed the film said that the creature was a seal. Captain Frazer later admitted that he had to endure a great deal of ridicule.

Sightings continued, and more photographs were taken; but the general public had ceased to be deeply interested in the monster. After the initial excitement, most people were willing to accept the view of sceptics that the monster had been a cynical invention of people involved in the Highland tourist business; if so, it had certainly succeeded, for Loch Ness hotels were crowded throughout the summer. One of the most interesting sightings of 1934 went virtually unnoticed. On 26 May Brother Richard Horan, of St Benedict's Abbey, was working in the abbey boathouse when he heard a noise in the water, and saw the monster looking at him from a distance of about thirty yards. It had a graceful neck with a broad white stripe down its front, and a muzzle like a seal's. Three other people corroborated his sighting. In the December of the following year, a Miss Rena Mackenzie also saw the monster fairly close, and noted that its head seemed tiny, and that the underside of its throat was white. A man named John Maclean, who saw the monster in July 1938, saw the head and neck only twenty yards away, and said that it was obviously in the act of swallowing food, opening and closing its mouth, and tossing back its head 'in exactly the same manner that a cormorant does after it has swallowed a fish'. When the creature dived Maclean and his wife saw two humps. They described it as being about eighteen feet long, and said that at close quarters its skin was dark brown and 'like that of a horse when wet and glistening'. Each of these sightings enables us to form a clearer picture of the monster. And in July 1958 the water bailiff Alex Campbell had a sighting which confirmed something he had believed for many years – that there must be more than one of the creatures; he saw one lying quietly near St Benedict's Abbey while another (visible as a large black hump) headed across the loch, churning the surface of the water. (Many accounts indicate that the animals can move at high speed.)

During the Second World War interest in the monster (or monsters) waned, although sightings continued to be reported. In 1943 Commander Russell Flint, in charge of a motor launch passing through Loch Ness on its way to Swansea, reported a tremendous jolt that convinced the crew that they had struck some floating debris. In fact, they saw the monster disappearing in a flurry of water. His signal to the Admiralty, reporting that he had sustained damage to the starboard bow after a collision with the Loch Ness monster, earned him in response 'a bit of a blast'.

In November 1950 the *Daily Herald* ran a story headed 'The Secret of Loch Ness', alleging that dozens of eight-foot-diameter mines had been anchored on the floor of the loch since 1918, some at a depth of a mile. (The *Herald* stated that at its greatest depth, the loch is seven miles deep.) The story apparently had some slight basis in fact; mines *had* been laid in 1918 by HMS *Welbeck* – Hugh Gray, who later took the first monster photograph, was on board – but when a vessel went to collect them in 1922, only the anchors remained. The mines, which were designed to have a life of only a few years, were probably at the bottom. Certainly none of the photographs looks in the least like an eight-foot mine, even one with horns.

In the following year another monster photograph was taken by a woodsman named Lachlan Stuart. He was about to milk a cow early on 14 July 1951 when he saw something moving fast down the loch, so fast that he at first thought it was a speedboat. He grabbed his camera, rushed down the hill, and snapped the monster when it was only fifty yards offshore. The result was a photograph showing three distinct humps.

Four years later a bank manager named Peter Macnab was on his way back from a holiday in the north of Scotland, and pulled up his car just above Urquhart Castle. It was a calm, warm afternoon – 29 July 1955 – and he saw a movement in the still water near the castle; he hastily raised his camera, and took a photograph which has joined the 'surgeon's photograph' and the Lachlan Stuart photograph as one of the classic views of the monster. But he was so anxious to avoid ridicule that he released the picture only three years later, in 1958.

Before that happened, interest in the case had been revived by the best book on it so far – *More Than a Legend*, published in 1957. The author was Constance Whyte, wife of the manager of the Caledonian canal, who became interested in the monster after she was asked to write an article about it for a small local magazine. Mrs Whyte interviewed every witness she could find, and produced the first overall survey of the evidence since Rupert Gould's book of 1934. *More Than a Legend* aroused widespread interest, the author was deluged with correspondence, and once again the Loch Ness monster was news. What Mrs Whyte had done, with her careful research, was to refute the idea that the monster was a joke, or the invention of the Scottish Tourist Board. No one who reads her book can end with the slightest doubt that the monster really exists, and that it shows itself with a fair degree of frequency.

The immediate result was a new generation of 'monster-hunters'. One of these, Frank Searle, was a manager for a firm of fruiterers in London; he bought Constance Whyte's book, and in 1958 decided to camp by Loch Ness. From then on he returned again and again. In June 1965 he was parked in a lay-by near Invermoriston and chatting to some hitch-hikers when he saw a dark object break the surface, and realized he had at last seen the monster. His excitement was so great that in 1969 he gave up his job and pitched his tent by Loch Ness, where he was to remain for the next four years. In August 1971 he saw the tail at close quarters as the monster dived; his impression was of an alligator's tail, 'seven feet long, dark and nobbly on top, smooth dirty white underneath'. In November 1971 he got his first photograph of the monster – a dark hump in a swirl of water; he admitted that it was 'inconclusive'. But in the following five years he obtained at least ten of the best pictures of the monster taken so far, including one showing the swan-like neck rising out of the water, and another showing both the neck and one of the humps; these were published in his *Nessie: Seven Years in Search of the Monster* in 1976. During that time his tent had become a 'Mecca for visitors' – mostly directed to him by the Scottish Tourist Board – and in 1975 he estimated that he had seen twenty-five thousand in eight months. On 7 June 1974, together with a girl visitor from Quebec, he had a memorable sighting. As they approached a barbed-wire fence near Foyers, they noticed a splashing sound. They crept up and peered over the fence, 'and saw two of the strangest little creatures I've ever seen. They were about two feet in length, dark grey in colour, something like the skin of a baby elephant, small heads with black protruding eyes, long necks and plump bodies. They had snake like tails which were wrapped along their sides, and on each side of the body, two stump-like appendages.' When he tried to get through the fence the small creatures 'scuttled away with a kind of crab-like motion' and were submerged in the loch within seconds.

But in his book *The Loch Ness Story* – perhaps the best comprehensive account of the hunt for the monster – Nicholas Witchell comments: 'It is a regrettable fact which can easily be proved that these 1972 photographs have been tampered with. Mr Searle has also produced another series identical with the original shots in all respects except that an extra hump has been added to them by some process of superimposition or by rephotography.' And he adds: 'Because of the highly suspicious content of some of Mr Searle's photographs and the inconsistencies of the facts surrounding the taking of them, it is not possible to accept them as being authentic photographs of animate objects in Loch Ness.'

In 1959 an aeronautical engineer named Tim Dinsdale read an article about the monster in a magazine called *Everybody's*, and was intrigued. He spent most of that winter reading everything he could find; it was in the following February that (as already described) he looked at the surgeon's photograph, and noticed the circle of ripples that convinced him that it was genuine. In April that year Dinsdale went off to Loch Ness to hunt the monster. But after five days he had still seen nothing. On the day before he was due to return home he was approaching his hotel in Foyers when he saw something out in the loch; his binoculars showed a hump. He snatched his 16-mm ciné-camera and began to film as the creature swam away. Then, almost out of film, he drove down to the water's edge; by the time he got there the creature had vanished. But Dinsdale had fifty feet of film showing the monster in motion. When shown on television it aroused widespread interest and – as Witchell says – heralded a new phase in the saga of the monster.

That June the first scientific expedition to Loch Ness embarked on a month-long investigation, with thirty student volunteers and a Marconi echo-sounder, as well as a large collection of cameras. A ten-foot hump was sighted in July, and the echo-sounder tracked some large object as it dived from the surface to a depth of sixty feet and back up again. The expedition also discovered large shoals of char at a depth of a hundred feet – an answer to sceptics who said that the loch did not contain enough fish to support a monster; the team's finding was that there was enough fish to support several.

But Dr Denys Tucker, of the British Museum of Natural History, who had organized this expedition, did not lead it as he had intended to; in June he was dismissed from his job – as he believed, because he had publicly expressed his belief in the existence of the monster.

Dinsdale became a close friend of Torquil MacLeod, who had seen the monster almost out of the water in February 1960. MacLeod had watched it for nine minutes, and admitted being 'appalled by its size', which he estimated at between 40 and 60 feet. It had a long neck, like an elephant's trunk, which kept moving from side to side and up and down, and 'paddles' at the rear and front. In August 1960 MacLeod had another sighting from the shore, while a family in a motor yacht belonging to a company director, R.H. Lowrie, saw the monster at close quarters for about a quarter of an hour, taking a few photographs. At one point they thought the monster was heading straight for them and about to collide; but it veered away and disappeared.

It was also in August 1960 that Sir Peter Scott, founder of the Wildfowl Trust, and Richard Fitter of the Fauna Preservation Society approached the Member of Parliament David James and asked for his help in trying to get government assistance for a 'flat-out attempt to find what exactly is in Loch Ness'. In April 1961 a panel decided that there was a prima facie case for investigating the loch. The result was the formation of the Bureau for Investigating the Loch Ness Phenomena, a registered charity. In October 1961 two powerful searchlights scanned the loch every night for two weeks, and on one occasion caught an eight-foot 'finger like object' standing out of the water. In 1962 another team used sonar, and picked up several 'large objects'; one of these sonar recordings preceded an appearance of the monster on the surface.

In 1966 Tim Dinsdale's film was subjected to analysis by Air Force Intelligence, which reported that the object filmed was certainly not a boat or a submarine, and by NASA's computer-enhancement experts, who discovered that two other parts of the body also broke the surface besides the main hump.

In August 1962 another 'monster-hunter', F.W.('Ted') Holiday, parked his van by Loch Ness, on the southern shore opposite Urquhart Castle. As darkness fell he had a feeling that 'Loch Ness is not a water by which to linger'. Two nights later, on a perfectly still night, he heard the crash of waves breaking on the stony beach, although there was no sound of a boat engine. Two days later he had his first sighting of the monster. On a hill close to the spot where Dinsdale had taken his 1961 film, he suddenly saw a black and glistening object rise three feet out of the water; then it dived like 'a diving hippopotamus'. He could still see the shape of the animal just below the surface. He judged it to be about 45 feet long. Then a man on a nearby pier started hammering, and the creature vanished.

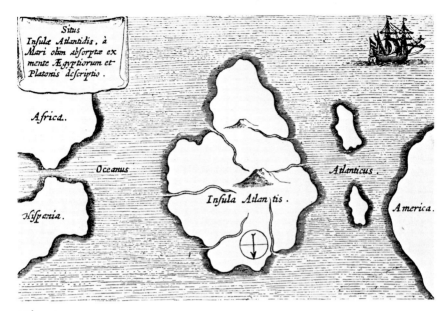

(Above)
Sketch-map showing the location of the mythical city of Atlantis, said to lie submerged beneath the waves of the Atlantic Ocean. (See Chapter 1)

(Below)
The Thera volcano erupting in 1925–6. (See Chapter 1)

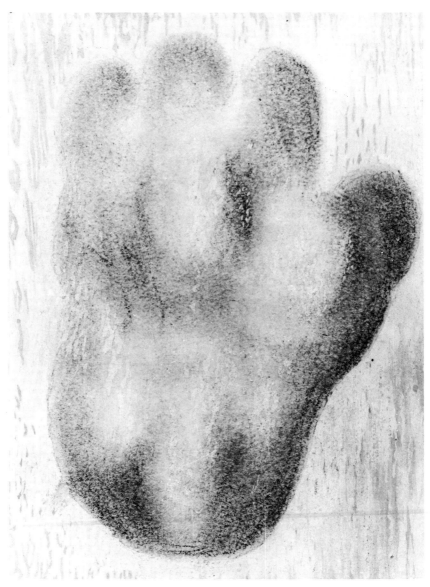

An artist's impression of a giant footprint found in the snow in the Himalayas, alleged to be that of a Yeti or Abominable Snowman (See Chapter 4)

(*Photo Source*)

£100 FREE CROSS-WORD COMPETITION: SEE PAGE 4

Daily Mirror

THE DAILY PICTURE NEWSPAPER WITH THE LARGEST NET SALE

CAMPAIGN TO MAKE LONDON STREETS SAFER

No. 7,199 | Registered at the G.P.O. as a Newspaper | TUESDAY, DECEMBER 7, 1926 | **[24 PAGES]** | One Penny

MYSTERY OF WOMAN NOVELIST'S DISAPPEARANCE

Mrs. Agatha Christie, the missing woman novelist, with her daughter.

A thorough search in the woods near the spot where Mrs. Christie's car was found.

EARL'S DAUGHTER TAKES THE AIR IN A CAGE

Jack Best at the place where he found the car abandoned.

Following an important clue received yesterday a special search will be made to-day for Mrs. Agatha Christie, the novelist wife of Colonel Archibald Christie, D.S.O., who disappeared after leaving her home at Sunningdale, Berks, in her motor-car. The car was found abandoned near Newlands Corner, Surrey.—(Daily Mirror photographs.)

The infant daughter of Earl and Countess De la Warr asleep in her perambulator inside a galvanised iron cage which her parents (inset) have had fixed outside the front of their home near Victoria. This enables her to take the air without risk.—(Daily Mirror.)

On 3 December 1926 the crime-writer Agatha Christie left her home at Sunningdale, in Berkshire, and disappeared. She was found living in a hotel in Harrogate under an assumed name. (Front page of the *Daily Mirror*, 7 December 1926.) (See Chapter 7)

(*Newspaper Library, Colindale*)

(*Above*)
Howard Carter examines the sarcophagus of Tutankhamon in 1923. (See Chapter 7)
(*Mary Evans Picture Library*)

(*Opposite*)
The Gold Mask of Tutankhamon, King of Egypt, who died at the age of eighteen after a reign of only six years. On 26 November 1922 the archaeologist Howard Carter and his colleague Lord Carnarvon investigated Tutankhamon's undisturbed tomb and found a clay tablet bearing the inscription 'Death will slay with his wings whoever disturbs the peace of the pharaoh'. The legend persists that anyone involved in investigating the tombs of the pharaohs will die prematurely. (See Chapter 7)
(*Photo Source*)

John Dillinger, a bank robber and gangster, who was gunned down by FBI agents in Chicago on 22 July 1934. (See Chapter 9)

(from *The Picture History of Crime*)

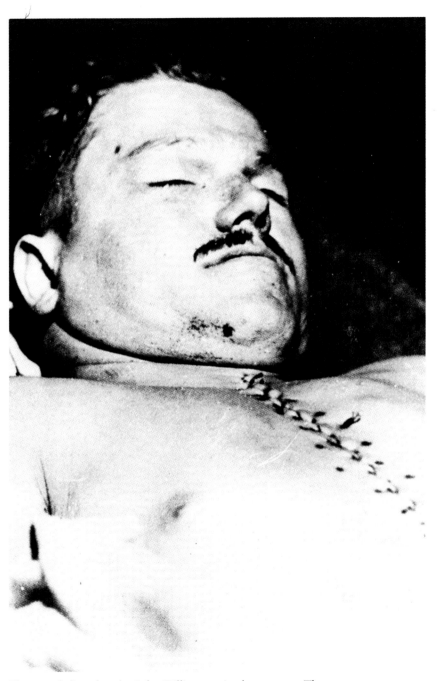

The man believed to be John Dillinger – in the morgue. The autopsy report cast doubt on whether the body really was Dillinger's. (See Chapter 9)

(from *The Picture History of Crime*)

Alchemy is the pursuit of the transmutation of baser metals into gold. An engraving of Medieval alchemists at work. (See Chapter 11)

Fort Lauderdale, the US Naval Air Station in Florida, from where Flight 19 took off at 2 p.m. on 5 December 1945.

The disappearance of Flight 19 – five US Navy bombers which vanished over the Bermuda Triangle on a routine training flight in December 1945 – has never been satisfactorily explained. This is a Grumman TBM Avenger of the type that went on Flight 19. (See Chapter 3)

(Photo: Paul Begg)

Kaspar Hauser.

(*Left*)
Probably the best-known of the hundreds of Hauser pictures, this engraving shows Kaspar as he looked when he first turned up in Nuremberg in May 1928. He is seen holding his letter of introduction. (See Chapter 13)

Germanisches National Museum

(*Below*)
Kaspar Hauser in the last years of his life – a portrait in striking contrast to the woebegone expression of the engraving above. (See Chapter 13)

Germanisches National Museum

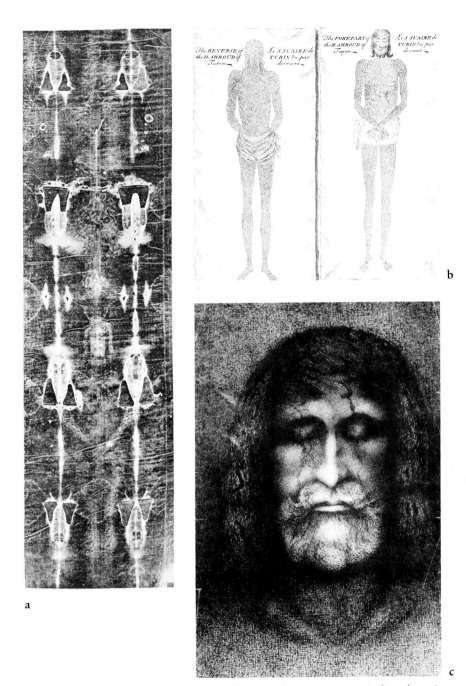

The Holy Shroud of Turin, a 14ft strip of linen said to be Christ's winding-sheet. It apparently bears the 'negative' of a crucified man. If the Shroud is genuine, this may be an image of Christ. (a) a photograph of the image on the Shroud; (b) a drawing of the front and reverse of the image; (c) photograph (detail) of 'Christ's' face on the Shroud. (See Chapter 14)

((a) and (c) *BBC Hulton Picture Library* (b) *Mary Evans Picture Library*)

(*Right*)
The burning of Joan of Arc, the 'Maid of Orleans', in the market-place at Rouen on 30 May 1431. Did she escape the flames?
(From the painting by Lenepveu, nineteenth-century French school.)

(*Photo Source*)

(*Left*)
Joan of Arc at the Siege of Paris. (Engraving by Philippoteaux.) (See Chapter 16)

(*Mary Evans Picture Library*)

The portrait of Kitchener on the right is similar to that on the famous recruiting poster – 'Your country needs YOU!', which was said to be responsible for 300,000 recruits enlisting in the First World War. (See Chapter 17)

(BBC Hulton Picture Library)

In June 1916 the distinguished soldier and British Secretary for War, Lord Kitchener, perished when *HMS Hampshire* was sunk by a German mine off the Orkneys. Was it a tragic accident or an act of sabotage? (See Chapter 17)

(BBC Hulton Picture Library)

Two photographs which allegedly show 'Nessie', the Loch Ness Monster. (See Chapter 18)

(Photo Source)

(Below)

On 19 November 1703 a prisoner died in the Bastille after an imprisonment of 34 years. To conceal his identity he wore an iron mask. Voltaire and Dumas, among others, have written of The Man in the Iron Mask and put forward solutions to the mystery. (See Chapter 19)

(Mary Evans Picture Library)

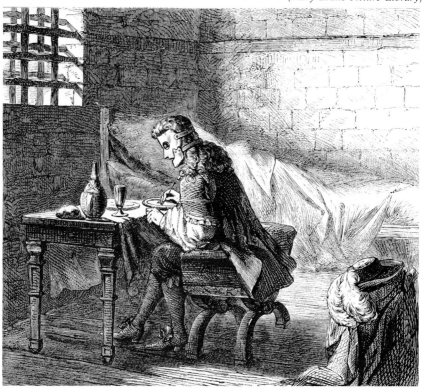

Leonardo da Vinci's painting in the Louvre, Paris. Is it of Mona Lisa?

The Isleworth Mona Lisa

Raphael's sketch of Mona Lisa, now in the Louvre. (See Chapter 21)

On a calm afternoon in December 1872 the two-masted brig *Mary Celeste* was found drifting in the North Atlantic. There was no sign of her Captain, his family or the crew of seven. How, or why, they disappeared is one of the great mysteries of the sea. (See Chapter 20)

(Mary Evans Picture Library)

Two pages from the Voynich manuscript. Ever since 1912, when it was acquired by a New York dealer in rare books, Wilfred M. Voynich, cryptologists have tried to unravel its secrets – without success.

(Beinecke Library, Yale University/Photo: Edward J. Hansen)

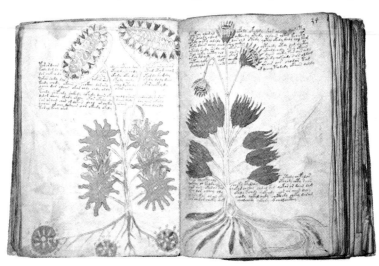

Every year from then on Holiday returned to the loch; but in 1963 and 1964 he was unlucky. Then in 1965 he saw it on two occasions; on the first he saw it (looking like an upturned boat) from three different positions as he raced his car along the loch to get a better view. But he had already reached a conclusion about the nature of the monster, that it was simply a giant version of the common garden slug, an ancestor of the squid and octopus. In his book *The Great Orm of Loch Ness* he argued that the monster is a type of *Tullimonstrum gregarium*, a creature looking a little like a submarine with a broad tail. He also came to believe that these monsters were once far more plentiful in the British Isles, that they used to be known as 'worms' (or 'orms'), and that they gave rise to the legend of dragons. A photograph in the book shows the Worm's Head peninsula in South Wales, and argues that it is so called because it resembles the 'orm' of legend and of Loch Ness.

In 1963 Holiday interviewed two fishermen who had seen the monster at close range, only 20 or 30 yards away. One said that the head reminded him of a bulldog, that it was wide and very ugly. The neck was fringed by what looked like coarse black hair. In a letter to Dinsdale, Holiday remarked: 'When people are confronted by this fantastic animal at close quarters they seemed to be stunned. There is something strange about Nessie that has nothing to do with size or appearance. Odd, isn't it?' He was intrigued by the number of people who had a feeling of horror when they saw the monster. Why were dragons and 'orms' always linked with powers of evil in medieval mythology? He also began to feel increasingly that it was more than coincidence that the monsters were so hard to photograph: he once had his finger on the button when the head submerged. Either the monsters had some telepathic awareness of human observation or they were associated with some kind of Jungian 'synchronicity', or meaningful coincidence.

Holiday, who was a fishing correspondent, had also had a number of sightings of UFOs (or Flying Saucers), and one or two close brushes with 'poltergeists' (or 'banging ghosts'). And he was intrigued to learn that Boleskin House, near Foyers, had been tenanted by the notorious 'magician' Aleister Crowley in the early years of the twentieth century, and that Crowley had sharted to perform there a lengthy magical ritual by a certain Abramelin the Mage. Crowley himself claimed that the house was filled with shadowy spirits while he was performing the ritual (which takes many months), and that they drove a coachman to drink and a clairvoyant to become a prostitute. Crowley failed to complete the ritual, and, according to Holiday 'misfortune stalked him' from then on. Although he never says so in so many words, Holiday seemed to entertain the suspicion that the monster may have been conjured up by Crowley: certainly he thought it a coincidence that a creature associated with evil should be seen so often from Foyers, near Boleskin House. He also thought it odd when American students exploring the cemetery near Boleskin found a tapestry and a conch shell beneath a grave slab. The tapestry – probably Turkish in origin – had 'worm like creatures' embroidered on it, and its freedom from mildew suggested that it had been hidden recently. Holiday suspected that it had been used in some magical ceremony, and that the ceremony had been hastily abandoned when someone walked into the churchyard. It looked as if black magic is still practised near Boleskin House.

Soon after this Holiday went to have dinner with a friend near Loch Ness, and met an American called Dr Dee, who was in England looking up his family tree. Dr Dee said that he had discovered that he had a celebrated Elizabethan ancestor of the same name. It was another coincidence: John Dee, the Elizabethan 'magician', had published the ritual of Abramelin the Mage.

In a letter to me in 1971 Ted Holiday described a further coincidence. Looking across the loch, he found himself looking at the word DEE in large yellow letters. Bulldozers engaged in road-widening had scraped away the soil running down to the loch, and the top half of the 'letters' was formed by the yellow subsoil. The bottom half of the letters was formed by the reflection of the top half in the perfectly still water.

In fact Holiday was coming to a very strange conclusion about lake monsters; it arose from some investigations he had undertaken in Ireland in 1968, where more monsters had been sighted in lochs (or 'loughs') in Galway. The sightings sounded very much like those of 'Nessie', and the witnesses were of unimpeachable reputation – on one occasion, two priests. Yet after weeks of careful observation, and even an attempt to 'net' a monster in Lough Nahooin, Holiday had failed to obtain the slightest bit of evidence for the monsters. What puzzled him was that these Irish lakes were too small to support a fifteen-foot monster, still less a colony of them. He began to wonder whether the *peiste* (as the Irish called the creature) was a thing of flesh and blood. Jung had suggested that UFOs are a 'projection' from the human unconscious, modern man's attempt to recreate lost religious symbols. Could it be, Holiday wondered, that the lake monsters are also some kind of 'projection'?

By 1971 Holiday had abandoned the notion that the lake monsters are simply 'prehistoric survivals'. He was coming round to the admittedly eccentric view that there is some influence at work that actively prevents the final solution of the mystery, just as in the case of Unidentified Flying Objects. And some time in 1972 this view seemed to be confirmed when he read a newspaper controversy between an 'exorcist', the Rev. Donald Omand, and some opponent who thought the Loch Ness monster was simply an unidentified animal. Omand had inherited 'second sight' from Highland ancestors, and had no doubt of the real existence of powers of evil – or at least of mischief; he often performed exorcisms to get rid of them. He had caught his first glimpse of a lake monster in Loch Long in Ross-shire in 1967. In June 1968, in a boat in Norway's Fjord of the Trolls, he saw another, which came straight towards them; the Norwegian captain who was with him told him not to be afraid: 'It will not hurt us – they never do.' And in fact the monster dived before it reached their boat. But the Captain, Jan Andersen, was convinced that the monsters were basically evil, that in some way they could do harm to men's characters (or, as Omand would have said, their souls). In 1972 Omand attended a psychiatric conference at which an eminent Swedish psychiatrist read a paper on the monster of Lake Storsjön, and said that he was convinced that the monsters had a malevolent effect on human beings, especially those who hunted them or saw them regularly. He thought their influence could cause domestic tragedies and moral degeneration. So Omand began to consider the theory that perhaps lake monsters are not real creatures, but 'projections' of something from the prehistoric past.

Holiday wrote to Omand, and the odd result was that in June 1973 Holiday and Donald Omand rowed out into the middle of Loch Ness, and Omand performed an exorcism of the loch. Holiday said they both felt oddly exhausted when it was over. And his suspicion that he was stirring up dangerous forces seemed to be confirmed two days later when he went to stay the night with a retired Wing Commander named Carey. Holiday was telling Mrs Carey about a Swedish journalist called Jan-Ove Sundberg who had been wandering through the woods behind Foyers when he had seen a strange craft in a clearing, and some odd-looking men; the craft had taken off at a great speed, and after his return to Sweden, Sundberg had been plagued by 'men in black' – people claiming to be officials who often seem to harass UFO 'contactees'.

Holiday said he intended to go and look at the place where the 'UFO' had landed, and Mrs Carey warned him against it. At this moment there was a rushing sound like a tornado outside the window and a series of violent thuds; a beam of light came in through the window, and focused on Holiday's forehead. A moment later, all was still. The odd thing was that Wing Commander Carey, who had been pouring a drink only a few feet away from his wife, saw and heard nothing. The next morning, as Holiday was walking towards the loch he saw a man dressed entirely in black – including helmet and goggles – standing nearby; he walked past him, turned his head, and was astonished to find that the man had vanished. He rushed to the road and looked in both directions; there was nowhere the man could have gone. One year later, close to the same spot, Holiday had a heart attack; as he was being carried away he looked over the side of the stretcher and saw that they were just passing the exact spot where he had seen the 'man in black'. Five years later, Holiday died of a heart attack.

Perhaps a year before his death, Ted Holiday sent me the typescript of his book *The Goblin Universe*, in which he attempted to justify the rather strange views he had gradually developed since starting his hunt for the Loch Ness monster. He had already discussed them in his second book *The Dragon and the Disc*, in which he linked UFOs ('discs') and 'worms' as symbols of good and evil. Then, to my surprise, he changed his mind about publishing the book.

There were, I suspect, two reasons. The team of investigators from the Academy of Applied Science at the Massachusetts Institute of Technology, led by Dr Robert H. Rines, had taken some remarkable underwater photographs in 1972 and 1975; one of the 1972 photographs showed very clearly an object like a large flipper, perhaps eight feet long, while a 1975 photograph showed very clearly a long-necked creature and its front flipper; this was particularly impressive because the sonar evidence – waves of sound reflected back from the creature – made it clear that this was not some freak of the light or piece of floating wreckage or lake-weed. By the time he was thinking about publishing *The Goblin Universe*, Holiday was probably wondering whether the book would be contradicted by some new evidence that would establish the physical reality of the monster beyond all doubt. Apart from this, the argument of *The Goblin Universe* was not quite as rigorous as it might be – he was attempting to explain why his views had changed so startlingly since 1962, and spent a great deal of time dwelling on 'the paranormal'. At all events, he decided not to publish the book, and instead wrote another typescript confined to lake monsters. (*The Goblin Universe* was recently published in America.)

This account of Holiday's activities may seem to be something of a digression; yet it illustrates the immense frustration experienced by monster-hunters in the 1970s and 1980s. When Gould wrote his book in 1934 the solution of the problem seemed close; then it receded. Constance Whyte's book revived interest in the mystery, and when the Loch Ness Phenomena Investigation Bureau began to co-operate with the team from the Academy of Applied Science, and to use all the latest scientific equipment, it began to look as if the mystery was about to be solved once and for all. Yet at the time of this writing – eleven years after that remarkable underwater picture of the monster – there has still been no major advance. Nicholas Witchell triumphantly concludes his book *The Loch Ness Story* (1975) with a chapter entitled 'The Solution', in which he describes his excitement when Rines telephoned him from America to describe the colour photograph of the monster; it contains the sentence: 'With the official ratification of the discovery of the animals in Loch Ness, the world will lose one of its most popular mysteries.' And he declares that it would be ignoble now to gloat about the short-sightedness of the scientific establishment for its sceptical attitude towards Loch Ness.

It is now clear that Witchell was premature. Most people still regard the question of the monster's existence as an open one, and the majority of scientists still regard the whole thing as something of a joke. In 1976 Roy Mackal, a director of the Loch Ness Investigation Bureau and Professor of biochemistry at the University of Chicago, published the most balanced and thoroughgoing scientific assessment so far, *The Monsters of Loch Ness*. He turns a highly critical eye on the evidence, yet nevertheless concludes that it is now proven that 'a population of moderate-sized, piscivorous aquatic animals is inhabiting Loch Ness'. If the scientific establishment was willing to change its mind, this book should have changed it; yet it seems to have made no real impact.

One thing seems clear: that Holiday's pessimism about the monster was unjustified; even at the time he was writing *The Dragon and the Disc*, Rines was taking the best underwater photographs of the monster so far. So there seems reason to believe that that science will finally solve the problem of establishing its existence beyond all doubt. The problems of capturing the monster either on film or in nets are epitomized in the following description by Dennis Stacy, of San Antonio, Texas, of his own encounter with 'Nessie'.

In 1972 I went to the Loch with the express purpose of looking for Nessie. The idea was to camp along the shoreline for about two weeks and see what was to be seen. I had a very distinct feeling of confidence that if I went to the Loch I would see Nessie. I met some students on vacation from Oxford and stayed with them just above Drumnadrochit. Every day I would take my camera down to the shoreline and have a good look around. Except for the day it was cold and drizzly and all of us went for a walk in the pinewoods there. A girl student and myself soon wandered off on our own from the others and made it down to the lochside. While we had been under the pines, the sky cleared remarkably and the wind died down. By the time we reached the loch, it was completely still and mirror-like. About three quarters of a mile across the loch, nearly under Crowley/Page's Boleskine, was Nessie, showing about six feet of neck and head above the water. We had jumped up on the little low rock wall skirting the road. We both saw it at the same time and nearly caused each other to tumble over the side by grabbing the other's shoulders and pointing and saying, Look! Do you see what I see?

And my camera, a 35mm, was miles away. My companion, however, had a little small, cheap camera, and the presence of mind to take a shot. All that was visible in the picture was a white wake, about a hundred feet in length, left by Nessie (or whatever), and which showed up clearly against the dark reflection of the trees on the other side in the water.

Nessie herself? The head was definitely angular, as described. Some say like a horse, with the very pronounced wedge-shape. In my own experience, I liken it to the shape of a rattlesnake's head, a square snout running back in a flare to the jaws. The length of neck out of the water, including the head, was five or six feet. The *impression* it gave, in the sense that spiders and snakes seem to exude their own peculiar aura, was one not so much of danger as power. I mean it was really cutting a wake through the water, raising a little wavelet on either side of the neck. At times the head was lowered down and forward, and would sweep a small angle from side to side, as if feeding, by lowering the bottom part of the jaw just into the water. But it was really too far away to be absolutely certain of this last manoeuver; the head, however, could be very plainly seen swinging from side to side.

It was swimming thusly when we first saw it and after no more than a minute, simply sank lower and lower in the water, much in the same way a person comes down from a round of water-skiing, or a submarine submerges.

(Letter to the author, 20 Sept 1980.)

Holiday might point out that some points in this narrative seem to support his own quasi-Jungian views. Dennis Stacy expected to see the monster. But he did not see it while he was patrolling the lake with his camera; it happened accidentally on a day he had decided to take off from his vigil. It certainly sounds as if the monster is playing some Jungian game of hide-and-seek. Yet all of us have experienced that same feeling that certain days are lucky or unlucky – everything seems to go right or everything seems to go wrong – and common sense tells us that this is purely subjective; an attitude of pessimism makes us careless and therefore accident-prone; an attitude of optimism awakens a new level of vigilance that anticipates problems.

What seems perfectly clear from Stacy's narrative (and many others quoted in the foregoing pages) is that the creatures of Loch Ness appear above the surface fairly frequently, particularly on calm days. If science can devise methods of detecting the presence of aeroplanes or jet-propelled missiles in the skies, and of submarines under the sea, it should surely be a simple matter to design a system that would detect all objects that move on the surface of Loch Ness on a calm day, and to film them? In these days of laser beams and electronic surveillance, it seems absurd that we should have to wait for chance sightings of the monster, like the one described above. It should also be obvious that attempts to 'hunt' it with motor launches, submarines, helicopters and searchlights are self-defeating, since they create exactly the kind of disturbance that drives the creature(s) to hide in the depths of the loch.

When the 'monster' is finally identified and classified it will undoubtedly be something of an anticlimax, and Loch Ness will probably lose most of its tourist industry at a blow. Half the fascination of the monster lies in the notion that it is terrifying and dangerous. In fact all the evidence suggests that like that other legendary marauder the 'killer' whale, it will turn out to be shy, amiable and quite harmless to man.

19 The Man in the Iron Mask

On 19 November 1703 a masked prisoner died in the Bastille after a brief illness. He had been imprisoned for thirty-four years, and even the king's Lieutenant in the Bastille, Etienne du Jonca, did not know his identity. He made a note in his journal: 'I have since learnt that they called him M. de Marchiel'. The unknown prisoner was buried the day after his death, under the name of Marchioly, and was quickly forgotten.

He became famous nearly half a century later, as a result of a book by Voltaire, *The Century of Louis XIV,* in which Voltaire finally exposed the mystery of the 'man in the iron mask'. According to Voltaire, a few months after the death of Cardinal Mazarin (which occurred in 1661), a young prisoner wearing an iron mask – or rather, a mask whose chin was composed of steel springs, so he could eat without removing it – was taken to the prison on the Ile Sainte Marguerite. Orders were given to kill him if he removed the mask. This prisoner, 'of majestic height . . . of a graceful and noble figure', was allowed to have anything he desired. His greatest pleasure was fine linen and laces. He was obviously a man of high rank, for the governor seldom sat down in his presence. Even the doctor who attended him was never allowed to see his face. The stranger died in 1704, said Voltaire (getting the date wrong by a year), and the strange thing is that when first he was incarcerated on the Isle of St Marguerite no person of any rank disappeared in Europe. According to Voltaire, the mysterious prisoner once scratched something on a plate, which he threw out of a window of his prison. It was picked up by a fisherman, who took it to the prison governor. 'Have you read what is written on it?' asked the governor. The fisherman confessed that he was unable to read. 'You are lucky,' said the governor . . . .

Voltaire's story created a sensation. There had been rumours about a masked prisoner, but no one had ever dared to speak about them openly. In fact a rather absurd novel called *The Iron Mask*, by the Chevalier de Mouhy, had been banned five years earlier, although its story took place in Spain and it bore no resemblance to the true story of the masked prisoner.

But who was the masked prisoner, and what had he done? Twenty years later, in *Questions on the Encyclopedia*, Voltaire revealed the answer or what he believed to be the answer. To understand his story, we must know a little of French history. King Louis XIII was rumoured to be impotent, and was in any case on bad terms with his wife, Anne of Austria. Anne was far closer to the king's great minister Cardinal Mazarin; politically they were hand in glove, and it is fairly certain that he was her lover; she may even have secretly married him after the death of the king. This then was Voltaire's theory: that Anne of Austria bore Mazarin a son, and that this happened before the birth of Louis XIV; the child, naturally, was kept secret from the king. So Louis XIV had an elder brother, who might have challenged his right to the throne. Which is why Louis kept his brother in prison, his face concealed by a mask, in case the family resemblance gave him away . . . .

Nearly a century after Voltaire's 'revelation', in 1847, Alexandre Dumas published his famous novel *The Man in the Iron Mask*, one of the many sequels to *The Three Musketeers*. This became by far the most famous account of the mystery, and was the basis of the popular Hollywood film. According to Dumas, the unknown prisoner was the twin brother of Louis XIV. This was not Dumas's own theory; it was first put forward in a work called *Memoires of the Duc de Richelieu*, published in London in 1790. This work claimed that Louis XIV was born at noon, and that his twin brother arrived at 8.30 in the evening, while his father was at supper. The younger twin was hidden away, so as not to cause problems with the succession. But these *Memoirs* are in fact a forgery by the Duc's secretary, the Abbé Soulavie, so this story is probably an invention.

In his introduction to an English translation of Dumas's novel the literary critic Sidney Dark writes:

Other wilder theories have identified the prisoner with the Duke of Monmouth, the illegitimate son of Charles II, with a certain Armenian Patriarch, with Fouquet, the ambitious minister of Louis XIV in his youth, who is one of the central figures in Dumas's novel, and, wildest guess of all, with Molière. It is said that after the successful production of Molière's famous comedy *Tartuffe* the Jesuits persuaded Louis XIV to order his disappearance. All these guesses are romantic and fantastic. Serious historians now hold that the Man in the Iron Mask was an Italian called Matthiolo, a minister of the Duke of Mantua, who aroused the enmity of Louis XIV through some obscure intrigues.

Sidney Dark was not quite correct. The man that many scholars thought was the masked prisoner was Ercole Mattioli, who was born in 1640, and was Secretary of State to the Duke of Mantua. The 'obscure intrigue' that aroused the wrath of Louis XIV was a piece of double-dealing. In 1632 France had bought a stronghold in italy called Pinerolo, or Pignerol. Thirty years or so later, Louis thought he saw a chance to acquire another useful piece of Italian territory by the same means: the town and citadel of Casale, near Turin, which belonged to the Duke of Mantua. Apparently the Duke was financially embarrassed and might be willing to sell. But negotiations had to be carried out with great caution, for Louis was quarrelling with Spain, and the Duke of Mantua was surrounded by friends of Spain. In fact Mattioli allowed news of the proposed deal to leak out to Louis's enemies, with the result that it fell through. Louis was furious, but there was not much he could do about it while Mattioli was on Italian territory. First of all, Mattioli had to be kept in the dark about the king's anger. Next he had to be lured to Pignerol, apparently to conclude the deal. The moment he was on French territory he was arrested, and thrown into gaol in the fortress of Pignerol, which was in the charge of a governor named Saint-Mars. The whole thing was kept secret; Mattioli simply 'disappeared', and remained in prison until his death; no one knows quite when this was, but the likeliest guess is that it was about fifteen years later, in 1694.

Mattioli is certainly a likely candidate – we may recall that Etienne du Jonca, the King's Lieutenant in the Bastille, said that the masked prisoner was known as 'M. Marchiel'; and we know he was buried as 'Marchiolly'. But *if* Mattioli was the man in the mask, then why did the king go to such lengths to keep his identity secret, especially after he was transferred to the Island of St Marguerite, then to the Bastille? It is true that Mattioli was kidnapped in Italy, which might cause diplomatic problems. But in that pragmatic age, no one would have bothered much about Mattioli after he was imprisoned. And why hide Mattioli's face? Not many people would recognize it.

Then what about the twin brother theory, which is still by far the most popular solution to the mystery? In fact this was exploded half a century before Dumas wrote his novel. After the fall of the Bastille during the French Revolution, its archives were published under the title *The Bastille Unveiled*. The chairman of the commission that investigated the archives, a certain M. Charpentier, studied every document he could lay his hands on relating to the man in the iron mask. Other royal archives were also at his disposal, and he found there was not a scrap of evidence that Anne of Austria had given birth either to an illegitimate son or to twins.

But Charpentier *did* uncover a few interesting facts about the 'ancient prisoner', as well as one curious legend. The legend was that the man in the mask was the illegitimate son of Anne of Austria by the Duke of Buckingham, the handsome, daredevil minister of James I and Charles I. Buckingham had risen to power as the favourite of the homosexual James I, but also acquired a strong influence over Charles I. It is known that he did his best to seduce Anne of Austria when he was in France in 1626, but a matter of some doubt whether he succeeded – it would not be easy for two people as well known as they were to find an opportunity for adultery. But according to the legend recorded by M. Charpentier, Anne bore the Duke a son in 1626 who bore a remarkable family resemblance to her later child Louis XIV, born twelve years later – hence the need to keep him masked . . . .

This legend had one strong point in its favour. It originated with a certain Madame de Saint-Quentin, who was the mistress of the Marquis de Louvois, Louis XIV's war minister. And if (as is practically certain) she heard it from the Marquis, then surely there must be a certain amount of truth in it? That is true; but the opposite may also be true. Perhaps the Marquis told her the story that Louis wanted people to believe – a story that was close enough to the truth to seem probable, but that would mislead the curious. In any case, this story also has one major drawback. If the man in the iron mask was born in 1626, then he would have been about seventy-three at the time of his death. But other clues about the prisoner suggest that he was at least ten years younger than that. Voltaire says he was young and graceful. But by 1669 – the date at which the Bastille archives revealed that the former prisoner had first been incarcerated – a man born in 1626 would have been forty-three – almost an old man in the Europe of that period.

At least Charpentier was able to find a few useful clues from the archives.

The prisoner had been in Pignerol, like Mattioli, as well as on the island of St Marguerite – also like Mattioli. But it was not Mattioli. For other archive material revealed that when Saint-Mars, the prison governor of Pignerol, was given another appointment at nearby Exiles in 1681 the 'ancient prisoner' went with him, while Mattioli stayed behind. And as more archive material came to light, it was discovered that various letters between the minister of war and Saint-Mars were in the file. And, more important, there were letters from the king. These proved beyond all doubt that the name of the man in the iron mask was Eustache Dauger. In July 1669 the Marquis de Louvois (the father of the one who told his mistress the fairy tale about the Duke of Buckingham) wrote to Saint-Mars:

The King has commanded that I am to have the man named Eustache Dauger sent to Pignerol. It is of the utmost importance .. that he should be securely guarded and that he should in no way give information about himself nor send any letters . . .. You must on no account listen to what he may want to say to you, always threatening to kill him if he opens his mouth . . .

And the archive contained two letters from the king himself that underlined the same point. They make one thing very plain: that Eustache Dauger knew some astonishing secret, and that the king was quite determined that no one else should know it. Then why not execute Dauger? Possibly because Louis XIV was not as ruthless and cruel as that; possibly because he had a certain affection for Dauger. Possibly even because the king was hoping that Dauger might one day reveal some great secret . . . .

It was a historian called Jules Lair who first advanced the theory that the man in the mask was Eustache Dauger; he did this in a life of the finance minister Nicholas Fouquet, who was also condemned to life imprisonment by the king. Fouquet, born in 1615, had been a protégé of Cardinal Richelieu, and when Mazarin – Richelieu's ally and successor – died in 1661 everyone expected Fouquet to become the king's chief minister. But the young king – he was only twenty-three – was sick of Fouquet, who had become immensely wealthy as a result of his office. He may also have been jealous of Fouquet, who had tried to seduce Louise de la Vallière, the officer's daughter who became the king's mistress. The king appointed Jean-Baptiste Colbert, a shopkeeper's son, assistant to Fouquet, and Colbert soon reported that Fouquet was handing the king falsified accounts every afternoon. Fouquet made the mistake of inviting the king to his château and entertaining him with extravagant magnificence, a magnificence the king knew was bought with public money. Fouquet was arrested, tried, and sentenced to life imprisonment in the fortress of Pignerol. And in 1675 the 'ancient prisoner', Eustache Dauger, was allowed to become Fouquet's valet. There can have been only two possible reasons. Either Fouquet already knew Dauger's secret of the 'ancient prisoner', or it did not matter if he found out, since he himself would never be released.

But who was Eustache Dauger, and what had he done? The first question proved slightly easier to answer than the second. In the late 1920s the historian Maurice Duvivier set out to track him down. The doctor who had attended him in the Bastille had mentioned his age as about sixty. That meant he must have been born in the late 1630s. Duvivier searched the records tirelessly for a Dauger – or D'Auger, or Danger, or Oger, or Daugé – who might fit the bill. Eventually he found one in the records of the Bibliothèque Nationale, a man called Oger de Cavoye, a member of the minor gentry of Picardy. Eustache Oger (also spelt Dauger) de Cavoye was the son of François de Cavoye, the captain of Cardinal Richelieu's musketeers, and he was born on 30 August 1637. He was one of six brothers, four of whom died in battle. The fifth, Louis Dauger de Cavoye, had become one of Louis XIV's most trusted officials. But Eustache seems to have been the ne'er-do-well of the family. And the more Duvivier studied him, the more certain he became that he was the man in the iron mask.

Eustache's father, François de Cavoye, went to court to seek his fortune about 1620. Like Dumas's D'Artagnan, he soon achieved celebrity for his courage. (D'Artagnan was in fact a real person, and he escorted Fouquet to Pignerol prison.) He married a young widow, Marie de Sérignan, and became the captain of the cardinal's guard in 1630. Marie was extremely popular in her own right, and became a friend of Richelieu and of the king, and a maid of honour to the queen. So her sons were brought up at court, and the young Eustache was a playmate of the young Louis XIV – which seems to explain why Louis was unwilling to have him executed. François de Cavoye was killed at the siege of Bapaume in 1641, but his widow's position ensured that the children continued to be favoured at court. But four of the brothers were to die in the army. Eustache, who was also a soldier, had served in seven campaigns by the time he was twenty-one.

In 1659, when he was twenty-two, Eustache Dauger seems to have been involved in an extremely strange incident. He was present on the Good Friday of that year at a black mass in the Castle of Roissy, in which a pig was christened and eaten. The scandal was tremendous, and a number of careers were ruined, but Eustache seems to have escaped punishment, probably because of the respect in which his mother was held at Court. But six years later he was involved in another scandal which forced him to resign his commission. There was some sort of quarrel with a page-boy outside the old castle of St Germain; one account (by the Duc d'Enghien) says that the page was drunk, and that he managed to strike the Duc de Foix with his pike as he staggered past him. A quarrel flared, and 'a man called Cavoye' killed the page. This was regarded as an act of sacrilege, since the place was sanctified by the king's presence. The Duc de Foix escaped unpunished, but Cavoye was forced to sell his commission. That the Cavoye referred to was Eustache Dauger is proved by the fact that he also ceased to be a guards officer in 1665, while his two surviving brothers Louis and Armand continued to serve the king.

Soon after the murder of the page, Eustache's mother died, and in her will declared that Louis Dauger, not his elder brother Eustache, should be the head of the family. She had apparently made this will fourteen months before the murder of the page, so we can only conclude that she already regarded Eustache as a scapegrace. She left him a pension for life of a thousand livres a year. Eustache seems to have been financially secure, and he and his brother Louis shared rooms in the Rue de Bourbon, not far from the Charity Hospital. But in 1668 Louis Dauger found himself in serious trouble. He had been trying to seduce a lady named Sidonia de Courcelles, whose husband objected. Louis fought a duel with him, and was arrested. The war minister Louvois was also interested in Sidonia, and he tried hard to get Louis sentenced to death. The finance minister Colbert saved him; but Louis spent the next four years in the Bastille. When he emerged he continued to rise in the world. But by then his brother Eustache was in Pignerol.

Why? What had Eustache done? Duvivier's theory is that he had played some part in the infamous 'affair of the poisons', or rather, in a curtain-raiser to it that occurred in 1668. The 'affair of the poisons' began in 1673, when the police chief, Nicolas de la Reynie, heard rumours of wealthy ladies who were admitting in the confessional that they had poisoned their husbands. It took La Reynie four years to uncover an incredible 'poisons ring' run by fortune-tellers and priests who practised the black mass. Many ladies of the court were involved, and so (this came as a deep shock to the king) was Madame de Montespan, the king's mistress. Her aim was to secure the king's love and to weaken the influence of her rival Louise de la Vallière, and she took part in a black mass, allowing her naked belly to be used as the altar, while a priest named Guibourg slit the throat of a baby. In another ceremony to concoct a love potion for the king, drops of a woman's menstrual blood were mixed with a man's sperm – the latter obtained by getting a man to masturbate into a holy chalice. All this so horrified the king that he ordered it to be investigated in the utmost secrecy in a room lit only by candles, known as the Chambre Ardente (lighted room) – and that no hint of it should be allowed to reach the public. Most of the leading figures in the affair of the poisons were burned alive. Mme de Montespan was disgraced.

In 1668, five years before La Reynie heard the first hints about the poison ring, there had been another 'poison scare' in Paris, and a 'sorcerer' named Le Sage and his assistant, the Abbé Mariette, were charged with witchcraft. There was much talk about love potions, black masses, and ladies of the court. The name of Madame de Montespan was mentioned for the first time, but hastily suppressed. Le Sage was sentenced to the galleys for life, while the Abbé Mariette, who had influential relatives, escaped with nine years' banishment.

Now in the later affair of the poisons, the Abbé Guibourg admitted that he had been paid to say a black mass at the home of the Duchesse d'Orléans by a surgeon who lived in the St-Germain quarter, near the Charity Hospital, with his brother. This is where Eustache Dauger and *his* brother lived in 1668. And another piece of evidence from the Chambre Ardente trial referred to a surgeon called d'Auger, who supplied 'drugs'. Duvivier speculates that this 'surgeon' d'Auger was Eustache, and that it was his involvement in the Le Sage-Mariette affair that led to his banishment. Evidence showed that Eustache Dauger had been arrested at Dunkirk by special order of the king; he was apparently about to flee to England. So Duvivier could be right. Eustache Dauger could be the surgeon d'Auger involved in the sorcery case.

But that still fails to explain why the king should conduct the whole affair with such secrecy. After all, the Abbé Mariette was banished, and so had plenty of opportunity to open his mouth about any sinister secrets he knew about the king and Dauger. Somehow Duvivier's theory that Dauger's crime was sorcery or selling poisons fails to carry conviction.

There is another and rather more interesting possibility that links Dauger with the mystery of Rennes-le-Château (see Chapter 28). In his book *The Holy Blood and the Holy Grail*, Henry Lincoln states that Fouquet, the disgraced finance minister, may have been the man in the iron mask. This as we know is impossible; Fouquet died in 1680, twenty-three years before the 'ancient prisoner'. But Lincoln also points out that in 1656 Fouquet's brother Louis was sent to Rome to see the painter Poussin, and that he wrote Fouquet a curious letter about some secret which would give him 'through M. Poussin, advantages which even kings would have great pains to draw from him'. This secret is assumed to be something to do with the hidden treasure of Rennes-le-Château. Poussin's painting *The Shepherds of Arcady*, which contains important keys to the mystery, was acquired by Louis XIV and kept in his private rooms where no one could see it. Is it possible that Fouquet knew the secret of Rennes-le-Château, and that the king had him imprisoned in Pignerol – where he was not allowed to speak to anyone – to try to force him to disclose the secret? There is yet another possibility linked with Rennes-le-Château. Lincoln reveals that an important part of the mystery concerns a secret order called the Priory of Sion, whose aim is to restore the Merovingian dynasty to the throne of France. In the seventeenth century the Merovingians – descendants of King Merovech – were the house of Lorraine. The younger brother of Louis XIII, Gaston d'Orléans, was married to the Duke of Lorraine's sister, and there was an attempt to depose Louis and put Gaston in his place – which would have meant that Gaston's Merovingian descendants would have been once more on the throne of France. The attempt failed, but it was still possible that Gaston's heirs would succeed to the throne, since Louis XIII was childless. Then, as we know, Anne of Austria astonished everyone by conceiving the child who became Louis XIV . . . .

Lincoln writes: 'According to both contemporary and later writers, the child's true father was Cardinal Richelieu, or perhaps a 'stud' employed by Richelieu . . ..'

And who could such a 'stud' have been? The obvious candidate is Richelieu's handsome young captain of musketeers, François Dauger de Cavoye. There are many stories about the conception of Louis XIV – how, for example, Richelieu plotted to bring the king and his queen together, and how Louis took refuge with Anne of Austria during a thunderstorm, as a result of which the child was conceived. It is of course possible that Louis XIV was conceived as a result of one single encounter between the king and queen, but far more likely that Richelieu arranged the encounter so that Louis would have reason to believe the child was his own . . . .

Several writers mention the resemblance between Louis Dauger de Cavoye, Eustache's younger brother, and Louis XIV. This would be understandable if the two were, in fact, half-brothers.

And so at last we have a theory that seems to explain the mystery of the man in the mask. François de Cavoye was the 'stud' who made sure that an heir to the throne was born, thus frustrating the aspirations of the Merovingians (and the Priory of Sion). Eustache and Louis Dauger both knew that the king was really their half-brother; this is why Louis became a royal favourite after his release from the Bastille. He could be relied upon to keep a secret. But the ne'er-do-well Eustache was a different story. After his downfall, his resignation from the guards, and the arrest and imprisonment of his brother, he began to talk too much. Perhaps he tried some form of blackmail on the king: release my brother or else . . . That would certainly explain why Louis had him whisked away to Pignerol and kept incommunicado, and why he later made sure that the 'ancient prisoner' always accompanied the governor Saint-Mars when he moved to another prison. It is also conceivable that Eustache became involved with the Priory of Sion and the plot to place a Merovingian on the throne of France – after all, what better reason could there be for replacing the king than revealing that he was not the true son of Louis XIII? Fouquet probably knew the secret already, since he also seems to have had connection with the Priory. (Lincoln speculates that this is why Fouquet was arrested and tried; Louis tried hard to have Fouquet sentenced to death, but the court refused.) That is why Eustache was allowed to become Fouquet's valet. But when another old acquaintance of Dauger's, the Duc de Lauzun, was imprisoned in Pignerol after an escapade, he and Dauger were carefully kept apart.

This theory could explain many things. It could explain, for example, why the war minister Louvois (who undoubtedly knew the secret) told his mistress that the masked prisoner was the son of the Duke of Buckingham and Anne of Austria. It was not too far from the truth; it explained why the king should want to keep the prisoner's existence a secret; but it made the prisoner the illegitimate child rather than the king. It would also explain why Dauger was obliged to wear a mask when other people were around: like his brother, he probably resembled the king. It is almost impossible to imagine why a man should be obliged to wear a mask unless his face itself is an important key to his secret.

It must be admitted that there is also one strong objection to this theory. When King Louis XV was finally told the secret of the man in the mask by his regent, the Duc d'Orléans, he is reported to have exclaimed , 'If he were still alive I would give him his freedom.' Would the king really have thought it unimportant that his grandfather was the son of Richelieu's captain of musketeers? Perhaps; after all, his own throne was now secure. But there is another story of Louis XV that casts rather more doubt on the theory. When the Duc de Choiseul asked him about the mysterious prisoner he refused to say anything except: 'All conjectures which have been made hitherto are false.' Then he added a baffling afterthought: 'If you knew all about it, you would see that it has very little interest.' If this comment is true – and not simply an attempt to allay the duke's curiosity – then it suggests that all the thousands of pages that have been written about the man in the iron mask are 'much ado about nothing'.

20 The Mystery of the Mary Celeste

On a calm afternoon of 5 December 1872 the English ship *Dei Gratia* sighted a two-masted brig pursuing an erratic course in the North Atlantic, midway between the Azores and the coast of Portugal. As they came closer they could see that she was sailing with only her jib and foretop mast staysail set; moreover, the jib was set to port, while the vessel was on a starboard tack – a sure sign to any sailor that the ship was out of control. Captain Morehouse of the *Dei Gratia* signalled the mysterious vessel, but received no answer. The sea was running high after recent squalls, and it took a full two hours before Morehouse could get close enough to read the name of the vessel. It was the *Mary Celeste*. Morehouse knew this American ship and its master, Captain Benjamin Spooner Briggs. Less than a month ago both vessels had been loading cargo on neighbouring piers on New York's East River. The *Mary Celeste* had set sail for Genoa with a cargo of crude alcohol on 5 November, ten days before the *Dei Gratia* had sailed for Gibraltar; yet now, a month later, she was drifting in mid-Atlantic with no sign of life.

Morehouse sent three men to investigate, led by his first mate Oliver Deveau, a man of great physical strength and courage. As they clambered aboard they saw that the ship's decks were deserted; a search below revealed that there was not a living soul on board. But the lifeboat was missing, indicating that Captain Briggs had decided to abandon ship.

There was a great deal of water below decks; two sails had been blown away, and the lower foretop sails were hanging by their corners. Yet the ship seemed seaworthy, and was certainly in no danger of sinking. Then why had the crew abandoned her? Further research revealed that the binnacle, the box containing the ship's compass, had been smashed, and the compass itself was broken. Two cargo hatches had been ripped off, and one of the casks of crude alcohol had been stoved in. Both forward and aft storage lockers contained a plentiful supply of food and water.

The seamen's chests were still in the crew's quarters, an indication of the haste in which the ship had been deserted. But a search of the captain's cabin revealed that the navigation instruments and navigation log were missing. The last entry in the general log was dated 25 November; it meant that the *Mary Celeste* had sailed without crew for at least nine days, and that she was now some 700 miles north-east of her last recorded position.

Apart from Captain Briggs and a crew of seven, the *Mary Celeste* had also sailed with Briggs's wife Sarah and his two-year old daughter Sophia Matilda. Faced with the mystery of why they had abandoned ship for no obvious reason, Morehouse experienced a certain superstitious alarm when Deveau suggested that two of the *Dei Gratia*'s crew should sail the *Mary Celeste* to Gibraltar; it was the prospect of £5,000 salvage money that finally made him agree to Deveau's scheme.

Both ships arrived in Gibraltar harbour six days later. And instead of the welcome he expected, Deveau was greeted by an English bureaucrat who nailed an order of immediate arrest to the *Mary Celeste*'s mainmast. The date significantly was Friday the 13th.

From the beginning the *Mary Celeste* had been an unlucky ship. She was registered originally as the *Amazon*, and her first captain had died within forty-eight hours. On her maiden voyage she had hit a fishing weir off the coast of Maine, and damaged her hull. While this was being repaired a fire had broken out amidships. Later, while sailing through the Straits of Dover, she hit another brig, which sank. This had occurred under her third captain; her fourth accidentally ran the ship aground on Cape Brenton Island and wrecked her.

The *Amazon* was salvaged, and passed through the hands of three more owners before she was bought by J.H. Winchester, the founder of a successful shipping line which still operates in New York. Winchester discovered that the brig – which had now been renamed *Mary Celeste* – had dry rot in her timbers, and he had the bottom rebuilt with copper lining and the deck cabin lengthened. These repairs had ensured that the ship was in excellent condition before she had sailed for Genoa under the experienced Captain Briggs – this helped to explain why she had survived so long in the wintry Atlantic after the crew had taken to the lifeboat.

British officials at Gibraltar seemed to suspect either mutiny or some Yankee plot – the latter theory based on the fact that Captain Morehouse and Captain Briggs had been friends, and had apparently dined together the day before the *Mary Celeste* had sailed from New York. But at the inquiry that followed, the idea of mutiny seemed to have gained favour. To back this theory the Court of Inquiry was shown an axe-mark on one of the ship's rails, scoring on her hull that was described as a crude attempt to make the ship look as if she had hit rocks, and a stained sword that was found beneath the captain's bunk. All this, it was claimed, pointed to the crew getting drunk, killing the master and his family, and escaping in the ship's boat.

The Americans were insulted by what they felt was a slur on the honour of the US Merchant Navy, and indignantly denied this story. They pointed out that Briggs was not only known to be a fair man who was not likely to provoke his crew to mutiny, but also that he ran a dry ship; the only alcohol on the *Mary Celeste* was the cargo. And even a thirsty sailor would not be likely to drink more than a mouthful of crude alcohol – it would cause severe stomach pains and eventual blindness. Besides, if the crew had mutinied, why should they leave behind their sea-chests together with such items as family photographs, razors and sea-boots?

The British Admiralty remained unconvinced, but had to admit that if the alternative theory was correct, and Briggs and Morehouse had decided to make a false claim for salvage, Briggs would actually have lost by the deal – he was part-owner of the ship, and his share of any salvage would have come to a fraction of what he could have made by selling his share in the normal way.

In March 1873 the court was finally forced to admit that it was unable to decide why the *Mary Celeste* had been abandoned, the first time in its history that it had failed to come to a definite conclusion. The *Dei Gratia*'s owners were awarded one-fifth of the value of the *Mary Celeste* and her cargo. The brig herself was returned to her owner, who lost no time in selling her the moment she got back to New York.

During the next eleven years the *Mary Celeste* had many owners, but brought little profit to any of them. Sailors were convinced she was unlucky. Her last owner, Captain Gilman C.Parker, ran her aground on a reef in the West Indies and made a claim for insurance. The insurers became suspicious, and Parker and his associates were brought to trial. At that time the penalty for deliberately scuttling a ship on the high seas was death by hanging; but the judge, mindful of the *Mary Celeste*'s previous record of bad luck, allowed the men to be released on a technicality. Within eight months Captain Parker was dead, one of the associates had gone mad, and another had committed suicide. The *Mary Celeste* herself had been left to break up on the reef.

Over the next decade or so, as no new evidence came to light, interest in the story waned. During the trial, when fraud was still suspected, a careful watch had been kept on the major ports of England and America. But there was no sign of any of the missing crew.

In the year 1882 a 23-year-old newly qualified doctor named Arthur Doyle moved to Southsea, a suburb of Portsmouth, and screwed up his nameplate. And during the long weeks of waiting for patients he whiled away the time writing short stories. It was in the autumn of 1882 that he began a story: 'In the month of December 1873, the British ship *Dei Gratia* steered into Gibraltar, having in tow a derelict brigantine *Marie Celeste*, which had been picked up in the latitude 38°40′ , longitude 70°15′ west.'

For such a short sentence, this contains a remarkable number of inaccuracies. The year was actually 1872; the *Dei Gratia* did not tow the *Marie Celeste*, the latter came under its own sail; the latitude and longitude are wrong; and the ship was called plain English Mary, not Marie. All the same, when 'J.Habakuk Jephson's Statement' was published in the Cornhill magazine in 1884 it caused a sensation, launching Arthur Doyle's career as a writer – he was soon using the name A.Conan Doyle. Most people took it for the truth, and from then on it was widely accepted that the *Mary Celeste* had been taken over by a kind of Black Power leader with a hatred of Whites. Mr Solly Flood, the chief investigator in the *Mary Celeste* case, was so indignant that he sent a telegram to the Central News Agency denouncing J.Habakuk Jephson as a fraud and a liar. From then on the *Cornhill* was willing to publish most of Conan Doyle's stories at thirty guineas a time instead of the three guineas he had been paid so far.

Doyle's story was the signal for a new interest in the mystery, and over the next few years there were a number of hoax accounts of the last days of the *Mary Celeste*. They told all kinds of stories from straightforward mutinies to mass accidents – such as everyone falling into the sea when a platform made to watch a swimming race gave way, or the finding of another derelict carrying gold bullion, which tempted Captain Briggs to leave his own ship drifting while he escaped in the other one. One author argued that all the crew had been dragged through the ship's portholes at night by a ravenous giant squid, while Charles Fort, the eminent paranormal researcher, suggested the crew had been snatched away by the same strange force that causes rains of frogs and live fish. Fort added, 'I have a collection of yarns, by highly individualized liars, or artists who scorned, in any particular, to imitate one another; who told, thirty, forty, or fifty years later, of having been members of this crew.' Even today the *Mary Celeste* often sails unsuspectingly into TV serials and Sci-Fi movies to become involved in time warps or attacked by aliens in UFOs.

In fact, a careful study of the facts reveals that the solution of this particular mystery is obvious.

The man most responsible for the perpetuation of the myth about the *Marie Celeste* was Conan Doyle: it was he who insisted that the ship's boats were still intact. This small inaccuracy made an otherwise simple problem virtually insoluble.

In fact, once we know that the boat was missing, we at least know one thing for certain: that the crew abandoned ship, apparently in great haste – the wheel was not lashed, an indication that the ship was abandoned in a hurry. The question then presents itself: what could have caused everyone on board to abandon the ship in such a hurry?

Captain James Briggs, the brother of the *Mary Celeste*'s skipper, was convinced that the clue lay in the last entry in the log, for the morning of 25 November 1872: it stated that the wind had dropped after a night of heavy squalls. James Briggs believed the ship may have become becalmed in the Azores, and started to drift towards the dangerous rocks of Santa Maria Island. The gash-marks found along the side of the *Mary Celeste* – which the British investigators had claimed were deliberately made by the ship's mutinous crew – may have been made when she actually rubbed against a submerged rock, convincing the crew that she was about to sink.

Oliver Deveau proposed that during the storms some water had found its way from between decks into the hold, giving the impression that the ship was leaking.

Another popular explanation is that a waterspout hit the *Mary Celeste*. The atmospheric pressure inside a waterspout is low; this could have caused the hatch-covers to blow open and forced bilge water into the pump well; this would have made it look as if the ship had taken on six to eight feet of water and was sinking fast.

There are basic objections to all these three answers. If the ship scraped dangerous rocks off Santa Maria Island, then the lifeboat would have been close enough to land on the Island. Since no survivors were found and no wreckage from the lifeboat, this seems unlikely.

Oliver Deveau's theory has a great deal more in its favour. There have often been panics at sea. When Captain Cook's *Endeavour* was in difficulties off the coast of eastern Australia the ship's carpenter was sent to take a reading of the water in the hold. He made a mistake, and the resulting hysteria might have ended with the crew leaving the ship if Cook had not been able to control the panic. On another occasion a ship which was carrying a hold full of timber dumped the whole lot into the sea off Newfoundland, before anyone realized that it would be next to impossible to sink a ship full of wood. But it seems unlikely that a captain of Briggs's known efficiency would allow some simple misreading to cause a panic.

The objection to the waterspout theory is that, apart from the open hatches, the ship was completely undamaged. If a waterspout was big enough to cause such a panic, it would surely have caused far more havoc.

In any case, the real mystery is why, if the crew left the *Mary Celeste* in the lifeboat, they made no attempt to get back on board when they saw that the ship was in no danger of sinking.

Only one explanation covers all the facts. Briggs had never shipped crude alcohol before, and being a typical New England puritan, undoubtedly mistrusted it. The change in temperature between New York and the Azores would have caused casks of alcohol to sweat and leak. The night of storms, in which the barrels would have been shaken violently, would have caused vapour to form inside the casks, slowly building up pressure until the lids of two or three blew off. The explosion, though basically harmless, might have blown the hatches off the cargo hold on to the deck in the positions in which Deveau later found them. Convinced that the whole ship was about to explode, Briggs ordered everyone into the lifeboat. In his haste, he failed to take the one simple precaution that would have saved their lives – to secure the lifeboat to the *Mary Celeste* by a few hundred yards of cable. The sea was fairly calm when the boat was lowered, as we know from the last entry in the log, but the evidence of the torn sails indicates that the ship then encountered severe gales. We may conjecture that the rising wind blew the *Mary Celeste* into the distance, while the crew in the lifeboat rowed frantically in a futile effort to catch up. The remainder of the story is tragically obvious.

21 Where is the Mona Lisa?

The answer to the above question may seem self-evident: in the Louvre. But the matter is not quite as straightforward as it looks.

The Mona Lisa is better known on the continent of Europe as 'La Gioconda', or the smiling woman – the word means the same as the old English 'jocund'. It was painted, as everyone knows, by the great Italian artist Leonardo, who was born in the little town of Vinci, near Florence, in 1452. Mona Lisa (Mona is short for Madonna) was a young married woman who was about twenty-four when Leonardo met her. She was the wife of a man twenty years her senior, the wealthy Francesco del Giocondo, and when Leonardo started to paint her around 1500 she had just lost a child. Leonardo's biographer Vasari says that her husband had to hire jesters and musicians to make her smile during the early sittings.

For some reason Leonardo became obsessed with her, and went on painting her for several years, always dissatisfied with his work. This has given rise to stories that he was in love with her, and even that she became his mistress; but this seems unlikely. Leonardo was homosexual, and took a poor view of sex, writing with Swiftian disgust: 'The act of coitus and the members that serve it are so hideous that, if it were not for the beauty of faces . . . the human species would lose its humanity.' Yet there was something about Madonna Lisa that made him strive to capture her expression for at least six years – possibly more. His biographer Antonia Vallentin says she fascinated him more than any other woman he met in his life. He gave the unfinished portrait to Mona Lisa's husband when he left Florence in 1505, but still continued to work on it at intervals when he returned.

In his *Lives of the Painters*, Giorgio Vasari says that Leonardo worked at the Mona Lisa for four years and left it unfinished. 'This work is now in the possession of Francis, king of France, at Fontainebleau . . .' And this, we assume, is the famous portrait now in the Louvre. Yet this raises a puzzling question. Leonardo gave the portrait to the man who had commissioned it, Mona Lisa's husband, in 1505, and a mere forty or so years later, when Vasari was writing, it is in the possession of Francis I of France. Surely the Giacondo family would not part with a masterpiece so easily? Besides, the Louvre picture is quite obviously finished . . . .

There is another interesting clue. In 1584 a historian of art, Giovanni Paolo Lomazzo, published a book on painting, sculpture and architecture, in which he refers to 'the Gioconda *and* the Mona Lisa', as if they were two seperate paintings. The book is dedicated to Don Carlos Emanuele, the Grand Duke of Savoy, who was a great admirer of Leonardo – so it hardly seems likely that this was a slip of the pen . . . .

Two Giocondas? Then where is the other one? And, more important, *who* is this second Gioconda?

The answer to the first question is, oddly enough: in the Louvre. The world-famous painting, which has been reproduced more often than any other painting in history, is almost certainly not the Mona Lisa that we have been talking about.

Then where *is* the painting of the woman who so obsessed Leonardo that he could not finish her portrait? There is evidence to show that this original Mona Lisa was brought from Italy in the mid-eighteenth century, and went into the stately home of a nobleman in Somerset. Just before the First World War it was discovered by the art connoisseur Hugh Blaker in Bath, and he picked it up for a few guineas, and took it to his studio in Isleworth. Hence it became known as the Isleworth Mona Lisa. It was bigger than the Louvre painting, and – more important – was unfinished; the background has only been lightly touched in. Blaker was much impressed by it. The girl was younger and prettier than the Louvre Mona Lisa. And Blaker felt that this new Mona Lisa corresponded much more closely to Vasari's description than the Louvre painting. Vasari rhapsodized about its delicate realism:

The eyes had that lustre and watery sheen which is always seen in real life, and around them were those touches of red and the lashes which cannot be represented without the greatest subtlety . . . The nose with its beautiful nostrils, rosy and tender, seemed to be alive. The opening of the mouth, united by the red of the lips to the flesh tones of the face, seemed not to be coloured, but to be living flesh.

Sir Kenneth Clark, quoting this passage in his book on Leonardo, asks: 'Who would recognise the submarine goddess of the Louvre?' To which Blaker would have replied: 'Ah, precisely.' But the description *does* fit the Isleworth Mona Lisa.

There is another point that seems to establish beyond all doubt that Blaker's picture is Leonardo's Mona Lisa. The painter Raphael saw it in Leonardo's studio about 1504, and later made a sketch of it. This sketch shows two Grecian columns on either side – columns that can be found in the Isleworth Mona Lisa, but not in the Louvre painting.

Blaker believes that the Isleworth Mona Lisa is a far more beautiful work, and many art experts have agreed with him. It is true that the Louvre painting has many admirers; Walter Pater wrote a celebrated 'purple passage' about it in *The Renaissance* beginning 'She is older than the rocks among which she sits; like the vampire, she has been dead many times . . .', and W.B. Yeats thought this so beautiful that he divided it into lines of free verse and printed it as a poem in his *Oxford Book of Modern Verse*. On the other hand, the connoisseur Bernard Berenson wrote about it: 'What I really saw in the figure of Mona Lisa was the estranging image of woman beyond the reach of my sympathy or the ken of my interest . . . watchful, sly, secure, with a smile of anticipated satisfaction and a pervading air of hostile superiority . . .' He felt the beauty of the Louvre Mona Lisa had been sacrificed to technique. No one could say this of the far more fresh and lively Isleworth Mona Lisa.

But if the lady in the Louvre is not Leonardo's Lisa del Giocondo, then who is she? Here the most important clue is to be found in a document by Antonio Beatis, secretary to the Cardinal of Aragon. When Leonardo went to the court of Francis I in 1517 he was visited by the cardinal, and the secretary noted down the conversation. The cardinal was shown works by Leonardo, including St John, the Madonna with St Anne, and 'the portrait of a certain Florentine lady, painted from life at the instance of the late Magnifico Giuliano de Medici . . .'

In her biography of Leonardo, Antonia Vallentin speculates that this work *was* the Mona Lisa, and asks: 'Did Giuliano [de Medici] love Mona Lisa in her girlhood . . . did he think with longing of her now she was married to Messer del Giocondo, and had he commissioned Leonardo to paint her portrait?' But this delightful romantic bubble is shattered by a mere consideration of dates. Giuliano de Medici, brother of Lorenzo the Magnificent, master of Florence, was murdered in Florence cathedral in 1478. The plotters – mostly rival bankers – hoped to kill Lorenzo too, but Lorenzo was too quick for them. All this happened in the year before Mona Lisa was born.

Then who *was* the lady that Leonardo painted at the orders of Giuliano de Medici? Almost certainly the answer is Costanza d'Avalos, Giuliano's mistress, a lady of such pleasant disposition that she was known as 'the smiling one' – la Gioconda . . . .

And so it would seem that the painting in the Louvre has been labelled 'the Mona Lisa' by a simple misunderstanding. Its subject is obviously a woman in her thirties not, like Mona Lisa del Giocondo, in her twenties. Leonardo took it with him to France, and it went into the collection of Francis I, and eventually into the Louvre. The unfinished Mona Lisa stayed in Italy, was brought to England, and was purchased by Hugh Blaker in 1914. In 1962 it was purchased for some vast but undisclosed sum – undoubtedly amounting to millions – by a Swiss syndicate headed by the art-collector Dr Henry F. Pulitzer, and Pulitzer has since written a short book, *Where is the Mona Lisa?*, setting out the claims of his own painting to be that of Madonna Lisa del Giocondo. Pulitzer's contention is simple. There are two Giocondas – for Madonna Lisa had a perfect right to call herself by her husband's name, with a feminine ending. But there is only one Mona Lisa. And that is not in the Louvre but in London.

22 Money Pit

Who Buried the Treasure?

Mahone Bay, Newfoundland, contains as many islands as there are days in the year, and in the summer of 1795, a youth named Daniel McGinnis decided to explore one of these. Unlike most of the other islands, this one was covered with oak-trees, a timber rarely found in the far north. Daniel was intrigued to find unmistakable signs of human habitation, although none was recent. And since settlers were unlikely to choose such a remote spot, it meant that the visitors had been either Indians or pirates. The teenager had lived all his life on the eastern shore of Mahone Bay, with its tales of piracy and hidden treasure. And when he came upon an oak-tree with a ship's tackle block hanging from one of its lower branches he had no doubt that he was on the trail of some buccaneer's treasure hoard. His excitement was increased when he noticed a depression under the oak-tree, suggesting that a hole had once been excavated there and then filled in again.

Daniel McGinnis rushed home and enlisted the aid of two close friends. The next day John Smith, twenty, and Anthony Vaughan, thirteen, returned with him to the island carrying picks and shovels. In a crescent-shaped cove on the island's south-eastern shore they found a half-buried boulder in which a heavy iron ring-bolt had been embedded, a ring solid enough to moor a large vessel. From there they struck inland, and discovered the remains of a tolerably well-made (if rather overgrown) road running between the north-east and south-west corners of the island. In the clearing they saw that a branch sixteen feet above the depression had been cut off about four feet from the trunk, and that the bark of the tree was deeply scored with rope-marks. But when they tried to retrieve the tackle block it fell to pieces.

The boys went to work with the picks and shovels and soon found themselves in a thirteen-foot-wide circular shaft, its walls of hard blue clay still showing the marks of the original picks used to dig it. At four feet they unearthed a layer of flagstones. These were not indigenous to the island, and must have come from Golden River, about two miles distant.

At a depth of 10 ft they came upon a platform of oak logs, extending across the shaft, the ends firmly embedded in the walls and all quite rotten, suggesting that they had been there for many years. They loosened the logs and dragged them out, every moment hoping to find chests of doubloons and precious gems just beneath. They were disappointed; there was only more clay. At 20 ft they came upon another layer of logs, then one at 30 feet.

Finally, realizing the task was too great for them, they decided to give up, although they were convinced they were only a few feet from the treasure. As they paddled dejectedly back home they could hardly have guessed their Tom Sawyer adventure would lead to the deaths of five men, and the expenditure of hundreds of thousands of dollars.

It was obvious that machinery would be needed to excavate the pit, and the boys tried to raise the capital among their friends. No one was interested. Many of the townspeople believed that the place was haunted; elderly inhabitants remembered seeing strange lights resembling bonfires on the island when they were children. It was rumoured that several local men had rowed over to investigate, and had never been seen again.

In the face of this lack of enthusiasm, the treasure-hunters were finally forced to admit defeat. But when Daniel and John got married they moved on to the island, which they had christened Oak Island. Nine years after that first visit John Smith's wife became pregnant, and her husband took her to the mainland for the delivery. While she was there she talked about her husband's discovery with a doctor named Simeon Lynds. He was interested enough to raise the necessary capital among his friends, and in 1803 work once again commenced on the Money Pit.

In the intervening years a quantity of mud had settled in the bottom of the pit, and this had to be removed before the diggers could find the sticks left to mark the spot by the three boys. Using a system of ropes, pulleys and buckets, they managed to reach a depth of eighty feet from the surface without finding any sign of the treasure they hoped was there. But below this they encountered a new barrier every ten feet. As is often the case with such ventures, no records were kept by the treasure-hunters, and there is some confusion over the sequence of the levels they encountered. One version gives the sequence of platforms like this: at forty feet a platform of oak sealed with putty; at fifty feet, plain oak; at sixty feet, oak sealed with coconut fibre and putty; at seventy feet, plain oak; and at eighty feet, another layer of oak sealed with putty.

By now the searchers were convinced that the pit had been dug by pirates; the putty was the type used on ships – enough of it was brought out of the pit to glaze the windows of over twenty houses around Mahone Bay – and the coconut fibre must have travelled at least two thousand miles to reach Nova Scotia, again suggesting sailors.

They dug deeper, and at ninety feet came upon a layer of ship's putty as hard as brick. Immediately beneath this there was a large stone of a type unknown in Nova Scotia, and on the underside of this stone the searchers found roughly cut figures and letters of no obvious significance. Smith took this home, and later built it into his fireplace. The treasure-hunters felt that at least it indicated they were close to their goal.

They pushed a crowbar into the earth, which was by then so waterlogged that they were having to raise a cask of water for every two of earth. Only a few feet below the last platform they struck a hard surface that seemed to stretch right across the shaft; they all agreed that it was wood, and that it was probably a chest. At last it looked as if their goal was in sight.

The discovery was made late on a Saturday evening, and as night fell they climbed out of the shaft. They did not work on the Sunday, and must have spent the time between then and Monday morning in an agony of expectation. Smith later said that they spent the time happily deciding how many shares each man was to receive.

The sight that met their eyes as they arrived on the Monday morning must have seemed to them like a nightmare; all but about thirty feet of the ninety-foot shaft was filled with muddy water. They tried to bail out the water with buckets, but the level remained the same. They brought in a pump to do the work; it burst from overwork, and the water-level remained the same. In total frustration, the men abandoned work.

In the spring of 1805 the treasure-hunters returned to try a new plan of attack. They sank a second shaft next to the old one, to a depth of 110 feet, about fifteen feet deeper than the original, and then started to tunnel towards what they hoped were the treasure chests from underneath. Unfortunately, they had dug too close to the original shaft; the pressure of the water split the intervening wall of clay, deluging the diggers with hundreds of gallons of muddy water. The second shaft filled so quickly that the men were lucky to escape with their lives.

The syndicate had now run out of money: there was nothing for it but to abandon the project. Smith, writing to a friend, said: 'Had it not been for the various mischiefs nature played on us, we would by now, all of us, be men of means.' He did not guess that the reason for his failure was not the mischief of nature but the skill of a long-dead pirate.

For more than forty years the Money Pit remained untouched. In 1849 a new syndicate, formed by investors from another part of Nova Scotia, made another attempt. Involved in the new venture were Dr David Lynds, a relative of Simeon Lynds, and Anthony Vaughan, the youngest of the original explorers, who was now in his late sixties. Of the other two, McGinnis was dead and Smith chose not to be actively involved.

On Oak Island they found that both shafts had caved in. Over the next twelve days they dug to a depth of eighty-six feet, and were glad to find no sign of flooding. Once again they finished work on a Saturday evening. The next morning they checked the pit for any sign of water, and found that it was still quite dry. At 2 p.m. they came back from church, only to find the pit filled with sixty feet of water.

The following day they began by trying to bail out the water with buckets; in the words of one account: 'The result appeared as unsatisfactory as taking soup with a fork.' When they saw just how difficult a task they were facing the searchers decided to find out what really lay at the bottom of the pit. To do this they used a pod auger, a horse-driven drill that brought up samples of whatever material it drilled through. A platform was erected above the water and five holes were drilled to a depth of 106 feet. The first two, drilled a little west of the centre of the pit, brought up only mud and stones. A statement made by the man who directed the drilling shows what was found by the borings east of the centre:

After going through the platform [at the level reached by the crowbar in 1804] which was five inches thick, and proved to be spruce, the auger dropped twelve inches and then went through four inches of oak; then it went through twenty-two inches of metal in pieces; but the auger failed to bring up anything in the nature of treasure, except three links resembling the links of an ancient watch chain. It then went through eight inches of oak, which was thought to be the bottom of the first box and the top of the next; then twenty-two inches of oak and six inches of spruce, then into clay seven feet without striking anything.

The next bore to be sent down was less successful, seeming to miss the chests, but the jerky motion of the drill suggested that it might have struck the edge of one or both of the chests. This time the bore brought up fragments of coconut fibre mixed with splinters of oak. These two borings suggested that the Money Pit contained two chests, one on top of another. But did they contain buried treasure? The nature of 'the metal pieces' is not recorded. Later one of the members of the syndicate described the 'links of watch chain' as 'a piece of gold chain', but this was probably a touch of embellishment.

The last boring was the most significant of the five. It was decided to carefully remove every scrap of metal that the pod auger brought to the surface so that they might be examined by microscope. This operation was going well until there was a disturbance among the men searching through the bore samples. One of the men had seen the foreman, James Pitblado, find something, examine it carefully, and put it in his pocket. When asked to produce it he refused, saying that he would show it at the next meeting of directors of the syndicate. They took him at his word, but he failed to put in an appearance. Instead he tried to persuade a local businessman to buy the east end of Oak Island. The businessman was willing, but the syndicate refused to sell. Pitblado is said to have died in a mining accident not long afterwards; he never revealed what it was that he had found, but the local legend insists that it was a jewel.

The treasure-hunters were now convinced that the pit contained two chests filled with treasure. The only question that remained was how to get at them. Undeterred by the near-disaster that befell the 1804 syndicate, they decided to dig another shaft next to the original, and try to tunnel their way to the chests from underneath. They reached a depth of 109 feet without encountering any sign of water, but as they started to dig towards the Money Pit the workmen were suddenly deluged with hundreds of gallons, and once again barely escaped with their lives. The new shaft filled to the same level as the original, thirty-three feet from the surface.

Incredibly, nobody up until then had really wondered where all the water was coming from. Then one of the drenched men observed that the water tasted salty. Watching the level in the pit over a twelve-hour period, they found that it rose and fell with the tide in the bay; the Money Pit was full of sea-water.

The soil at that end of the island was mostly clay, so it was quite impossible that the water might have seeped through to the pit. There had to be a tunnel. Now the treasure-hunters shifted their attention to the nearest beach, Smith's Cove, 500 feet to the north-east. And as the tide went out they observed that the sand 'gulched water like a sponge being squeezed'.

Digging revealed a layer of coconut fibre under three feet of sand. Directly beneath the fibre was a layer of eel grass or kelp, four or five inches deep, and beneath that a quantity of flat stones. This huge man-made sponge stretched for 150 feet along the beach between the high and low water marks. At a depth of five feet they found five box drains, evenly spaced, solidly built of flat stones, which led to a funnel-shaped sump set just above the high-water mark.

The drains were so well constructed that when they uncovered one of them they found that no soil had seeped through to obstruct the water flow in what might have been a hundred years. From the sump the water passed along a downward sloping passage for the five hundred feet to the Money Pit, reaching it just below the ninety-foot level.

If the construction of the pit itself was impressive, the flood-tunnel system was surely the work of an engineering genius. As the tide rose in the bay the water was soaked up by the coconut fibre sponge and channelled through the drains and tunnel to the pit. As long as the shaft was full of soil the water would be held back by the pressure. The removal of earth lessened the pressure, and when the diggers got to the ninety-foot level the force of the tide would be able to push the water through to flood the shaft.

The searchers were elated; such elaborate precautions suggested an immense treasure. And now all that remained was to stop off the water, and pump out the pit. . ..

Working with new enthusiasm, they began to construct a 150-foot-long coffer dam across the mouth of the bay, but nature seemed determined to frustrate their efforts. Before the dam was finished an unusually high tide knocked the whole thing down. The syndicate decided to try to block off the tunnel from the beach. When the tides made this impossible they decided to intersect the tunnel between the beach and the pit. Their first shaft, near Smith's Cove, missed it completely. They dug another shaft close to the pit, but at thirty-five feet came upon a large boulder. When this was removed the shaft filled once more with the familiar rush of water. Now utterly confused, they decided that this must be the flood tunnel, failing to see that the sea tunnel must be another sixty feet down, or the shaft would have flooded when the original excavators had reached a depth of thirty feet. In an attempt to stop the 'leak' they drove timbers into the ground. When this failed they even tried to approach the chests from below. At 118 feet the workmen started to tunnel towards the original shaft. When the workmen were breaking for lunch the water from the Money Pit once more broke through and flooded the shaft. After this blow work was suspended for nine years.

In 1859 the syndicate was resurrected. Once again shafts were sunk with the intention of either draining the Money Pit or diverting the flood tunnel. Yet even with a workforce of sixty-three men, they were unable to stem the flood. In 1861 the manual pumps were replaced with steam pumps. The boiler promptly burst, scalding a workman to death. So once again work was suspended.

In the ensuing years many more attempts were made, mostly by prospectors who showed more enthusiasm than ingenuity or common sense. Most of them settled for digging more shafts around the Money Pit to try to stop the flow of water; none of them seemed to understand that it would be simpler to dig near Smith's Cove, where the shafts would only have to be ten to fifteen feet deep, instead of the ninety-foot holes they were digging near the pit. As a result of all this activity the area around the Money Pit became honeycombed with water-filled shafts, making the task even more difficult.

In 1866 operations were taken over by the newly formed Halifax syndicate. They also attempted to dam up Smith's Cove, but were defeated by unusually high tides. At one point they actually discovered the place where the flood tunnel entered the Money Pit, and became aware of the amazing expertise that had gone into its construction. The mouth was two and a half feet wide and four feet high, entering the tunnel at 110 feet from the surface. To strengthen it the builders had carefully laid beach stones around the lip of the tunnel.

This new discovery should have solved their problems, since all they now had to do was to block up the tunnel and prevent more sea-water from entering. Unfortunately, the entire area was so honeycombed with shafts by this time that the water could now enter from several other directions.

Yet one thing was obvious: all this skill would be wasted if the pirates had not meant to come back to collect their treasure. That being so, they must have built in a way to cut off the flow of sea-water. The most straightforward method would be a floodgate to block off the tunnel. In that case, where was it? A careful search of the 500-foot strip of land between Smith's Cove and the Pit failed to locate it. And so once again the treasure-hunters had to admit defeat. A member of the company, Isaac Blair, later told his nephew Frederick: 'I saw enough to convince me that there was treasure buried there, and also enough to convince me that they will never get it.'

At the age of twenty-four, Frederick Blair himself had a try at finding the treasure; he joined a group of prospectors calling themselves the Oak Island Treasure Company. The year was 1891, nearly a hundred years since Daniel McGinnis had first landed on the island. Their intention was 'to use the best modern appliances for cutting off the flow of water through the tunnel . . .' Unfortunately, 'the best modern appliances' made virtually no difference mainly because the treasure-hunters once again attempted to cut off the flow of water at the Money Pit end of the tunnel. By the time their money ran out the new syndicate had still achieved as little as its predecessors.

They rethought their plans, and in 1897 did what they should have done to begin with, to dig at the Smith's Cove end of the tunnel. At about fifteen feet below the surface they encountered sea-water. This time, instead of trying to block off the tunnel with a wall of logs, they placed a 160lb charge of dynamite in the hole. When it was detonated there was a sudden rush of turbulence in the water of the Money Pit, 450 feet away. The flood tunnel had almost certainly collapsed. Yet when they attempted to pump out the Pit the water rushed back in just as quickly.

Faced with these discouraging results, they decided to try another approach: to see if they could locate the treasure chests in the waterlogged clay. They drove down a three-inch pipe, in which a drill would work more efficiently. At 126 feet the pipe and its drill were brought to a halt by an obstruction, described as 'an edge of iron'. A larger drill succeeded in boring through it, and continued down to 151 feet. At this level it was stopped by a layer of soft stone, later identified as cement. Twenty inches below this the drill bored through five inches of oak wood; this looked altogether more promising. At this point the drill began to behave rather oddly; it dropped a few inches to rest on what seemed to be a metal object that could be moved a fraction of an inch from side to side. Could this be the lid of the chest? They drilled on, and the drill seemed to encounter smaller metal objects, possibly coins or jewellery. Moreover, when the drill was raised again a piece of parchment was found stuck to it; written on it were the letters 'V.I.'

And now, when it looked as if they were finally on the brink of success, their luck ran out. When they tried to drill down to the chest a second time they failed to find it. Hope revived when another drill struck something that might have been the edge of a chest. But a third drill broke through into a channel of underground water, which surged up the pipe at a rate of four hundred gallons a minute, soaking everything within range.

So it looked as if there was a second flood tunnel, a great deal lower than the first. To test this Frederick Blair poured a heavy red dye into the Money Pit, and his theory was confirmed when the dye reappeared off the south side of the island. This indicated that the deeper tunnel must be at least six hundred feet long.

The syndicate sank six more shafts in their attempt to block off this newly discovered tunnel, and each had to be abandoned when water gushed in. It was pointless to continue. They had spent over $225,000 on the operations; even if they finally recovered the treasure there would be no guarantee that it would reimburse them for such enormous costs. So reluctantly, they decided to call a halt.

During the next thirty years there were several more attempts to excavate the Money Pit, none of them as ambitious as the Oak Island Treasure Company. Each attempt made it less likely that the treasure would ever be recovered. The original site had now been totally destroyed, and there was little more than a quagmire in its place. In 1931 William Chappell, who had been in the Oak Island syndicate in 1897, found a pick, a miner's seal-oil lamp, and an axe-head buried in the mud; examination showed them to be about 250 years old, suggesting that the date of the original Money Pit may have been as early as 1680.

With the passage of the years the geological formation of Oak Island became better understood, and it was realized that its limestone base contained many cavities and sink-holes; if the 'treasure' had sunk into one of these, then it would probably be virtually unrecoverable. Nevertheless, in 1937 a wealthy New England businessman, Gilbert D. Hedden, spent two seasons digging and drilling, and reached the discouraging conclusion that the treasure chests had broken up in the waterlogged soil. He decided that if the second flood tunnel could be blocked off the quagmire would slowly dry out.

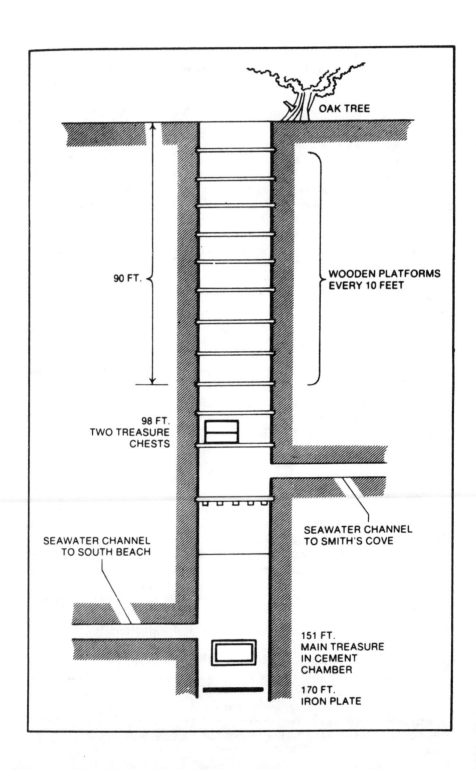

OAK TREE

90 FT.

WOODEN PLATFORMS
EVERY 10 FEET

98 FT.
TWO TREASURE
CHESTS

SEAWATER CHANNEL
TO SMITH'S COVE

SEAWATER CHANNEL
TO SOUTH BEACH

151 FT.
MAIN TREASURE
IN CEMENT
CHAMBER

170 FT.
IRON PLATE

The simplest way to block off the influx of sea-water was obviously to find the tunnel's floodgate. Unlike his predecessors, Hedden decided against searching between the Money Pit and the sea. Instead he tried logic. Why had the pirates never returned for their treasure? The likeliest possibilities were shipwreck or capture by the authorities. In that case the clues to the mystery might be hidden in the biography of some famous pirate captain. If such a man had died at the end of a rope, the vital clue might be contained in court transcripts, or the man's confession. Hedden began spending his days in libraries. And in a short while he found the man who seemed to fit his theories: Captain Kidd.

In fact, William Kidd had not been a murderous cutthroat, like so many of his predecessors; he was a privateer – that is, a sailor who was paid by his government to attack only ships belonging to enemy nations. Many privateers considered themselves to be loyal patriots who were essentially a part of their country's navy. Britain's most famous 'pirate', Sir Francis Drake, was a privateer.

In 1696 Kidd had been commissioned by King William III to suppress piracy and confiscate pirate loot. But Kidd was a weak and ambitious man who found attacking merchant ships easier than pursuing pirates. Over the next five years his ship the *Adventure* roamed the sea-lanes and attacked ships of all nations, enemy or otherwise. The British government had no strong objection, since Kidd only attacked 'foreigners'. The decision to outlaw him seems to have been based on the suspicion that they were not getting a fair share of his loot. Thoroughly upset at this slur on his name, Kidd hurried to New England with the intention of defending himself. Lord Bellomont, the governor, immediately clapped him in irons, and confiscated about £14,000 worth of treasure from his ship. Kidd was then sent back to England, where he was tried and executed; his tarred body was hung at Tilbury Point as a warning to other 'pirates'.

What Hedden discovered was that on the eve of his execution Kidd was said to have sent to the Speaker of the House of Commons saying that if his life was spared he would lead the authorities to his buried treasure, which he valued at £100,000. Kidd had claimed that his treasure was buried on an island in the China Seas, but this may have been a deliberate attempt to mislead. It also struck Hedden that the French *chêne* means oak, and that Kidd may have been dropping a clue about the location of his treasure.

Hedden was reading a book called *Captain Kidd and his Skeleton Island*, written in 1935 by Harold Wilkins, when he came upon a map purporting to be Kidd's treasure island. It had an obvious similarity to Oak Island, despite notes written on the edge claiming that it was situated in the China Seas. On its lower edge were an intriguing set of directions:
18W and by 7E on Rock
30SW 14N Tree
7 by 8 by 4

Book in hand, Hedden wandered around the Money Pit and found a large granite stone, due north of the pit, in which a hole had been drilled. This reminded him of a similar stone that had been found in Smith's Cove many years before. Searching the Cove, they uncovered the stone, and found that the distance between the two boulders was just over 25 rods, a rod equalling sixteen-and-a-half feet.

Hedden called in a surveyor who calculated a position 18 rods from the drilled stone to the west, and 7 rods from the drilled stone to the east. Thirty rods south-west of this point brought them to an area of flat ground covered with low scrub. Clearing the ground, they came upon various beach stones which had obviously been laid out in some form of pattern. As they worked on they found that it took the form of an arrowhead with an outwardly curving lower side, perhaps representing a rough sextant. Its apex pointed due north to the Money Pit and the large oak-tree that had once stood over it. The map, apparently, was inaccurate; the tree had stood slightly more than 14 rods away from the arrow. Despite this, Hedden was convinced that the treasure map represented Oak Island, and that the Money Pit had been constructed by Captain Kidd.

In high spirits he set off for England, and went to interview the author of the book, Harold Wilkins. He was hoping that Wilkins would have further information that might lead him to discover the hidden floodgate. Wilkins was astonished; he'd never heard of Oak Island, and pointed out that the map in his book was probably inaccurate – he'd been forced to draw it from memory after seeing the original in a private collection. When Hedden pointed out that the directions on the map were almost precisely accurate he was even more surprised. He insisted that he had invented them simply to fill in an empty space on the map; he was later so impressed by what Hedden had found on the island that he began to entertain the curious conviction that he was the reincarnation of Captain Kidd.

All this carried Hedden no further. He failed to locate his 'confession' that would help him to locate the floodgate to cut off the sea. So, like all his predecessors, Hedden reached a dead end.

Next came Edwin H. Hamilton, a machine engineer who drilled down to 180 feet, deeper than anyone before him. He made an interesting discovery: that the mouth of the second flood tunnel joined the Money Pit from the same side as the first one. This suggested that both tunnels originated from Smith's Cove, and that the lower tunnel did not run south as Blair's red dye had seemed to suggest. Hamilton concluded that there must be an underground stream below the second flood tunnel (which was at 110 feet) and that this had carried the dye into the sea on the south side of the island, creating still more confusion. It was obviously fortunate for Hedden that he gave up when he did.

After Hamilton abandoned his excavations, an ex-circus stunt rider called Robert Restall died in the Money Pit when exhaust gas from a pump filled the shaft. His 22-year-old son and two other men also died trying to save him.

Finally, in 1965, an American petroleum geologist called Robert Dunfield once again tried the brute-force approach, and brought in a seventy-foot clam digger. In six weeks he excavated a hole 80 feet wide by 130 feet deep. He found nothing, and managed to obliterate all traces of the treasure pit.

So the mystery remains: who built the Money Pit and why? The obvious answer, pirates, is less convincing than it sounds. Most of the booty accumulated by pirates would be of the perishable variety: food, drink, spices, silks and satins. When they found money they promptly shared it out among themselves and spent it. Even the notorious Blackbeard only managed to accumulate one chestful of valuables. Besides, it seems unlikely that pirates could have constructed the Money Pit – it would have taken a very strong-willed captain to force a crew of lazy cutthroats to spend more than a week digging tunnels on a remote island.

An altogether more plausible suggestion is made in Rupert Furneaux's book *The Money Pit*. He suggests that the skill and precision involved in the pit's construction point to a military operation. The army would have the men and the skilled engineers to complete such a project. Furneaux suggests that the pit was constructed around 1780, at the time the British army was losing the American War of Independence. The British were making plans for a speedy withdrawal, and the garrison at New York was scheduled to retreat to Halifax in Nova Scotia – at the time the nearest large settlement to Oak Island. Furneaux suggests that the Corps of Royal Engineers might have been ordered to build the pit to hide the garrison's war chests, containing the supply of money to pay the British army. It is possible that the money was never actually buried in the pit, or that if it was it was later retrieved and taken back to England. This seems to be the likeliest explanation of the total failure of all the syndicates to find the slightest sign of treasure. It is a sad reflection, that almost two centuries of effort have been wasted on what finally amounts to a hoax.

23 'The Most Mysterious Manuscript in the World'

The Voynich Manuscript

It was in 1912 that an American dealer in rare books, Wilfred Voynich, heard of a mysterious work that had been discovered in an old chest in the Jesuit school of Mondragone, in Frascati, Italy, and succeeded in buying it for an undisclosed sum. It was an octavo volume, six by nine inches, with 204 pages; it had originally another 28 pages, but these are lost. It is written in cipher, which at first glance looks like ordinary medieval writing. And the pages are covered with strange little drawings of female nudes, astronomical diagrams, and all kinds of strange plants in many colours.

There was a letter accompanying the manuscript, dated 19 August 1666, and written by Joannes Marcus Marci, the rector of Prague University. It was addressed to the famous Jesuit scholar Athanasius Kircher – remembered today mainly for some interesting experiments in animal hypnosis – and stated that the book had been bought for 600 ducats by the Holy Roman Emperor Rudolf II of Prague. Kircher was an expert on cryptography, having published a book on the subject in 1663, in which he claimed to have solved the riddle of hieroglyphics. This in itself may be taken to indicate that Kircher was inclined to indulge in wishful thinking, since we know that it would be another century and a half before Champollion succeeded in reading hieroglyphics. Kircher had apparently already attempted to decipher a few pages of the book, sent to him by its previous owner, who had devoted his whole life to trying to decode it. Now he sent him the whole manuscript.

We do not know how the manuscript came to be in Prague, but the likeliest possibility is that it was taken there from England by the famous Elizabethan 'magician' Dr John Dee, who went there in 1584; one writer speculates that Dee may have obtained it from the Duke of Northumberland, who had pillaged monasteries at the behest of Henry VIII. The English writer Sir Thomas Browne said later that Dee's son Arthur had spoken about 'a book containing nothing but hieroglyphics' which he had studied in Prague. Marci believed the mysterious book to be by the thirteenth-century monk and scientist Roger Bacon.

The Voynich manuscript (as it came to be known) is a baffling mystery because it *looks* so straightforward; with its drawings of plants it looks like an ordinary medieval 'herbal', a book describing how to extract healing drugs from plants. One would expect astronomical or astrological diagrams in a herbal, because the plants were often supposed to be gathered by the full moon, or when the stars or planets were in a certain position.

Kircher obviously had no success with the manuscript; he finally deposited it in the Jesuit College in Rome, whence it came into the hands of the Jesuits of Frascati.

Voynich was fairly certain that the manuscript would not remain a mystery once modern scholars had a chance to study it. So he distributed photostats to anyone who was interested. The first problem, of course, was to determine what language it was in – Latin, Middle English, perhaps even Langue d'Oc. This should have been an easy task, since the plants were labelled, albeit in some sort of code. But most of the plants proved to be imaginary. Certain constellations could be recognized among the astronomical diagrams but again, it proved impossible to translate their names out of code. Cryptanalysts tried the familiar method of looking for the most frequent symbols and equating them with the most commonly used letters of the alphabet; they had no difficulty recognizing 29 individual letters or symbols, but every attempt to translate these into a known language was a failure. What made it so infuriating was that the writing didn't *look* like a code; it looked as if someone had sat down and written it as fluently as his mother tongue. Many scholars, cryptanalysts, linguists, astronomers, experts on Bacon, offered to help; the Vatican Library offered to throw open its archives to the researchers. Still the manuscript refused to yield up its secret – or even one of its secrets.

Then in 1921 a professor of philosophy from the University of Pennsylvania, William Romaine Newbold, announced that he had solved the code; he explained his discovery before a meeting of the American Philosophical Society in Philadelphia. What he had done, he explained, was to start by translating the symbols into Roman letters, reducing them in the process from 29 to 17. Using the Latin *conmuto* (or *commuto*: to change) as a key word, he then went on to produce no less than four more versions of the text, the last of which was (according to Newbold) a straightforward Latin text mixed up into anagrams. These merely had to be unscrambled and the result was a scientific treatise which revealed that Roger Bacon was one of the greatest intellects of all time.

This had, of course, always been suspected. It was Bacon who had inspired Columbus to seek out America by a passage in his *Opus Majus* in which he suggested that the Indies could be reached by sailing westward from Spain. In the days of alchemy and a dogmatic and muddled science derived from Aristotle, Bacon advocated learning from nature by experiment and observation, and was thrown into prison for his pains. In rejecting the authority of Aristotle he was also by implication rejecting the authority of the Church. In his *City of God*, St Augustine had warned Christians to shun science and intellectual inquiry as a danger to salvation. Roger Bacon, like his Elizabethan namesake Francis, could see that such an attitude was tantamount to intellectual suicide. Yet when all this is said, it has to be admitted that Bacon was very much a man of his time, and that the *Opus*

Majus is full of statements that a modern scientist would regard as gross errors and superstitions.

But if Newbold was correct, Bacon was one of the greatest scientists before Newton. He had made a microscope and examined biological cells and spermatozoa – these were the tadpole-drawings in the margins – and had made a telescope long before Galileo; he had even recognized the Andromeda nebula as a spiral galaxy. Newbold translated a caption to what he claimed to be a sketch of the nebula: 'In a concave mirror I saw a star in the form of a snail . . . between the navel of Pegasus, the girdle of Andromeda and the head of Cassiopeia.' (It is known that Bacon understood how to use a concave mirror as a burning-glass.) Newbold declared that he had no idea of what he would find by looking in the region indicated, and was surprised to find that the 'snail' was the Andromeda nebula.

But in *The Codebreakers* cipher expert David Kahn has pointed out one of the basic flaws in Newbold's system. Newbold's method depended on 'doubling up' the letters of a word, so that, for example, 'oritur' became or-ri-it-tu-ur, and this text was solved with the aid of the key word 'conmuto' and the addition of a q. But how would this process be carried out in reverse – in other words, when Bacon was turning his original text into a cipher? Kahn says: 'Many one-way ciphers have been devised; it is possible to put messages into cipher, but not to get them back out. Newbold's seemed to be the only example extant of the reverse situation.'

Newbold died in 1926, only sixty years old; two years later his friend Roland G.Kent published the results of Newbold's labours in *The Cipher of Roger Bacon*. It was widely accepted – for example, by the eminent cultural historian Étienne Gilson.

But one scholar who had been studying Newbold's system was far from convinced. He was Dr John M.Manly, a philologist who headed the department of English at Chicago University, and who had become assistant to the great Herbert Osborne Yardley – described as the greatest codebreaker in history – when US Military Intelligence set up a cryptanalysis department in 1917. Manly had produced the definitive edition of Chaucer in eight volumes, comparing more than eighty versions of the medieval manuscript of the *Canterbury Tales*. One of his most remarkable feats was the deciphering of a letter found in the baggage of a German spy named Lothar Witzke, who was captured in Nogales, Mexico, in 1918. In three days of non-stop application Manly had solved the twelve-step official transposition cipher, with multiple horizontal shiftings of three and four letter groups finally laid out in a vertical transcription. In a military court he was able to read aloud a message from the German minister in Mexico beginning: 'The bearer of this is a subject of the empire who travels as a Russian under the name of Pablo Waberski. He is a German secret agent. . .' It was the spy's death warrant (although President Wilson commuted it to life imprisonment).

Now Manly studied Newbold's *Cipher of Roger Bacon*, and concluded that in spite of his undoubted integrity, Newbold had been deceiving himself. The weak point of the cipher was the anagramming process. Most sentences can be anagrammed into a dozen other sentences, a method by which admirers of Francis Bacon have had no difficulty proving that he wrote the plays of Shakespeare (see Chapter 34). With a sentence involving more than a hundred letters, there is simply no way of guaranteeing that some particular rearrangement provides the only solution – David Kahn points out that the words 'Hail Mary, full of grace, the Lord is with thee' can be anagrammed in thousands of different ways.

Newbold had also made certain 'shorthand signs' a basic part of his system of interpretation. When Manly looked at these through a powerful magnifying glass he found out that they were not 'shorthand' at all, only places where the ink had peeled off the vellum. By the time he had pointed out dozens of cases in which Newbold had allowed his interpretation to be influenced by his own twentieth-century assumptions, Manly had totally demolished Newbold's claim to have solved 'the cipher of Roger Bacon'.

Since that time, 1931, there have been many attempts to decipher the Voynich manuscript. In 1933 a cancer specialist, Dr Leonell C.Strong, published his own fragments of translation, and proved to his own satisfaction that the work was a herbal by an English scholar, Anthony Ascham; he even published a recipe for a contraceptive which apparently works. But Strong failed to explain the method by which he arrived at his translations, so they have never achieved wide acceptance.

William F. Friedman, who organized a whole group of specialists to work on the problem in the last year of the Second World War, was frustrated by the end of the war and the disbandment of his group. But Friedman pointed out that the Voynich manuscript differs from other codes in one basic respect. The inventor of a code attempts to frustrate would-be cryptanalysts by trying to remove repetitions that would give him away (for example, a repeated group of three words would almost certainly be 'and' or 'the'). The Voynich manuscript actually has far more repetitions than an ordinary text. This led Friedman to hypothesize that the text is in some artificial language which, because of a need for simplicity, would inevitably have more repetitions than a highly complex 'natural' language. But this presupposes that Roger Bacon (or whoever wrote the manuscript) was so anxious to conceal his meaning that he went to far greater lengths than even a code-expert would consider reasonable. And for a thirteenth-century monk, who had little reason to fear code-breakers, this seems unlikely. . . .

And this, of course, is the very heart of the mystery. We do not know when the manuscript was written, or by whom, or in what language, but even if we knew the answers to these questions it is difficult to think of any good reason for inventing such a baffling code. The earliest ciphers in the Vatican archive date from 1326 (when Roger Bacon was a boy) and these are merely 'coded' names relating to the struggle between Ghibellines and Guelphs. These were respectively supporters of the Holy Roman Emperor and the Pope; the Ghibellines are called Egyptians and the Guelphs Children of Israel. (It is easy to guess what side the inventor of the code was on.) The earliest Western 'substitution' cipher dates from 1401. The first treatise on codes, the *Polygraphia* of Johannes Trithemius, was not printed until 1518, two years after the death of its author. So it is hard to imagine why Roger Bacon or anyone within a century of his death should have gone to so much trouble to invent a code of such apparent sophistication when something much simpler would have sufficed.

Kahn offers one clue to why the author of a herbal (which is what the Voynich manuscript looks most like) should want to conceal his meaning when he speaks of one of the earliest encipherments, a tiny cuneiform tablet dating from about 1500 BC. 'It contains the earliest known formula for the making of glazes for pottery. The scribe, jealously guarding his professional secret, used cuneiform signs . . . in their least common values.' The author of the Voynich manuscript may have been a highly skilled professional herbalist who wrote down his secrets for his own use and those of his pupils, and was determined to keep them out of the hands of rivals.

This view would have struck the antiquarian bookseller Hans Kraus as altogether too commonplace. When Ethel Voynich died at the age of ninety-six, in 1960, Kraus purchased the manuscript from her executors and put it up for sale at $160,000; he explained that he thought that it could contain information that might provide new insights into the record of man, and that if it could be deciphered it might be worth a million dollars. No one took it at that price, and Kraus finally gave it to Yale University in 1969, where it now lies, awaiting the inspiration of some master-cryptographer.

24 Orffyreus and the Perpetual Motion Machine

The dream of perpetual motion is undoubtedly a delusion. The law of the conservation of energy states that energy cannot be created or destroyed; in other words, you cannot get more energy out of a machine than you put into it. So it is irritating to have to admit that there is one well-authenticated story of a perpetual motion machine that has defied all attempts at explanation. It was invented by a man who called himself Orffyreus, and it is described in the Leipzig *Acta Eruditorum* for 1717.

Its inventor's real name was Johann Ernst Elias Bessler, and he was born in Zittau, Saxony, in 1680. When he decided to choose himself a *nom de guerre* he wrote the alphabet in a circle, then selected the thirteenth letter after each of the letters of Bessler; the result was Orffyre, which he latinized to Orffyreus. Like Leonardo, he seems to have been a man of many talents, and studied theology, medicine and painting as well as mechanics. And in his early thirties he announced that he had discovered the secret of perpetual motion.

Now, perpetual motion *sounds* a practical possibility. Suppose, for example, that you construct an upright wheel, which spins on a well-greased axle. If you stick a very small weight on the top edge of the wheel (say a piece of putty) it will descend by its own weight to the bottom, and will then continue on, through its own momentum, until it comes *very nearly* to the top again. Suppose one could think of some ingenious means to add just that tiny extra push which would carry it over the top, some method of making little weights alter their position on the rim of the wheel, for example. . . But in practice it proves to be impossible without cheating – that is, giving the wheel a tiny extra push.

In 1712 Orffyreus appeared in the town of Gera, in the province of Reuss, and exhibited a 'self-moving wheel'. It was three feet in diameter and four inches thick. When given the slightest push it started up, then quickly worked itself up to a regular speed. Once in motion it was capable of raising a weight of several pounds. And this in itself is incredible. If an empty spacecraft was drifting through space, far from the influence of any star, it would continue moving in a straight line for ever, because there would be nothing to stop it. (This is Newton's first law of motion.) Similarly, if a wheel was given the slightest spin in empty space, it would go on spinning for ever. But it could not be made to do any 'work' – to raise a weight, for example. As soon as its original energy was exhausted, it would stop. Yet according to Orffyreus his wheel could not only keep on spinning for ever, but could also raise weights.

This was done by winding a rope round the axis, with a weight attached to it.

Oddly enough, the burghers of Gera do not seem to have been impressed by his demonstrations. It may be simply that they were not sufficiently mechanically minded to realize that he was offering them an invention that could transform the world. (If rediscovered today, his secret would enable us to dispense with coal, oil and atomic energy.) Or it may have been simply that Orffyreus was a singularly irritating person, self-assertive, boastful and dogmatic. At all events, he made far more enemies than friends, and soon had to move on. He left Gera without regret, and moved to Draschwitz, near Leipzig, where in 1713 he constructed a still larger wheel, this one five feet in diameter and six inches in width; it could turn at 50 revolutions a minute and raise a weight of 40lb. Then he moved again to Merseburg, and constructed a wheel six feet in diameter and a foot thick. A number of local 'learned men' examined his wheel, agreed that it was not moved by any outer force, and signed a certificate to that effect. But this minor triumph moved Orffyreus's enemies to fury. One published a pamphlet offering Orffyreus a thousand thalers if he could make a wheel revolve in a locked room for a month. Another offered to construct a wheel – admittedly a trick – that would do everything that Orffyreus's wheel could do. And J.G.Borlach of Leipzig published a pamphlet in which he demonstrated (what is undoubtedly true) that a perpetual motion machine is against the laws of nature.

In that same year, 1716, Orffyreus left Merseburg for the small independent state of Hesse-Cassel, in which he was to score his greatest triumph. Here at last his luck seemed to change. The reigning Landgrave (or Count), whose name was Karl, was sufficiently impressed by the homeless inventor to make him a town councillor and offer him rooms in the ducal castle at Weissenstein. (Half a century later another wandering inventor, the Count de Saint-Germain – see Chapter 32 – would be taken under the protection of yet another Duke Karl of Hesse-Cassel.) And during the year 1717 he constructed at the castle his largest wheel so far, this one being twelve feet in diameter and fourteen inches thick. In spite of its size, it was fairly light-weight. It was described in a letter to Sir Isaac Newton by a Professor 'sGravesande of Leyden,

> . . . a hollow wheel, or kind of drum .. covered over with canvas, to prevent the inside from being seen .. I have examined the axles and am firmly persuaded that nothing from without the wheel in the least contributes to its motion. When I turned it but gently, it always stood still as soon as I took away my hand. . . .

When set in motion, the wheel revolved twenty-five or twenty-six times a minute. An 'Archimedean screw for raising water' could be attached to its axle by means of a rope; in that case the speed dropped to twenty revolutions a minute.

The wheel remained on exhibition in the castle for several months, and was examined by many learned men, who all concluded that there could be no deception. Then on 31 October 1717 Orffyreus was requested to transfer the wheel to another room in the castle presumably a larger one, 'where there were no contiguous walls'. On 12 November the Landgrave and various officials came to look at the wheel, observed it in motion for a while, then watched as the doors and windows of the room were tightly sealed, in such a way that no one could enter without leaving traces behind. Two weeks later the seals were broken and the room opened; the wheel was still revolving. The door was resealed, and this time it remained closed until 4 January 1718. The wheel was still revolving at twenty-six revolutions per minute.

Deeply impressed, his doubts now laid at rest, the Landgrave asked Orffyreus how much he wanted for his secret and turned pale when Orffyreus replied, 'Twenty thousand pounds.' It was his greatest invention and his life's work, he reminded them, and he deserved adequate compensation. The Landgrave and his retinue of scientists was inclined to agree, but he didn't have that much money to hand. Baron Fischer, architect to the Emperor of Austria, pointed out that it should be easy to raise the money in London, and accordingly wrote to Dr J.T. Desaguliers of the Royal Society. The arrangement he proposed was that if the movement of the wheel should prove to be 'a perpetual one', then the £20,000 should be given to the inventor; if not, the money would be returned.

Meanwhile Professor 'sGravesande had made a thorough examination of the axle of the machine, and wrote a report to the effect that as far as he could see there was no way in which the wheel could be a fake. Unfortunately, the paranoid inventor suspected that 'sGravesande was asked to examine the axle in the hope of discovering the secret without paying for it. Orffyreus exploded. He locked himself in the room, and smashed the wheel. Then he wrote a message on the wall, declaring that it was the impertinent curiosity of 'sGravesande that had provoked him.

And now, regrettably, Orffyreus and his machine vanish into obscurity. If Orffyreus had lived a century later he would have been pursued by prying journalists, and we would have a detailed history of the rest of his life. But these were the days before the invention of newspapers, and all we know is that Orffyreus was rebuilding his machine ten years later, in 1727, and that 'sGravesande had agreed to examine it again. But there is no record that it was ever tested. All we know is that Orffyreus died in 1745, at the age of sixty-five. And his secret, whatever it was, died with him.

The mystery here is surely psychological rather than scientific. If we accept that energy cannot be created or destroyed, then we must conclude that the wheel was a fraud, no matter how well its inventor succeeded in concealing it. Orffyreus, according to one contemporary, had been a clockmaker at some point, and we must assume that he had found some method of concealing a spring mechanism somewhere in the supports. We may assume that other explanations such as that a man was concealed inside it are ruled out by the crucial test in which the machine was left in a locked room for three months.

Yet if we assume that Orffyreus was a fraud, the puzzle remains. What could he hope to gain from it? There was no way in which he could have absconded with the £20,000, for as we can see from Baron Fischer's letter, the money would not even be handed over unless they were first satisfied that he had genuinely discovered the principle of perpetual motion.

It must also be admitted that Orffyreus's character makes it seem unlikely that he was a straightforward swindler. Charm and smoothness are an essential part of the equipment of the confidence man; and while there is no guarantee that paranoia and bad temper are a sign of genius, there is no denying that we find it hard to associate such characteristics with a deliberate confidence trickster. They are more likely to be accompanied by a certain obsessive quality, a conviction of one's own remarkable talents. It is easier to believe that Orffyreus was a self-deceiver than that he was a crook. But could a self-deceiver construct a wheel that would run for three months in a locked room?

On the other hand, let us suppose that Orffyreus was a man with a grudge – a man who was quite certain about his own genius, but who resented his lack of recognition. It *is* conceivable that in a mood of rage and contempt he decided to practise a deliberate swindle, and then use the money to devote the rest of his life to his researches. How could he hope to carry out such a swindle?

A careful study of the case suggests some possible answers. Orffyreus himself published a pamphlet, typically entitled *The Triumphant Orffyrean Perpetual Motion* (1719), in which he offers an exceedingly obscure account of his basic principles. He admits that his wheel depends upon weights, which 'constitute the perpetual motion itself, since from them is received the universal movement which they must exercise so long as they remain out of the centre of gravity'. These weights, he says, are so placed that they can 'never obtain equilibrium'. Professors who examined his machine described being able to hear the movements of about eight weights, presumably placed on the rim of the wheel. This principle is known as the 'overbalancing wheel', and has been the mainstay of inventors who have tried to produce perpetual motion. The basic idea can be seen in Rupert Gould's drawing. If in fact the wheel has two rims, one inside the other, and some ingenious inventor could devise a method for transferring the weights automatically from one rim to another, then the problem of perpetual motion would be solved. As they transfer to the outer rim, they cause it to outweigh the weights on the inner rim on the opposite side, so that side of the wheel descends. As it begins to rise again under its own momentum the 'grabs' – or whatever – transfer the weight on to the inner rim, and since they are now closer to the centre, they become in effect lighter than those on the descending outer rim, and rise to the top of the wheel, where they are again transferred to the outer rim. It sounds foolproof.

But the Marquis of Worcester (who originally thought of the idea) overlooked one basic point. The outer rim is of course longer than the inner one, so there are less weights on the descending rim than on the other side. (In Gould's drawing, it can be seen that there are twenty weights on one side of the wheel compared to eighteen on the other.) So the two sides exactly counterbalance one another, and the wheel soon comes to a halt.

But this is not a point that would immediately strike anybody who studied a drawing or model of the overbalancing wheel. And it is conceivable that Orffyreus may have reckoned on this in deceiving the Landgrave and his wise men. We may suppose that he secreted some kind of powerful clockspring inside the supports of his machine, with a cog-wheel that turned the axle. When the time came to hand over his secret he would remove the canvas cover

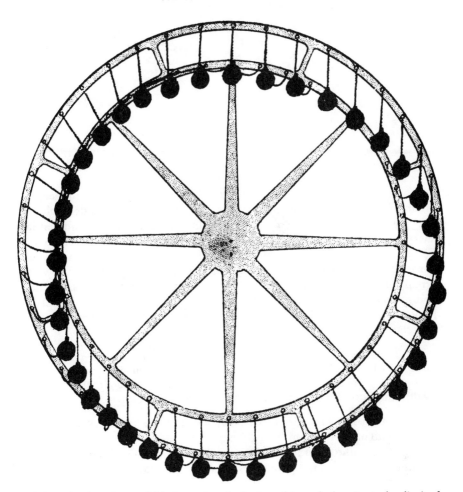

of the wheel and reveal his ingeniously designed 'overbalancing wheel'. And unless the savants were extremely astute, or had given long consideration to the problem, they would agree that Orffyreus had indeed solved the problem of perpetual motion in an absurdly simple way. And by the time they dismantled the wheel and found the clock-spring mechanism, Orffyreus would be a hundred miles away.

But there is also an objection to this explanation. It is easy to design a modern clock or watch that will run for a year, because the 'moving parts' are so light that they can be driven by a tiny battery. But a twelve-foot wheel with weights round the rim would require a great deal more energy: a heavy-duty car battery might do it, but a clock-spring that would drive such a wheel for two months would have to be enormous. There is no obvious room inside Orffyreus's wheel for such a spring. And unless Orffyreus had invented the principle of the dynamo a century and a half before Faraday, there seems to be no other possibility. And so we are left once more with the tantalizing possibility that perhaps Orffyreus *did* stumble upon some simple but profound secret that has eluded all his successors.

25 The 'People of the Secret'

Early in 1883 a book called *Esoteric Buddhism* caused an immediate sensation, and quickly went into a second edition. It was by a slender, balding little man called Alfred Percy Sinnett, editor of India's most influential newspaper the *Pioneer*. What caused the excitement was Sinnett's claim, on the very first page, that he had obtained his information from 'hidden masters', men who lived in the high mountains of Tibet and who were virtually immortal. Coming from the editor of a newspaper that was regarded as the mouthpiece of the British government in India, this could not be dismissed as 'occultist' lunacy. Such a man deserved serious attention when he declared:

For reasons that will appear as the present explanations proceed, the very considerable block of hitherto secret teaching this volume contains, has been conveyed to me, not only without conditions of the usual kind, but to the express end that I might convey it in my turn to the world at large.

Many people took Sinnett very seriously indeed. The poet W.B. Yeats read the book and handed it to his friend Charles Johnston, who was so impressed that he rushed off to London for permission to set up a Dublin branch of the Theosophical Society, the publishers of Sinnett's book.

It was almost three years later that the general public learned how Sinnett had obtained his 'hitherto secret teaching', and the sceptics felt confirmed in their cynicism. In October 1880 Sinnett and his wife had played host to that remarkable lady Madame Blavatsky, who told him that most of her knowledge had been obtained from her 'secret Masters' who lived in the Himalayas. She convinced Sinnett of her genuineness by a series of minor miracles. On a picnic, when an unexpected guest had turned up, she ordered another guest to dig in the hillside with a table knife; he unearthed a cup and saucer of the same pattern as the rest of the china. When a woman remarked casually that she wished she could find a lost brooch Madame Blavatsky told the other guests to go and search in the garden; the missing brooch was found in a flower-bed wrapped in paper. And when Sinnett expressed his desire to correspond directly with the 'Masters' Madame Blavatsky promised to do what she could, and a few days later Sinnett found lying in his desk the first of what were to become known as 'the Mahatma letters'. It was from this series of letters that Sinnett obtained his knowledge of 'esoteric Buddhism'.

Unfortunately, this information about the Mahatma letters was revealed in a report on Theosophy published by the Society for Psychical Research towards the end of 1885, and the rest of the report was damning. It was the result of an investigation by a young man named Richard Hodgson, who had talked to Madame Blavatsky's housekeepers and learned that most of the 'miracles' were fraudulent; their most convincing demonstration was to cause a letter – addressed to Hodgson and referring to the conversation they had only just had – to fall out of the air above his head. Hodgson's report had the effect of totally destroying Madame Blavatsky's credibility, and demolishing the myth of the 'hidden Masters' in Tibet.

Having said all this, it is necessary to admit that there are still a number of things to be said in Madame Blavatsky's favour. The evidence of many observers shows that she was undoubtedly a genuine 'spirit medium'. Constance Wachtmeister, a countess who became Madame Blavatsky's factotum in 1884, found it at first a little unnerving. She was sharing a room (divided by a screen) with Madame Blavatsky, and as soon as Madame was asleep the raps would begin, continuing at intervals of ten minutes until about 6 a.m. A lamp was burning by Madame Blavatsky's bed; on one of the first nights the countess was kept awake and slipped behind the screen to extinguish it. She had only just got back into bed when the lamp was relit. Madame Blavatsky was obviously asleep, and in any case the countess would have heard the scrape of a match or tinder box. Three times she extinguished it; three times it promptly relit itself. The raps also continued. The third time she put it out, she saw a disembodied brown hand turning up the wick. She woke Madame Blavatsky, who looked pale and shaken, and explained that she had been 'with the Masters' and that it was dangerous to awaken her suddenly.

Charles Johnston describes how he sat watching HPB (as her admirers called her), tapping her fingers idly on a table-top. Then she raised her hand a foot or so above the table and continued the tapping movement; the sounds continued to come from the table. Then she turned towards Johnston, and began to send the 'astral taps' on to the back of his hand. 'I could both feel and hear them. It was something like taking sparks from the prime conductor of an electric machine; or, better still, perhaps, it was like spurting quicksilver through your fingers.'

It is of course possible that all this was fraudulent; but it seems unlikely. If we can accept the hypothesis that there are genuine mediums that is, mediums who either possess, or are possessed by, certain 'magical' powers then it seems fairly certain that Madame Blavatsky was such a person. And if we can accept that there are genuine mediums, then the next question is whether their powers are the result of some mysterious activity of the unconscious mind, or whether they involve some external force – some emanation of the 'collective unconscious', or even 'spirits'. Most students of the paranormal end up by conceding (however reluctantly) that there does seem to be some external force, although understandably many of them find it impossible to concede the existence of spirits.

The psychiatrist Wilson Van Dusen, who studied hundreds of patients suffering from hallucinations in the Mendocino State Hospital, reached the remarkable conclusion that the nature of the hallucinations had been accurately described by the eighteenth-century mystic Emanuel Swedenborg.

They seemed to fall into two types, which he calls 'higher order' and 'lower order'. Lower-order hallucinations seemed to be stupid and repetitive; they 'are similar to drunken bums at a bar who like to tease and torment just for the fun of it'. But higher-order hallucinations seemed 'more likely to be symbolic, religious, supportive, genuinely instructive'. A gas-fitter experienced a higher-order hallucination of a beautiful woman who showed him thousands of symbols. Van Dusen was able to hold a dialogue with this 'woman', with the help of the patient, and after the conversation the patient asked for just one clue to what they had been talking about.

If we can accept this much, then we can also see that Madame Blavatsky's 'secret masters' may not have been her own invention. She told Constance Wachtmeister that the raps that resounded from above her bed were a 'psychic telegraph' that linked her to the Masters, who watched over her body while she slept. If we are willing to concede that the Masters may have been what Swedenborg calls 'angels', or what Van Dusen calls higher-order hallucinations, then it suddenly ceases to be self-evident that HPB was an old fraud. We have at least to consider the hypothesis that *something* was going on which is slightly more complicated.

Madame Blavatsky was not the inventor of the idea of secret masters; the notion is part of an ancient 'occult' tradition. The composer Cyril Scott, who was also an 'occultist', writes in his *Outline of Modern Occultism* (1935) of the basic tenets of 'Occult science':

Firstly, the occultist holds that Man is in process of evolving from comparative imperfection to much higher states of physical and spiritual evolution. Secondly, that the evolutionary process in all its phases is directed by a Great Hierarchy of Intelligences who have themselves reached these higher states.

Now, many modern thinkers would agree that man is involved in an evolutionary process that involves his mind as well as his body, and many would insist that the process is not entirely a matter of Darwinian mechanisms (see, for example, the contributors to Arthur Koestler's *Beyond Reductionism*). But it is clearly a very long step from this kind of evolutionism to the belief that the evolutionary process is being directed by 'higher intelligences'.

Such a step was, in fact, taken (on purely scientific grounds) by the cybernetician David Foster, in his book *The Intelligent Universe*. Foster's basic assertion is simply that, to the eye of the cyberneticist, evolution seems to suggest some intelligent intervention. Cybernetics is basically the science of making machines behave as if they are intelligent – as does, for example, a modern washing machine, which performs a number of complex processes, heating water up to a certain temperature, washing the clothes for a certain period, rinsing them, spin-drying, etc. But these processes are 'programmed' into the machine, and can be selected by merely turning a dial, or inserting a kind of plastic biscuit – each of whose edges contains a different programme – into a slot. An acorn could be regarded as a device containing the programme for an oak-tree. But to the eye of a cybernetician the acorn, like the plastic biscuit, suggests some form of programming. Could an acorn be programmed solely by Darwinian natural selection? Foster points out that one basic rule about computer-programming is that the intelligence that does the programming must be of a higher, more complex, order than the programme itself. Similarly, in order to drive a car or use an electric typewriter my mind must work faster than the machine; if the machine goes faster than my mind, the result will be disaster or confusion. In cybernetics, blue light could be a programme for red light, but not vice versa on the same principle that Dickens can create Mr Pickwick, but a Mr Pickwick could not create a Dickens. And Foster argues that the energies involved in programming DNA would need to be higher than any form of energy found on earth. He argues that the process would require energies of the same order as cosmic rays. Such an argument obviously implies that the complexity of life on earth can only be accounted for by some intelligence 'out there'.

We may reject this argument, pointing out that 'instinct' may create a complexity that looks like superintelligence. Mathematical prodigies, who can work out problems of bewildering complexity within seconds, are often of otherwise low intelligence. There is no evolutionary necessity for the human brain to work out such problems; so why *has* the brain developed such a power? The physiologist would reply: as a kind of by-product, just as a simple calculating device like an abacus could be used to multiply numbers far beyond the grasp of the human imagination. But those who believe that evolution is basically purposive use such examples as mathematical prodigies to argue that the evolution of man's higher faculties cannot be explained in purely Darwinian terms.

Since Madame Blavatsky (who died in 1891) there have been many 'occultists' (I use the word in its broadest sense, as meaning those who are interested in the paranormal) who have believed that they were in contact with higher intelligences. Alice Bailey became an active member of the Theosophical Society after the death of Madame Blavatsky, and was convinced she was in touch with Sinnett's 'Mahatma' (it means 'great soul') Koot Hoomi. In 1919, disgusted by the power struggles within the society, she founded her own group, and produced a large number of books dictated by an entity called 'the Tibetan'.

The Rev. Stainton Moses, an early member of the Society for Psychical Research, used 'automatic writing' to produce large quantities of a script that was published after his death under the title *Spirit Teachings*. Although Moses published extracts from these in *Light*, he was too embarrassed to admit that some of the 'spirits' who dictated them claimed to be Plato, Aristotle and half a dozen Old Testament prophets. Yet there was strong evidence that these scripts were not simply the product of his own unconscious mind. On one occasion Moses asked the 'spirit' if it would go to the bookcase, select the last book but one on the second shelf, and read out the last paragraph on page 94. The spirit did this correctly. Moses was still not convinced, so the spirit selected its own book. It dictated a passage about Pope, then told Moses precisely where to find it; when Moses took the book off the shelf, it opened at the right page. The spirit dictated these passages while the books remained closed on the shelf.

In 1963 two Americans, Jane Roberts and her husband Rob, began experimenting with an ouija board, inspired to some extent by 'Patience Worth' (see Chapter 42). Various personalities identified themselves and gave messages; then after a while a character who identified himself as 'Seth' began to come through:

It was immediately apparent that the board's messages had suddenly increased in scope and quality. We found ourselves dealing with a personality who was of superior intelligence, a personality with a distinctive humor, one who always displayed outstanding psychological insight and knowledge that was certainly beyond our own conscious abilities.

'Seth' went on to dictate a number of books, with titles like *The Seth Material* and *Seth Speaks*, which achieved tremendous popularity. They certainly demonstrate that Seth, whether an aspect of Jane Roberts's unconscious mind or a genuine 'spirit', was of a high level of intelligence. Yet when Jane Roberts produced a book that purported to be the after-death journal of the philosopher William James, it was difficult to take it seriously. James's works are noted for their vigour and clarity of style; Jane Roberts's 'communicator' writes like an undergraduate:

Yet, what a rambunctious nationalistic romp, and it was matched with almost missionary fervour by the psychologists, out to root from man's soul all of those inconsistencies and passions that were buried there; and to leash these as well for the splendid pursuits of progress, industry and the physical manipulation of nature for man's use.

There is a clumsiness here that is quite unlike James's swift-moving, colloquial prose. 'And to leash these as well. . .' is simply not William James; he would simply have said 'And to harness these..'

Yet Seth himself often says things of immense and profound importance – for example, his emphasis (in *The Nature of Personal Reality*) on the importance of the conscious mind and conscious decision.

I quite realise that many of my statements will contradict the beliefs of those of you who accept the idea that the conscious mind is relatively powerless, and that the answers to problems lie hidden beneath – i.e., in the 'unconscious'. Obviously the conscious mind is a phenomenon, not a thing. It is ever-changing. It can be concentrated or turned by the ego in literally endless directions. It can view outward reality or turn inward, observing its own contents. . . . It is far more flexible than you give it credit for.

Comments like these are so opposed to our familiar dogmas about the unconscious and the 'solar plexus' that they make an impact of startling freshness. This is not the usual diffuse verbiage of 'inspirational' writing, but the communication of a vision into the powers of the mind. If Seth is an aspect of Jane Roberts, then she is a philosopher of considerable insight.

The experience of the Londoner Tony Neate is typical of the 'psychic' who finds himself 'in communication' with Van Dusen's 'higher order hallucinations'. In 1950, at the age of twenty, he began as a sceptic playing with a primitive form of ouija board, a glass on a polished table-top; the glass flew off the table with such violence that it knocked a man over backward. He began to practise psychometry – receiving 'pictures' from objects that are held in the hand – and found that his visions of the history of such objects were often accurate. One day when he was practising psychometry he went into a trance, and 'spirits' spoke through him. A 'spirit' who claimed to be Freud quoted a German book giving the exact page; Tony Neate was able to track down the book in the London Library and found the quotation accurate. A spirit who claimed to be the singer Melba told of a concert she had given in Brussels; again, the statement was found to be accurate.

Then, during the Christmas of 1955, Tony Neate found himself tuned in to a character who called himself Helio-Arcanophus (H-A for short), who claimed to be an inhabitant of Atlantis – the name means high priest of the sun. Tony Neate and his associates founded a society called the Atlanteans, and they moved into a farm complex in West Malvern. The writer Annie Wilson spent some time there, and her book about her experiences, *Where There's Love*, makes it clear that, like Seth, 'H-A' has many important and some original things to say. Reading these utterances, it is natural for the sceptic to assume that they originate in the unconscious mind of Tony Neate. But if that is the case, then how can we explain the Freud quotation and the information obtained from 'Melba'? And if we are willing to admit that this information was obtained 'paranormally' or that *any* information can be obtained paranormally, as in the case of the Glastonbury scripts (see *Time in Disarray*) then it is obviously possible that the same applies to the utterances of Seth and Helio-Arcanophus.

Not all 'occult teachings' claim to originate with disembodied entities; others are accompanied by the claim that they have been preserved down the ages by secret societies or brotherhoods. George Gurdjieff, one of the most original thinkers of the twentieth century, spent much of his youth in search of a certain 'Sarmoung Brotherhood', and claimed to have received his basic teachings from a monastic brotherhood in the northern Himalayas. The essence of Gurdjieff's teaching consists in the notion that ordinary consciousness is a form of 'sleep', that nearly all human activities are entirely 'mechanical', and that if man wishes to cease to be mechanical he has to make a tremendous effort of will. But books like *In Search of the Miraculous* (by Gurdjieff's leading follower P.D.Ouspensky) make it clear that behind Gurdjieff's 'psychological' teachings lay a highly complex cosmological system, which has no obvious relevance to the psychological teachings, and which it seems unlikely that Gurdjieff invented himself.

This cosmology is further elaborated in the four-volume work of another leading Gurdjieff follower, J.G.Bennett, *The Dramatic Universe*, which is founded on the assertion that 'there is a class of cosmic essences called Demiurges that is responsible for maintaining the universal order', and that these Demiurgic Intelligences 'work upon time scales far exceeding the span of a human life'. Bennett calls the universe 'dramatic' to underline his sense of the importance of free will; because the universe is not dead and predetermined, the final outcome is uncertain. 'The key to the whole scheme is will-time or Hyparxis. This is the region in which the will is free to make decisions that introduce something new and *uncaused* into the world process.' The demiurges have far greater power than man to introduce something new and uncaused into the world process; but they are not infallible. Although their main task is 'to guide the evolution of the world from its first lifeless beginning', they have 'guided the process by experiment and trial, sometimes making mistakes and retracing their steps, sometimes making great leaps forward, as when life came out of the ocean and land creatures began.' Bennett adds that Gurdjieff calls the demiurges 'angels', 'but this had so many meanings that it is best avoided'.

The existence of a secret tradition of hidden teachings is hinted at in Idries Shah's book *The Sufis*, and it was in a review of this book in the *London Evening News* that its literary editor, Edward Campbell, wrote:

For many centuries there has been a strange legend in the East. It suggests that in some hidden centre, perhaps in the Highlands of Central Asia, there exists a colony of men possessing exceptional powers. This centre acts, in some respects at least, as the secret government of the world.

Some aspects of this legend came to the West during the Crusades; the idea was renewed in Rosicrucian guise in 1614; it was restated with variations last century by Mme Blavatsky and the French diplomat Jacoliot; was suggested again by the English author Talbot Mundy, and most recently by the Mongolian traveller Ossendowski in 1918.

In the mysterious Shangri-la of this legend, certain men, evolved beyond the ordinary human situation, act as the regents of powers beyond this planet.

Through lower echelons – who mingle unsuspected in ordinary walks of life, both East and West – they act at critical stages of history, contriving results necessary to keep the whole evolution of the earth in step with events in the solar system.

And in his book *The People of the Secret* (1983), Campbell (under the punning pseudonym Ernest Scott) goes on to suggest that 'in the first quarter of the 20th century, Western science had not only reached a critical stage but an impasse and that, simultaneously, material possibly capable of resolving that situation appeared unobtrusively from the East'. He goes on to suggest that 'this interpretation derives from a source superior to, and qualitatively different from, ordinary intellect', and that 'similar "intervention" occurs at critical points in human history and has done so in all cultures and all ages in a form appropriate to the moment'. Campbell refers to the sources of this influence as 'the Tradition', and suggests that between 1920 and 1950 part of the intention appears to have been to 'reveal publicly *the mechanism of the Tradition's own operation*'. And he mentions that two men who were in contact with 'the Tradition' were J.G.Bennett and Rodney Collin, both followers of Gurdjieff.

Campbell goes on to suggest a close analogy between the human organism and a civilized culture.

A sperm cell originates a new individual. Suppose a conscious man originates a new culture. Suppose that within life there are a few men, unsuspected and hidden, who are able to process conscious energy and are therefore in touch with the pattern of conscious energy outside life. (In J.G.Bennett's terminology this would correspond to the Demiurgic level.) Such conscious men would be to a human culture as a sperm cell is to tissue cells in the human body.

Campbell then sketches out the 'cultural systems' outlined by Rodney Collin in his book *The Theory of Celestial Influence* (Chapter XVI): Aurignacian man, Magdalenian man, Middle and Far Eastern Man (Egypt, Sumer, Ancient India), Graeco-Roman Man, Early Christian Man, Mediaeval Christian Man, Renaissance Man, Modern Man. In this scheme Egypt gave birth to the world of the Greeks, and the Greeks transmitted the 'energy of fertilization' to Rome via the philosophy of the Stoics and Epicureans. 'Again a period of dazzling achievement seemingly from nowhere.' Early Christianity sprang out of Rome, but by the eighth century had fossilized into the corrupt church of the mediaeval papacy. The next culture, according to Campbell, is the medieval church, which originated in Cluny, whose Gothic cathedral 'encapsulated all the Gothic cathedrals to come'. 'In each of these there was a suggestion of a whole unseen cosmology; each an encyclopedia in stone containing, for those who could read . . . a summary of the Plan and Purpose of evolution.' Campbell clearly agrees with the author of *The Mystery of the Cathedrals* (see Chapter 11) that Gothic cathedrals were alchemical textbooks. The medieval masons were exponents of 'the Tradition'. Campbell also notes that this was also the period of 'esoteric building in Islam', and mentions the joint mission from Cluny and Chartres to Saracen Spain, which returned with knowledge of logarithms, algebra and alchemy.

This was the preparation for the next major stage: the Renaissance. And Renaissance culture finally gave way to the modern epoch around the mid-nineteenth century – Campbell mentions 1859, the year of *The Origin of Species*. Our modern age, Campbell suggests, reached the peak of its development about 1935 with road and air transport and radio and cinema – and indeed, we can see that these developments transformed the mental outlook of the human race just as the invention of printing did in the Renaissance. The modern epoch may well continue for another six or seven hundred years; but the new epoch that will replace it will struggle into being long before our own period comes to an end.

Campbell's starting-point, then, is the 'Demiurgic intelligences' of J.G.Bennett. He assumes that these are a reality, and that their activities can be seen in human history. From the point of view of this 'Hidden Directorate', early Christianity took the wrong turning. He sees the mission of Jesus as an event of universal significance, an attempt to introduce certain energies into the evolutionary process – the energies of a selfless love. Campbell suggests that the Early Fathers 'rejected the wisdom component within which lay the techniques of developing consciousness'. They reasoned that nothing is necessary for spiritual evolution except the Christ. The 'heretic' Arius felt instinctively that this was a mistake. His heresy consisted of the assertion that the Son was *not* the equal of the Father – a dim recognition that Jesus had been 'sent' into history at a particular time for a particular purpose. When the Council of Nicaea rejected this view in AD 325, they turned their back on the

'Demiurgic Tradition'. 'Yet', says Campbell,

Demiurgic responsibility for evolution remained. The Demiurges were still obligated to achieve evolutionary gains, in harmony with growth beyond the earth. Their agents, the Hidden Directorate on earth, were still required to contrive the social environment which would provide the necessary opportunities. The mandate of both is to raise the level of consciousness of mankind in general and of suitable individuals exceptionally. Mankind in the West had subconsciously decided that this was no longer necessary.

The coming of Mohammed once again allowed the Demiurges a foothold. A 'school' for the oral transmission of his ideas formed around him. 'This inner group of 90 took an oath of fidelity and are said to have adopted the name Sufi.' (A moment later, Campbell confuses the issue by stating that this is not to say that Sufism derives from Mohammedanism, and that the Sufic tradition actually goes back through Plato, Hippocrates, Pythagoras and Hermes Trismegistos. But the main thrust of his argument is clear.) In due course the Arabs invaded Spain, and planted the seeds that would become the Renaissance.

Campbell's chapter on 'Rome, Christianity and Islam' contains a clear example of what he means by Demiurgic intervention in human history. The monasteries of western Europe, which preserved learning during the Dark Ages, were too remote and inaccessible to serve as real cultural centres. But St Patrick's conversion of Ireland – beginning in AD 432 – caused 'the rebirth of Celtic culture by a "shock" from Christianity'. Ireland became a centre of learning – so much so that in 550 a ship had to be chartered to carry scholars from Gaul to Cork. Celtic Christianity valued pagan literature. St Columba and his pupil Columbanus directed the missionary flow back to Europe, and Columbanus founded more than a hundred monasteries. Rome finally brought the Celtic Church to heel in 664 at the Synod of Whitby, but the impulse could not be destroyed. Two Celtic monks were established as dispensers of wisdom at the court of Charlemagne. Campbell makes the fascinating suggestion that the Celtic Church obtained some of its wisdom through 'psychokinetic techniques'. Psychokinesis is the term invented by students of parapsychology for 'mind over matter', and Campbell suggests elsewhere in the book that this is the basic secret of alchemy; it is not quite clear how he believes the Celtic Church used these techniques.

In the ninth century, says Campbell, schools of initiates began to flourish in Córdoba and Toledo, and their efforts were to have far-reaching influences, which can still be traced in the world today. The doctor Al Razi and the scholar Avicenna, both Persians, were only two of an immense number of scholars who 'provided the raw material for the coming injection of intellect into Europe'. Among these intellectual impulses were the schools of thought that would later become known as Freemasonry and Illuminism, 'impulses which at their seventh harmonic were to encompass the French Revolution'.

The next five chapters of *The People of the Secret* are an interpretation of European history from the 'interventionist' point of view. They consider the Kabbalah, the Tarot and alchemy as vehicles of 'the Tradition', and study the historical significance of Catharism, the rise of the Troubadors, and the legends of King Arthur. Again and again, Campbell traces the original seed of these movements back to their Sufic origins.

In the chapter on Gurdjieff, Campbell comments:

Since the early 1950s, a great deal of hitherto unknown material has become available, and in the nature of things this cannot have happened by accident. If it has leaked, it is because those in charge of it have decided to 'leak' it.

Separately, the various hints amount to little. Taken together, they suggest for the first time the nature of the organisation, long suspected but never identified, which is concerned with injecting developmental possibilities into the historical process at certain critical points.

On the basis of internal evidence, it may be legitimate to suggest that this organisation is the expression of one of the Centres inferred by J.G.Bennett as directing the evolution of the whole human race. In *The Dramatic Universe*, the Centres of Transformation are the four hypothetical regions where, 35,000 to 40,000 years ago, the human mind was endowed with creativity and man became *Homo sapiens sapiens*. Twelve thousand years ago, these Centres withdrew for some 80 generations to prepare for the debut of modern man. The suggestion is that one of these, immediately responsible for the West, has decided to come, partially at least, into the open in the second half of the 20th century. It may be that the intellectual development of the West is now at such a stage that the parent can only guide the offspring further by taking it into its confidence.

Campbell mentions that attempts by Gurdjieff's pupils to make contact with the monasteries or other teaching centres where Gurdjieff gained his 'occult' knowledge were all unsuccessful.

In the 1930s it is believed that Ouspensky made contact with the Mevlevi (Order Dervishes) and asked them to send someone to England. This they declined to do, but indicated that they were prepared to receive a representative from him. One of Ouspensky's senior pupils was ready to leave for the East in 1939 when War broke out and the project was abandoned.

But in 1961 a journalist seeking material for an article on Sufi practices 'was unaccountably introduced to every facility for getting material . . . This journalist, Omar Burke, found himself allowed to visit a secret Dervish community whose location has been identified as Kunji Zagh ("Raven's Corner") in Baluchistan.' Burke then wrote up his findings in an article in *Blackwood's Magazine* in December 1961. It was seen by a member of a London Gurdjieff group who realized that one trail to Gurdjieff's source was being openly revealed in a magazine. But when the London group made contact with the 'source' they were told that it would be pointless to come to Baluchistan because the current focus of activity was in England.

Campbell argues that Gurdjieff's 'source' was the Sufic tradition. What is implied, presumably, by the comment about the 'current focus' in London is that this is to be found in the group run by Idries Shah, author of the book *The Sufis*. Bennett had in fact handed over his own teaching centre at Coombe Springs to Shah. In his autobiography *Witness* Bennett describes how in 1962 he was told by an old friend about Idries Shah, who had come to England from Afghanistan to seek out followers of Gurdjieff and 'complete their teaching'. At a meeting with Shah his first impressions were unfavourable.

He was restless, smoked incessantly, talked too much, and seemed too intent on making a good impression. Halfway through the evening our attitude completely changed. We recognised that he was not only an unusually gifted man, but that he had the indefinable something that marks the man who has seriously worked upon himself.

Shah, he says, did not claim to be a teacher, but he claimed to have been sent by his own teacher, and that 'he had the support of the "Guardians of the Tradition." ' He goes on to quote a document Shah gave him, 'Declaration of the People of the Tradition', which stated that a 'secret, special, superior form of knowledge' really exists, and could be transmitted

to the people to whom this material is addressed . . .This knowledge is concentrated, administered and presided over by three forms of individual . . . They have been called an 'Invisible Hierarchy' because normally they are not in communication or contact with ordinary human beings: certainly not in two-way communication with them.

Bennett then goes on to tell how he was persuaded by Shah to hand over Coombe Springs, with no strings attached, and a note of bitterness creeps in when he describes how Shah sold the house for £100,000 only a year later. Yet it remains clear that in spite of a certain personal animosity towards Shah, Bennett still does not discount the possibility that he is precisely what he says he is.

In any case, Campbell's thesis does not stand or fall by whether the reader is willing to accept Idries Shah as a representative of 'the secret people'. It was Bennett himself who invented the phrase 'the Hidden Directorate' in *The Dramatic Universe*. Campbell summarizes the thesis of his book:

The script for the long human story was written by intelligences much greater than man's own . . . Responsibility for this process on Earth lies with an Intelligence which has been called The Hidden Directorate. This may correspond to the level symbolised in occult legend as an Individual (*eg* 'The Regent' or 'The Ancient of Days', etc). It is to be equated either with the Demi-Urgic level or with the level immediately below.

Side by side with action on humanity-in-the-mass, the Executive and its subordinates are concerned with local attempts to raise the conscious level of individual men exceptionally.

Such specially selected ordinary individuals may aspire to qualify for participation in the work of the Executive. The process by which they may so qualify is the Magnum Opus – the 'Great Work'.This is equivalent to a vertical ascent to a higher level as opposed to a gradual rise with the evolutionary tide.

In 1857 an American schoolmistress and authoress, Delia Bacon, produced her controversial work *Philosophy of the Plays of Shakespeare Unfolded* (see Chapter 34) in which she suggested that 'Shakespeare' was actually a group of Elizabethan scholars, probably led by Francis Bacon, whose aim was to express new ideas that would otherwise have led to torture and imprisonment. The book was received with derision, and Delia Bacon went insane and died soon after. Campbell expresses the same theory at two points in *The People of the Secret*, and sceptics will undoubtedly feel that his whole thesis deserves the same reception as Delia Bacon's. The commonsense objection is that men who represented turning-points in human history – Mohammed, Cosimo de' Medici, Darwin, Einstein – were obviously not members of some 'Hidden Directorate'. And if no 'hidden directorate' is needed to explain their existence or their impact on history, then why bother to entertain such an unnecessary hypothesis?

On the other hand, cultural historians have often observed how certain ideas seem to be 'in the air' at certain times, and the Germans coined a word to express this phenomenon, the *Zeitgeist*. Every major discovery and invention seems to have been made by at least two people at the same time (evolution, photography, relativity, sound-recording, television). The biologist Rupert Sheldrake has even produced a theory ('morphic resonance') arguing that once *any* difficult process has been achieved, from crystallization of a new substance to the creation of a new idea, it 'spreads' like a wave on the surface of a pond, facilitating the process wherever it occurs. Again, Jung's idea of synchronicity (see Chapter 36) suggests some connection between the mind and the world of physical matter which finds no support in the western philosophy of science. Such ideas indicate a movement away from the 'dead' universe of nineteenth-century science and towards the 'intelligent universe' posited by Dr David Foster. It could be argued that a 'hidden directorate', responsible for evolution, is only a logical extension of this idea.

Campbell mentions Yeats's book *A Vision* as an example of a work inspired by 'the Tradition'. This work is a 'system' of human types, expressed in terms of the phases of the moon, and was produced by Yeats's wife Georgie through automatic writing. Yeats's 'communicators' also sketched out their own vision of history, which has much in common with that advanced in *People of the Secret*. But when Yeats offered to 'spend what remained of life explaining and piecing together' this complex system, he received the reply: 'No, we have come to give you metaphors for poetry.' Even if the 'Hidden Directorate' is accepted only on this level, it remains a fascinating and fruitful hypothesis.

26 Poltergeists

The poltergeist or 'noisy ghost' is one of the most baffling phenomena in the whole realm of the paranormal. There are thousands of people who do not believe in ghosts, but who will reluctantly admit that the evidence for the poltergeist is too strong to ignore. The favourite theory of such sceptics is that the poltergeist is some unexplained freak of the human mind.

If the poltergeist is a 'ghost' or spirit, as its name implies, then its chief characteristic is as a spirit of mischief. Poltergeists cause objects to fly through the air, doors to open and close, pools of water to appear from nowhere. And they are by no means a rarity; at this very moment some case of poltergeist activity is probably going on within a dozen miles of the reader of this book. (I know of a case that is going on within a dozen miles of me as I write this.)

One of the earliest known cases was recorded in a chronicle called the *Annales Fuldenses* and dates back to AD 858. It took place in a farmhouse at Bingen, on the Rhine; the chronicle describes an 'evil spirit' that threw stones, and made the walls shake as if men were striking them with hammers. Stone-throwing is one of the most typical of poltergeist activities. The poltergeist also caused fires – another of their favourite activities (although, for some reason, they seldom do serious damage) – in this case burning the farmer's crops soon after they were gathered in. It also developed a voice – a much rarer feature in poltergeist cases – and denounced the man for various sins, including fornication and adultery. Priests sent by the Bishop of Mainz apparently failed to exorcise it; in fact, it is virtually impossible to get rid of a poltergeist by exorcism ceremonies.

It was only after the formation of the Society for Psychical Research in 1882 that the poltergeist was carefully studied. Then it was observed that in the majority of cases there were adolescent children present in the houses where such occurrences took place; it seemed a reasonable assumption that the children were somehow the 'cause' of the outbreak. And in the age of Freud the most widely held theory was that the poltergeist is some kind of 'unconscious' manifestation of adolescent sexual energies; but no one has so far offered a theory as to exactly how this can occur.

In England one of the most spectacular cases is also one of the earliest to be thoroughly recorded: the so-called 'phantom drummer of Tedworth'. It took place in the home of a magistrate called John Mompesson in March 1661. The whole household was kept awake all night by loud drumming noises. The magistrate had been responsible for the arrest of a vagrant named William Drury, who attracted attention in the street by beating a drum.

Mompesson had the drum confiscated, in spite of Drury's appeals. Drury escaped from custody – he was being held for possessing forged papers – without his drum. It was after this that the disturbances in Mompesson's household began, and continued for two years. The 'spirit' also slammed doors, made panting noises like a dog, and scratching noises like huge rats, as well as purring noises like a cat. It also developed a voice and shouted, 'A witch, a witch!' It emptied ashes and chamberpots into the children's beds, and caused various objects to fly through the air. In 1663 Drury, who was in prison for stealing a pig, admitted to a visitor that he was somehow responsible for the disturbances, and said they would continue until Mompesson made him satisfaction for taking away his drum. But the phenomena finally seem to have faded away.

A famous poltergeist haunting took place in the home of the Rev.Samuel Wesley – grandfather of the founder of Methodism – at his rectory at Epworth in Lincolnshire. 'Old Jeffrey', as the family came to call it, kept the family awake on the night of 1 December 1716 with appalling groans, and – a few nights later – with loud knocking noises. It also produced sounds of footsteps walking along the corridors and in empty rooms. The 'focus' of the disturbances seemed to be nineteen-year-old Hetty Wesley, who was usually asleep when the disturbances began, and who trembled in her sleep. As usual, the disturbances gradually faded away.

The famous case of the 'Cock Lane' ghost ended with an innocent man going to prison for two years. The 'focus' of the disturbances was ten-year-old Elizabeth Parsons, daughter of a clerk called Richard Parsons. The Parsons family had two lodgers: a retired innkeeper named William Kent and his common-law wife Fanny Lynes, whose sister Elizabeth had been Kent's previous wife. (This was why they could not marry, the law preventing a man from marrying his deceased wife's sister.) One night when Kent was away Fanny Lynes asked the ten-year-old girl to sleep with her to keep her company; they were kept awake by scratching and rapping noises from behind the wainscot. Soon after this Fanny Lynes died of smallpox, and Kent moved elsewhere. The strange rappings continued, and a clergyman named Moore tried to communicate with the 'spirit', using a code of one rap for yes, two for no. By this means the 'spirit' identified itself as Fanny Lynes, and accused her ex-'husband' of poisoning her with arsenic.

Parsons was unfortunately unaware that poltergeists tell lies more often than not. And he was not displeased to hear that Kent was a murderer, for he was nursing a grudge against him. Kent had lent him money which he had failed to repay, and was now suing him. So Parsons overlooked the fact that the knockings began before the death of Fanny Lynes, and made no attempt to keep the revelations secret.

In due course, Kent heard that he was being accused of murder by a 'spirit', and came to the house in Cock Lane, to hear for himself. When the raps accused him of murder he shouted angrily, 'Thou art a lying spirit'

The 'ghost' became famous. But when a committee – including Dr Johnson – came to investigate, it preferred to remain silent, convincing Johnson that it was a fraud. Then Kent decided to prosecute for libel. The burden of proof lay on Elizabeth's father who was for legal purposes the accuser. There was another test, and Elizabeth was told that if the ghost did not manifest itself this time, her mother and father would be thrown into prison; naturally, she made sure something happened. But servants peering through a crack saw that she was making the raps with a wooden board. She was denounced as a fake. At the trial Parsons was sentenced to two years in prison, as well as to stand three times in the pillory. His wife received a year; a woman who had often 'communicated' with the spirit received six months. Even the parson was fined £588 – a huge sum for those days. But when Parsons was standing in the pillory the crowd was distinctly sympathetic and took up a collection for him – an unusual gesture in that age of cruelty, when crowds enjoyed pelting the malefactor in the pillory, sometimes even killing him. Regrettably, we know nothing of what happened to any of the protagonists after the trial. But it is very clear that the unfortunate Parsons family suffered a great injustice. Many witnesses testified earlier that it would have been impossible for Elizabeth to have faked the rapping noises.

One of America's most famous cases occurred on the farm of a Tennessee farmer named John Bell; the case of the 'Bell witch' is also unusual – in fact, virtually unique – in that the poltergeist ended by causing the death of its victim, Bell himself. Bell had nine children, one of whom, Betsy, was a girl of twelve; she was almost certainly the 'focus'. The disturbances began in 1817 with scratching noises from the walls, and occasional knocks. Then invisible hands pulled bedclothes off the beds, and there were choking noises that seemed to come from a human throat. Then stones were thrown and furniture moved. The 'spirit' frequently slapped Betsy, and her cheek would redden after the sounds of the blow; it also pulled her hair. After about a year the poltergeist developed a voice – a strange asthmatic croak. (Poltergeist voices seldom sound like human voices – it is as if the 'entity' is having to master an unfamiliar medium). It made remarks like 'I can't stand the smell of a nigger.' After its manifestations Betsy was usually exhausted – she was obviously the source of its energy.

Then John Bell began to be attacked; his jaw became stiff and his tongue swelled. The poltergeist, which had now developed a normal voice, identified itself as an Indian, then as a witch called Old Kate Batts. (It used several voices.) It also declared that it would torment John Bell until he died, which it then proceeded to do. It pulled off his shoes, hit him in the face, and caused him to have violent physical convulsions. All this continued until one day in 1820 he was found in a deep stupor. The 'witch' claimed that she had given 'old Jack' a dose of a medicine that would kill him. And when Bell did in fact die the witch filled the house with shrieks of triumph. Then the disturbances abated. One day in 1821, as the family was eating supper, there was a loud noise in the chimney, and an object like a cannonball rolled out from the fireplace and turned into smoke. The witch's voice cried: 'I am going and will be gone for seven years.' But she stayed away for good.

One expert on poltergeists, Nandor Fodor, has suggested that the explanation of the Bell witch lies in an incestuous attack made on Betsy by her father, and that the poltergeist is a 'personality fragment' that has somehow broken free of the rest of the personality. There is no real evidence for either of these claims.

Another famous American case took place in the home of the Rev. Eliakim Phelps in 1850. This poltergeist began by scattering furniture around and making curious dummies out of stuffed clothes. They were extremely lifelike and were constructed in a few minutes. Then the poltergeist entered the stone-throwing stage (most disturbances seem to go through a number of definite phases), breaking seventy-one window-panes. Paper burst into flames and all kinds of objects were smashed. The twelve-year-old boy, Harry, was snatched up into the air, and on one occasion tied to a tree. His elder sister Anna, sixteen, was pinched and slapped. But when mother and children went off to Pennsylvania for the winter the disturbances ceased.

It was in fact a series of poltergeist disturbances that started the extraordinary nineteenth-century craze known as Spiritualism, which began with typical knocking noises in the home of the Fox family in Hydesville, New York State, in 1848; two daughters – Margaret, fifteen, and Kate, twelve – were obviously the 'focuses'. A neighbour who questioned the 'spirit' (with the usual code one knock for yes, two for no) was told that it was a peddler who had been murdered in the house. (Many years later, human bones and a peddler's box were found buried in the cellar.) The notoriety of the case caused many other Americans to take up 'spiritualism', sitting around a table in the dark with clasped hands, and asking for spirits to 'manifest' themselves. The Hydesville 'spirit' finally delivered a message announcing a new era in spirit communication. And in fact spiritualism swept across the United States, then across Europe.

In the early 1850s a French educator named Léon-Denizard-Hyppolyte Rivail became interested in the new spiritualist craze; when two daughters of a friend proved to be proficient in 'automatic writing' Rivail asked the 'spirits' all kinds of questions, and received unusually constructive and serious answers. In due course these were published in *The Spirits' Book*, which Rivail published under the pseudonym of Allan Kardec. It became for a while a kind of Bible of Spiritualism, although there was later a split within the movement, many influential Spiritualists rejecting Kardec's belief in reincarnation.

In Paris in 1860 there had been a series of violent disturbances in a house in the Rue des Noyers – the usual window-smashing and furniture-throwing. Rivail requested to speak to the 'spirit' responsible, and an entity that claimed to be a long-dead rag and bone man declared that it had used the 'electrical energy' of a servant girl in the house to cause the disturbances. The girl, it said, was quite unaware of this – in fact, she was the most terrified of them all. He had been doing these things merely to amuse himself.

'Kardec' was convinced that poltergeists are 'earth-bound spirits' – that is, dead people who for various reasons have been unable to advance beyond the purely material plane.

One of the most remarkable American cases of the nineteenth century was recorded in a book called *The Great Amherst Mystery* by Walter Hubbell, a stage magician who moved into the house of the Teed family in Amherst,

Nova Scotia, in 1869 to investigate a poltergeist that concentrated its attention on an eighteen-year-old girl named Esther Cox. The disturbances had begun in the previous year, when Esther's boy-friend, Bob MacNeal, had tried to order her into the woods at gunpoint, presumably to rape her; when interrupted he fled and never returned. Soon after this Esther and her sister Jane were kept awake by mouse-like rustling noises, and a cardboard box leapt into the air. Two nights later, Esther's body seemed to swell like a balloon, but returned to normal after a sound like a thunder-clap. Bedclothes were thrown around the room. Esther's pillow inflated like a balloon. In front of many witnesses, writing appeared on the wall saying, 'Esther, you are mine to kill.' Esther often complained of an 'electric feeling' running through her body. When the poltergeist got into its stride small fires broke out, objects flew around the room, furniture moved, and Esther turned into a kind of human magnet, to which knives and other metal objects stuck firmly. Hubbell succeeded in communicating with the 'spirits', who were able to prove their authenticity by telling him the number inside his watch and the date of coins in his pockets. When a barn burned down Esther was accused of arson and sentenced to four months in prison. When she came out again the manifestations stopped.

The Society for Psychical Research was founded in 1882 to investigate 'psychical phenomena' scientifically. One of its most influential members, Frank Podmore, author of a valuable two-volume history of Spiritualism, was firmly convinced the poltergeists were usually fakes, caused by stone-throwing children, although he *was* willing to admit that a well-known case at Durweston, on Viscount Portman's estate, was probably genuine. Podmore later had a lengthy correspondence with Andrew Lang, who found Podmore's scepticism too wholesale; Lang is generally conceded to have won this controversy.

In 1900 the famous criminologist Cesare Lombroso investigated a case of poltergeist haunting in a wine shop in Turin. As Lombroso stood in the wine cellar bottles gently rose from the shelves and exploded on the floor. At first Lombroso suspected that the proprietor's wife was the cause of the disturbances, but they continued while she was away. Lombroso's suspicions then focused on a thirteen-year-old waiter. When this boy was dismissed the haunting stopped.

So it was fairly clear to the early investigators that poltergeist phenomena were connected, more often than not, with some particular person, usually an adolescent. (The word poltergeist was seldom used in the early days of psychical research, although it *had* been used to describe various cases by Mrs Catherine Crowe in her best-seller *The Night Side of Nature* in 1848.) But it was not until the late 1940s that the 'unconscious mind' theory became popular. Nandor Fodor put forward his theory that poltergeists are 'personality fragments' in *The Journal of Clinical Psychopathology* in 1945. Frank Harvey's play *The Poltergeist* had a successful West End run in 1946; it was based on a case that had taken place at Pitmilly House, Boarshill, near Fife, in which £50 worth of fire damage had been caused – Harvey transferred it to a Dartmoor vicarage. His play popularized the 'unconscious mind' theory, which had first been put forward about 1930 by Dr Alfred Winterstein, in discussing the case of the Austrian medium Frieda Weisl; the latter's husband described how, when they were first married, ornaments would fly off the mantelpiece when she had an orgasm. The Countess Zoe Wassilko-Serecki had reached similar conclusions when she examined a young Rumanian girl named Eleanore Zugun, who was continually slapped and punched by a poltergeist-bite-marks that appeared on her were often damp with saliva. By the end of the 1940s the 'unconscious mind' theory was generally accepted by those psychical investigators who were willing to believe that the poltergeist was not a fraud. This theory was summarized by BBC investigator Brian Branston in his book *Beyond Belief* (1976):

I believe that, on the evidence, we may claim as a working hypothesis that poltergeist phenomena are produced unconsciously by an individual whose psyche is disturbed, that the disturbed psyche reacts on the oldest part of the brain, the brain stem, which by means unknown to science produced the commonly recognisable poltergeist phenomena. And these phenomena are the overt cry for help: as the poem says . . . .. 'I was not . . . waving but drowning.'

Yet Branston's own theory has been contradicted by a case he has cited earlier in the chapter on poltergeists – one that took place at Northfleet in Kent. Branston records that 'spooks so upset the various tenants that the house finally became empty. Previous tenants named Maxted had young children, and the usual poltergeist phenomena had taken place – mouse-like scratching noises, then the bedclothes pulled off the bed, ornaments disappearing and reappearing, and so on. When Mrs Maxted saw the ghost of a six-year-old girl they decided to move out. The next tenants had no children; they heard strange noises in the bedrooms, and smelt an unpleasant, rotting smell, but it was only after a year that they woke up to find one end of the bed rising up into the air, while beside the bed stood a pinkish-orange phantom, partly transparent, of a woman with no head. They also moved out. But even when the house was empty the next door tenants were able to hear thumping noises, and were alarmed when their own bed began to vibrate. So here, it seems, is a case where the 'poltergeist' remained in the house throughout two tenancies, and stayed on when the house was empty.

A similar case was investigated by the present writer.[1] It took place in the Yorkshire town of Pontefract, in the home of the Pritchard family. Furniture moved, ornaments flew around, green foam gushed out of the taps, the house was shaken by thunderous crashes. A 'ghost' – apparently a monk dressed in black – was also seen. But the 'haunting' began when the eldest son, Phillip, reached the age of fifteen, and lasted a few days. When his younger sister Diane was fourteen the disturbances began again, and were this time more violent. (Diane had been away on holiday during the first outbreak.) Practically every breakable object in the house was smashed, Diane was thrown repeatedly out of bed and attacked by moving furniture, and a crucifix flew off the wall and stuck to her back, making a red mark. Then, as

---

[1] *Poltergeist, A Study in Destructive Haunting*, by Colin Wilson, 1981, Chapter 4.

before, the manifestations faded. Diane herself was aware that the entity was somehow using her energy, and also felt intuitively that it meant her no real harm.

Cases like these suggest that the poltergeist is not a manifestation of the unconscious mind of an unhappy teenager but – as Kardec stated – an actual entity or 'spirit', which remains associated with some place, but which can only manifest itself through the surplus energy of a human being – not necessarily a teenager.

This was the conclusion reached by Guy Lyon Playfair, a paranormal-investigator who went to Rio de Janeiro in the early 1960s. Brazil, unlike England and France, remained faithful to Allan Kardec's version of spiritualism, and his two works, *The Spirits'Book* and *The Medium's Book*, became the basic scriptures of Brazil's most influential religion, 'spiritism'. He investigated a poltergeist for the Brazilian Institute for Psycho-biophysical Research, and began to accept the Brazilian belief that poltergeists are spirits, and that they can be controlled by witch doctors, who may send them to haunt someone they dislike. One young girl named Maria was continually attacked by a poltergeist which tried to suffocate her and set her clothes on fire. A medium relayed a message saying that Maria had been a witch in a previous existence, through whom many people had suffered, and now she was paying for it. Maria committed suicide with poison at thirteen. Playfair's books *The Flying Cow* and *The Indefinite Boundary* present highly convincing evidence that most poltergeist disturbances are due to 'spirits'.

In 1977 Playfair and his fellow SPR member Maurice Grosse went to investigate a poltergeist at Enfield in north London. The case is described in detail in a classic book *This House is Haunted*. There were four children in the Harper family, aged respectively thirteen, eleven, ten and seven; it was a one-parent family, and there was considerable psychological tension. The disturbances began with vibrating beds and moving furniture. Playfair tried holding a chair in position with wire; the wire was snapped. A medium who came to the house said that there were several entities, and that eleven-year-old Janet was the 'focus'. Playfair and Grosse finally established communication with the entity by means of a code of raps; it stated that it had been a previous tenant of the house thirty years ago and was now dead. It began to write messages in pencil. Eventually it developed a strange, harsh voice, identifying itself as Joe Watson. On another occasion the entity called itself Bill Haylock, and claimed that it had come from a nearby graveyard in Durant's Park. One of its standard replies to questions (such as 'Do you know you are dead?') was 'Fuck off.' Bill Haylock was later identified as a local resident, now deceased. Finally, in 1978, a Dutch clairvoyant, Dono Gmelig-Meyling, spent some time in the house, and somehow put an end to the 'haunting'. He reported going on an 'astral trip', and meeting a 24-year-old girl who was somehow involved in the case. Maurice Grosse's daughter Janet, who was the right age, had been killed in a motor-cycle crash in 1976. Playfair speculates that it was Janet who drew her father's attention to the case, putting it into the head of a neighbour to ring the *Daily Mirror*, and into the head of a *Daily Mirror* journalist to contact the Society for Psychical

Research. (Kardec insisted that our minds are far more influenced by 'spirits' than we realize.) But the energy required by the poltergeist or poltergeists was undoubtedly supplied by the children, primarily by Janet Harper. (Playfair commented at one stage that half the contents of the local graveyard seemed to be haunting the house.)

The view that poltergeists are 'spirits' who make use of some form of human energy remains highly unfashionable among psychical investigators, who prefer the more 'scientific' theory of Fodor. Yet the case of the phantom drummer of Tedworth seems to support Playfair's view that poltergeist phenomena can be caused by 'witchcraft'; and witches have traditionally claimed to perform their 'magic' through the use of spirits. One thing is certain: that Podmore's view that poltergeists are usually due to deliberate fraud is untenable in the face of the evidence. Sceptics point out that most 'psychical phenomena' are intermittent, and that they are so much the exception that they may safely be ignored. But there have been literally thousands of cases of poltergeist phenomena, and they continue to occur with a regularity that makes them easy to record and investigate. No one who considers the phenomenon open-mindedly can fail to be convinced that the poltergeist is a reality that defies 'purely scientific' explanation.

27 Psychometry

'Telescope into the Past'

In the winter of 1921 members of the Metapsychic Institute in Paris met together to test a clairvoyant. Someone produced a letter and asked someone to pass it to her; before it could reach her it was grabbed by a novelist called Pascal Forthunny, who said scathingly: 'It can't be difficult to invent something that applies to anybody.' He then closed his eyes and pronounced solemnly: 'Ah yes, I see a crime, a murder . . .' When he had finished the man who had brought the letter said: 'That was written by Henri Landru.' Landru was the 'Bluebeard' who was then on trial for the murders of eleven women. The sceptic Forthunny had discovered that he possessed the curious ability known as psychometry – the ability to 'sense' the history of an object by holding it in the hand.

According to the man who invented the word – an American doctor named Joseph Rodes Buchanan – it is an ability we all possess, although most of us have unconsciously suppressed it. Buchanan – who was a professor of medicine in Kentucky – came to suspect the existence of such a faculty in 1841, when he met a bishop named Leonidas Polk, who claimed that he could always detect brass when he touched it – even in the dark – because it produced a peculiar taste in his mouth. Buchanan was interested in the science known as phrenology – the notion that the 'bumps' on our skulls reveal our characters – and he was interested to discover that Polk seemed to have a highly developed 'bump' of sensibility. So he decided to perform a scientific test on students who had a similar bump. Various metals were wrapped in paper, and Buchanan was delighted to discover that many of his students could detect brass, iron, lead and so on by merely pressing their fingertips against the paper. They could also distinguish substances like salt, sugar, pepper and vinegar.

Buchanan concluded that the answer lay in some 'nerve aura' in the fingertips, which can detect different metals exactly as we could distinguish them by touching them with the tip of the tongue. This appeared to be confirmed by his observation that it seemed to work better when the hands are damp with perspiration – for after all, a damp skin is more 'sensitive' than a dry skin. But this explanation began to seem inadequate when he discovered that one of his best 'sensitives' – a man named Charles Inman – could sense the contents of sealed letters, and the character of the writers. Buchanan's explanation was that the 'nerve aura' of the writer had left some kind of trace on the letter, and Inman was able to pick up this trace through his own nerve aura. In other words, Inman's 'sensitivity' was abnormally developed, in much the same way as a bloodhound's sense of smell. But that theory also broke down when he discovered that Inman displayed the same insight when presented with photographs – daguerreotypes – in sealed envelopes. Even the argument that the photograph had been in contact with the 'sitter', and had therefore picked up something of his 'nerve aura', ceased to be convincing when Buchanan discovered that newspaper photographs worked as well as daguerreotypes.

The professor of geology at Boston University, William Denton, read Buchanan's original paper on psychometry – the word means 'soul measurement' – and decided to try it himself. His sister Anne was 'highly impressible', and she proved to be an even better psychometrist than Inman; she was not only able to describe the character of letter-writers; she was even able to describe their physical appearance and surroundings.

This led Denton to ask himself whether, if a writer's image and surroundings could be 'impressed' on a letter, 'why could not rocks receive impressions of surrounding objects, some of which they have been in the immediate neighbourhood of for years'. So in 1853 Denton began testing his 'sensitives' with geological and archaeological specimens, 'and was delighted to find that without possessing any previous knowledge of the specimen, or even seeing it, the history of its time passed before the gaze of the seer like a grand panoramic view.' When he handed his sister a piece of volcanic lava from Hawaii, she was shaken to see 'an ocean of fire pouring over a precipice and boiling as it pours'. Significantly, she also saw the sea with ships on it, and Denton knew that the lava had been ejected during an eruption in 1840, when the American navy had been in Hawaii. A fragment of bone found in a piece of limestone evoked a picture of a prehistoric beach with dinosaurs. A fragment of Indian pottery brought a vision of Red Indians. A meteorite fragment brought visions of empty space, with the stars looking abnormally large and bright. A fragment of rock from Niagara brought a vision of a boiling torrent hurling up spray (which she thought was steam). A piece of stalactite brought an image of pieces of rock hanging down like icicles. To make doubly sure that his sensitives were not somehow picking up unconscious hints or recognizing the specimens, Denton wrapped them in thick paper. He also discovered that when he tried the same specimen a second time – perhaps a month later – it produced the same result, although the picture was never identical.

In one of his most interesting experiments he showed his wife a fragment of Roman tile which came from a villa that had belonged to the orator Cicero. She described a Roman villa and lines of soldiers; she also saw the owner of the villa, a genial, fleshy man with an air of command. Denton was disappointed; Cicero had been tall and thin. But by the time Denton came to write the second volume of *The Soul of Things* he had discovered that the villa had also belonged to the dictator Sulla, and that Sulla *did* fit his wife's description.

Another impressive 'hit' was the 'vision' induced by a piece of volcanic rock from Pompeii. Mrs Denton had no idea what it was, and was not allowed to see it; but she had a vivid impression of the eruption of Vesuvius and the crowds fleeing from Pompeii. Denton's son Sherman had an even more detailed vision of ancient Pompeii, complete with many archaeological details – such as an image of a boat with a 'swan's neck' – which proved to be historically accurate.

Denton was immensely excited; he believed that he and Buchanan had discovered a so far unknown human faculty, a kind of 'telescope into the past' that would enable us to relive great scenes of history. In effect, everything that had ever happened to the world was preserved on a kind of 'newsreel' (although this was not, of course, an image that occurred to Denton) and could be replayed at will.

But while the evidence for the psychometric faculty is undoubtedly beyond dispute, Denton was not aware of how far it can be deceptive. The third volume of *The Soul of Things*, published in 1888, contains 'visions' of various planets that we now know to be preposterous. Venus has giant trees like toadstools and animals that sound as if they were invented by Hieronymus Bosch; Mars has a summery temperature (in fact it would be freezing) and is peopled with four-fingered men with blue eyes and yellow hair; Jupiter also has blue-eyed blondes with plaits down to their waists and the ability to float like balloons. Denton's son Sherman (who was responsible for most of these extraordinary descriptions) had clearly developed the faculty that Jung calls 'active imagination', and was unable to distinguish it from his genuine psychometric abilities.

What impresses the modern reader about Denton's *Soul of Things* and Buchanan's *Manual of Psychometry* (optimistically sub-titled The Dawn of a New Civilization) is their thoroughly scientific approach. This also impressed their contemporaries at first. Unfortunately, the period when they were conducting their experiments was also the period when the new craze known as Spiritualism was spreading across America and Europe. It had started with curious poltergeist manifestations in the home of the Fox family in New York state (see Chapter 26) in the late 1840s. By 1860 it was a world-wide phenomenon. Scientists were appalled, and most of them dismissed it as sheer delusion. Anything that seemed remotely connected with the 'supernatural' became the object of the same scepticism, and the researches of Buchanan and Denton never attracted the attention they deserved. Denton died in 1883, Buchanan in 1900, both in relative obscurity.

The next major experiments in psychometry were made by Dr Gustav Pagenstecher, a German who moved to Mexico City in the 1880s, and who regarded himself as a hard-headed materialist. Some time after the First World War, Pagenstecher was treating the insomnia of a patient called Maria Reyes de Zierold by hypnosis. One day, as she lay in a hypnotic trance, she told him that her daughter was listening at the door. Pagenstecher opened the door and found the daughter there. He began testing Maria for paranormal abilities and discovered that while under hypnosis she could share his own sensations; if he put sugar or salt on his tongue she could taste it; if he held a lighted match near his fingers she felt the heat of the flame. Then he began testing her for psychometric abilities. Like Denton's subjects, she could describe where some specimen came from. Holding a sea-shell, she described an underwater scene; holding a piece of meteorite, she described hurtling through space and down through the earth's atmosphere. ('I am horrified! My God!') Dr Walter Franklin Prince, who tested her on behalf of the American Society for Psychical Research, handed her what he thought was a 'sea bean' which he had found on the beach. She described a tropical forest. Professional botanists confirmed that the 'bean' was a nut from a tree that grew in the tropical forest, and that was often carried down to the sea by the rivers.

Another eminent experimenter of the 1920s was Dr Eugene Osty, director of the Metapsychical Institute at which the novelist Pascal Fortunny correctly identified the letter from the mass murderer Landru. In his classic work *Supernormal Faculties in Man*, Osty described many experiments in psychometry with various 'sensitives'. In 1921 he was handed a photograph of a sealed glass capsule containing some liquid; it had been found near the great temple at Baalbek. One of his best psychics, a Mme Moral, held the photograph in her hand – it was so blurred it could have been of anything – and said immediately that it reminded her of 'a place with dead people', and of one old man in particular. She 'saw' a vast place, like an enormous church, then went on to describe the man, who was obviously a high priest. The capsule in the photograph contained the blood of a man who had been sacrificed in some distant land, and had been placed in the priest's grave as a memento.

At the time Osty himself had no idea what the photograph represented, and was surprised when the engineer who had found it was able to confirm that it had been discovered in a rich tomb in the Bekaa valley.

This story raises again the central problem about psychometry. Buchanan's original hypothesis – that it was simply a matter of 'nerve aura', so the psychometrist could be regarded as a kind of human bloodhound – ceases to be plausible if the information can be picked up from a photograph, which could not be expected to retain any kind of 'scent'. Even Denton's assumption that every object somehow 'photographs' its surroundings seems dubious. In that case a piece of Roman pavement could only have 'photographed' a limited area, and Mrs Denton's view of Roman legionaries would have been simply of hairy legs towering up above her.

The likeliest hypothesis is that the faculty involved is what is traditionally known as 'clairvoyance', a peculiar ability to 'know' what is going on in some other place or at some other time. But Bishop Polk's ability to distinguish brass in the dark is obviously not clairvoyance. Here, as in so many other areas of the 'paranormal', it is practically impossible to draw neat dividing lines.

Many modern psychometrists – like Gerard Croiset, Peter Hurkos and

Suzanne Padfield – have been able use their faculty to help the police solve crimes: Suzanne Padfield was even able to help the Moscow police catch a child-murderer without leaving her home in Dorset.[1] But it is significant that Croiset disliked being called a psychometrist or clairvoyant, and preferred the more ambiguous word 'paragnost' – meaning simply the ability to 'know' what lies beyond the normal limits of the senses.

See *The Psychic Detectives* by Colin Wilson.

28 Rennes-le-Château

The Treasure of Béranger Saunière

The mystery of Rennes-le-Château is the riddle of a poor priest who discovered a secret that made him a millionaire and which profoundly shocked the priest to whom he confided it on his deathbed.

In June 1885 a new curé came to the little village of Rennes-le-Château, on the French side of the Pyrenees; he was 33-year-old Béranger Saunière, and he was returning to the area in which he had been brought up. His early account books survive, and they show that he was very poor – the income on which he supported himself and his housekeeper was the equivalent of six pounds sterling a year.

It was six years later that Saunière decided to restore the church altar, a stone slab cemented into the wall and supported at the other end by two square Visigothic pillars. One of these proved to be hollow, and inside it Saunière found four parchments in wooden tubes. Two were genealogies of local families; the other two were texts from the New Testament, but written without the usual spaces between the letters. It seemed fairly obvious that these were in some sort of code – in fact, the code of the shorter text was straightforward. Saunière only had to write down the letters that were raised above the others, and he had a message that read: 'A Dagobert II roi et à Sion est ce trésor et il est la mort': to Dagobert II, king, and to Sion belongs this treasure, and he is there dead. (The final phrase 'et il est la mort' could also be translated 'and it is death' – meaning, perhaps, 'it is death to interfere with it.') So these secret messages were about a treasure. Dagobert was a seventh-century French king of the Merovingian dynasty. The author of these parchments was almost certainly a predecessor of Saunière, a priest named Antoine Bigou, who had been the curé of Rennes-le-Château at the time of the French Revolution.

Saunière took the parchments to the Bishop of Carcassonne, Monseigneur Félix-Arsène Billard, and the bishop was sufficiently intrigued to send Saunière to Paris to consult with various scholars and experts in cryptography. Among these were the Abbé Bieil, director of St Sulpice. Bieil's nephew was a brilliant young man named Emile Hoffet, who was a student of linguistics. Although Hoffet was training for the priesthood, he was in touch with many 'occultists' who flourished in Paris in the 1890s, an era which had seen a revival of interest in ritual magic; Hoffet introduced Saunière to a circle of distinguished artists, which included the poet Mallarmé, the dramatist

Maeterlinck and the composer Claude Debussy. It was probably Debussy who introduced Saunière to the famous soprano Emma Calvé, and the relationship that developed between them may have been more than friendship – Saunière was a man who loved women and food.

Before he left Paris, Saunière visited the Louvre and purchased reproductions of three paintings, including Nicolas Poussin's *Les Bergers d'Arcadie* – the Shepherds of Arcady – which shows three shepherds standing by a tomb on which are carved the words 'Et in Arcadia Ego' – usually translated as 'I [Death] am also in Arcadia.'

When Saunière returned to Rennes-le-Château three weeks later he was hot on the trail of the 'treasure'. He brought in three young men to raise the stone slab set in the floor in front of the altar, and discovered that its underside was carved with a picture of mounted knights; it dated from about the time of King Dagobert. When his helpers dug farther down they discovered two skeletons, and – according to one of them who survived into the 1960s – a pot of 'worthless medallions'. Saunière then sent them away, locked the church doors, and spent the evening there alone.

Now Saunière, accompanied by his housekeeper – a young peasant girl named Marie Denarnaud – began to spend his days wandering around the district with a sack on his back, returning each evening with stones which he used to construct a grotto in his garden. Whether this was the only purpose of his explorations is not known. He also committed a rather curious piece of vandalism on a grave in the churchyard. It belonged to Marie, Marquise de Blanchefort, whose headstone had been designed by the same Abbé Bigou who had concealed the parchments in the column. Saunière obliterated the inscriptions on the stone that covered the grave, and removed the headstone completely. However, he was unaware that both inscriptions had already been recorded in a little book by a local antiquary. The inscription on the gravestone is shown opposite:

The vertical inscriptions on either side of the gravestone are easy to read: a mixture of Greek and Latin letters carries the inscription *Et in Arcadio Ego* – linking it with the Poussin painting. The central inscription: 'Reddis Regis Cellis Arcis' may be read: 'At royal Reddis, in the cave of the fortress.' 'Reddis' is one of the ancient names for Rennes-le-Château, which was also known to the Romans as Aereda.

The inscription on the headstone has many odd features. In the first line, the *i* of *ci* (*ci gît* means 'here lies') has been carved as a capital T. The M of Marie has been left at the end of the first line. The 'e' of 'noble' is in the lower case. The word following 'negre' should read 'Dables' not 'Darles', so should have an R, not a B. Altogether there are eight of these anomalies in the inscription, making up two sets of four, one in capital letters and one in lower case. The capitals are TMRO, while the lower case are three e's and a p. Only one word can be formed of the capitals: MORT – death. Only one word can be formed of the lower-case letters: *epée* – sword. In fact these two words proved to be the 'keyword' to decipher the longer of the two parchments found in the pillar. . . .

Whether Saunière deciphered it alone, or whether his obliging friends at St

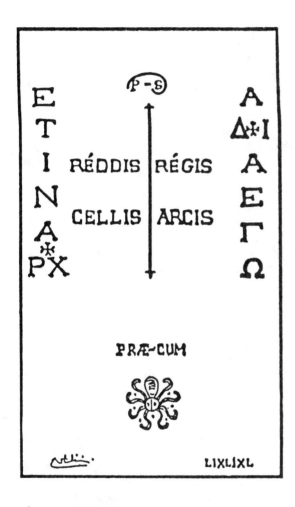

CT GIT NOBLe M

ARIE DE NEGRe

DARLES DAME

DHAUPOUL De

BLANCHEFORT

AGEE DE SOIX

ANTE SEpT ANS

DECEDEE LE

XVII JANVIER

MDCOLXXXI

REQUIESCAT IN

PACE

(P.S.) PRAE-CUM

Sulpice unknowingly handed him the vital clues, may never be known. All that *is* known is that shortly after this Saunière began spending money at a remarkable rate. He contacted a Paris bank, who sent a representative to Rennes-le-Château solely to attend to Saunière's business. Then he built a public road to replace the dirt track that had run to the village, and also had a water supply piped in. He built a pleasant villa with a garden that had fountains and shady walks. To house his library he built a gothic tower perched on the edge of the mountainside. He began to collect rare china, antiques and precious fabrics. He began to entertain distinguished visitors like Emma Calvé and the Secretary of State for Culture. One of his visitors was recognized as the Archduke Johann von Habsburg, cousin of Franz-

Josef, Emperor of Austria. His guests were given the very best of food and wine (and it may be significant that Saunière eventually died of cirrhosis of the liver).

Understandably, Saunière's superiors were curious about his wealth and wanted to know where it came from. Saunière told them coolly that he was not at liberty to divulge the source of his wealth – some of it came from rich penitents who had sworn him to secrecy. He had also been paid well for saying masses for the souls of the dead. The old bishop decided to mind his own business, but a new one later revealed a pertinacious curiosity, and when Saunière declined to satisfy it, ordered his transfer to another parish. Saunière declined to be transferred. A new priest was appointed to Rennes-le-Château, but the villagers still continued to treat Saunière as their spiritual pastor. Eventually, in 1917, Saunière suffered a stroke, and died at the age of sixty-four. A priest from a neighbouring parish who was called to his deathbed emerged looking pale and shaken, and a local account, doubtless exaggerated, says that he 'never smiled again'.

His housekeeper, Marie Denarnaud, lived on until 1953 in considerable affluence. When after the Second World War the French government issued new currency, and demanded to know the source of any large sums (the aim being to trap tax-evaders and profiteers) she burned piles of ten-franc notes in the garden, and lived for the remainder of her life on the proceeds of the sale of Saunière's villa. She was evidently determined not to betray Saunière's secret. Just before her death she confided to the purchaser of the villa that she would tell him a secret that would make him both rich and powerful; but she died after a stroke that left her speechless.

The obvious solution to the mystery is that Saunière discovered the treasure mentioned in the parchment, and somehow turned it into modern currency. In which case the mystery is simply what clues he found in the parchment, and how he followed them up to discover the concealed hoard.

Henry Lincoln, a modern investigator, became fascinated by the problem after reading a book called *Le Trésor Maudit* [*The Accursed Treasure*], by Gérard de Sède, in 1969. He made many visits to Rennes-le-Château, and eventually made a programme for BBC television called 'The Lost Treasure of Jerusalem . . .?' Lincoln went to Paris to see Gérard de Sède, and before the programme was made de Sède had presented him with the solution of the 'long cipher' from the Visigothic column. De Sède claimed that this had been broken with the help of French army experts who had used a computer. Lincoln suspected that this was untrue, and British Intelligence confirmed his suspicion that the code could not have been broken by computer.

The code was unbelievably complex – so complex that Lincoln does not even attempt to explain it in the book he later wrote on the mystery. Cracking it involved a technique known to cipher experts as the Vigenère process, which involves writing out the alphabet twenty-six times in a square, with the first line beginning with A, the second with B, the third with C, and so on. Then the key word Mort Epée is placed over the whole message in this case, of the longer of the two parchments and the letters are transformed by a simple process using the Vigenère table. But the new text is still meaningless.

The next step is to move each letter one letter farther down the alphabet. It is still meaningless. The next step is to use a new key word on the jumble. This new key word is the entire text of the headstone beginning 'Ci gît noble Maria' etc, and to take from the gravestone the two lots of letters 'P.S' and 'Prae cum' (Latin for 'before' and 'with'). This new 'keyword' is applied backward to the text, ending with 'P.S.' and 'Prae cum.' Then all the letters are moved two spaces down the alphabet. Next, the text is divided into two groups of 64, and these are laid out on two chessboards, and the knight makes a series of knight's moves on the chessboards. Then the letter contained in each square of this series is written down. And now at last the message emerges – although it still looks quite absurd. The message runs: BERGERE PAS DE TENTATION QUE POUSSIN TENIERS GARDENT LE CLEF PAX DCLXXXI PAR LA CROIX ET CE CHEVAL DE DIEU J'ACHEVE CE DAEMON DE GARDIEN A MIDI POMMES BLEUES. This may be translated: SHEPHERDESS WITHOUT TEMPTATION TO WHICH POUSSIN AND TENIERS HOLD THE KEY PEACE 681 WITH THE CROSS AND THIS HORSE OF GOD I REACH THIS DAEMON GUARDIAN AT MIDDAY BLUE APPLES.

This message, we must presume, led Saunière to the treasure. Which raises the interesting question: *how* did he succeed in deciphering the message? True, he had the all-important 'key words' from the grave of Marie de Blanchefort. But even if he also knew about the Vigenère table and the knight's moves, that would still make the decipherment an unbelievably complex task for an ordinary parish priest without training in cryptography. Leaving aside for the moment the actual meaning of the message, who handed Saunière the thread that guided him through this complex labyrinth?

Lincoln concluded, logically, that there must be someone who had already known some of the basic answers to the mystery or, more likely, some group or organization. This, presumably, was the organization from which his own informant, Gérard de Sède, had received his own information. This guess seemed to be supported by the number of books and pamphlets about Saunière and Rennes-le-Château that had appeared since 1956. Many of these were under obvious pseudonyms like 'Anthony the Hermit'. They proved to be available in the Bibliothèque Nationale, although some of them were curiously difficult to get hold of one of them was constantly engaged for three months. And it was in the Bibliothèque Nationale that Lincoln found one of his most vital clues: a number of miscellaneous items gathered together in stiff covers under the title *Dossiers secrets*. And one of these documents spoke about a secret order called the Priory of Sion. We may recall that the shorter of the two documents Saunière found in the pillar ended with the letters P.S., while the longer document – the one containing the 'shepherdess' message – is signed with the letters NO-IS which back to front reads 'Sion'. According to this document, the Grand Masters of this secret order included the alchemist Nicolas Flamel (who is reputed to have made gold), Leonardo da Vinci, Isaac Newton, Victor Hugo – and Claude Debussy. Saunière had met Debussy in Paris. This then could explain where he had received the key to the code.

And what exactly *was* the Priory of Sion? It was, according to the *Secret Dossiers*, the inner hierarchy of the order of 'warrior monks' called the

Knights Templars. In the year AD 1118, after the first Crusade had opened the Holy Land to Christian pilgrims, a knight called Hugues de Payens conceived the apparently absurd idea of policing the dangerous roads of the Holy Land with a small band of knights. They were successful beyond all expectation, and were granted a wing of Solomon's temple on Mount Sion in Jerusalem as their headquarters. As grateful pilgrims left them legacies they became immensely wealthy – they were also virtually the bankers of the Holy Land. Their downfall came two centuries later when the French king Philip the Fair (Philippe le Bel) had them all arrested in one sudden swoop – it was 13 October 1307 – and accused them of all kinds of horrible blasphemies and indecencies. Dozens of them were tortured and executed, and in 1312 the order was dissolved. Philip had gained his chief objective – to lay his hands on their wealth – but he was unsuccessful in his attempt to seize the treasures of one of their major strongholds, Bezu, which is near Rennes-le-Château. . . .

Mount Sion is just outside Jerusalem, and Jerusalem is often referred to as Sion in the scriptures. According to the *Secret Dossiers*, the Order of Sion (as it was at first called) was the secret society that originally created the Templars, and it was unaffected by the latter's downfall in 1307. And what was the purpose of the Priory? It was apparently to restore the Merovingians – the dynasty founded by King Clovis at the beginning of the sixth century AD – to the throne of France. Later Merovingian kings were distinctly feeble – in fact, they became known as 'the feeble kings' (*rois fainéants*) – and left most of the work to their major-domos (or Mayors of the Palace). In AD 679 one of these major-domos organized the murder of King Dagobert II – a lance was driven through his eye while he was asleep – and in due course the major-domos became kings: they were known as the Carolingians.

According to the *Secret Dossiers*, Dagobert's son Sigisbert fled south to Languedoc, and inherited the title duke of Razés and count of Rhedae from his uncle. Rhedae is another old name for Rennes-le-Château (which was then a large town), and Razés is the name of the county (or comté) in which Rennes is situated. And three centuries later, another descendant of Dagobert, Godfrey de Bouillon, led the First Crusade and freed Jerusalem from the Moslems.

It seems rather a strange ambition – to restore to the throne of France a dynasty known as 'the feeble kings'. Why should anyone bother? It seems as irrelevant and absurd as wanting to restore the Tudors or Stuarts to the English throne. And what connection could there be between this curious aspiration and the 'treasure' that made Saunière a rich man? As Lincoln pursued his researches, he found himself drawn into an increasingly bewildering labyrinth of mystery and rumour.

To begin with, Gérard de Sède told him, while he was preparing the original television programme, that the tomb shown in Poussin's painting had now been discovered. It was at a place called Arques, a few miles east of Rennes-le-Château. The tomb is close to the Château of Arques, and is in fact an exact duplicate of the tomb in Poussin's painting. One can even see Rennes-le-Château in the background of the painting. The first vertical line of the tombstone inscription on Marie de Blanchefort's grave reads 'Et in

Arc'. The central inscription reads 'At royal Reddis in the caves of the fortress.' An odd-looking circle surrounds the letters P.S. which starts *before* the P and curls back so that it ends before the S. The letter before P is O. The letter before S is R. O and R together spell 'or', the French for gold. The message seems to be saying that the gold is at Royal Reddis in the caves of the fortress. Why royal Reddis? Because it is associated with the Merovingian line of kings. . . .

So we can begin to see why the coded message on the parchment said that Poussin held the key; it was presumably to this painting it was referring. But the message also mentioned the painter Teniers, a Flemish artist who was a contemporary of Poussin. What part does he play in the mystery? Lincoln discovered that there is a copy of Poussin's *Shepherds of Arcady* at Shugborough Hall, in Staffordshire – a bas relief which is a reversed mirror image of the painting. But also at Shugborough Hall there is a painting of St Anthony by Teniers. The temptation of St Anthony was one of Teniers's favourite subjects. But this one is different – it simply shows St Anthony in meditation: no temptation. And in the background there is a shepherdess. 'Shepherdess, no temptation, that Poussin and Teniers hold the key . . .' Shugborough Hall is the seat of the earls of Lichfield, and Lincoln discovered that it had been a hotbed of masonic activity in the seventeenth century. In 1715 one of the earls helped his cousin when he escaped from Newgate prison. The cousin was called Charles Radclyffe, and he is listed in the *Secret Dossiers* as one of the Grand Masters of the Priory of Sion. The offence for which Radclyffe was imprisoned was, significantly, aiding the Old Pretender in his attempt on the throne of England. Radclyffe became the secretary of the Young Pretender in France – and presumably Grand Master of the Priory of Sion – and was executed after Culloden in 1746. So there could be good reasons why more clues to the Rennes-le-Château mystery are to be found at Shugborough Hall. Unfortunately, Lincoln found himself unable to decipher these clues.

What precisely *is* the treasure of Rennes-le-Château? The obvious guess is that it is the treasure of the Templars of Bezu, which Philippe le Bel failed to lay his hands on. And this could well be correct. But there is another clue that is contained in the longer of the two coded parchments. In the middle of the message there are twelve letters raised above the others; these have to be discarded before the decoding process begins. But in addition there are eight small letters that occur at random throughout the text, and these spell the words Rex Mundi, King of the World. This links the message with a religious sect called the Cathars, which might be regarded as an early form of Protestantism. The Cathars or 'Pure Ones' held a belief that was derived from a much older sect called the Manichees: that everything to do with the world of matter is evil, and everything to do with the world of spirit is good. They believed that this world was not created by God but by a 'demiurge' or demon, who is the King of this world. Although they accepted salvation through Christ, they did not believe that he was crucified on the cross. This sect of early puritans became so powerful in the Languedoc – where Rennes-le-Château is situated – that the pope called a crusade against them, and in

1209 a huge army invaded Languedoc and murdered thousands of people. The last stand of the Languedoc Cathars occurred in 1244; the Cathars took refuge in the citadel of Montségur, situated on a mountain-top. After a ten-month siege they surrendered, and were offered lenient terms by the besiegers – all who renounced their faith could go free. Heretics who refused to surrender would be burned alive. They were given two weeks to think about it; at the end of that time two hundred heretics were dragged down the mountain (about two hundred family members were spared) and burnt on a huge pyre. But during those two weeks four men escaped from the citadel carrying the 'treasure' of the Cathars – two months earlier another two Cathars had escaped with more 'treasure'. These were not caught.

So Saunière's treasure may have been that of the Cathars of Montségur. But surely this cannot have been very substantial – after all, six men scrambling down a steep mountain-side cannot carry much gold and silver. It is, of course, conceivable that they were carrying some other form of treasure – the holy objects of the Cathars. But if that is so, what were these holy objects?

For completeness we should mention yet another treasure associated with the area: the treasure of the Visigoths (or Western Goths), the German 'barbarians' who played an important part in the downfall of Rome. In Dagobert's time Rennes-le-Château was a Visigoth bastion, and Dagobert was married to a Visigoth princess. In their triumphant march across Europe the Visigoths accumulated vast treasures, which seem to have included some of the treasures from the Temple at Jerusalem, removed after the Roman emperor Titus took Jerusalem in AD 69. Much of this treasure was never recovered.

But for Henry Lincoln the Priory of Sion materials in the *Secret Dossiers* were leading to another and far stranger line of ènquiry. After his first television programme on Rennes-le-Château (he went on to make three) he received a curious letter from an Anglican priest which claimed that the treasure did not involve gold or precious stones. It consisted of 'incontrovertible proof' that the Crucifixion was a fraud, and that Jesus was still alive as late as AD 45. (The date of the crucifixion is usually assumed to be about AD 33.) Lincoln went to see the priest, who declined to go into detail. But he admitted that his information came from an Anglican scholar named Canon Alfred Leslie Lilley. Lilley had maintained contacts with Catholic scholars based at St Sulpice, and had been acquainted with Emile Hoffet, the trainee priest who had introduced Saunière to Debussy and others.

And it gradually became clear that this was in fact the 'great secret' of the Priory of Sion. The real founder of the Merovingian dynasty was not the legendary King Merovech (or Merovée), but Jesus himself, and *this* was why the descendants of the Merovingians felt that they had a right to the throne of France. In the course of his investigations Lincoln had encountered repeated mentions of the Holy Grail or 'Sangreal'. One legend asserted that it was in the possession of the Templars, another that it was the 'treasure' carried down Montségur by the four Cathars. But 'sang real' also means 'royal blood'. The Grail was supposed to be the cup from which Jesus drank at the last supper, and Glastonbury legends assert that it was taken there by Joseph of Arimathea. In two of the Gospels, Jesus is described as being a descendant of King David, and therefore of royal blood; the notice 'The King of the Jews' displayed above the cross is generally assumed to be sarcasm, but it may have referred to a claim actually made by the close followers of Jesus.

It was in a book, *The Holy Blood and the Holy Grail* (1982), co-authored by Michael Baigent and Richard Lee, that Lincoln finally revealed this astonishing theory. It is difficult to discover from the book how far this is his own deduction from the evidence, and how far he received the information from sources like Gérard de Sède, or from M. Pierre Plantard de Saint-Clair, who claims to be a lineal descendant of Dagobert II, and the chief Merovingian pretender to the throne of modern France. But the theory itself is straightforward enough. It is that Jesus did not die on the cross – that the sponge that was proffered to him contained a drug. Lincoln points out that Jesus seems to have taken only a few hours to die, while most people took days, even weeks. His death forestalled the breaking of his legs – an act of mercy that prevented a crucified man from supporting himself on his nailed feet, and ensured his swift suffocation as his weight dragged on his arms. The sponge was offered in the nick of time. The theory also involves the assumption that Jesus was married, and that his wife was probably Mary Magdalene, who may have been identical with Mary the sister of Martha and of Lazarus. According to the theory, Jesus left Palestine and came to Languedoc, although he may have ended his life at the siege of Masada in AD 74. The hillside tomb depicted by Poussin could well be the actual tomb of Jesus.

Whether or not there is historical evidence for this theory, there is certainly evidence that this is the belief held by the Priory of Sion and by Saunière himself. He built himself a tower to house his library and called it the Magdala tower (Magdala being the name of the village from which Magdalene came). He called his house the Villa Bethania, after Bethany, the home of the other Mary, and the place from which two of the disciples fetch the ass on which Jesus rides into Jerusalem. Lincoln suggests that the man who provided the ass was Lazarus, and that it was all part of a carefully laid plan which would involve the false crucifixion.

There is a curious and baffling piece of evidence concerning Nicolas Poussin. In 1656 Nicolas Fouquet, Louis XIV's Minister of Finance, dispatched his younger brother Louis to Rome on a mission that involved a visit to Poussin. On 17 April Louis wrote Nicolas a letter commenting that Poussin had displayed 'overwhelming joy' on receiving the letter Fouquet had sent him. It then goes on:

He and I have planned certain things of which in a little while I shall be able to inform you fully; things which will give you, through M.Poussin, advantages which kings would have great difficulty in obtaining from him, and which, according to what he says, no one in the world will ever retrieve in centuries to come; and, furthermore, it would be achieved without much expense and could even turn to profit, and they are matters so difficult to enquire into that nothing on earth at the present time could bring a greater fortune nor perhaps ever its equal. . .

The comment about 'advantages which kings would have great difficulty in obtaining (or drawing) from him' is fairly clearly a reference to Louis XIV. It looks as if Fouquet is involved in some interesting plot behind Louis's back. Five years later Fouquet was arrested on vague charges of misappropriation of funds, and finally sentenced to life imprisonment. (One theory suggests that he was the Man in the Iron Mask.) Louis XIV went to great trouble to obtain the painting of the *Shepherds of Arcady* – which is also engraved on Poussin's tomb – yet instead of placing it on display, kept it in his private apartments.

Let us then see if we can begin to piece together the basic outline of this incredibly complicated story. It begins with Jesus, who is alleged to have arranged his own crucifixion and subsequent 'resurrection', presumably with the aim of 'creating faith' and establishing Christianity. Whether or not this is true, we are invited to believe that the Merovingian dynasty believed that it was descended directly from Jesus.

When Dagobert was murdered the Church endorsed the regicide; Pepin the Short, first of the Carolingians, repaid the pope by taking an army to Italy, inflicting defeats on the pope's enemies the Lombards, and handing over the captured territory, which became the basis of the Papal States. So the Merovingians came to regard themselves as the enemies of the Church of Rome. A secret society called the Priory of Sion was formed, with the object of placing the Merovingians back on the throne of France. It held some important sacred object – possibly the Grail, possibly some 'incontrovertible proof' of the descent of the Merovingians from Jesus. Its secret password was probably the phrase 'Et in Arcadia Ego.' In the twelfth century the Knights Templars became the military arm of this secret society – which means, presumably, that they shared the secret about the crucifixion – a secret, we must bear in mind, that could have undermined the foundations of the Catholic Church, which was founded upon the notion of the Vicarious Atonement. No crucifixion, no atonement, no Church. . . .

The oddest aspect of the destruction of the Templars was the accusations of blasphemy and worship of demons. But if the Templars *did* possess this knowledge, then they *were* dangerous, both to the Church and to the State (*i.e.*, to the kings of France). There is also much historical evidence of a close alliance between the Templars and the Cathars. The Cathars gave large amounts of land to the Templars, and Bertrand de Blanchefort, fourth Grand Master of the Templars, came of a Cathar family. Bertrand's descendants fought besides the Cathars of Languedoc against the invaders who were sent by the pope to stamp out Catharism.

By the sixteenth century the Merovingians were represented by the house of Lorraine (which became Habsburg-Lorraine – so the Habsburgs were also Merovingians). They tried hard to depose the ruling house of Valois, but although they finally succeeded in bringing about their extinction, they had exhausted themselves in the process and had no eligible candidate to put forward. When Louis XIII died there was another determined attempt by the conspirators to prevent Louis XIV coming to the throne; but this again failed. (Readers who wish to study this historical aspect in more detail are recommended to read Lincoln's fascinating book.)

The story of Fouquet's downfall seems to suggest that he was hoping to use the secret of the Priory of Sion to overthrow the king. It is not clear how Poussin was associated with the mystery, but he was presumably a member of the Priory, and was asked to encode its major secret – probably that of the 'incontrovertible evidence', or of the Grail – in his picture *The Shepherds of Arcady*. Lincoln argues that the painting embodies some secret geometry involving a pentagram which would enable the 'treasure' to be located. King Louis's interest in the painting suggests that he hoped to find the treasure first.

During the early years of Louis's reign the Grand Master of the Priory was, according to the *Secret Dossiers*, a German minister named Johann Valentin Andreae; and this introduces an interesting new complication. Andreae is believed to have been the author of a curious work called *The Fama Fraternitas of the Worthy Order of the Rosy Cross*, published in 1614. This claimed that an ascetic called Christian Rosenkreuz, who lived to be 106, had spent his whole life in a search for occult wisdom, and had founded an order called the Brotherhood of the Rosy Cross, or Rosicrucians. He lay buried in a secret tomb for 120 years, surrounded by lighted candles, before a brother found the tomb. Now, anyone who wished to become party to this secret wisdom only had to make their interest known and they would be contacted. . . . Many people published pamphlets announcing their desire to be initiated but (as far as is known) none of them were ever contacted. Two more Rosicrucian works were published, and scholarship has established that the author of the third of these, *The Chemical Wedding of Christian Rosenkreuz*, was Andreae. Rosicrucianism exerted a powerful influence on the minds of scholars and occultists in the seventeenth, eighteenth and nineteenth centuries. Now, according to Lincoln's sources, Andreae is revealed as a Grand Master of the Priory (twenty years after publication of the *Fama*), and we are apparently to assume that the Priory of Sion became closely identified with the Rosicrucians, and later with the various Masonic lodges.

Lincoln writes:

It was in the eighteenth century, however, that the Merovingian bloodline probably came closest to the realisation of its objectives. By virtue of its intermarriage with the Habsburgs, the house of Lorraine had actually acquired the throne of Austria, the Holy Roman Empire. When Marie Antoinette, daughter of François de Lorraine, became queen of France, the throne of France, too, was only a generation or so away. Had not the French Revolution intervened, the house of Habsburg-Lorraine might well, by the early 1800s, have been on its way to establishing dominion all over Europe.

With the Revolution, these hopes evaporated. And for some reason the Abbé Antoine Bigou, the priest of Rennes-le-Château and confessor of the Blanchefort family (of which, we may recall, one member had been a Master of the Templars) felt that both he and the secret of Rennes-le-Château were in danger. Why is not clear – the sans-culottes could hardly kill every priest in France. Possibly he thought they had been betrayed or were likely to be. At all events, he went to the trouble of writing the two coded parchments and concealing them, together with the two genealogical tables, in the Visigothic pillar. We do not know what the two tables contained – perhaps the line of descent from Jesus down to the living members of the Priory of Sion. (According to Lincoln's informant, M.Plantard, the Merovingian Pretender, they are now in a London bank vault.) Then Bigou fled to Spain, where he soon died.

So the scene was set for Saunière's appearance nearly a century later, and for his discovery of the parchments. What happened then? Saunière went to Paris, and contacted the very person – Emile Hoffet – who was able to put him in touch with the modern Priory of Sion. The Priory may well have lost touch with the secrets of Rennes-le-Château, if Bigou had hidden the 'treasure', and so would have been delighted to see him. We must assume that Saunière accepted the 'incontrovertible proof' that Jesus had not died on the cross but had founded a royal dynasty, and became a member of the Priory. He then returned to Rennes-le-Château, and used the knowledge he had gained – presumably from Debussy – to find the 'treasure'. Those excursions in the area, when he claimed to have been collecting stones for a grotto, must have been part of the treasure-hunt. He found his 'treasure', and became a rich man. But we know that much of his money came from the Habsburg family – at one point he was accused of being an Austrian spy because he was being paid by the Habsburgs – but that some of it was paid to him by the Abbé Henri Boudet, curé of nearby Rennes-les-Bains. Boudet also passed on money to the Bishop of Carcassonne. It would seem, then, that Boudet too was a member of the Priory of Sion.

When Saunière died, after enjoying his new-found wealth for less than a quarter of a century, he shocked the priest who administered the final rites by admitting that he was not, in the strict sense of the word, a Christian. He had dropped hints to the same effect in the restorations in his church: the devil inside the door (Rex Mundi) – Asmodeus, the legendary guardian of Solomon's treasure – and many baffling touches in the tableau of the crucifixion, such as a money bag at the foot of the cross. Over the door he had inscribed the words TERRIBILIS EST LOCUS ISTE: this place is terrible. The words are from the dedicatory mass sung for new churches, and 'terrible' here means 'awe-inspiring'; but it still seems odd that Saunière should have chosen them for the motto of his church, seen immediately before the visitor encounters its 'demon guardian'.

Lincoln seems to feel that the solution to the mystery of Saunière's wealth is that it came from the Priory of Sion. But this is disputed by other writers. Brian Innes, who conducted a four-part investigation of the mystery in a magazine called *The Unexplained* in 1980, points out that quantities of gold have been found in the area. In 1645 a shepherd boy called Ignace Paris was executed for theft; he was in possession of gold coins, and claimed that he had found these after falling down a ravine and finding his way into a cave full of treasure. Innes says that more recently a slab of gold weighing nearly 45lb has been found near Rennes-le-Château, made from fused Arab (or Crusader) coins, and that in 1928 the remains of a large gold statue were found in a hut on the edge of a stream that flows below the village.

In their book *The Holy Grail Revealed: The Real Secret of Rennes-le-Château*, Patricia and Lionel Fanthorpe also argue strongly that Saunière found real treasure, not merely some ancient secret. Yet they are also inclined to agree with Lincoln that there was also some 'object' referred to as the Grail which could confer power on those who owned it: they compare it to the Ring of Power in Tolkien's *Lord of the Rings*, and even suggest in one place, that it might be of 'extra-terrestrial origin', linking Rennes-le-Château with the 'ancient astronaut' theories of Erich von Däniken.

None of the theories can provide a complete solution to the mystery of Rennes-le-Château, but on the whole Lincoln comes closest to it. For the twentieth-century reader, the notion that Jesus survived the crucifixion and founded a dynasty is not particularly 'terrible'. Yet we can see that for Nicolas Poussin and Louis Fouquet this notion would have seemed hair-raising, a kind of spiritual dynamite, sufficient to undermine sixteen centuries of Christianity and the authority of the pope. Even for Saunière, living at the end of the sceptical nineteenth century, it must have seemed quite startling.

Is it likely that we shall ever get to the bottom of the mystery? It is well within the realms of possibility. Presumably the Priory of Sion knows precisely what Saunière found near Rennes-le-Château in the hillside tomb or the old fortress, and its increasing tendency to 'go public' may mean that we shall sooner or later be told the whole story. But even if that does not happen, the solution could still lie in the message on the second parchment – in solving the puzzle contained in Poussin and Teniers, in working out the meaning of 'Peace 681' (which could refer to the year 1799, since Templar Freemasons dated the calendar from the year 1118), the horse of God, the demon of the guardian at noon, and the blue apples. But whoever discovers the secret can be reasonably certain of one thing: that the treasure itself will be missing.

29 Did Robin Hood Really Exist?

Next to King Arthur, Robin Hood is the most famous of British heroes, and he shares with King Arthur the indignity of having his existence doubted by modern scholarship. The folklorist Lord Raglan concluded that he was really a Celtic god, while in *The God of the Witches* Margaret Murray argues that his name means *Robin of the Hood*, and that he was probably the devil (or horned god) in ancient witchcraft festivals. Yet there is also convincing evidence that Robin was a real person, and that – as the ballads declare – he plundered the king's deer in Sherwood Forest and had a long-standing feud with the Sheriff of Nottingham.

The first literary reference to Robin Hood occurs in William Langland's *Piers Plowman*, dating from around 1377. Langland makes a priest remark that he could not say his paternoster without making mistakes, but 'I know rhymes of Robyn Hood and Randolf Earl of Chester.' So there were already ballads of Robin Hood by that date. In 1510 Wynkyn de Worde, one of the earliest printers, brought out *A Lytell Geste of Robyn Hood*, which did for Robin Hood what Malory had done for King Arthur in the middle of the previous century. And by the time he appears in Sir Walter Scott's *Ivanhoe* (1847) Robin had become the boon-companion and ally of Richard the Lion Heart, the heroic outlaw of the woods. All that was needed then was for some folklorist to notice how often Robin Hood's name is associated with folk festivals, like the Hobby Horse ceremony which takes place on May Day in Padstow, Cornwall,[1] to suggest that Robin Hood was really Robin Wood, and that his name is derived from the Norse god Woden . . . In fact he appears as Robin Wood in T.H.White's *Sword in the Stone*, in which he becomes a contemporary of King Arthur, who (if he ever existed) was said to have died about AD 540.

Those who assume there is no smoke without fire are inclined to believe that Robin Hood was a real outlaw who at some time lived in Sherwood Forest, and who became so popular during his own lifetime that, like Billy the Kid, he soon became the subject of tales and ballads. Yet it seems unlikely that he was around as early as Richard the Lion Heart (1157–99), or he would surely have been mentioned in manuscripts before *Piers Plowman* two centuries later. In his *Chronicle of Scotland*, written about 1420, Andrew Wyntoun refers to Robin Hood and Little John for the year 1283, which sounds altogether more likely – about a century before *Piers Plowman*.

And where precisely did he operate? One important clue is that there is a

---

[1] Actually 8 May, but the date has become displaced over the centuries.

small fishing town called Robin Hood's Bay in Yorkshire, not far from Whitby, and that up on the nearby moors there are two tumuli (or barrows) called Robin Hood's Butts. Another is that in medieval England the forest of Barnsdale in Yorkshire joined Sherwood Forest in Nottinghamshire. A sixteenth-century life of Robin Hood among the Sloane Manuscripts says he was born in Locksley, in Yorkshire, about 1160. *The Chronicle of Scotland* associates Robin with 'Barnysale' presumably Barnsdale. So the evidence suggests that he was a Yorkshireman.

Later legends declare that he was 'Sir Robin of Locksley', or even the Earl of Huntingdon. But it is clear from the earlier ballads that he was a yeoman – a farmer who owns his own land – and that this is partly why he became such a hero: not because he was a nobleman, but because he was a representative of the people. (A small tenant farmer would be only one stage above a landless peasant.)

One of the most important clues to Robin's identity emerged in the mid-nineteenth century, when the Historic Documents Commission was cataloguing thousands of documents which represented eight centuries of British history. It was in 1852 that the antiquary Joseph Hunter claimed that he had stumbled upon a man who sounded as if he might be the original Robin Hood. His name in fact was Robert, and he was the son of Adam Hood, a forester in the service of the Earl de Warenne. (Robin was simply a diminutive of Robert – not, in those days, a name in its own right.) He was born about 1280, and on 25 January 1316 Robert Hood and his wife Matilda paid two shillings for permission to take a piece of the earl's waste ground in 'Bickhill' (or Bitch-hill) in Wakefield. It was merely the size of a kitchen garden – thirty feet long by sixteen feet wide. The rent for this was sixpence a year. The Manor Court Roll for 1357 shows a house 'formerly the property of Robert Hode' on the site – so by that time Robert Hood was presumably dead.

Now, 1316 was midway through the reign of Edward the Second, the foppish, homosexual king who was finally murdered – by having a red-hot spit inserted into his entrails – in September 1327. After his coronation (in 1307) he dismissed his father's ministers and judges and made his lover, Piers Gaveston, Earl of Cornwall – to the fury of his barons. It was the most powerful of these, Thomas, Earl of Lancaster, who forced Edward to accept the rule of twenty-eight barons (called Ordainers), and who finally executed Piers Gaveston in 1312. Edward's lack of attention to affairs of state allowed the Scots – against whom his father Edward I had fought so successfully – to throw off their English masters. Edward II was defeated at Bannockburn in 1314, two years before Robin Hood hired the piece of waste ground and set up home with his wife Matilda. So it is understandable that when the Earl of Warenne was ordered by the king to raise a troop to fight the Scots Robert Hood failed to oblige, and the records show that he was accordingly fined. But when a second muster was raised in 1317 Hood's name was not listed among those fined – which led J.W.Walker, a modern historian, to conclude that this time Robin Hood joined the army. Five years later it was the Earl of Lancaster who raised the army, to fight against the king. Again, Hood's name is not among those fined, so it again seems that he answered the summons. Lancaster's army was defeated at Boroughbridge, and Lancaster was captured and beheaded. The quarrel had been about Edward's new favourites, the Despensers, father and son, whom he had been forced to banish; now he was able to recall them.

Many of Lancaster's supporters were declared outlaws, and Walker discovered a document that stated that a 'building of five rooms' on Bichhill, Wakefield, was among the property confiscated. Walker believes that this was Robert Hood's home, and that the outlaw now took refuge in the nearby forest of Barnsdale, where he soon became a highly successful robber.

Now, it must be understood that if Robert Hood *was* the legendary Robin, and he took refuge in the forest, living off the deer population, he was risking horrible penalties. When William the Conqueror brought the Normans to England he declared that the forests – which covered a third of the land – were his own property; any peasant who killed deer risked being literally flayed alive. Under William the Saxons suffered as much as countries occupied by the Nazis in the Second World War. Two and a half centuries later the Normans regarded themselves as Englishmen, and the French language had ceased to be used in England, but the laws were still harsh. The 'forest laws' had been mitigated, so a man could no longer have his hands or his lips sliced off for poaching a deer; but the penalty was still a heavy fine, a year's imprisonment, and sureties for his future good behaviour. If he could not find guarantors he had to 'abjure the realm' – quit the kingdom for ever.

The battle of Boroughbridge was fought on 16 March 1322, near the Ure river in Yorkshire; dismounted men-at-arms and archers drove back the cavalry, then another royalist army moved up behind the rebels and forced them to surrender. Lancaster was captured and tried; evidence revealed that he had been contemplating an alliance with the king's old enemy Robert the Bruce. Lancaster – the king's cousin – was beheaded. And Robin Hood, deprived of his home, became an outlaw in the king's forest.

But if Walker is correct in identifying Robert Hood of Wakefield as Robin Hood, he was not an outlaw for long. In the spring of the following year the king made a progress through the north of England, reaching York on 1 May. From 16 May to 21 May he stayed at Rothwell, between Wakefield and Leeds, and spent three days hunting at Plumpton Park in Knaresborough Forest. And the *Lytell Geste* makes this visit a part of the story of Robin Hood, describing how the king 'came to Plompton Park / And failed [missed] many of his deer.' Where the king was accustomed to seeing herds of deer, now he could find only one deer 'that bore any good horn'. Which made the king swear by the Trinity 'I wish I could lay my hands on Robin Hood':

I wolde I had Robyn Hode
With eyen I myght hym se.

So, according to this ballad, one of the foresters suggested that the king should disguise himself as an abbot, riding through the greenwood with a band of monks. The ruse was successful; Robin and his men stopped the 'abbot', but recognized him as the king. And the king thereupon found Robin so likable that he invited him to join the royal household as a *vadlet*, a gentleman of the royal bedchamber. The king continued on his travels until February 1324, when he returned to Westminster. The royal household accounts for April record payment of the past month's wages to Robyn Hod and twenty-eight others. The first record of a payment to Robyn Hod is in the previous June. The ballad tells us that after being a servant of the king for somewhat over a year Robin asked the king's permission to return to Barnsdale. And the household accounts for November 1324 record that Robyn Hod, formerly one of the 'porteurs' (gentlemen of the bedchamber) had been given five shillings 'because he is no longer able to work'. The ballad says that Robin asked the king's leave to return to Barnsdale, and was given permission to stay for seven days. But he never returned; instead he regrouped his merry men, and lived on in the greenwood for another twenty-two years. If this is based on fact, then he died about 1346, in his mid-sixties.

The king's fortunes took a downward turn after Robin's departure. He had recalled the banished Despensers, and the younger of the two had become his 'favourite' – to the disgust of his queen, who had already had to contend with Piers Gaveston. She was a Frenchwoman, daughter of Philip the Fair. Now she began to take a romantic interest in an unpleasant and ambitious young baron called Roger de Mortimer, who had been thrown into the Tower for his opposition to the Despensers. Queen Isabella became his mistress, and it was probably she who plotted Mortimer's escape. He fled to Paris, and was joined there by Isabella, who was on a mission for the king. They landed at Orwell, in Suffolk, with an army of almost three thousand. When the king heard the news he fled, and was captured, and imprisoned in Berkeley Castle. He was forced to abdicate, and his son (aged fifteen) was crowned Edward III. On the night of 21 September 1327 horrible screams rang through the castle. The next morning it was announced that the king had died 'of natural causes'. There were no marks on the body, but it is said that his features were still contorted with agony. A chronicle of some thirty years later states that three assassins entered his cell when he was asleep, and held down the upper half of his body with a table. Then a horn was inserted into the anal orifice, and a red-hot iron bar was used to burn out the king's insides.

Mortimer and Isabella ruled England as regents for four years; then the young king asserted himself, had Mortimer seized in Nottingham Castle, and had him executed as a traitor at Tyburn. The loss of her lover almost drove the queen mad. But she was restored to favour, and lived on for another twenty-eight years.

It is of course conceivable that the Robin Hood who lived in Edward's reign had no connection with the legendary outlaw of Sherwood Forest; one reference book (*Who's Who In History*) says that he was alive in 1230, in the reign of Henry III, on the grounds that records show that the Sheriff of Yorkshire sold his possessions in that year (for 32s 6d) when he became an outlaw; but the same reference book admits that the Robyn Hode of Wakefield is also a good contender. There is something to be said for this earlier dating, for it would give more time for the legend of Robin Hood to spread throughout England. But there is also a great deal to be said for Robin Hood of Wakefield. If he became an outlaw in 1322, as a result of the Lancaster rebellion, then he spent only one year in Sherwood Forest before the king pardoned him. The story of his pardon by the homosexual king certainly rings true – as does his appointment as a gentleman of the bedchamber. It is natural to speculate that he may have found that his duties in the bedchamber involved more than he had bargained for, although at this time the king's favourite was the younger Hugh le Despenser (executed by Mortimer and Isabella in 1326). So he returned to the greenwood, and became a hero of legend. We do not know whether he became the arch-enemy of the Sheriff of Nottingham, but the sheriff – who would be the equivalent of a modern Chief Constable – would have been responsible for law and order in Nottinghamshire and south Yorkshire, and would certainly have resented a band of outlaws who lived off the king's deer. One chronicle states that Robin also had a retreat in what became known as Robin Hood's Bay, and ships in which he could escape to sea. (He is also said to have operated as far afield as Cumberland.) If a concerted attempt had been made to flush him out, it would probably have succeeded. But most of the peasants and tenant farmers would have been on Robin's side. There had been a time when the forests of England were common land, and half-starved peasantry must have felt it was highly unreasonable that thousands of square miles of forest should be reserved for the king's hunting, when the king could not make use of a fraction of that area.

But there could be another reason that Robin was allowed to operate without too much opposition. When he was at court he must surely have met the fourteen-year-old boy who would become Edward III, and Edward would be of exactly the right age to look with admiration on a famous outlaw. This is only speculation, but it could undoubtedly explain why Robin was allowed to become the legendary bane of authority in the last decades of his life.

Authority has its own ways of striking back. According to the Sloane Manuscript, Robin fell ill, and went to his cousin, the Prioress of Kirklees, to be bled – the standard procedure for treating any illness in those days. She decided to avenge the many churchmen he had robbed, and allowed him to bleed to death. Another account says that she betrayed him at the request of her lover, Sir Roger de Doncaster. Still another source states that the man responsible for Robin's death was a monk who was called in to attend him, and who decided that the outlaw would be better dead. He was buried in the grounds of the nunnery, within a bowshot of its walls. Grafton's Chronicle (1562) says he was buried under an inscribed stone, and a century later another chronicle reported that his tomb, with a plain cross on a flat stone, could be seen in the cemetery; in 1665 Dr Nathaniel Johnstone made a drawing of it; Gough's *Sepulchral Monuments* also has an engraving of the tombstone. In the early nineteenth century navvies building a railway broke up the stone – it is said they believed its chips to be a cure for toothache. So the last trace of the real existence of Robin Hood disappeared. But by that time the grave of the prioress had been discovered among the ruins of the nunnery, and it bore some resemblance to the tomb of Robin Hood. It also mentioned her name – Elizabeth Stainton.

The real significance of Robin Hood is that he lived in a century when the peasants were beginning to feel an increasing resentment about their condition – a resentment that expressed itself in the revolutionary doctrines of John Ball, and which exploded in the Peasants' Revolt of 1381, only a short time after Robin is first mentioned in print by Langland. The Peasants' Revolt is generally considered to mark the end of the Middle Ages; but it is in the ballads of Robin Hood that we can see that the state of mind known as the Middle Ages is coming to an end.

30 The Mystery Death of Mary Rogers

The mysterious death of the 'cigar girl' Mary Rogers, which caused a sensation in New York in the summer of 1841, would hardly cause a raised eyebrow in the same city today. That the mystery has never been forgotten is largely the work of Edgar Allan Poe, who transformed it into a classic detective story. Half a century after the death of the cigar girl, information came to light that suggested that Poe's 'guess' had been at least partly correct – and that led one writer to suggest that Poe himself may have committed the murder.

Mary Cecilia Rogers was born in New York in 1820; her mother, who became a widow when the child was five, supported herself by running a boarding-house in Nassau Street. Mary grew up into a tall, very beautiful young woman with jet-black hair. This led a cigar-store owner named John Anderson, whose shop was on Broadway, to offer her a job as a salesgirl. In 1840 this was regarded as an imaginative piece of business enterprise, for New York was even more 'Victorian' than London, and young unmarried girls did not exhibit themselves behind shop counters, particularly in shops frequented exclusively by young men. Mary's mother objected to the idea, but her daughter's enthusiasm finally won her over. She drew many new customers to the shop, although – as Thomas Duke is careful to note in his *Celebrated Criminal Cases of America* (1910) – 'the girl's conduct was apparently a model of modest decorum, and while she was lavish in her smiles, she did not hesitate to repel all undue advances'.

She had been working in the store about ten months when one day in January 1841 she failed to appear. Her mother had no idea where she was, and according to Duke, 'Mr Anderson was unable to account for her absence'. The police searched for her and the newspapers reported her disappearance. Six days later she reappeared, looking tired and rather ill, and explained that she had been visiting relatives in the country. Her mother and her employer apparently corroborated the story. But when a rumour began to circulate that she had been seen during her absence with a tall, handsome naval officer Mary abruptly gave up her job – only a few days after returning – and was no longer seen on Broadway. A month later she announced her engagement to one of her mother's boarders, a clerk called Daniel Payne.

Five months later, on Sunday 25 July 1841, Mary knocked on her fiancé's door at 10 a.m. and announced that she was going to see her aunt in Bleecker Street; Payne said that he would call for her that evening. Payne also spent the day away from home, but when a violent thunderstorm came on towards evening he decided not to call for Mary, but to let her stay the night with her aunt. Mrs Rogers apparently approved. But when Mary failed to return home the following day she began to worry. When Payne returned from work and learned that Mary was still away, he rushed to see the aunt in Bleecker Street – a Mrs Downing – and was even more alarmed when she told him that she had not seen Mary in the past forty-eight hours.

It was two days later on Wednesday morning that three men in a sailing-boat saw a body in the water off Castle Point, Hoboken. It was Mary, and according to the *New York Tribune* 'it was obvious that she had been horribly outraged and murdered'. She was fully clothed, although her clothes were torn, and the petticoat was missing. A piece of lace from the bottom of the dress was embedded so deeply in the throat that it had almost disappeared. An autopsy performed almost immediately led to the conclusion that she had been 'brutally violated'. Oddly enough, Daniel Payne did not go to view the corpse, although he had earlier searched for her all over New York, including Hoboken. But after being interrogated by the police, Payne was released.

A week passed without any fresh clues, and a large reward was offered. Then the coroner received a letter from some anonymous man – who said he had not come forward before from 'motives of perhaps criminal prudence' – and who claimed to have seen Mary Rogers on the Sunday afternoon of her disappearance. She had, the writer said, stepped out of a boat with six rough-looking characters, and gone with them into the woods, laughing merrily and apparently under no kind of constraint. Soon afterwards a boat with three well-dressed men had come ashore, and one of these accosted two men walking on the beach and asked if they had seen a young woman and six men recently. They said that they had, and that she had appeared to go with them willingly. At this the trio turned their boat and headed back for New York.

In fact, the two men came forward and corroborated this story. But although they both knew Mary Rogers by sight, neither of them could swear that the girl they had seen was definitely Mary.

The next important piece of information came from a stagecoach-driver named Adams, who said he had seen Mary arrive on the Hoboken ferry with a well-dressed man of dark complexion, and that they had gone to a roadhouse called 'Nick Mullen's'. This tavern was kept by a Mrs Loss, who told the police that the couple had 'taken refreshment' there, then gone off into the woods. Some time later she had heard a scream from the woods; but since the place 'was a resort of questionable characters' she had thought no more of it.

Two months after the murder, on 25 September, children playing in the woods found the missing petticoat in a thicket; they also found a white silk scarf, a parasol and a handkerchief marked 'M.R.' Daniel Payne was to commit suicide in this spot soon after.

A gambler named Joseph Morse, who lived in Nassau Street, was arrested and apparently charged with the murder; there was evidence that he had been seen with Mary Rogers on the evening she disappeared. The following day, he had fled from New York. But Morse was released when he was able to prove that he had been at Staten Island with another young lady on the

Sunday afternoon. One odd story in the *Tribune* declared that Morse believed that the young lady *was* Mary Rogers, and that when he heard of the disappearance he assumed she had committed suicide because of the way he had treated her – he had tried to seduce her in his room. He was relieved to learn that the girl with whom he had spent the afternoon was still alive.

In the following year, 1842, Poe's 'Mystery of Marie Roget' was published in three parts in *Snowden's Ladies' Companion*. But for anyone looking for a solution of the Mary Rogers mystery, it should be treated with extreme caution. Poe argues that Mary Rogers was not murdered by a gang but by a single individual. His original view seems to have been that the motive was rape; later he heard the rumour that Mary had died as a result of an abortion, and made a few hasty alterations in his story to accommodate this notion. He argues that the signs of a struggle in the woods, and the battered state of her face, indicate that she was killed by an individual – a gang would have been able to overpower her easily. He also speaks of a strip from the girl's skirt that had been wound around the waist to afford a kind of handle for carrying the body; but the evidence of two witnesses who dragged the body out of the water makes no mention of this 'handle'. In spite of this, there can be no doubt that Poe's objections to the gang theory carry a great deal of weight.

In an issue of a magazine called *The Unexplained* (No. 152) Grahame Fuller and Ian Knight suggest that Poe himself may have been the killer of Mary Rogers. A witness thought he had seen her with a tall, well-dressed man of swarthy complexion on the afternoon she died; the authors point out that Poe had an olive complexion and was always well dressed. But Poe was only five feet eight inches tall – hardly a 'tall man'. They also argue that Poe may have killed Mary Rogers in a fit of 'alcoholic insanity'. In 1841 Poe's wife Virginia was dying of tuberculosis and he was under considerable stress; he wrote later: 'I became insane, with long intervals of horrible sanity. During these fits of unconsciousness I drank, God only knows how often or how much.' Yet none of Poe's biographers have ever suggested that he was a violent person – on the contrary, most emphasize his gentleness and courtesy. There have been plenty of alcoholic men of genius, a few of whom – like Ben Jonson or Caravaggio – have killed men in duels or quarrels; but there is not a single example of one who has ever committed a murder. Besides, no witness suggested that the man who was seen with Mary Rogers was blind drunk. On the whole, the notion of Poe as a demonic killer, writing 'The Mystery of Marie Roget' to boast about his crime, must be relegated to the realm of fantasy.

What was not known to Poe in 1842 is that Mary's employer, John Anderson, had been questioned by the police as a suspect; like all the others, he was released. But fifty years later – in December 1891 – new evidence was to emerge. By that time Anderson had been dead ten years; he became a millionaire, and died in Paris. Apparently he had told friends that he had experienced 'many unhappy days and nights in regard to her' (Mary Rogers), and had been in touch with her spirit. His heirs contested his estate, and in 1891 his daughter tried to break her father's will on the grounds that when he signed it he was mentally incompetent. The case was settled out of court, and the records destroyed. But a lawyer named Samuel Copp Worthen, who had been closely associated with Anderson's daughter Laura Appleton, knew that his firm had kept a copy of the testimony in the Supreme Court of New York in 1891, and he made it his business to read it. He finally revealed what he had learned in the periodical *American Literature* in 1948. It revealed that Anderson had been questioned by the police about the death of Mary Rogers, and that this had preyed on his mind, so that he later declined to stand as a candidate for mayor of New York, in case someone revealed his secret.

The most significant part of the testimony was the assertion that Anderson had admitted to paying for an abortion for Mary Rogers and had got 'in some trouble over it'. But he had insisted that he had not 'had anything, directly, himself, to do with her problems'.

This would obviously explain Mary's week-long disappearance from the cigar store, and the fact that she looked tired and ill when she returned. It probably also explains why she decided to leave the store a week later – not because of gossip about the naval officer, but because she needed more time to convalesce.

Worthen's theory is that in the six months after leaving the cigar store Mary again got herself pregnant, and once more appealed to Anderson for help. When she left home that Sunday morning she intended to go to Hoboken for an abortion. (In fact, there was a story that Mrs Loss, the tavern-owner, had admitted on her deathbed that Mary Rogers had died during an abortion; there is no hard evidence for this confession, but it *is* known that the District Attorney was inclined to the abortion theory of Mary's death.) She died during the abortion, and her body was dumped in the river to protect the abortionist – the dark-skinned man with whom she was seen on the ferry – and Mrs Loss's family.

How does this theory fit the known facts? The answer is: very well indeed, particularly if we make the natural assumption that the father of the second unborn child was Daniel Payne – for it seems unlikely that Mary agreed to marry him, then continued her affair with her former lover. (Nothing is known about this former lover, but Anderson is obviously a suspect.) We must assume, then, that Payne knew perfectly well that Mary was on her way to Hoboken to have an illegal operation. We may also probably assume that the pregnancy was still in its early stages, and that Mary anticipated very little trouble – after all, she had recovered from the earlier abortion in a week, though it still left her feeling ill. Mary's mother was probably also in the secret. Duke comments: 'It was generally believed at the time that the murdered girl's mother knew more about her daughter's mysterious admirer than she chose to tell.'

What of the evidence about the gang? It is possible, of course, that a young girl was actually seen entering the woods with a gang of men, and that this was nothing to do with Mary Rogers. But it far more probable that the anonymous letter claiming that Mary had entered the woods with six ruffians was sent by Mrs Loss or one of her friends – it came from Hoboken. Then all she had to do was to persuade two of her relatives or friends to claim that they were the men on the beach, and that they had seen Mary enter the woods and seen the boat with three men that landed shortly afterwards. . . . The result would be a perfect red herring, directing the attention of the police away from her own abortion parlour.

What of the petticoat found later in the woods? This, significantly enough, was found by Mrs Loss's children. We may assume that the petticoat, the umbrella and the handkerchief were left behind in Mrs Loss's roadhouse when Mary's body was dragged to the water in the middle of the night, and were later planted in the woods, in a place where the bushes were broken, to suggest evidence of a struggle.

And what of the evidence that Mary had been raped? This, apparently, was the coroner's report; we do not know whether she was examined by a doctor or if so what the doctor concluded. What we *do* know is that Mary's body was already decomposing, and that because of the hot July weather it was buried within a few hours of being taken out of the water; so any inquest would have been performed in haste. In 1841 the science of legal medicine was in its infancy, and it is doubtful whether anyone took a vaginal swab and examined it under a microscope for spermatozoa. What was probably taken for evidence of rape was actually evidence of an abortion that had gone wrong.

Duke reports that Daniel Payne committed suicide 'at the same spot in the woods where his sweetheart was probably slain'. Other writers on the case have questioned this (notably Charles E. Pearce in *Unsolved Murder Mysteries*, 1924). But Payne's suicide would certainly be consistent with the theory that he was the father of the unborn child.

It is a disappointing – if obvious – solution to one of the great 'murder mysteries', that Mary Rogers died in the course of an abortion. Why is it not more generally known? Partly because Poe himself obscured the truth. In the 1850 edition of Poe's works published in the year after his death 'Marie Roget' appeared with a footnote that stated:

It may not be improper to record . . . that the confessions of *two* persons (one of them the Madame Dulac of the narrative [Mrs Loss]) made at different periods long subsequent to the publication confessed, in full, not only the general conclusion but absolutely *all* the chief hypothetical details by which the conclusion was attained.

But this is obviously impossible. Mrs Loss only seems to have confessed that Mary had died in the course of an abortion in her tavern. Poe's theory was that she was murdered by a man 'in a passion' who then dragged her body to the seashore. The likely truth seems to be that she died of an air embolism, and that the abortionist, with the aid of Mrs Loss, made the death look like murder by tying a strip of cloth round her throat; the two of them then probably carried it to the water. Poe's 'Marie Roget', far from being an amazingly accurate reconstruction of the murder, is simply a bad guess. Poe may not have been a murderer, but he was undoubtedly a liar.

31 What Became of the Russian Royal Family?

According to the history books, the last tsar of Russia was murdered, together with his family, in a cellar in the small town of Ekaterinburg (now Sverdlovsk) in the Urals. It happened on the night of 16 July 1918. Revolution had broken out in Petrograd (formerly St Petersburg) on 8 March of the previous year the immediate cause being riots due to shortage of bread, and in the autumn the Bolsheviks ousted Kerensky's provisional government. The royal family – Tsar Nicholas II, the Tsarina Alexandra, their son Alexei and their four daughters Olga, Tatiana, Maria and Anastasia – became prisoners in the royal palace. The provisional government had planned to send them to England, but agitation by Lloyd George prevented it; in August 1917 they were sent to Tobolsk, in Siberia, then – in the following spring – to Ekaterinburg.

They apparently had no reason to suspect that they were about to be killed. They were told that, since the White Russian (counter-revolutionary) armies were drawing near, they were about to be evacuated to Czechoslovakia. That evening they were ordered down to the cellar. Alexei, the thirteen-year-old heir to the throne, had to be carried by his father; he suffered from hereditary haemophilia, a condition in which the blood lacks a clotting agent, so that a scratch can prove fatal. The Tsar was given a chair to sit on. Their gaoler, a Siberian Jew named Yurovsky, said 'Nicholas Alexandrovich, your followers have tried to set you free. They failed. Now you are going to be shot.' 'What?' asked the Tsar. 'This', said Yurovsky, and shot him in the chest with a revolver. He fell dead. The others dropped on their knees, and were all shot in that position – according to the 'records', ten of them: the Tsarina and her five children, their doctor Botkin, their cook and two servants, and the pet spaniel. Meanwhile, a lorry revved its engine outside to drown the noise. The bodies were then destroyed with vitriol and thrown down a mine shaft. A few days later – on the 25th – the town fell to the Whites, and an investigation was ordered. The result of that investigation was a book, *Judicial Enquiry into the Assassination of the Russian Imperial Family* by Nikolai Sokolov, which stated the facts as they have been summarized above.

Yet one of these 'facts' already stands out as peculiar. Why destroy the bodies with vitriol before disposing of them? It would have required a vast quantity of vitriol to dispose of ten bodies. And why bother anyway? The living tsar might become the focus of a counter-revolution, but a dead tsar is harmless, whether or not he is recognizable. . . .

Two days after the murders described by Sokolov, an official statement announced that the Tsar had been executed, but stated that 'his wife and son have been sent to a safe place'. Two days later still, on the 20th, a workers' meeting was told that the town would soon fall to the Whites, but that they would not free the Tsar because he had been shot. He added that the rest of the royal family had been sent away.

In the 1970s two investigative reporters, Anthony Summers and Tom Mangold – both of the BBC – heard about certain photographs taken during the Sokolov investigation, which had turned up in the attic of a Paris antique dealer in 1962. But the actual documentation was missing. Sokolov had accumulated a seven-volume dossier, from which he had written his book. But obviously, his book had been selective. Summers and Mangold set out upon the almost impossible task of trying to track down the rest of the 'file on the tsar'. A tsarist officer in Paris, General Pozdnyshev, asserted that the documents had been stolen by the Germans, but that there was a second set, which was safe 'in the hands of neutrals'. The investigators discovered that this set had been entrusted to a British journalist, Robert Wilton of *The Times*. They tracked down Wilton's last known landlady, but she was unable to help. They advertised in the personal columns of *The Times*, and learned from a relative that Wilton's widow had auctioned the dossiers at Sotheby's in 1937. Sotheby's advised the investigators to check their old records in the British Museum. These revealed that the dossiers had been sold to a dealer in rare books in Mayfair. The dealer eventually got permission from the widow of the purchaser to reveal his identity. She told them that the dossier had been sold for a four-figure sum to an executive of the Bell Telephone Company. And finally, the retired executive was able to tell them that he had donated the dossier to the Houghton Library of Harvard University. And so the investigators finally tracked down Sokolov's evidence for the death of the Russian royal family.

This, they discovered, cast considerable doubt on the story told in Sokolov's book. The problem faced by Sokolov and other 'White' investigators was simple. It was to their advantage to prove that the Tsar and his family had been brutally murdered by the Reds. And obviously, if their final evidence was inconclusive, then it would be understandable if they ended by accepting the horrific story of the Ekaterinburg cellar. But there was one problem. The investigation failed to reveal any of the corpses. According to Sokolov, this is because the corpses were all taken to a nearby mine – the Four Brothers – where they were hacked to pieces, soaked in vitriol, then burned with large quantities of petrol. But Summers and Mangold spoke to several noted pathologists who all denied that it would be possible totally to destroy bodies like this, in the open air; a great deal of bone would be left over – and presumably thrown down the mine. And the mine did in fact contain a few tell-tale items, including a finger and set of false teeth – identified as being those of Dr Botkin. And the corpse of a dog, identified as 'Jemmy', the pet of the royal family, was also found in the mine (although much later). But apparently nothing that might be interpreted as bone-fragments of the royal family and its servants, not even a single tooth. (Teeth are the most difficult part of a body to destroy).

In late September 1918 the British Foreign Office sent a trained observer, Sir Charles Eliot, to Ekaterinburg to study the evidence for the murders. In October, Sir Charles wrote a long report, in which he described the 'death room', with seventeen bullet-holes in the wall and door – all close to the floor (apparently supporting the suggestion that the victims were kneeling at – the time). He suggests that the evidence indicates that there were five victims – the Tsar, Dr Botkin, and the three servants. He goes on to say that the next day a train with the blinds down left Ekaterinburg for an unknown destination. If he is correct in counting only seventeen bullet-holes (Sokolov speaks of twenty-seven), it seems that most of the eleven victims were finished off with just one bullet, which seems unlikely. Eliot adds that it is the general opinion that the empress and her five children were sent off to the north or west.

There was another piece of evidence that supported this view. The girls all had shoulder-length hair, and a priest saw them with hair intact two days before the disappearance. But four lots of hair, identified as coming from the four girls, was found in the Ipatiev house where they were supposedly murdered. So was part of the Tsar's beard. Why cut their hair to murder them? On the other hand, if they were to be taken elsewhere, then it might be just as well to 'disguise' them; the Tsar's beard was quite distinctive.

In December 1918 a report of the murder, originating from the 'White government' in Omsk, spoke of the girls being repeatedly raped while the Tsar, chained to a chair, was forced to look on. Another report said that the girls had been raped for days before their murder, and that a Lett called Biron, who had fired the first shot, had shouted in front of several witnesses: 'Now I can die, I have had the empress . . .' This seems to have been pure invention, but it reveals why the Whites should have preferred the tale of the Ekaterinburg massacre to some less definite story about the family having been moved 'north' by train, and then having disappeared. It was far better propaganda.

There is one interesting and notorious complication in this tale of the fate of the imperial family: the mystery of 'Anastasia'. Anastasia was the youngest of the four daughters. She was seventeen in July 1918. Two years later, in February 1920, a girl of about twenty tried to commit suicide by jumping into a Berlin canal. During six weeks in hospital she refused to speak, and she preserved her silence in a mental home at Dalldorf. In 1922 a fellow-patient told a former tsarist officer that she had recognized the patient as the Grand Duchess Tatiana, the second eldest of the Tsar's children, who was twenty-one at the time of the 'massacre'. A former police official, Baron Arthur von Kleist, took 'Tatiana' into his own home, and in June 1922 she told Kleist that she was the Grand Duchess Anastasia, and that she had been present at the 'massacre'. She had been knocked unconscious, rescued by a soldier named Tchaikovsky, and later moved with Tchaikovsky and his family to Rumania, where she bore him a son who was placed in an orphanage. Tchaikovsky was killed in a street fight in Bucharest, and Anastasia had drifted to Berlin, where she attempted suicide. . . .

The royal families of Europe began to take an interest in 'Anastasia'. The Tsarina's sister Olga sent the ex-tutor of the royal family, Pierre Gilliard, to see 'Anastasia', and he was apparently at first convinced; Olga later went with Gilliard; her own conclusion was that the girl was not her niece Anastasia, but that she was not consciously trying to deceive. In 1926 she stated publicly that she did not believe the girl to be Anastasia. Gilliard himself is suspect; when he later denounced 'Anastasia' as an impostor one of the reasons he gave was that she spoke only German, and the real Anastasia knew no German. Yet Gilliard himself had taught her German, as her school exercise books later proved.

Another uncle, Grand Duke Andrei, who knew the original Anastasia far better than Olga did, had no doubt that she was his niece. Many more relatives and acquaintances became equally convinced of her genuineness. Felix Dassel, an officer who knew her well, was suddenly convinced when he referred to an old colonel, and Anastasia giggled: 'The man with the pockets.' She had given the colonel this nickname because he had forgotten himself and addressed the Grand Duchesses with his hands in his pockets. When Dr Botkin's daughter said to Anastasia, 'I will undress you just as my father did' the girl replied immediately, 'Yes, measles.' The only time Botkin had stayed with the girls was when they had measles.

In 1927 a private detective claimed to have proved that Anastasia was really a Polish factory worker, Franziska Schanzkowska, who had vanished in Berlin in 1920, but Franziska's brother flatly denied this when he confronted her.

So far Anastasia had made no attempt to take advantage of her alleged identity; on the contrary, she often refused to see people who wanted to 'help'. But in 1938 she agreed to allow a German lawyer to attempt to establish her right to her title – and presumably to her share of the remainder of the Tsar's fortune which had been lodged in foreign banks. But these legal efforts, which dragged on for years, were finally a failure. In 1957 the judges allowed themselves to be heavily influenced by a man called Hans Johann Mayer, an Austrian, who claimed that he had been in the Ipatiev house on the night of the massacre, and who insisted that he had seen the entire imperial family lying dead. It was later revealed that he had earlier offered to testify on Anastasia's behalf in exchange for a large sum of money, and was completely discredited, but the damage was done. Finally, Anastasia – now calling herself Anna Anderson – married a history professor at the University of Virginia, Dr John Manahan, and settled down in Charlottesville. There Summers and Mangold interviewed her, and seem to have been impressed – their book *The File on the Tsar* indicates that they are strongly inclined to believe that she is genuine, and photographs they publish certainly show a remarkable resemblance between the original Anastasia and 'Anna Anderson'. They admit that their long evening with her was a failure from the evidential point of view, and that she spoke for only a few minutes about her past. If indeed she was the Grand Duchess Anastasia, she could have told them once and for all what happened in the Ipatiev house. But all she said was: 'There was no massacre there . . . but I cannot tell the rest.'

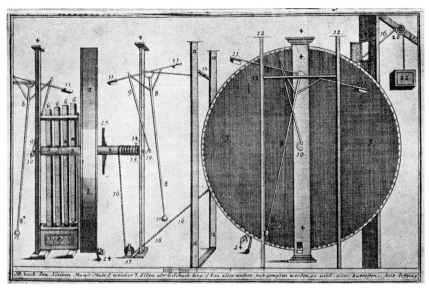

(*Above*)
Orffyreus' Wheel – a perpetual motion machine invented by 'Orffyreus', alias Johann Ernest Elias Bessler, who was born in Zittau, Saxony, in 1680. In 1712 he exhibited a 'self-moving wheel' three feet in diameter and four inches thick. This illustration is taken from a pamphlet published by 'Orffyreus' in 1715. (See Chapter 24)

The Russian mystic Madame Blavatsky (*above*) who claimed that her knowledge had been obtained from her 'secret Masters' who lived in the Himalayas. George Gurdjieff (*right*), one of the most original thinkers of the twentieth century. He, too, claimed to have received his basic teachings from a monastic brotherhood in the northern Himalayas. (See Chapter 25)

(*Mary Evans Picture Library*)

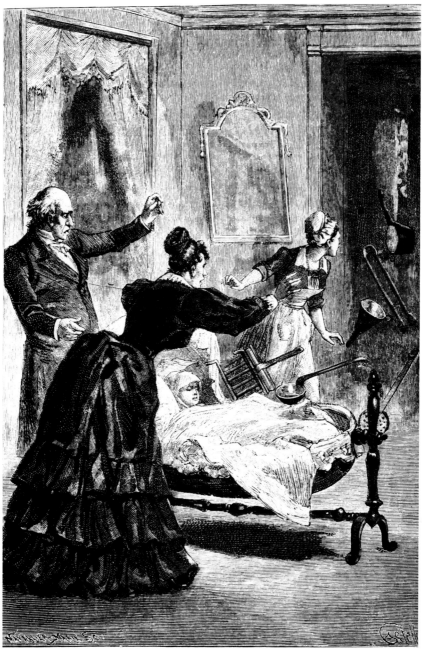

A poltergeist is a noisy, mischievous spirit often associated with adolescent children. An engraving of a poltergeist at work at Guillonville, France, in March 1849, where it was associated with 14-year-old Adolphine Benoit. (From Figuier's *Mystères de la Séance*.) (See Chapter 26)

(*Above*)
Errol Flynn in *The Adventures of Robin Hood* (1938), one of the many films based on the story of the legendary outlaw of Sherwood Forest. (In this particular film, Sherwood Forest was recreated in California.) Copyright in film poster: Ronald Grant. (See Chapter 29)
(*Mary Evans Picture Library*)

(*Right*
Engraving by Stephanoff of Robin Hood, Maid Marion, and Robin's Merry Men in Sherwood Forest. (See Chapter 29)
(*Mary Evans Picture Library*)

(*Above, left*)
Contemporary sketch of Mary Rogers behind the counter at Anderson's cigar store. Her murder inspired a novel. (See Chapter 30)

(*Above, right*)
An advertisement for an 1843 *Almanack* makes use of the tragedy of Mary Rogers. (See Chapter 30)

(*Left*)
A contemporary sketch of Mary Rogers, published in the New York *Atlas* of 6 August 1841. (See Chapter 30)

Nicholas II, the last Tsar of Russia, with his wife and five children. In 1918 the whole family were supposedly murdered by the Bolsheviks. This photograph was taken c.1905.

(*BBC Hulton Picture Library*)

(*Above*)
Four members of the Russian royal family during their imprisonment. From left to right: Maria, Alexis, Tatiana, Olga. (See Chapter 31)

Guards patrol (*above*) and (*below*) the house at Ekaterinburg where the Russian royal family were held captive. (See Chapter 31)

(*Above: Photo Source; below, Mary Evans Picture Library*)

(*Opposite, below*)
Nicholas II and three of his four daughters during their captivity in Siberia and a few weeks before their alleged assassination. From left to right: Maria, Anastasia, Olga. Bolshevik guards are in the background. Did Anastasia escape? (See Chapter 31)

(*Photo Source*)

The Comte de Saint-Germain, known as 'Saint-Germain the Deathless', claimed to be four thousand years old. He is regarded by many 'occultists' as one of the most exciting and mysterious figures in the history of magic, but by sceptics as a charlatan.

Artist's impression of an interview with the Comte de Saint-Germain at Holstein, c. 1785. (See Chapter 32)

An engraving of the cemetery of Saint-Médard, Paris, where some bizarre 'miracles' are said to have taken place in the eighteenth century. (See Chapter 33)

Droeshout print of Shakespeare commissioned by John Heminge and Henry Condell, fellow-actors. It appeared as the frontispiece to the First Folio, 1623. (See Chapter 34)

(Mary Evans Picture Library)

Bust of Shakespeare in Holy Trinity Church, Stratford-upon-Avon. It is believed to have been made by Gerard Johnson, i.e. Gheerart Janssen, before 1623, and to have been commissioned specially by Shakespeare's son-in-law, John Hall. The memorial is of white marble inlaid with black panels. The bust itself was originally coloured. (See Chapter 34)

(BBC Hulton Picture Library)

Drawing by Phiz for Dickens' *Bleak House* showing an act of spontaneous human combustion. (See Chapter 35)

Carl Gustav Jung (1875–1961), Swiss psychiatrist. He coined the word 'complex' to describe memories of emotions or events which affect the individual concerned, though suppressed by the conscious mind. He also coined the word 'synchronicity' for meaningful coincidence. (See Chapter 36)

(Mary Evans/Sigmund Freud copyrights)

The gardens at Versailles where, in 1901, two English women, Eleanor Frances Jourdain (*above, right*) and Charlotte Anne Moberly (*above, left*) experienced a 'time slip' and found themselves back in Versailles in 1789. In the background is Le Petit Trianon (photograph taken 1900). (See Chapter 37)

(*Mary Evans Picture Library/Society for Psychical Research*)

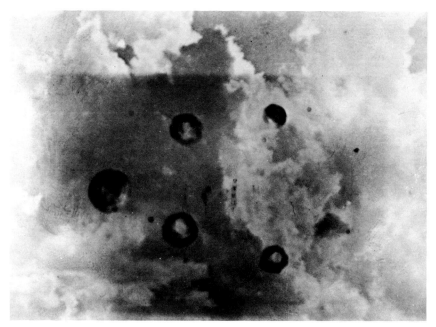

Examples of flying saucers or UFOs (Unidentified Flying Objects).

The photograph below was taken by a US coastguard at Salem, Massachusetts. He was in the station photo-laboratory preparing to clean a camera when he noticed several brilliant lights in the sky. He seized the camera, clicked the shutter and this photograph was the result.
Various theories have been put forward to account for UFOs. (See Chapter 39)
(First two photographs *Photo Source*; third photograph *Mary Evans Picture Library*)

A ouija board – a board lettered with the alphabet and other signs, used with a movable pointer (often a tumbler) to obtain messages from the spirit world during seances. (See Chapter 42)

(*Mary Evans Picture Library*)

This comment fits in very well with the basic thesis of the authors – which is that the Tsarina and her daughters were sent from Ekaterinburg to Perm, two hundred miles north-west of Ekaterinburg. There a nurse named Natalya Mutnykh stated that she was taken to a basement to see the empress and her four daughters. But Summers and Mangold also cite information that makes it unlikely that Anna Anderson is the Grand Duchess Anastasia. There is evidence that Anastasia escaped in Perm, and was recaptured. In fact the head of the Swedish Red Cross Mission, Count Carl Bonde, has described how in 1918 the special train in which he was travelling was stopped and searched for Anastasia. (The Perm documents indicate that she escaped in the spring of 1919, but Bonde was writing in 1952, and may easily have got the year wrong.) But if she was recaptured, then it seems unlikely that she could have escaped to Berlin. And the conviction of Summers and Mangold that Anna Anderson was Anastasia itself becomes suspect. After all, 'Anastasia's' original story was that she *was* present at the 'massacre' in Ekaterinburg and was rescued by a soldier named Tchaikovsky. The evidence shows that she and her mother and sisters went to Perm, so the Ekaterinburg story must presumably be a lie. Summers and Mangold would have made a far more convincing book if they had decided that Anna was an impostor. But her statement that 'there was no massacre' happened to fit their own thesis (which, presumably, they had already explained to 'Anastasia' and her husband), so they have decided to accept her as genuine.

Nevertheless, the evidence they present for their basic thesis is very strong indeed. They argue that the 'massacre' involved only the Tsar, Tsarina, Dr Botkin and two servants – perhaps not even the Tsar and Tsarina. The rest of the family was taken to Perm, the aim being to use them as bargaining counters with the British and the Germans (both of whose royal families were related to them). At one point the Russians expected a German invasion; later, when this fear proved groundless, they considered an exchange of the royal prisoners for a socialist leader, Leo Jogiches, held in Berlin – the name of socialist Karl Liebknecht (later murdered) was also mentioned. But opposition in England to the idea of receiving the Russian royal family finally caused King George V to change his mind about inviting them. The British ambassador in Paris, Lord Bertie, was asked to see if the French would be willing to take the Russians; he replied that he thought they would be unwelcome, since the empress was regarded as 'a criminal or a criminal lunatic'. (It was widely believed at the time – even in Russia – that the Tsarina wanted the Germans to win; she was herself a German.) And after the German defeat of 1918 the Kaiser was in no position to aid his Russian cousins. So, one by one, the doors slammed on the survivors of the Russian royal family.

Summers and Mangold admit that there is no evidence whatever to indicate what finally happened to Alexandra and her daughters. All we know is that when the Whites captured Perm in December 1918 the Tsarina was no longer there. In the January of the following year, four Grand Dukes were taken from their prison in Petrograd and shot. The bloody civil war which the Reds would eventually win was at its most savage, and the Russian royal family had become an irrelevance.

No doubt the question of whether the empress and her daughters died at Perm or Ekaterinburg is also an irrelevance. Yet it is impossible not to hope that the uncertainty will one day be dissipated perhaps – by some document in the Soviet archives, perhaps by the discovery of five skeletons buried in the woods around Perm. . ..

32 'Saint-Germain the Deathless'

He is still regarded by many 'occultists' as one of the most exciting and mysterious figures in the history of magic; some even believe that he is still alive. But everyone who has written about him has ended by wondering whether the secrets of 'Saint-Germain the deathless' are a matter of mystery or merely of mystification. Since the enormous dossier on him collected at the orders of Napoleon III was destroyed by fire during the Commune, the question must remain unanswered. 'Thus', says one historian, 'once again an "accident" upheld the ancient law which decrees that the life of an adept must always be surrounded by mystery.'

When the Comte de Saint-Germain (he admitted the name was false) first appeared in France about 1756 he looked about fifty years old. He was a brilliant conversationalist, spoke many languages, possessed a knowledge of medicine, and was a first-rate experimental chemist. He was a small man, who dressed in black velvet with a white satin cravat (a sign of self-restraint in those days of magnificent male wardrobes), and whose manners were meticulously correct. He was obviously wealthy – he wore many diamonds and he had numerous servants. These seem to have been extremely well trained. When a sceptic said to one of them: 'Your master is a liar' the man replied: 'I know that better than you. He tells everyone that he is four thousand years old. But I have been in his service only a hundred years, and when I came the count told me that he was three thousand years old. Whether he has added nine hundred years by error, or whether he is lying, I do not know.' Another servant – his valet – was asked about some point of ancient history and replied: 'Perhaps the count forgets that I have been in his service only five hundred years.'

It sounds as if he was an accomplished leg-puller, or perhaps merely a charlatan; but if so, it is not clear what he hoped to gain. He seems to have been wealthy; he was an accomplished violinist, a skilful painter, and had a wide knowledge of music and painting – apparently he could identify most paintings at a glance. In *Historical Mysteries*, Andrew Lang suggests that he was the son of the ex-queen of Spain, Marie de Neuberg, who lived in Bayonne after the death of her husband Charles II. Marie's lover was the finance minister, Count Andanero, and Lang thinks it possible that Saint-Germain was his son.

Before going to France, Saint-Germain had been in Vienna. He had met the Marshal de Belle-Isle, who had contracted some illness while campaigning in Germany; Saint-Germain cured him, and the marshal brought him back with him to Paris. Soon after, he cured a lady of the court of mushroom poisoning, and became a friend of Madame de Pompadour, mistress of Louis XV. The ladies of the court found him intriguing. Countess von Gergy, whose husband had been ambassador to Venice around 1710, thought she recollected his name, and asked him if his father had been there; Saint-Germain replied – typically – that he himself had been there at the time. 'Impossible' said the countess; the man she had known had been at least forty-five at the time. Saint-Germain smiled mysteriously. 'I am very old.' He then added various details about Venice, which convinced the countess that he knew what he was talking about. 'You must be a devil!' exclaimed the countess, at which Saint-Germain began to tremble as if he had cramp and hurriedly left the room.

A decade earlier, Saint-Germain had been in London, and in 1745 was arrested as a spy of the Young Pretender, who was just marching on Derby. Horace Walpole noted in a letter:

.. the other day they seized an odd man who goes by the name of Count Saint-Germain. He has been here these two years and will not tell who he is, or whence . . . He sings, plays on the violin wonderfully, composes, is mad, and not very sensible. He is called an Italian, a Spaniard, a Pole; a somebody that married a great fortune in Mexico, and ran away with her jewels to Constantinople; a priest, a fiddler, a vast nobleman. The Prince of Wales has had unsatisfied curiosity about him, but in vain. . . .

No one knows where he was between 1745 and 1755. But by the late 1750s he was the talk of Paris. Madame du Hausset, a *femme de chambre* of Madame de Pompadour, wrote:

A man who was as amazing as a witch came often .. This was the Count de Saint-Germain, who wished to make people believe that he lived for several centuries. One day Madame said to him, while at her toilet, 'What sort of man was Francis I. . .?' 'A good sort of fellow,' said Saint-Germain, 'too fiery – I could have given him a useful piece of advice but he would not have listened.' He then described, in very general terms, the beauty of Mary Stuart and La Reine Margot. 'You seem to have seen them all . . .' 'Sometimes,' said Saint-Germain, 'I amuse myself, not by making people believe, but by letting them believe that I have lived from time immemorial.' Then Madame de Pompadour asked him about Madame de Gergy, who thought she had known Saint-Germain in Venice fifty years ago. 'It may be so,' said Saint-Germain, 'But I admit that even more possibly the respected lady is in her dotage.'

It seems clear from this that Saint-Germain treated the tales of his great age as a joke, and made no real attempt to impose them on Madame de Pompadour. The king's foreign minister, the Duc de Choiseul, further confused the issue by hiring an impostor to impersonate Saint-Germain in the salons of Paris, and to discredit him by making absurd claims – such as claiming to have been a close friend of Saint Anne, mother of the Virgin Mary, and making remarks like 'I always knew Christ would come to a bad end.'

So what do we actually know of the life of Saint-Germain? An autograph letter of 1735 proves that he was in The Hague in November of that year, but does not tell us why. Saint-Germain would then be about twenty-five years old. We know he was in England from 1743 to about 1745, and was arrested as a spy. The story given in Mrs Cooper-Oakley's book on him is that someone who was jealous of him (because of a rivalry about a lady) planted a treasonable letter in his pocket, then had him arrested; he was able to prove his innocence.

By 1755 he was wealthy and was living in Vienna, where he was taken up by the Marshal de Belle-Isle and brought to Paris, where – as already noted – his conversation and his wide culture soon made him a favourite of the salons. He claimed to live off some food or elixir which he made himself, and would sit through dinners without eating. In fact his greatest interest seems to have been chemistry, and he had apparently discovered some process for dyeing silk and leather. He told the king that he could remove flaws from diamonds, and went off with a stone worth six thousand francs. A month later he returned the stone flawless, and a jeweller valued it at ten thousand francs. In all probability Saint-Germain simply substituted another stone, and gained the king's gratitude at the low price of four thousand francs. The result was that the king set up a laboratory at the Trianon, and installed Saint-Germain in apartments at the castle of Chambord, to work on his dyeing processes – the king hoped these would eventually bring large sums to the royal treasury, which badly needed replenishing. He became so much a familiar of Louis that the Duc de Choiseul wrote indignantly: 'It is strange that the King is so often allowed to be almost alone with this man, though when he goes out he is surrounded by guards. . . .' He also referred to Saint-Germain as 'the son of a Portuguese Jew'.

In 1760 the king apparently sent Saint-Germain on a diplomatic mission to Holland – although this was kept secret from his ministers; Saint-Germain's mission was to investigate overtures of peace with England – the king was hoping to persuade England to abandon her ally Prussia. Saint-Germain found himself staying in the same hotel as that other amusing adventurer Casanova, who was trying to negotiate a loan for France. They already knew one another, and Casanova was convinced that Saint-Germain was a charlatan. He says of him in his Memoirs:

This extraordinary man, intended by nature to be the king of impostors and quacks, would say in an easy and assured manner that he was three hundred years old, that he knew the secrets of universal medicine, that he possessed a mastery over nature, that he could melt diamonds. . . . Notwithstanding his boastings, his bare-faced lies and his manifold eccentricities, I cannot say I thought him offensive.

Nevertheless, Casanova seized the opportunity to destroy Saint-Germain's credit by producing a bogus 'cabalistic' oracle warning against him. Meanwhile the Duc de Choiseul had got wind of the plot – he was against making peace – and sent orders for Saint-Germain to be arrested and conveyed to the Bastille. But the Dutch Ambassador decided to drop a word in Saint-Germain's ear, and he took the next boat to London. Louis was too embarrassed to admit that he and Belle-Isle had been behind Saint-Germain's mission.

Saint-Germain's enemies had succeeded in bringing about his downfall – although there can be no doubt that his own tactlessness and naivety also played their part; he buttonholed the most unsuitable people and told them about his mission. In England he met the German ambassador, and may have hoped to go and join Frederick the Great in Saxony; the ambassador wrote in haste to the Prussian secretary of state begging him to do his best to hinder Saint-Germain's journey, on the grounds that he was dangerously impetuous, and might fascinate the king and persuade him to undertake 'many disastrous measures'. He seems to have had no doubt of Saint-Germain's power to fascinate. Saint-Germain was apparently obliged to return secretly to Holland, where he purchased an estate, calling himself Count Surmont – he seems to have been short of cash, for he paid only part of the purchase price. The French ambassador described him as 'completely discredited'. But he had found himself a new patron – or dupe – in Cobenzl, minister in the Austrian Netherlands, who wanted to exploit Saint-Germain's chemical processes in factories at Tournai. Cobenzl told Kaunitz, the Austrian chancellor, of all kinds of 'miracles', such as turning base metals into gold, dyeing silks and other materials all kinds of glorious colours, and tanning skins to produce marvellously soft leather. Cobenzl seemed positively infatuated with Saint-Germain, although he added: 'The only thing I can reproach him with is frequent boasting about his talents and origins.' And although Cobenzl later came to take a dim view of the 'genius's' character, he never doubted the tremendous commercial value of his processes. The factories in Tournai were set up, and Saint-Germain managed to pocket a hundred thousand gulden for secrets he had promised to give gratis. Even so, he vanished without parting with all the promised secrets. But the factories in Tournai apparently did well – from which we may infer that Saint-Germain's 'processes' were genuine enough.

Saint-Germain's movements during the next decade are unknown, but he himself claimed to have been twice to India, and to have been involved in the Russo-Turkish war in the Mediterranean (1768–74). He certainly went to St Petersburg and became a friend of Count Alexei Orlov, commander of the Russian expedition to the Archipelago. His favourite beverage, tea made from sennapods (a mild laxative), became known as Russian tea and was supplied in bulk to the Russian navy. For reasons that are not clear, he was raised to the rank of a Russian general. In 1774 he was living at Schwabach, in Anspach, and found himself a new patron, Charles Alexander, Margrave of Brandenburg. The margrave was duly impressed when he went with Saint-Germain to meet Orlov and saw the latter embrace him with great warmth. Soon Saint-Germain was the margrave's guest in his castle at Triersdorf, living quietly and continuing his experiments. He was now calling himself Count Tzarogy. But one day his desire to impress and astonish led him to tell his host that he was really Prince Rakoczy of Transylvania. But when the margrave visited Italy in the following year, and began to tell stories about his astonishing guest, he learned that the last three sons of the royal house of Transylvania were dead, and that his guest sounded like the notorious trickster Saint-Germain, who was really the son of a tax-collector of San Germano. Gemmingen, the Anspach minister who was sent to confront Saint-Germain, reported that 'Prince Rakoczy' did not deny that he called himself Saint-Germain. He had had occasion to use many aliases to avoid his enemies; but he had never disgraced any of the names he bore. This on the whole was true, and the margrave had to admit that his guest had always behaved quietly and modestly, and never tried to part him from large sums of money. All the same, he was disillusioned, and declined to see Saint-Germain again. So in 1776, in his mid-sixties, Saint-Germain once again took to the road. He visited Leipzig, Dresden, Berlin and Hamburg, then went to Berlin hoping to see Frederick the Great; but the king had no wish to make the acquaintance of a discredited adventurer.

Finally, Saint-Germain found another patron, Prince Charles of Hesse-Cassel, who was cool and uninterested to begin with, but gradually succumbed to Saint-Germain's charm and enthusiasm. Prince Charles was not disposed to doubt any of Saint-Germain's stories, including that he was Prince Rakoczy, that he had been brought up in the household of the last of the Medici, and that he was now eighty-eight years old. He set Saint-Germain up in a factory in Eckenforde, in Schleswig-Holstein, and there the adventurer lived out his last years quietly, suffering periodically from depression and rheumatism, and dying in February 1784, to the grief of Prince Charles, who described him as 'one of the greatest sages who ever lived'.

No sooner was Saint-Germain dead than rumours that he was still alive began to circulate. A journal published in the following year said he was expected to return soon. Madame de Genlis was convinced she had seen him in Vienna in 1821. In 1836 a volume of *Souvenirs* by the Countess d'Adhémar, who claimed to be familiar with the court at Versailles in the last days of the monarchy, claimed that she had seen Saint-Germain as late as 1793, and that he had warned her about the death of Marie Antoinette. He told her she would see him five times more, 'and do not wish for a sixth', and she claims that she saw him five times between then and 1820. But G.B. Volz, who conducted an investigation of the life of Saint-Germain in the 1920s, asserts that the countess never existed and that the *Souvenirs* are a forgery. In 1845 Franz Graffer declares in his *Memoirs* that he had seen Saint-Germain, and that he had announced that he would appear in the Himalayas towards the turn of the century – a claim that in due course led Madame Blavatsky to include him among her 'Secret Masters' in Tibet, and to quote him with respect in *The Secret Doctrine*. But again, the *Memoirs* of Franz Graffer are thought to be a forgery. On the other hand, Madame Blavatsky went to the trouble of visiting the then Countess d'Adhémar in 1885, and Mrs Cooper-Oakley, whose book on Saint-Germain appeared in 1912, discovered that there were still documents about him in the possession of the d'Adhémar family. As late as January 1972, a young man called Richard Chanfray appeared on French television claiming to be Saint-Germain, and apparently transformed lead into gold, using only a camping stove.

When all the claims and counter-claims have been taken into account, what can we say of the 'man of mystery'? First – regretfully – that he cannot be taken seriously as a mage or a secret Master. Whether the Prussian ambassador in Dresden is correct when he says 'inordinate vanity is the mainspring of his mechanism', there can be no doubt that Saint-Germain *was* a vain man who talked too much – too many contemporaries make this comment for it to be untrue. But a man may be vain and talkative, and still possess genius (Bernard Shaw being the example who immediately springs to mind). It is also perfectly clear that Saint-Germain was a genuine enthusiast, with an extraordinary range of talents. He himself never claimed to be a 'mage', or a student of occultism. In fact, he insisted that he was a materialist whose chief desire was to benefit humanity. Diderot and D'Alembert would no doubt have found him an ideal contributor to their *Encyclopedia*.

The real mystery about Saint-Germain is that he *was* a man of genius, and at the same time a charlatan. He had what we would now call a strongly developed sense of publicity, a desire to intrigue and fascinate. And this in itself argues that he was not what he claimed to be. He was undoubtedly *not* the last surviving member of the Transylvanian royal family – precise details are known about its last three surviving members. But this desire to pose as a king in exile suggests that Saint-Germain was born in fairly humble circumstances, and that he spent a great deal of his childhood and youth daydreaming about fame and glory. The annals of charlatanism are full of Walter Mittys and Billy Liars, but it is difficult to recollect a swindler who was really born in a palace or a stately home. We may probably assume, then, that Saint-Germain was not the bastard son of the Queen of Spain. But it seems equally clear that he managed to acquire himself a good education, and that chemistry was the love of his life. In different circumstances he might have become a Lavoisier or Robert Boyle or Michael Faraday. His natural brilliance made him contemptuous of the intelligence of his fellow-men, and when he claimed to be three hundred years old, or dropped hints about his acquaintance with Francis I, he probably told himself that he was poking fun at human stupidity.

The only real mystery is where he acquired the money to pose as a prince. Since he seems to have been an honest man (if we except the little affair of the Tournai factory), the answer, presumably, is that he was able to turn his chemical researches to commercial use. It is a disappointing conclusion that the Man of Mystery, the Secret Master, was merely a brilliant industrial chemist. But it is the only theory that corresponds to the facts as we know them.

33 The Miracles of Saint-Médard

The strange events that took place in the little Paris churchyard of Saint-Médard between 1727 and 1732 sound so incredible, so preposterous, that the modern reader is tempted to dismiss them as pure invention. This would be a mistake, for an impressive mass of documents, including accounts by doctors, magistrates and other respectable public figures, attests to their genuineness. The miracles undoubtedly took place. But no doctor, philosopher or scientist has even begun to explain them.

They began with the burial of François de Pâris, the Deacon of Paris, in May 1727. François was only thirty-seven years old, yet he was revered as a holy man, with powers of healing. He was a follower of Bishop Cornelius Jansen, who taught that men can be saved only by divine grace, not by their own efforts. The Deacon had no doubt whatever that his own healing powers came from God.

Great crowds followed his coffin, many weeping. It was laid in a tomb behind the high altar of Saint-Médard. Then the congregation filed past, laying their flowers on the corpse. A father supported his son, a cripple, as he leaned over the coffin. Suddenly, the child went into convulsions; he seemed to be having a fit. Several people helped to drag him, writhing, to a quiet corner of the church. Suddenly the convulsions stopped. The boy opened his eyes, looking around in bewilderment, and then slowly stood up. A look of incredulous joy crossed his face; then to the astonishment of the spectators he began to dance up and down, singing and laughing. His father found it impossible to believe, for the boy was using his withered right leg, which had virtually no muscles. Later it was claimed that the leg had become as strong and normal as the other.

The news spread. Within hours cripples, lepers, hunchbacks and blind men were rushing to the church. At first few 'respectable' people believed the stories of miraculous cures – the majority of the Deacon's followers were poor people. The rich preferred to leave their spiritual affairs in the hands of the Jesuits, who were more cultivated and worldly. But it soon became clear that ignorance and credulity could not be used as a blanket explanation for all the stories of marvels. Deformed limbs, it was said, were being straightened; hideous growths and cancers were disappearing without trace; horrible sores and wounds were healing instantly.

The Jesuits declared that the miracles were either a fraud or the work of the Devil; the result was that most of the better-off people in Paris flatly refused to believe that anything unusual was taking place in the churchyard of Saint-Médard. But a few men of intellect were drawn by curiosity, and they invariably returned from the churchyard profoundly shaken. Sometimes they recorded their testimony in print: some, such as one Philippe Hecquet, attempted to explain the events by natural causes. Others, such as the Benedictine Bernard Louis de la Taste, attacked the people who performed the miracles on theological grounds, but were unable to expose any deception or error by them, or any error on the part of the witnesses. The accumulation of written testimony was such that David Hume, one of the greatest of philosophers, wrote in *An enquiry concerning human understanding* (1758):

> There surely never was a greater number of miracles ascribed to one person. . . . But what is more extraordinary; many of the miracles were immediately proved upon the spot, before judges of unquestioned integrity, attested by witnesses of credit and distinction, in a learned age . . . . Where shall we find such a number of circumstances, agreeing to the corroboration of one fact?

One of those who investigated the happenings was a lawyer named Louis Adrien de Paige. When he told his friend, the magistrate Louis-Basile Carré de Montgéron, what he had seen the magistrate assured him patronizingly that he had been taken in by conjuring tricks – the kind of 'miracles' performed by tricksters at fairgrounds. But he finally agreed to go with Paige to the churchyard, if only for the pleasure of pointing out how the lawyer had been deceived. They went there on the morning of 7 September 1731. And de Montgéron left the churchyard a changed man – he even endured prison rather than deny what he had seen that day.

The first thing the magistrate saw when he entered the churchyard was a number of women writhing on the ground, twisting themselves into the most startling shapes, sometimes bending backward until the backs of their heads touched their heels. These ladies were all wearing a long cloth undergarment that fastened around the ankles. M.Paige explained that this was now obligatory for all women who wished to avail themselves of the Deacon's miraculous powers. In the early days, when women had stood on their heads or bent their bodies convulsively, prurient young men had begun to frequent the churchyard to view the spectacle.

However, there was no lack of male devotees of the deceased Abbé to assist in the activities of the churchyard. Montgéron was shocked to see that some of the women and girls were being sadistically beaten – at least, that is what at first appeared to be going on. Men were striking them with heavy pieces of wood and iron. Other women lay on the ground, apparently crushed under immensely heavy weights. One girl was naked to the waist: a man was gripping her nipples with a pair of iron tongs and twisting them violently. Paige explained that none of these women felt any pain; on the contrary, many begged for more blows. And an incredible number of them were cured of deformities or diseases by this violent treatment.

In another part of the churchyard, they saw an attractive pink-cheeked girl of about nineteen, who was sitting at a trestle table and eating. That seemed normal enough until Montgéron looked more closely at the food on the plate, and realized from its appearance as well as from the smell that reached him that it was human excrement. In between mouthfuls of this sickening fare she drank a yellow liquid, which Paige explained was urine. The girl had come to the churchyard to be cured of what we would now call a neurosis: she had to wash her hands hundreds of times a day, and was so fastidious about her food that she would taste nothing that had been touched by another human hand. The Deacon had indeed cured her. Within days she was eating excrement and drinking urine, and did so with every sign of enjoyment. Such cases might not be remarkable in asylums; but what was more extraordinary – indeed, preposterous – was that after one of these meals she opened her mouth as if to be sick, and milk came pouring out. Monsieur Paige had collected a cupful; it was apparently perfectly ordinary cow's milk.

After staggering away from the eater of excrement, Montgéron had to endure a worse ordeal. In another part of the churchyard a number of women had volunteered to cleanse suppurating wounds and boils by sucking them clean. Trying hard to prevent himself vomiting, Montgéron watched as someone unwound a dirty bandage from the leg of a small girl; the smell was horrible. The leg was a festering mass of sores, some so deep that the bone was visible. The woman who had volunteered to clean it was one of the *convulsionnaires* – she had been miraculously cured and converted by her bodily contortions, and God had now chosen her to demonstrate how easily human beings' disgust can be overcome. Yet even she blenched as she saw and smelt the gangrened leg. She cast her eyes up to heaven, prayed silently for a moment, then bent her head and began to lap, swallowing the septic matter. When she moved her face farther down the child's leg Montgéron could see that the wound was now clean. Paige assured him that the girl would almost certainly be cured when the treatment was complete.

What Montgéron saw next finally shattered his resistance and convinced him that he was witnessing something of profound significance. A sixteen-year-old girl named Gabrielle Moler had arrived, and the interest she excited made Montgéron aware that, even among this crowd of miraculous freaks, she was a celebrity. She removed her cloak and lay on the ground, her skirt modestly round her ankles. Four men, each holding a pointed iron bar, stood over her. When the girl smiled at them they lunged down at her, driving their rods into her stomach. Montgéron had to be restrained from interfering as the rods went through the girl's dress and into her stomach. He looked for signs of blood staining her dress. But none came, and the girl looked calm and serene. Next the bars were jammed under her chin, forcing her head back. It seemed inevitable that they would penetrate through to her mouth; yet when the points were removed the flesh was unbroken. The men took up sharp-edged shovels, placed them against a breast, and then pushed with all their might; the girl went on smiling gently. The breast, trapped between shovels, should have been cut off, but it seemed impervious to the assault. Then the cutting edge of a shovel was placed against her throat, and the man wielding it did his best to cut off her head; he did not seem to be able even to dent her neck.

Dazed, Montgéron watched as the girl was beaten with a great iron truncheon shaped like a pestle. A stone weighing half a hundredweight (25 kilograms) was raised above her body and dropped repeatedly from a height of several feet. Finally, Montgéron watched her kneel in front of a blazing fire, and plunge her head into it. He could feel the heat from where he stood; yet her hair and eyebrows were not even singed. When she picked up a blazing chunk of coal and proceeded to eat it Montgéron could stand no more and left.

But he went back repeatedly, until he had enough materials for the first volume of an amazing book. He presented it to the king, Louis XV, who was so shocked and indignant that he had Montgéron thrown into prison. Yet Montgéron felt he had to 'bear witness', and was to publish two more volumes following his release, full of precise scientific testimony concerning the miracles.

In the year following Montgéron's imprisonment, 1732, the Paris authorities decided that the scandal was becoming unbearable and closed down the churchyard. But the *convulsionnaires* had discovered that they could perform their miracles anywhere, and they continued for many years. A hardened sceptic, the scientist La Condamine, was as startled as Montgéron when, in 1759, he watched a girl named Sister Françoise being crucified on a wooden cross, nailed by the hands and feet over a period of several hours, and stabbed in the side with a spear. He noticed that all this obviously hurt the girl, and her wounds bled when the nails were removed; but she seemed none the worse for an ordeal that would have killed most people.

So what can we say of the miracles from the standpoint of the twentieth century? Some writers believe it was a kind of self-hypnosis. But while this could explain the excrement-eater and the woman who sucked festering wounds, it is less plausible in explaining Gabrielle Moler's feats of endurance. These remind us rather of descriptions of ceremonies of dervishes and fakirs: for example, J.G.Bennett in his autobiography *Witness* describes watching a dervish ritual in which a razor-sharp sword was placed across the belly of a naked man, and two heavy men jumped up and down on it – all without even marking the flesh. What seems to be at work here is some power of 'mind over matter', deeper than mere hypnosis, which is not yet understood but obviously merits serious attention.

It would be absurd to stop looking for scientific explanations of the miracles of Saint-Médard. But let us not in the meantime deceive ourselves by accepting superficial 'sceptical' explanations.

34 Who Was Shakespeare?

Early in 1616, a respectable middle-class gentleman of Stratford-upon-Avon decided it was time to make his will; a few months later in April he died, apparently after a drinking bout with two old friends from London, the playwrights Ben Jonson and Michael Drayton. And then, for a considerable time, he was more or less forgotten. Within seven years of his death, a monument was erected to him in the parish church. In 1656 the antiquary Sir William Dugdale, who was interested in coats of arms, reproduced an inaccurate sketch of it in his *Antiquities of Warwickshire*. It showed a gentleman with a drooping moustache, whose hands rested on a woolsack – a symbol of trade. Few people in Stratford seemed to be aware that this mournful-looking tradesman was a famous actor-playwright who had performed before Queen Elizabeth.

More than a century later, in the 1770s, a clergyman named James Wilmot retired to his native Warwickshire, and devoted his declining years to the study of his two favourite writers, Francis Bacon and William Shakespeare. Since the village of which he was now the rector – Barton-on-the-Heath – was only half a dozen miles from Stratford, he began making inquiries to find out if any stories and traditions of the great actor-playwright now survived in his native town. Apparently no one knew of any. But from the study of Shakespeare's plays, Wilmot had concluded that he must have been a man of wide learning, and must therefore have possessed a considerable library. Over the course of many years he made diligent inquiries in the area, investigating small private libraries for fifty miles around. He found nothing whatever – not a single volume that might have belonged to Shakespeare. And finally he was struck by an astonishing conviction: that the man called Shakespeare was not the author of the plays attributed to him. The man who possessed all the qualifications for writing them was his other favourite author, Francis Bacon.

Wilmot was apparently so overwhelmed by this realization – for by this time, Shakespeare was becoming recognized as one of the greatest of English playwrights – that he decided to keep his strange convictions to himself. But almost thirty years later, when he was eighty, some of his caution had evaporated. And when he was visited by an Ipswich Quaker in 1803 Wilmot finally revealed his embarrassing secret. The Quaker, James Cowell, was researching Shakespeare's life because he had agreed to read a paper about him to his local philosophical society, and no standard biography had yet been published. Cowell was shaken, but more than half convinced. Two years later he read his paper on Shakespeare, and told his astonished fellow-townsmen about the remarkable old vicar and his alarming theories. The Ipswich philosophers were apparently 'thrown into confusion'. Perhaps Wilmot heard about their reaction; at all events, he left instructions in his will that all his Shakespeare papers should be burnt, and this was duly carried out. And Cowell's lecture lay undiscovered until more than a century later, when an eminent Shakespearian scholar described Wilmot in *The Times Literary Supplement* as 'The first Baconian'.[1] Professor Allardyce Nicoll did not intend it as a compliment, for he regarded the proponents of the Baconian theory of Shakespeare's authorship as cranks.

And why should anyone reach such an apparently eccentric conclusion? Why should the gentleman of Stratford-upon-Avon not be the author of *Hamlet* and *Lear*, just as most people assumed he was? In fact the notion is not quite as absurd as it sounds. The most baffling thing about Shakespeare is the lack of actual connection between the 'gentleman of Stratford' and the author of the plays. Shakespeare went to London in his twenties; within a few years he was a successful actor and playwright, and by the time he reached his mid-thirties (in 1601) he was one of the most popular writers of the time. The author of *Coriolanus* and *The Tempest* must have known he possessed genius – he says as much in sonnet 55, beginning:

Not marble, nor the gilded monuments
Of princes, shall outlive this powerful rime.

And when he returned to Stratford in his mid-forties he had become a wealthy man through the use of his talents. Is it conceivable that he did not even bother to take a single printed copy of any of his works with him – there were many extant – and that he even left behind in London the library he must have accumulated over the years? Of course, he may have done so – but in that case, what happened to them? Why are they not mentioned in his will?

Shakespeare scholars reply that in Elizabethan times acting was not regarded as a particularly respectable profession – hardly more so than pimping – and that Shakespeare may have preferred to keep it to himself. This is true. But writers, then as now, were regarded as a cut above most other professions, and Shakespeare was also the author of the sonnets, *The Rape of Lucrece* and *Venus and Adonis*. The sonnets appeared in 1609, two years before he retired to Stratford – surely he would have taken a few copies with him to distribute to his friends and family? Surely he would have made sure that copies of his works went to his beloved daughter Susanna to whom he left most of his estate in the will, and to her husband, the distinguished physician Dr John Hall, who was later to refuse a knighthood from Charles I? Again, the scholars reply that he may well have done so, and that Shakespeare's books simply vanished over the next fifty years or so – by which time admirers were beginning to show an interest in the playwright. It could be true, but it sounds somehow unlikely.

The Rev. Wilmot had another reason for doubting that the gentleman of

[1] 25 February 1932.

Stratford wrote the plays. They seem to reveal a man of wide learning and experience: a knowledge of medicine, law, botany and foreign countries, as well as of court life. Where would a butcher's son from Stratford have the opportunity of gaining such knowledge? Francis Bacon, on the other hand – philosopher, essayist and Lord Chancellor – was known as one of the most erudite men of his time. . . .

For Wilmot one of the main problems was that Shakespeare's reputation had increased so much since his death that it was difficult to sort out the truth from the later legends. Until 1660 – when the theatres opened again after the Puritan interregnum – he remained half forgotten (although his collected plays had appeared in 1623). There was a Shakespeare revival during the Restoration, but his plays were 'adapted' and almost totally rewritten. John Aubrey's *Brief Lives* (1682) has an extremely 'brief' life of Shakespeare – a mere two pages – in which he says that Shakespeare was a butcher's son, and that he would make dramatic speeches when he had to kill a calf. By that time the Stratford vicar John Ward had noted in his diaries (1661–3) the legend about Shakespeare dying after a drinking bout with Jonson and Drayton. By 1670 Shakespeare's reputation with the playgoing public was as high as it had been in 1600, and unscrupulous booksellers were getting rid of all kinds of old plays by declaring they were by Shakespeare. The 'Shakespeare boom' was largely the work of Sir William Davenant, who was reputed to be Shakespeare's godson – perhaps his son – and who devoted much of his life to reviving the reputation of his idol. The first *Life* of Shakespeare appeared in 1709, as the introduction to Nicholas Rowe's six-volume edition of Shakespeare; Rowe obtained much of his information from the actor Thomas Betterton, another worshipper of the bard, who had made a pilgrimage to Stratford to collect stories and traditions in about 1708. It was Rowe who first printed the story about how Shakespeare fled from Stratford after being caught poaching the deer of Sir Thomas Lucy. From then on the legends multiplied: stories of carousing in Warwickshire villages – notably 'drunken Bidford' – of rhymes about fellow-townsmen, of holding horses' heads outside the theatre when he first came to London, of his love affairs, his appearances before Queen Elizabeth and King James, and dozens more. In 1769 Shakespeare was now regarded with such reverence that the burghers of Stratford decided to hold bicentenary celebrations, and asked the famous actor David Garrick to take charge of the Jubilee. (They were, in fact, five years too late – Shakespeare was born in 1564 – but no one seemed to mind this.) Shakespeare had already become a source of income to the tradesmen of Stratford. Rain spoiled the celebrations, and Garrick lost a small fortune; nevertheless, the Jubilee may be said to have established the 'Shakespeare Industry' as Stratford's chief source of income.

But in the same year, 1769, Herbert Lawrence, a friend of Garrick's, published an amusing allegory called *The Life and Adventures of Common Sense* which describes how a plausible rogue and habitual thief named Shakespeare stole some of the attributes of Wisdom, Genius and Humour and used them to write plays. It was not meant to be a serious accusation, but it seemed to demonstrate a mildly satirical attitude to the Shakespeare

Industry. Soon after this the Rev. James Wilmot moved to Barton-on-the-Heath and began those researches that led him to conclude that Shakespeare's real name was Francis Bacon. But when the Quaker James Cowell imparted these conclusions to the Ipswich Philosophical Society in 1803 he swore them to silence about the name of their author, and they seem to have kept their word.

The absurd episode of the Ireland forgeries demonstrates the extent to which 'Bardolatry' (as Shaw was to call it) had gained a foothold by the 1790s. Samuel Ireland, a prosperous author of travel books, worshipped Shakespeare, and allowed various tradesmen of Stratford to sell him a large number of Shakespeare relics, including a goblet carved from the mulberry tree planted in Shakespeare's garden and the chair on which Shakespeare sat in his courting days. Ireland's youngest son William craved his father's affection, and began forging small Shakespeare items, such as a mortgage deed. His father's greed led him finally to forge whole Shakespeare plays which for a while fooled many experts. The bubble finally burst in 1796, when Ireland's play *Vortigern* was presented at Drury Lane; at the line: 'And when this solemn mockery is ended' the audience burst into boos and jeers. When William finally confessed to the forgeries his father flatly refused to believe him, remaining convinced that such 'works of genius' were beyond the powers of his untalented son. In the previous century there had been a far more sensible and balanced attitude – Samuel Pepys thought *Twelfth Night* 'but a silly play' and *A Midsummer Night's Dream* 'the most insipid, ridiculous play that I ever saw in my life'. By the mid-nineteenth century, Shakespeare was regarded as a godlike genius whose feeblest lines were regarded as beyond criticism. Matthew Arnold expressed this attitude of mindless worship in a sonnet that began:

Others abide our question. Thou art free.
We ask and ask: Thou smilest and art still,
Out-topping knowledge. For the loftiest hill
That to the stars uncrowns his majesty . . . etc.

It was probably this kind of uncritical veneration that lay at the root of the various heresies that began to spring up in the mid-nineteenth century. In 1848 the American consul at Vera Cruz, Joseph C. Hart, wrote a book on *The Romance of Yachting* in which he paused to reflect: 'Ah, Shakespeare – Immortal Bard – who were you?' And in the next thirty-five pages, Hart digresses from yachting to suggest the theory that the Stratford actor was merely a hack who inserted bawdy lines into plays that had been written by starving poets. In 1857 William Henry Smith published *Bacon and Shakespeare* in which he pointed out that nothing we know about Shakespeare indicates that he could be the author of the plays, while Bacon had all the necessary qualifications.

He had already been anticipated by a brilliant and attractive American lady, Delia Bacon, who had started life as a schoolteacher, then become an author and lecturer. Her special subjects were history and literature, and her study of Shakespeare convinced her – for the reasons we have already discussed – that the retired actor of Stratford was an unlikely author for the plays. She became convinced that the evidence for Bacon's authorship lay in England, probably in the tomb itself. She gained the support of that eminent Bostonian Ralph Waldo Emerson, and of a New York banker who admired Bacon, Charles Butler; she sailed for England in the spring of 1853, armed with an introduction to Carlyle from Emerson. Carlyle took to her at once and gave her support; so did Nathaniel Hawthorne, who was American consul in Liverpool. She spent three years living in lodgings and writing her book to prove that Bacon was Shakespeare. The publishers Chapman and Hall sent her a rejection note declining to have any part in 'an attack on one of the most sacred beliefs of the nation and indeed of all nations' – a phrase that expresses the almost religious bigotry that had become typical of the British attitude to Shakespeare. In 1856 she moved to Stratford and charmed the clerk of the church into allowing her to spend some time locked alone in the church; but at the last minute her nerve failed her – or perhaps she was merely demoralized at the thought of trying to rip up the floor of the church and dig down seventeen feet, the reputed depth of the grave.

In 1857, Delia Bacon finally brought out her *Philosophy of the Plays of Shakespeare Unfolded*. (Hawthorne, with whom she had quarrelled, paid for it.) But it proved to be a confused and confusing book – it is not even clear whether her 'suspect' is Bacon, Raleigh, Spenser, Sidney or the Earl of Oxford. Her main thesis was obviously absurd – that a group of enlightened scholars concocted the plays, using the Stratford actor as a 'front', in order to express convictions that might otherwise have led to imprisonment and torture. Reviewers were understandably scathing. After so many years of effort, Delia was shattered, and her mind gave way soon after. A nephew found her in a lunatic asylum, and took her back to New England, where she died at the age of forty-eight.

Delia Bacon's success was greater than she lived to realize; she had raised the question of Shakespeare's authorship, and now many others took it up, including Emerson, Whitman, Oliver Wendell Holmes and Henry James senior. In England the prime minister, Lord Palmerston, read William Henry Smith's book and became a Baconian.

In 1867 there came to light one of the most interesting and convincing pieces of evidence connecting Bacon and Shakespeare. A librarian commissioned by the Duke of Northumberland to examine manuscripts in Northumberland House came upon a folio volume consisting of twenty-two sheets folded double. It seemed clear that it had belonged to Francis Bacon – at least, it contained mostly copies of works written by him. Nine pieces remained in the folder, and there were probably more. The cover, headed 'Mr ffrauncis Bacon', also has the word 'Nevill' written twice at the top. Just below this are the words 'Ne vele velis', the family motto of Bacon's nephew Sir Henry Nevill. The script contains two different sets of handwriting, probably those of amanuenses – presumably Bacon's. The cover contains a list which seems to be a table of contents – since it mentions a number of pieces which are actually in the folder, such as four essays by Bacon, 'Philipp

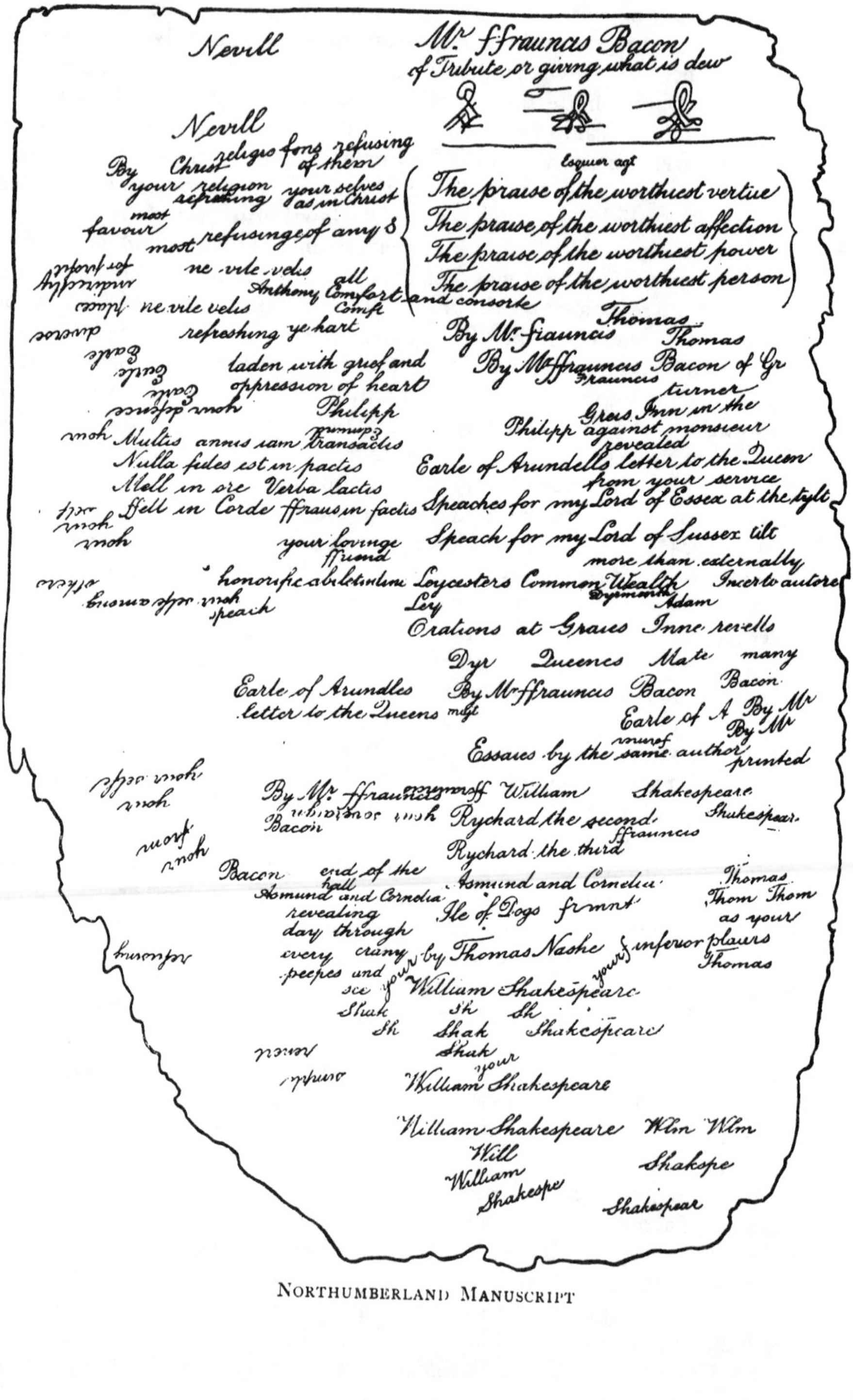

Northumberland Manuscript

against monsieur' – a letter from Sir Philip Sidney dissuading the Queen from marrying the Duke of Anjou, 'Speeches for Lord Essex at the tylt' – speeches by Bacon written for the Earl of Essex, and 'Loycester's Common Wealth' – an incomplete copy of Leicester's Commonwealth. But the cover also lists items that were no longer in the folio, including Nashe's banned play *The Isle of Dogs*, and 'Richard the Second' and 'Richard the Third'. And immediately above these Shakespeare titles: 'By Mr ffrauncis William Shakespeare.'

In fact this evidence is less powerful than it looks at first. 'Richard the Second', while not actually banned, was something of a 'sensitive' play, and Shakespeare had been obliged to omit some lines from the first quarto edition of 1597 (which is also the likeliest date for the Northumberland manuscript). When Essex rebelled in 1601 he paid for a special performance of *Richard II*, hoping that a play about a king who was deposed might inspire Londoners to join his insurrection. (It was unsuccessful, and he was executed.) The 'sensitive' lines about deposition were restored in an edition after Queen Elizabeth's death. *Richard III* was about the same sensitive subject, and may also have been regarded as dubious. As a Privy Councillor of the queen, and her legal adviser, it was Bacon's job to study 'sensitive' works – he had also read a work by Dr Hayward on Richard II which had 'much incensed Queen Elizabeth'; Dr Hayward was committed to the Tower for treason, but Bacon told the queen the book was harmless.

So we may assume that the Northumberland folder originally contained several 'banned' works on which Bacon had been asked to give an opinion. A closer look at the cover shows that the name 'Mr ffrauncis Bacon' and 'Mr ffrauncis' has been doodled several times perhaps by Bacon himself; Shakespeare's name has also been doodled repeatedly. But a close examination of the manuscript shows that it is quite untrue to claim that someone has doodled 'Mr ffrauncis William Shakespeare'. 'ffrauncis' and 'William Shakespeare' are on different levels, and the surname Bacon is written directly below 'Mr ffrauncis' (with the phrase 'your sovereign' written upside down between them). 'William Shakespeare' is written directly above the titles of his two plays and obviously refers to them.

So, regretfully, the Northumberland MS must be abandoned as a proof that there was a closer connection between Bacon and Shakespeare than is generally supposed; all it proves is that Bacon had read *Richard II* and *Richard III* in the course of his duties as the queen's adviser.

Thirty-one years after Delia Bacon's book there appeared the most influential of all the works of the 'Shakespeare heretics', Ignatius Donnelly's *The Great Cryptogram, Francis Bacon's Cipher in the So-called Shakespeare Plays*. Donnelly was an American congressman, famous for *Atlantis: the Antediluvian World*, which is still regarded as a sourcebook by those who believe in the existence of Plato's sunken continent. But in the vast two-volume work on Bacon he tried to prove that Bacon had hidden ciphers about himself in the plays of Shakespeare, to prove his own authorship. (Bacon was in reality fascinated by ciphers.) After years of studying the plays and trying out every possible key to the cipher he finally began to perceive such obscure messages as: 'Seas ill said that More low or Shak'st spur never writ a word of them', meaning, according to Donnelly: 'Cecil said that Marlowe or Shakespeare never writ a word of them.' The book inspired thousands of cranks to seek for 'ciphers' in Shakespeare and other famous authors, and provoked a few wits and satirists to demonstrate that almost any sentence can be rearranged to produce astonishing messages – Ronald Knox wrote a delightful essay proving by this method that Queen Victoria was the real author of *In Memoriam*, describing herself, for example, as 'Alf's pen-poet'.

Another Baconian who was convinced that Bacon concealed his identity under various ciphers and anagrams was Dr Orville W. Owen of Detroit, who finally extracted a long message in blank verse from the plays, and found that it ordered him to cut up all the works of Bacon and Shakespeare into separate pages and stick them around the outside of a wheel. Owen used two wheels, and a thousand-foot strip of canvas that passed around them, with the pages stuck on to it. By incredibly complex reasoning, he extracted more codes from this dismembered text, and used it to extract the information that Bacon was really the son of Queen Elizabeth and her lover the Earl of Leicester; *Hamlet* was written as a personal attack on his mother, who retaliated by sending Bacon to exile in France. . . . The cipher also revealed that the Queen had finally been strangled by her chief minister Robert Cecil. The deciphered material also informed Owen that Bacon had concealed vital manuscripts proving his authorship in various boxes hidden near a castle at the confluence of the rivers Severn and Wye. Owen and a band of faithful followers spent fifteen years searching the countryside in the region of Chepstow (where there is a ruined castle). They dug dozens of holes and tunnels around the castle, and even under the river Wye, but eventually had to admit defeat. Another party hired boatmen to take them up and down the river, looking for hidden flights of steps that might lead to secret chambers. To the armchair student of human eccentricity, it all sounds marvellously funny; but the people who wasted their fortunes and their lives on this wild-goose chase must have felt that it was closer to tragedy.

In fact, anyone who takes the trouble to read a biography of Francis Bacon will see why it is impossible that he could have written Shakespeare's plays. Their characters are utterly different. The author of *A Midsummer Night's Dream* and *Twelfth Night* is obviously a kindly and good-natured human being; it is easy to understand why his friends referred to him as 'gentle Shakespeare'. No one would have called Bacon gentle. He was a man of immense intelligence who was permanently dissatisfied with himself and with his lot in life. He was driven by the most superficial kind of ambition: 'political power is what I want, power over men and affairs'. He was a calculating, rather heartless man who believed that successful men should learn how to 'work' their friends by discovering their weaknesses. His father died before he had time to make provision for him in his will, and Bacon found himself practically penniless at the age of nineteen. His uncle Lord Burghley (William Cecil) was Lord Treasurer, and could easily have procured his nephew advancement; but he preferred to help his son Robert. Bacon became a lawyer. Then he decided to pay court to the Queen's favourite, the accomplished and dashing Earl of Essex; with charm and flattery he had soon gained the earl's friendship. Essex frequently gave him money – Bacon was a spendthrift – and tried hard to persuade the Queen to grant him various offices. When she passed over Bacon in favour of another candidate for Master of the Rolls, Essex soothed his protégé's disappointment by presenting him with a large estate. In 1596 Essex captured Cadiz, and became one of the most popular men in England. But – to Bacon's alarm – he began to overreach himself. After an unsuccessful expedition against the Irish, Essex was politically ruined. He tried to foment a rebellion, and was arrested and put on trial. Everyone recognized that he was guilty of hot temper rather than a desire to overthrow the Queen, and it seemed likely that his punishment would not be heavy. At this point Bacon betrayed his friend; he delivered a brilliant speech in which he accused Essex of treason, and declared that, 'as a friend', he knew Essex meant to seize the throne. Essex was sentenced to death and executed.

It is impossible to exonerate Bacon. He did it to gain favour with the Queen and further his own career; in return for sending Essex to his death he received twelve hundred pounds. But not the advancement he hoped for. Elizabeth distrusted him.

When Elizabeth died Bacon set out to flatter James I, and succeeded. He was knighted, and became Attorney-General in 1613. Five years later he finally reached the climax of his ambition, was ennobled and became Lord Chancellor. Three years later he was impeached for accepting bribes; he admitted his guilt and was banned from office and fined £40,000. He devoted the last five years of his life to writing.

Bacon is a baffling character, a strange mixture of greatness and pettiness. He was the most intelligent man of his time, and in some ways one of the nastiest. It would be difficult to conceive a character more totally unlike Shakespeare's. The dramatist had genius; yet in a sense was not particularly intelligent. He wrote as naturally as a bird sings. The pessimism in which he frequently indulges is the pessimism of a child who has just lost a favourite toy, not the gloomy cynicism of the brilliant intellectual who despises his own craving for success. It is as impossible that Bacon could have written Shakespeare as that Schopenhauer could have written *Alice in Wonderland*.

Bacon was only the first of many candidates. In 1891 an archivist named James Greenstreet wrote a series of articles in *The Genealogist* suggesting that Shakespeare was the Earl of Derby, William Stanley. In 1599 a Jesuit spy had told a correspondent on the continent that the earl was not available to take part in a plot against the Queen because he was 'busy in penning comedies for the common players'. Greenstreet died soon after publishing the articles, but the theory was revived fifteen years later by an American, Robert Frazer, in a book called *The Silent Shakespeare*. A later exponent of the theory, Professor Abel Lefranc, wrote four large volumes whose purpose was to prove that Shakespeare was thoroughly familiar with France and the French. He also pointed out that the plot of *Measure for Measure* was based on a real-life story from Paris in which there was a distinct similarity between the names of the characters and Shakespeare's inventions.

The dramatist Christopher Marlowe was another candidate, advanced in

1895 in a novel called *It Was Marlowe* by a San Francisco attorney, William G. Ziegler. It was not taken seriously, but the theory was revived in 1955 by an American scholar, Calvin Hoffman, in *The Murder of the Man Who Was Shakespeare*. Marlowe became famous with his first play, *Tamburlaine*, in 1587, when he was only twenty-three, and he probably collaborated with Shakespeare on Henry VI. In 1593 he was murdered in a quarrel about how much he owed towards a bill in a tavern; his murderer was acquitted. At the time of his murder Marlowe was in serious trouble; his fellow-playwright Thomas Kyd had been charged with atheism, and alleged that the papers found in his room actually belonged to Marlowe. Kyd was tortured but released, and seems to have died not long after. Marlowe had a powerful protector, Sir Thomas Walsingham, the cousin of the queen's spy-master Sir Francis Walsingham. At the time of his death he was due to stand trial, and might well have been executed. Hoffman's theory is that Marlowe was spirited away to Europe, and that another man was killed in his place and buried in his grave. And Marlowe went on to write the plays of Shakespeare. Hoffman's chief argument is that an analytical method invented by Dr Thomas Corwin Meadenhall – it involves noting the average length (in letters) of an author's words – demonstrated that Bacon could not have written Shakespeare, but that Marlowe *could*.

But once again a reading of the works of the two men reveals that they were quite different in character. One of the most basic differences was that Marlowe was homosexual, and Shakespeare was clearly not. The Shakespeare scholar Dr A.L.Rowse has pointed out that one major difference between the work of Marlowe and that of Shakespeare is that Shakespeare is fond of bawdy jokes and sexual *double entendres*, while Marlowe's work shows the prudery that is often characteristic of homosexuals – the distaste for crude smut. This observation leaves Calvin Hoffman's case with very little support.

Around 1914 an elementary schoolmaster named John Thomas Looney (an unfortunate name, but pronounced Loney) became convinced that the Stratford actor could not have written the plays, and began a systematic search for an Elizabethan who possessed the right qualifications. He deduced the character of the author from his work, then made a list of the basic requirements of such a person: he ended with a list of seventeen. By 1920 he had decided that only one man fitted the picture: Edward de Vere, the seventeenth Earl of Oxford. His book *Shakespeare Identified* is generally agreed to be as absorbing as a detective story, but his 'unfortunate name' prevented it being taken seriously by the general public. (Other writers on the Shakespeare problem included S.E.Silliman, who supported Marlowe's case, and George Battey, who believed Shakespeare was Daniel Defoe.) But although his book was soon forgotten, the theory was taken up by another American scholar, Charlton Ogburn, whose huge tome *The Mysterious William Shakespeare* (1984) is, in spite of its size, immensely readable. But although Ogburn argues convincingly that Oxford was a fine lyric poet who might well have written 'Hark, hark the lark' and 'Full fathom five', he has an almost impossible task convincing the reader that late plays like *A Winter's*

Tale, Lear and *The Tempest* were written before 1604, the year Oxford died. Looney overcame that problem by suggesting that these plays were written by other people – Raleigh being the author of *The Tempest* and Fletcher of *Henry VIII;* Ogburn argues vigorously that they were all written much earlier than supposed; but his arguments will leave most people as unconvinced as Looney's did.

One of the minor problems of Shakespeare scholarship is the identity of the lady called Anne Whateley, to whom, according to an entry in the Bishop of Worcester's register, Shakespeare was due to be married in November 1582; a licence was issued to William Shakespeare just before his marriage to Anne Hathaway. 'Whateley' could have been a slip of the pen on the part of the clerk, but surely he would not have written 'of Temple Grafton' when he should have written 'Shottery'? Says Sir Sidney Lee: 'He was doubtless another of the numerous William Shakespeare's who abounded in the diocese of Worcester.' This view is disputed by William Ross, a Scottish architect, who became convinced that Anne was the true author of Shakespeare's plays. In *The Story of Anne Whateley and William Shaxpere* (1939), Ross tells a touching story of how in 1581 the seventeen-year-old Shakespeare, employed in his father's business, called at a nunnery in Temple Grafton, near Stratford, and became acquainted with a nun called Anne Whateley, who fell in love with him. She began to write sonnets to him, the first of which began 'From fairest creatures we desire increase.' But after she had given him thirty-two sonnets, the youth confessed that he was having a love affair with an older woman, Anne Hathaway, and in sonnet 33 she becomes the 'basest cloud' that hides the face of the sun. When Anne Hathaway became pregnant Shakespeare experienced revulsion, and persuaded Anne Whateley to marry him; but the Hathaway family stepped in and took legal steps to force 'Shaxpere' to marry Anne Hathaway. Anne is of course the 'dark Lady', for whom Anne Whateley began to experience a tormented, ambivalent kind of love. In fact, according to Ross, Anne Whateley eventually wrote about Shakespeare's desertion – to London – from Anne Hathaway's point of view, the result being *A Lover's Complaint,* a triumph of identification of one woman with another.

But how did a girl who had spent most of her life in a nunnery become such an excellent craftsman? The answer, according to Ross, is that she was also the collaborator of one of the major poets of the age, Edmund Spenser. Spenser met Anne Whateley about 1576, when Shakespeare was only twelve, and fell in love with her. Spenser's first major poem, *The Shephearde's Calender,* appeared three years later, and, according to Ross, 'the surmise that she collaborated in it is not an improbable one'. And she then went on to write Spenser's most celebrated work, *The Faerie Queene.* A few years later she also dashed off Marlowe's *Hero and Leander.* In fact, 'a perusal of the plays attributed to Marlowe makes it quite evident that their real author was Anne Whateley. These plays . . . were preliminary efforts, written when she was acquiring proficiency in the technique of the theatre. Her full achievement as a creative artist was reserved for Shakespeare alone.' The question of whether she was also responsible for the bawdy passages is not explored, but we may probably assume that these vulgar touches were added by the Stratford actor.

The reader of *Anne Whateley and William Shaxpere* may experience a sudden suspicion that the author is pulling his leg, and that the book is intended as a satire on the whole anti-Shakespeare industry. This would be unfounded. William Ross presented the present writer with a copy in 1963, when he was seventy-three, and it was perfectly clear from his accompanying letter that he was totally sincere, and that since publishing the book in 1939 he had been working assiduously on his theory and accumulating more evidence. And it was also clear that nothing would convince him that the different styles of *The Faerie Queene*, *Hero and Leander* and *King Lear* indicate the presence of three different authors.

This seems to be the major problem with most of the anti-Shakespearians. They examine the problem through a magnifying glass, and cannot see the wood for the trees. And most of them are so lacking in any faculty of literary criticism that they cannot tell a good poem from a bad one. Most of them can be highly convincing for a few pages at a time, but the whole argument is always less than the sum of its parts. Neither Bacon nor Derby nor Oxford nor Marlowe nor even Anne Whateley finally emerge as a more convincing candidate than the Stratford actor.

But what of the Stratford actor? It seems, to put it mildly, unlikely that a man whose father was illiterate and whose children were illiterate, and who could not even be bothered to keep copies of his own books in the house, should have written *Hamlet* and *Othello*. We may reject all the other candidates as absurd; but at the end of the day we still find ourselves facing the same problems that made the Rev. James Wilmot conclude that, whoever wrote the plays and sonnets, it was not William Shakespeare.

35 Spontaneous Human Combustion

On the evening of Sunday 1 July 1951 Mrs Mary Reeser, aged seventy-seven, seemed slightly depressed as she sat in her overstuffed armchair and smoked a cigarette. At about 9 pm her landlady, Mrs Pansy Carpenter, called in to say goodnight. Mrs Reeser showed no disposition to go to bed yet; it was a hot evening in St Petersburg, Florida.

At five the next morning, Mrs Carpenter awoke to a smell of smoke; assuming it was a water pump that had been overheating, she went to the garage and turned it off. She was awakened again at eight by a telegraph boy with a telegram for Mrs Reeser; Mrs Carpenter signed for it and took it up to Mrs Reeser's room. To her surprise, the doorknob was hot. She shouted for help, and two decorators working across the street came in. One of them placed a cloth over the doorknob and turned it; a blast of hot air met him as the door opened. Yet the place seemed empty, and at first they could see no sign of fire. Then they noticed a blackened circle on the carpet where the armchair had stood. Only a few springs now remained. In the midst of them there was a human skull, 'charred to the size of a baseball', and a fragment of liver attached to a backbone. There was also a foot encased in a satin slipper; it had been burnt down to the ankle.

Mrs Reeser was a victim of a baffling phenomenon called spontaneous human combustion; there are hundreds of recorded cases. Yet in their standard textbook *Forensic Medicine,* Drs S.A.Smith and F.S.Fiddes assert flatly: 'Spontaneous combustion of the human body cannot occur, and no good purpose can be served by discussing it.' This is a typical example of the kind of wishful thinking in which scientists are prone to indulge when they confront a fact that falls outside the range of their experience. In the same way the great chemist Lavoisier denied the possibility of meteorites.

The example of Mrs Reeser is worth citing because it is mentioned by Professor John Taylor in his book *Science and the Supernatural,* a book whose chief purpose is to debunk the whole idea of the 'paranormal', which, according to Professor Taylor, tends to 'crumble to nothing' as it is scientifically appraised. Yet he then proceeds to admit that there are instances that seem 'reasonably well validated', and proceeds to cite the case of Mrs Reeser.

Twenty-nine years later, in October 1980, a case of spontaneous combustion was observed at close quarters when a naval airwoman named Jeanna Winchester was driving with a friend, Leslie Scott, along Seaboard Avenue in Jacksonville, Florida. Suddenly, Jeanna Winchester burst into yellow flames, and screamed, 'Get me out of here.' Her companion tried to beat out the flames with her hands, and the car ran into a telegraph pole. When Jeanna Winchester was examined it was found that 20 per cent of her body was covered with burns. But Jeanna Winchester survived.

Michael Harrison's book on spontaneous combustion, *Fire From Heaven* (1976), cites dozens of cases; they make it clear that the chief mystery of spontaneous combustion is that it seldom spreads beyond the person concerned. On Whit Monday 1725, in Rheims, Nicole Millet, the wife of the landlord of the Lion d'Or, was found burnt to death in an *unburnt* armchair, and her husband was accused of her murder. But a young surgeon, Claude-Nicholas Le Cat, succeeded in persuading the court that spontaneous human combustion *does* occur, and Millet was acquitted – the verdict was that his wife had died 'by a visitation of God'. The case inspired a Frenchman called Jonas Dupont to gather together all the evidence he could find for spontaneous combustion, which he published in a book *De Incendiis Corporis Humani Spontaneis*, printed in Leyden in 1763.

Another famous case of this period was that of Countess Cornelia di Bandi, of Cesena, aged sixty-two, who was found on the floor of her bedroom by her maid. Her stockinged legs were untouched, and between them lay her head, half burnt. The rest of the body was reduced to ashes, and the air was full of floating soot. The bed was undamaged and the sheets had been thrown back, as if she had got out – perhaps to open a window – and then been quickly consumed as she stood upright, so the head had fallen between the legs. Unlike the wife of innkeeper Millet, the countess had not been a heavy drinker. (One of the most popular theories of spontaneous combustion at this period was that it was due to large quantities of alcohol in the body.)

Two nineteenth-century novelists used spontaneous combustion to dispose of unwanted characters. Captain Marryat borrowed details from a *Times* report of 1832 to describe the death of the mother of his hero Jacob Faithful (in the novel of the same name), who is reduced to 'a sort of unctuous pitchy cinder' in her bed. Twenty years later, in 1852, Dickens put an end to his drunken rag-and-bone dealer Krook in *Bleak House* by means of spontaneous combustion – Krook is charred to a cinder that looks like a burnt log. G.H.Lewes, George Eliot's lover, took issue with Dickens and declared that spontaneous combustion was impossible, so in his preface to *Bleak House* Dickens contradicts Lewes and cites thirty examples from press reports. Yet at the end of his article on Krook in *The Dickens Encyclopedia* (1924), Arthur L. Hayward states dogmatically: 'The possibility of spontaneous combustion in human beings has been finally disproved.' He fails to explain what experiments have 'finally disproved' it.

Harrison's book, which gathers together the result of many studies, leaves no possible doubt of the reality of spontaneous combustion. But what causes it? At present it must be confessed that the phenomenon baffles medical knowledge. But Harrison offers some interesting clues. He speaks of the researches of an American doctor, Mayne R. Coe junior, who was interested in the subject of telekinesis – mind over matter. Coe was able to move aluminium strips pivoted on the points of needles by moving his hand over them – this was obviously due to some natural physical 'magnetism'. He began various yoga exercises in an attempt to develop his bioelectricity; sitting one day in an easy-chair, he felt a powerful current passing downward from his head throughout his body; he thought it was of high voltage but low amperage. He suspended a cardboard box from the ceiling on a length of string, and found that he could cause it to move from a distance – when the room was dry, from as much as eight feet. He then charged his body with 35,000 volts DC, using an electric current, and found that he could move the box in exactly the same way. This seemed to prove that he was in fact generating a high voltage current with his mental exercises. He also went up in an aeroplane to an altitude of 21,000 feet, where the air was extremely dry, and produced electric sparks after he had charged his body to 35,000 volts. Coe theorized that this could explain the phenomenon of levitation – when the yogi's body floats off the ground – with the positively charged human body repelling the negatively charged earth.

Harrison also cites cases of human 'batteries' and magnets people (usually children) who have developed a powerful electric charge. In 1877 Caroline Clare of London, Ontario, turned into a human magnet, who attracted metal objects and could give a powerful electric shock to as many as twenty people holding hands. She was suffering from adolescent depressions at the time. Frank McKinistry of Joplin, Missouri, developed a magnetic force which caused his feet to stick to the earth. In 1895 fourteen-year-old Jennie Morgan of Sedalia, Missouri, generated a charge sufficient to knock a grown man on his back, and when she touched a pump handle sparks flew from her fingertips. It is also worth noting that many teenagers who became the focus of 'poltergeist effects' (see Chapter 26) developed magnetic or electrical properties; in 1846 a French girl named Angélique Cottin became a kind of human electric battery; objects that touched her flew off violently, and a heavy oak loom began to dance when she came near it. On the other hand, Esther Cox, the 'focus' of the disturbances at Great Amherst in Nova Scotia, developed a magnetism that made cutlery fly to her and stick fast. It seems that there must be two kinds of charges, positive and negative.

According to Dr Coe, each human muscle cell is a battery, and a cubic inch could develop 400,000 volts. (The inventor Nicola Tesla used to demonstrate that the human body can take immense electrical charges – enough to light up neon tubes – provided the amperage is kept very low.)

But this seems unlikely to explain spontaneous combustion: the whole point of Tesla's experiments was that he did *not* burst into flame. It is high amperage that can cause 'burn-ups.' (If two 12-volt car batteries are connected by thin wire, the wire will melt; even thick wire becomes hot.) And this could begin to explain why the surroundings of victim – of spontaneous combustion are undamaged; they are non-conductors.

Victims of spontaneous combustion tend to be the old and the young. On 27 August 1938, the 22-year-old Phyllis Newcombe was dancing vigorously in Chelmsford, Essex, when her body glowed with a blue light which turned into flames; she died within minutes. In October of the same year a girl called Maybelle Andrews was dancing in a Soho nightclub with her boy-friend, Billy Clifford, when flames erupted from her back, chest and shoulders. Her boy-friend, who was badly burned trying to put her out, said that there were no flames in the room – the flames seemed to come from the girl herself. She died on the way to hospital. In such cases it seems just conceivable that the activity of dancing built up some kind of static electricity. Michael Harrison even points out that 'ritual dancing' is used by primitive tribes to build up emotional tension in religious ceremonies, and suggests that this is what has happened here.

Michael Harrison also points out some curious geographical links. On 13 March 1966 three men were 'spontaneously combusted' at the same time. John Greeley, helmsman of the SS Ulrich, was burnt to a cinder some miles west of Land's End; George Turner, a lorry-driver, was found burnt at the wheel of his lorry at Upton-by-Chester – the lorry overturned in a ditch; in Nijmegen, Holland, eighteen-year-old Willem ten Bruik died at the wheel of his car. As usual in such cases, the surroundings of all three were undamaged. Harrison points out that the three men were at the points of an equilateral triangle whose sides were 340 miles long. Is it conceivable that the earth itself discharged energy in a triangular pattern?

Another investigator, Larry Arnold, put forward his own theory in the magazine *Frontiers of Science* (January 1982): that so-called 'ley lines' – lines of 'earth force' may be involved. The man who 'discovered' ley lines, Alfred Watkins, noted how frequently places called 'Brent' occur on them (brent being an old English form of 'burnt'). Other 'ley-hunters' have suggested that megalithic stone circles are placed at crucial points on ley lines – often at crossing-points of several leys. It is again interesting to note how many stone circles are associated with the idea of dancing – for example, the Merry Maidens in Cornwall; Stonehenge itself was known as 'the Giants' Dance'. It has been suggested that ritual dances occurred at these sites, so that the dancers would somehow interact with the earth energy (or 'telluric force').

Larry Arnold drew a dozen or so major leys on a map of England, then set out to find if they were associated with mystery fires. He claims that one 400-mile-long 'fire-leyne' (as he calls them) passed through five towns where ten mysterious blazes had concurred. He also notes several cases of spontaneous combustion occurring on this 'leyne'. He cites four cases which occurred on it between 1852 and 1908.

Harrison believes that spontaneous combustion is basically a 'mental freak', where the mind somehow influences the body to build up immense charges. The answer could lie in either of the two theories, or in a combination of the two.

36 Synchronicity or 'Mere Coincidence'?

The *Sunday Times* journalist Godfrey Smith was thinking of writing something about the 'saga of lost manuscripts' – Carlyle's manuscript of *The French Revolution*, burnt by a careless maid, T.E.Lawrence's *Seven Pillars of Wisdom*, left in a taxi, Hemingway's suitcase full of early manuscripts, stolen from a train – and decided to call on the literary agent Hilary Rubinstein, a treasure-house of similar stories. But before he could introduce the subject into the conversation a girl sitting with them – the wife of the novelist Nicholas Mosley – mentioned that her husband was upset because he had just had the first 150 pages of his new novel stolen from his car. Smith remarked in his *Sunday Times* column: 'We are back in what J.W.Dunne called serial time, and Arthur Koestler called synchronicity, and some of us still call coincidence . . .'

It was Jung in fact who coined the word 'synchronicity' for meaningful coincidence. But Arthur Koestler was equally intrigued by the subject, and discussed it in a book called *The Roots of Coincidence* in 1972. In the following year he wrote an article about coincidence in *The Sunday Times* and appealed to readers for examples. Many of these were utilized in his book *The Challenge of Chance* (1973), co-authored by Sir Alister Hardy and Robert Harvie. He begins with a section called 'The Library Angel', describing coincidences involved with books. In 1972 Koestler had been asked to write about the chess championship between Boris Spassky and Bobbie Fischer, so he went to the London Library to look up books on chess and books on Iceland. He decided to start with chess and the first book that caught his eye was entitled *Chess in Iceland* by Williard Fiske.

He then tells of how Dame Rebecca West was trying to check up on an episode related by one of the accused in one of the Nuremberg war-crimes trials, and how she discovered to her annoyance that the trials are published in the form of abstracts under arbitrary headings and are therefore useless to a researcher. After an hour of fruitless searching she approached a librarian and said: 'I can't find it . . .', and casually took a volume off the shelf and opened it. It opened at the page she had been searching for.

This anecdote is particularly interesting because it involved an apparently 'random' action, a casual reaching out without logical purpose. The word 'synchronicity' was coined by Jung in connection with the *I Ching*, the Chinese *Book of Changes*, which the Chinese consult as an 'oracle'. The method of 'consulting' the *I Ching* consists of throwing down three coins at random half a dozen times and noting whether there are more heads or tails. Two or three tails gives a line with a break in the middle, thus: ; three heads gives an unbroken line. The six lines, placed on top of one another, form a 'hexagram':

```
——    ——
—————————
—————————
——    ——
—————————
—————————
```

The above hexagram is number 58, 'The Joyous – Lake', with a 'Judgement:': 'The Joyous, Success – Perseverance is favourable.' But from the logical point of view it is obviously impossible to explain how throwing down coins at random can provide an answer – even if the question has been very clearly and precisely formulated in the mind before the coins are thrown.

The experience of Rebecca West can provide a glimmering of an answer. She was looking for a particular passage. We may assume that some unconscious faculty of 'extra-sensory perception' guided her to the right place before she began to speak to the librarian, and then guided her hand as she casually reached out. But could it also cause the book to open in the right place? This would seem to require something more than 'ESP', something for which Horace Walpole coined the word 'serendipity', 'the faculty of making happy and unexpected discoveries by chance'. And what of the 'chance' that caused the librarian to be standing in the right place at that moment? We have here such a complex situation that it is difficult to conceive of some purely 'passive' faculty – a kind of intuition – capable of accounting for it. Unless we wish to fall back on 'coincidence', we have to think in terms of some faculty capable to some extent of 'engineering' a situation as well as merely taking advantage of it. And the use of the *I Ching* also seems to presuppose the use of such a faculty in causing the coins to fall in a certain order.

For most of his life Jung was unwilling even to conceive of such a possibility – at least publicly. (He was, in fact, using the *I Ching* as an oracle from the early 1920s.)

In 1944, when he was sixty-eight years old, Jung slipped on an icy road and broke his ankle; this led to a severe heart attack. While hovering between life and death, Jung experienced curious visions, in one of which he was hovering above the earth, out in space, then saw a kind of Hindu temple inside a meteor. 'Night after night I floated in a state of purest bliss.' He was convinced that if he recovered his doctor would have to die – and in fact the doctor died as Jung started to recover. The result of these strange experiences was that Jung ceased to be concerned about whether his contemporaries regarded him as a mystic rather than a scientist, and he ceased to make a secret of his lifelong interest in 'the occult'. In 1949 he wrote his influential introduction to Richard Wilhelm's edition of the *I Ching*, in which he speaks about the 'acausal connecting principle' called synchronicity; in the following year he wrote his paper *On Synchronicity*, later expanded into a book. Unfortunately, Jung's fundamental premise in both these seminal works is basically nonsensical. Western science, he says, is based on the principle of causality. But modern physics is shaking this principle to its foundations; we now know that natural laws are merely statistical truths, and that therefore we must allow for exceptions. This is, of course, untrue. The philosopher

Hume had argued that causality is not a basic law of the universe; a pan of water usually boils when we put it on a fire, but it *might* freeze. Kant later used this argument to demonstrate that the stuff of the universe is basically 'mental'. We can now see that these arguments were fallacious. It is true that a pan of water might freeze when placed on a fire, if the atmospheric pressure were suddenly increased a thousandfold. But this would not be a defiance of the law of causality, merely a change in some of the basic conditions of the experiment. And by the same argument, we can see that modern physics has *not* demonstrated that the laws of nature are 'statistical', and that once in a billion times they might be 'broken'. A law of nature cannot be broken except for some very good 'legal' reason.

So Jung's talk about an 'acausal connecting principle' may be dismissed as verbal mystification, designed to throw dust in the eyes of scientists who would otherwise accuse him of becoming superstitious in his old age. The example Jung gives of synchronicity makes this clear. He tells how, on 1 April 1949, they had fish for lunch, and someone mentioned the custom of making an 'April fish' (i.e., April fool) of someone. In the afternoon a patient showed him pictures of fish which she had painted. In the evening he was shown a piece of embroidery with fish-like monsters on it. The next morning another patient told him a dream of a fish. At this time Jung was studying the fish symbol in history, and before this string of coincidences began had made a note of a Latin quotation about fish. It is, says Jung, very natural to feel that this is a case of 'meaningful coincidence' – i.e., that there is an 'acausal connection'. But if the coincidence is 'meaningful', then there must be a causal connection – even if (as Jung is implying) it is not one that would be recognized by science. Jung is in fact suggesting that there is some hidden connection between the mind and nature.

Jung was not the first to consider this possibility. The Austrian biologist Paul Kammerer – who committed suicide after being accused of faking some of his experiments – was fascinated by odd coincidences, and wrote a book, *The Law of Series*, about it. The book contains a hundred samples of coincidence. For example, in 1915 his wife was reading about a character called Mrs Rohan in a novel; on the tram soon after she saw a man who resembled her friend Prince Rohan; that evening Prince Rohan dropped in to see them. In the tram she had heard someone ask the man who looked like Rohan whether he knew the village of Weissenbach on Lake Attersee; when she got off the tram she walked into a delicatessen shop, and the assistant asked her if she knew Weissenbach on Lake Attersee. . . .

Kammerer's theory was that events *do* happen in 'clusters', which are natural but not 'causal'. He thought of it as some unknown mathematical law – a 'law of seriality'. In short, 'absurd' coincidences *are* a law of nature. He spent his days carefully noting all kinds of things – the age, sex and dress of people walking past him in a park or sitting on a tram – and observed the typical 'clustering'.

Jung offers one of the most amusing examples of 'clustering' in his book on synchronicity – it was originally told by the scientist Camille Flammarion in his book *The Unknown*. The poet Emile Deschamps was given a piece of plum pudding by a certain M. Fortgibu when he was at boarding-school – the dish was then almost unknown in France, but Fortgibu had just returned from England. Ten years later Deschamps saw plum pudding in the window of a Paris restaurant and went in to ask if he could have some. He was told that unfortunately the pudding had been ordered by someone else – M.Fortgibu, who was sitting there, and who offered to share it. Years later he attended a party at which there was to be plum pudding, and he told the story about M.Fortgibu. As they sat eating plum pudding the door opened and a servant announced 'Monsieur Fortgibu.' In walked Fortgibu, who had been invited to another apartment in the same building, and had mistaken the door.

This seems to be a good example of Kammerer's seriality; if there is any 'meaning' in the coincidence, it is not apparent. But another example given by Flammarion is a different matter. When he was writing a book a gust of wind carried the pages out of the window; at the same moment it began to rain. He decided there would be no point in going to get them. A few days later the chapter arrived from his printer. It seemed the porter of the printing office had walked past, seen the pages on the ground, and assumed he had dropped them himself; so he gathered them together, sorted them, and delivered them to the printer. What was the subject of the chapter? The wind. . . .

So it would seem there are two types of coincidence: serial 'clusterings', which are purely 'mechanical', and synchronicities, which might seem to imply that the mind itself has been able to influence the laws of nature – as when Rebecca West snatched the book at random off the shelf.

Koestler gives an even stranger example of synchronicity. The writer Pearl Binder was planning a satirical novel in association with two collaborators. They invented a situation in which camps for the homeless had been set up in Hyde Park. They decided to have a refugee Viennese professor, a broken-down old man with a Hungarian-sounding name – such as Horvath-Nadoly. Two days later they read in the newspaper that a homeless foreign old man had been found wandering alone at night in Hyde Park, and had given his name as Horvath-Nadoly. Here all three collaborators had contributed to the impossible coincidence. So if it is to be regarded as 'meaningful' rather than an example of 'serial clustering', then it has to be supposed that all three participated in some odd form of telepathy and/or precognition; i.e., that called upon to 'invent' a situation at random, their unconscious minds preferred to cheat by supplying them with details about a real person – just as, asked to invent a name on the spur of the moment, we shall probably choose a name we have just seen or heard. . . .

This 'unconscious' explanation – preferred by Jung – can explain dozens of curious coincidences involving literature. In 1898 a novelist named Morgan Robertson wrote a book about a ship called the *Titan*, 'the safest vessel in the world', which hit an iceberg on her maiden voyage across the Atlantic; fourteen years later his story came to life in the tragic maiden voyage of the *Titanic*. Moreover, the editor W.T.Stead had written a story about a ship that sank, and concluded: 'This is exactly what might take place, and what will take place, if liners are sent to sea short of boats.' Like the liner in Morgan Robertson's novel, the *Titanic* did *not* have enough boats. And W.T.Stead was one of those who drowned.

In 1885 a playwright named Arthur Law wrote a play about a man called Robert Golding, the sole survivor of the shipwreck of a vessel called the *Caroline*. A few days after it was staged, Law read an account of the sinking of a ship called the *Caroline*; the sole survivor was called Robert Golding.

In 1972 a wrter named James Rusk published a pornographic novel called *Black Abductor* under a pseudonym; its plot was so similar to the true story of the kidnapping of heiress Patty Hearst in 1974 by the 'Symbionese Liberation Army' – even to the name of the victim, Patricia – that the FBI later interrogated Rusk to find if he had been involved in the kidnapping plot. He had not; it was again 'pure coincidence'.

In the month preceding the Allied invasion of Normandy – D-Day – the *Daily Telegraph* crossword puzzle gave most of the codewords for the operation: Utah, Mulberry, Neptune and Overlord (the last being the name of the whole operation). MI5 was called to investigate, but found that the compiler of the crosswords was a schoolmaster named Dawe who had no idea of how the words had come into his head.

To explain 'synchronistic' events, Jung was inclined to refer to a phrase of the French psychologist Pierre Janet, *abaissement du niveau mental*, 'lowering of the mental threshold', by which Janet meant a certain lowering of the vital forces – such as we experience when we are tired or discouraged and which is the precondition for neurosis. Jung believed that when the mental threshold is lowered 'the tone of the unconscious is heightened, thereby creating a gradient for the unconscious to flow towards the conscious'. The conscious then comes under the influence of what Jung calls the 'archetypes' or 'primordial images'. These images belong to the 'collective unconscious', and might be – for example – of a 'great mother', a hero-god, a devil-figure, or an image of incarnate wisdom. Jung thought that when the archetype is activated odd coincidences are likely to happen.

Jung worked out his idea of synchronicity with the aid of the physicist Wolfgang Pauli. Pauli himself seemed to have some odd power of causing coincidences. Whenever he touched some piece of experimental apparatus it tended to break. One day in Göttingen a complicated apparatus for studying atomic events collapsed without warning, and Professor J.Franck is said to have remarked: 'Pauli must be around somewhere.' He wrote to Pauli, and received a reply saying that at the time of the accident his train had been standing in the station at Göttingen, on its way to Copenhagen. Pauli, understandably, was intrigued by Jung's ideas about synchronicity, and Jung's book on the subject was published together with a paper by Pauli on archetypal ideas in the work of Kepler – Kepler had apparently stumbled on the idea of archetypes three centuries earlier, although he meant something closer to Plato's 'ideas'. Pauli had created a hypothesis called 'the exclusion principle', which says that only one electron at a time can occupy any 'planetary orbit' inside an atom. He gave no physical reason for this notion; it simply seemed to him to have a pleasing mathematical symmetry, rather like Avogadro's hypothesis that equal volumes of gases will have equal numbers of molecules. In his own essay on Kepler in *The Encyclopedia of Philosophy*, Koestler tried to show that Kepler had arrived at his correct results about the solar system through completely nonsensical ideas about the Blessed Trinity and other such notions, the implication being that creative minds have some instinct or intuition that *shows* them scientific truths, on some principle of symmetry or beauty, rather than through logical reasoning. And this in itself implies that there is some strange basic affinity between mind and nature, and that mind is not some accidental product that has no 'right' to be in the universe. It was this intuition that drew Jung and Pauli together.

More to the point is a passage in the writing of the medieval 'magician' Albertus Magnus:

A certain power to alter things indwells in the human soul and subordinates the other things to her, particularly when she is swept into a great excess of love or hate or the like. When therefore the soul of man falls into a great excess of any passion, it can be proved by experiment that the [excess] binds things together [magically] and alters them in the way it wants. Whoever would learn the secret of doing and undoing these things must know that everyone can influence everything magically if he falls into a great excess.

That is to say, a psychological state can somehow affect the physical world. But Albertus's 'great excess' is clearly the opposite of Jung's 'lowering of the mental threshold'. One is a lowering of vitality, the other an intensification of it.

Some of the concepts of 'split-brain physiology' – a science developed after Jung's death in 1961 – may be able to throw a useful light on these problems. The brain is divided into two hemispheres, rather like a walnut. Brain physiology has established that the left cerebral hemisphere is concerned with our conscious objectives – language, logic, calculation – while the right deals with intuition, pattern-recognition and insight. The remarkable discovery made by Roger Sperry was that when the bridge of nerves – called the corpus callosum – which connects the two halves is severed to prevent epilepsy the patient turns into two people. One split-brain patient tried to hit his wife with one hand while the other held it back. The person I call 'me' lives in the left hemisphere; the person who lives in the other half – the 'intuitive self' – is a stranger. When a female patient was shown an indecent picture with her right brain, she blushed; asked why she was blushing, she replied: 'I don't know.'

The right-brain 'stranger' is an artist; the left-brain 'me' is a scientist. There is some interesting evidence that it is this right-brain 'stranger' who is involved in so-called 'extra-sensory perception' – telepathy, dowsing, 'second sight' – and that his main problem is somehow to communicate the things he knows to the logical self, which is too preoccupied in its own practical purposes to pay attention to the 'still, small voice' of the 'other self'.

The 'stranger' can at times 'take over'. When the English boxer Freddie Mills fought Gus Lesnevitch in 1946 he was knocked down in the second round and concussed. He remembered nothing more until he heard the referee announcing the tenth round. But in the intervening seven rounds he had boxed brilliantly against the much heavier Lesnevitch, and was ahead on points. As soon as he 'recovered' consciousness he began to lose. His 'other self' had taken over when he was knocked down in the second round. Here is an example where a 'lowering of the mental threshold' produced positive results.

If, then, we credit the 'other person' with some kind of 'extra-sensory perception', it would be possible to explain such phenomena as the activities of 'the library angel' – for example, how Rebecca West located the trial she was looking for by reaching out casually. It knows where the trial is located, but it cannot communicate its knowledge to the left brain, which is obsessively searching through the catalogues. Then a librarian approaches, and it sees its chance as he stops near the book. She is prompted to go and complain to the librarian – a relatively easy task, since she is seething with exasperation – and then the 'other self' reaches out for the book and, with that intuitive skill that we see in great sportsmen, opens it at the right place. . . . (It would be interesting to know if Rebecca West reached out with her left hand – for the left side of the body is controlled by the right brain, and vice versa.)

And how does the ESP hypothesis apply to another story told by Rebecca West and quoted by Koestler? Again she was in the London Library, and had asked an assistant for Gounod's Memoirs. As she was waiting she was approached by an American who had recognized her, and who wanted to know if it was true that she possessed some lithographs by the artist Delpeche. She said she did, and they were still talking when the assistant returned with the book. She opened it casually, and found herself looking at a passage in which Gounod describes how kind Delpeche had been to his mother.

Now here, we can see, the chain of coincidences had been set in motion – by her request for the book – before the stranger came and asked her about Delpeche; so we cannot accuse her 'other self' of engineering the whole situation. What we *can* suppose is that the 'other self' was somehow aware that the Gounod Memoirs contained a reference to the artist they were speaking about at that very moment, and drew her attention to it by causing her to open the book in the right place. . . .

Why? One possible answer is self-evident. Modern man has become a 'split-brainer'; for the most part, he lives in the left brain. This means that he is only aware of *half* his identity. Whenever he is reminded of that other half – for example, when music or poetry produce a sudden 'warm glow', or when some smell reminds him vividly of childhood – he experiences the strange sense of wild elation that G.K.Chesterton called 'absurd good news'. The more he feels 'trapped' in his left-brain self by fatigue, discouragement, foreboding – the more he actually cuts himself off from that deep inner sense of purpose and well-being. If he had some instant method of re-establishing contact with this inner power – Abraham Maslow called such contacts 'peak experiences' – his life would be transformed. It must be irritating for that 'other self' to see the left-brain self plunging itself into states of gloom and boredom that are completely unnecessary, and so wasting its life – *both* their lives. So, as a fruitful hypothesis, we might regard 'synchronicities' – like the one involving Gounod's Memoirs – as attempts by the 'other self' to remind the left-brain personality of its existence, and to rescue it from its sense of 'contingency' – the feeling that Proust describes, of feeling 'mediocre, accidental, mortal'.

There is, unfortunately, another type of synchronicity that cannot be explained on the ESP hypothesis and this is the very type that Jung originally set out to explain. ESP cannot explain how the *I Ching* could produce a 'meaningful' answer to a question (if, of course, it actually does so). Common sense tells us that the throwing down of coins can only produce a chance result, *unless* the coins are somehow 'interfered with' as they fall. The Chinese believe that the *I Ching* is some kind of living entity – presumably a supernatural – one and we may assume that this entity answers the question by causing the coins to fall in a certain way. The Western psychologist, rejecting the supernatural explanation, can only fall back on the notion that the unconscious mind – the 'other self' – can somehow influence the fall of the coins by some form of psychokinesis, 'mind over matter'. And while this may be more or less satisfactory in explaining how the *I Ching* works, it still fails to explain, for example, the fish synchronicities that Jung found so intriguing: the Latin inscription about a fish, the mention of 'April fish', the patient who had painted fish, the embroidery with fish-like monsters, the other patient with the dream of a fish. Psychokinesis can hardly explain this series of coincidences.

This is true also of a type of 'cluster' coincidence described by Koestler. A doctor wrote to him commenting that if a patient with some rare and unusual complaint turns up at a surgery, he could be fairly certain that a similar case would turn up later during the same surgery, and that if a patient with a certain name – say, Donnell – should ring him, then another patient called Donnell would be almost certain to turn up at the surgery. Another letter mentioned similar 'clusters' of various types: a dentist noting how often he had 'runs' of patients with the same kind of extraction problem, an eye specialist noting how often he had runs of patients with the same eye problem, even a typewriter-repairer noticing how often he had runs of the same make of machine for repair, or runs of different machines with the identical problem.

Obviously there can be no 'explanation' for such oddities unless a mathematician discovers some completely new law of seriality. But again, we can note that such coincidences tend to produce in us much the same effect as more personal experiences of 'serendipity' – a sense that perhaps the universe *is* less meaningless and inscrutable than we assume. And this – as every reader of Jung's book will agree – is what Jung felt about synchronicity. In fact, a hostile critic might object that Jung – who was the son of a parson – is trying to introduce God by the back door. All his attempts to argue in favour of a 'scientific' principle of synchronicity are unconvincing because the words 'acausal connecting principle' involve a contradiction in terms – unless, that is, he is willing to admit that it is 'pure chance', in which case he has undermined his own argument. A coincidence is either 'meaningful' or it is not; and if it is meaningful, then it is not a coincidence.

In the last analysis, accepting or rejecting 'synchronicity' is a matter of individual temperament. I personally am inclined to accept it because my own experience of 'coincidences' inclines me to the belief that they *are* often 'meaningful'. On the morning when I was about to begin the article on Joan of

Arc in the present book, I noticed in my library a bound series of the *International History Magazine*, and decided to spend half an hour looking through it in case it contained material for this book. I opened the first volume at random, and found myself looking at an article on Joan of Arc, whose editorial introduction raised the question of whether she survived her 'execution'. In fact, the article proved to be useless: the author made no mention of the controversy about the Dame des Armoires. Does this not in itself suggest that the coincidence was 'non-meaningful'? Not necessarily. I have cited elsewhere (see Chapter 39) Jacques Vallee's interesting theory about synchronicity. When he was researching a cult that used the name of the prophet Melchizedek he spent a great deal of time looking up every reference to Melchizedek he could find. In Los Angeles he asked a woman taxi-driver for a receipt: it was signed M. Melchizedek. A check with the Los Angeles telephone directory revealed that there was only one Melchizedek in the whole area.

Vallee points out that there are two ways in which a librarian can store information. One is to place it in alphabetical order on shelves. But computer scientists have discovered that there is a simpler and quicker method. They prefer to store information as it arrives – the equivalent of a librarian putting books on the shelves side by side as they come into the library – and having a keyword or algorithm that will retrieve it. (In a library, the equivalent might be as follows: as each new book comes into the library, some kind of 'beeping' mechanism is attached to its spine; each beeper is adjusted to respond to a certain number code, like a telephone. When the librarian requires a certain book, he dials the number on his pocket beeper, and then goes straight to the book that is beeping.)

Vallee suggests that 'the world might be organised more like a randomised data base than a sequential library'. It was as if he had stuck on the universal notice-board a note saying; 'Wanted, Melchidezeks', and some earnest librarian had said: 'How about this one?' 'No, that's no good – that's just a taxi driver . . .'

This picture, like Jung's, suggests that there *is* some mutual interaction between the mind and the universe, and that the key to 'retrieving information' is to be in the right state of mind: a state of deep interest or excitement: Albertus Magnus's 'excess of passion'.

Another personal example. I was led to write the present article partly by the 'Joan of Arc coincidence', partly by another coincidence that happened a day or two later. I had received in the post a copy of the biography of the American novelist Ayn Rand by Barbara Branden. I was reading this in bed the next day when the post arrived. This included a paperback novel sent to me by an American reader, with a letter enclosed. The letter began: 'In Barbara Branden's recent biography of Ayn Rand you are mentioned in a footnote . . .'

Half an hour later, about to go to my study, I noticed a newspaper clipping that my wife had left for me outside the door. I asked her 'What's this?', and she said: 'It's an article that mentions Hemingway – I thought it might interest you.' In fact it was the article about coincidence and lost manuscripts by

Godfrey Smith, quoted at the beginning of the present article.

As it happened, I decided not to write the coincidence article immediately; I had planned first of all to write a piece about the disappearance of Mary Rogers. I took Poe's short stories from my bookshelf and opened it at 'The Mystery of Marie Roget'. The opening paragraph reads: 'There are few persons, even among the calmest thinkers, who have not occasionally been startled into a vague yet thrilling half-credence in the supernatural, by *coincidences* of so seemingly marvellous a character that, as mere coincidences, the intellect has been unable to receive them.' It confirmed my decision to write this article.

As if to underline this point, a further coincidence occurred after I had written the preceding sentence, which happened to be at the end of a day's work. About to leave my study, I noticed among an untidy pile of books a title I had no recollection of seeing before: *You Are Sentenced to Life* by W.D.Chesney, published by a private press in California; it was a book about life after death. I had obviously bought it a long time ago and had never – as far as I know – even glanced into it. I decided it was time to remedy this. Later in the afternoon, I spent an hour glancing through it, reading a section here and there; then, just before closing it, I decided to glance at the very end. The top of the last page was headed: ORDER OF MELCHIZEDEK, and was a reprint of a letter from Grace Hooper Pettipher, 'Instructor within the Order of Melchizedek', requesting a copy of another book published by the same press. I doubt whether, in two thousand or so books in my study, there is another reference to Melchizedek; but I had to stumble upon this one after writing about Melchizedek in an article about synchronicity.

It is my own experience that coincidences like this seem to happen when I am in 'good form' – when I am feeling alert, cheerful and optimistic, and not when I am feeling tired, bored or gloomy. This leads me to formulate my own hypothesis about synchronicity as follows. As a writer, I am at my best when I feel alert and purposeful; at these times I feel a sense of 'hidden meanings' lurking behind the apparently impassive face of everyday reality. But this is not true only for writers; it applies to all human beings. We are *all* at our best when the imagination is awake, and we can sense the presence of that 'other self', the intuitive part of us. When we are tired or discouraged we feel 'stranded' in left-brain consciousness. We feel, as William James says, that 'our fires are damped, our draughts are checked'. We can be jarred out of this state by a sudden crisis, or any pleasant stimulus, but more often than not these fail to present themselves. It must be irritating for 'the other self' to find its partner so dull and sluggish, allowing valuable time and opportunity to leak away by default. A 'synchronicity' can snap us into a sudden state of alertness and awareness. And if the 'other self' can, by the use of its peculiar powers, bring about a synchronicity, then there is still time to prevent us from wasting yet another day of our brief lives.

The Melchizedek coincidence seems to me of another kind, designed to confirm that we are on 'the right track'. When in the late 1960s I first turned my attention to the field of the paranormal, and began writing a book called *The Occult*, such coincidences became commonplace. I have described in that book how I needed a reference from some alchemical text. I knew that the book containing the reference was in one of the books facing my desk; but it was towards the end of the day, and I was feeling tired and lazy. Besides, I had forgotten where to find the reference, and my heart sank at the prospect of a fruitless search through half a dozen volumes. . . . Conscience finally triumphed and I heaved myself to my feet, crossed the room, and took a book off the shelf. As I did so the next book fell off the shelf; it landed on the floor, open, at the passage I was looking for. And I felt that curious flash of gratitude and delight that we always experience in these moments, as if some invisible guardian angel has politely tendered his help.

Now, a book falling off a shelf and opening at the right page is obviously closer to the procedure of the *I Ching* than, for example, Mrs Kammerer's chain of coincidences about Prince Rohan and Lake Attersee, or Flammarion's story about M.Fortgibu. Yet it seems equally obvious that, in a basic sense, there is a family resemblance between them. The problem arises if we attempt some kind of classification. When Rebecca West reached out and found the right book, this sounds like ESP. But a book falling off a shelf at the right page obviously involves some extra element besides ESP – something closer to psychokinesis. But neither ESP nor psychokinesis can begin to explain Mrs Kammerer's chain of coincidences; and in the case of M.Fortgibu and the plum pudding, it becomes absurd. We seem to be dealing with the mysterious entity that Charles Fort called 'the cosmic joker', and any respectable parapsychologist is bound to draw back in horror at the very idea.

But even if synchronicity declines to fit into any of our scientific theories, this is no reason to refuse to believe in its existence. Science still has no idea of how or why the universe began, of the nature of time, or of what lies beyond the outermost limit of the stars. In fact, science continues to use terms like space, time and motion *as if* they were comprehensible to the human intellect; no one accuses Cantor of being an occultist or mystic because he devised a mathematics of infinity. Science continues to grow and develop in spite of its uneasy metaphysical foundations.

From the purely practical point of view, the chief problem of human existence is individual lack of purpose. In those curious moments of relaxation or sudden happiness that we all experience at intervals, we can *see* that it is stupid to lose purpose and direction, and that if only we could learn to summon this insight *at will*, this fatal tendency to forgetfulness could be permanently eradicated, and life would be transformed. It is obvious in such moments that if we could train ourselves to behave *as if* there were hidden meanings lurking behind the blank face of the present, the problem would be solved. If 'synchronicities' can produce that sense of meaning and purpose, then it is obviously sensible for us to behave *as if* they were meaningful coincidences, and to ignore the question of their scientific validity.

37 Time in Disarray

Time Slips and Precognitions

The late Ivan T. Sanderson, the eminent naturalist and scientist, once had a curious experience of Paris. But it was the Paris not of today, but of five centuries ago; and, to make the story still more paradoxical, it happened in Haiti.

Before beginning his account (in *More 'Things'*), Sanderson is careful to note that he has never taken any interest in 'the occult' – not because he actively disbelieves in it, but because 'I have only one life to lead .. and I've been far too busy trying to catch up with the more pragmatic facts of it'.

Sanderson and his wife were living in a small village named Pont Beudet in Haiti; together with his assistant Frederick G.Allsop, he was engaged in a biological survey. One beautiful evening the three of them decided to drive to Lake Azuey in their ancient Rolls-Royce. Taking a short cut down an old dirt road, they drove into a squashy mass of mud, and went in up to their axles. They got out and began to walk. They walked through most of the night until they were exhausted. They encountered a car with an American doctor on his way to a case, but he had no room for three of them; he promised to try and pick them up on his way back. They plodded on in the moonlight. Then:

. . . suddenly, on looking up from the dusty ground I perceived absolutely clearly in the now brilliant moonlight, *and casting shadows appropriate to their positions*, three-storied houses of various shapes and sizes lining both sides of the road. These houses hung out over the road, which certainly appeared to be muddy with patches of large cobblestones. The houses were of (I would say) about the Elizabethan period of England, but for some reason I *knew* they were in Paris! They had pent roofs, some with dormer windows, gabled timbered porticos, and small windows with tiny leaded panes. Here and there, there were dull reddish lights burning behind them, as if from candles. There were iron-frame lanterns hanging from timbers jutting from some houses and they were all swaying together as if in a wind, but there was not the faintest movement of air about us. I could go on and on describing this scene as it was so vivid: in fact, I could *draw* it. But that is not the main point.

I was marvelling at this, and looking about me, when my wife came to a dead stop and gave a gasp. I ran smack into her. Then she went speechless for a time while I begged to know what was wrong. Finally she took my hand and, pointing, described to me *exactly what I was seeing*. At which point, *I* became speechless.

Finally pulling myself together, I blurted out something like 'What do you think's happened?' but my wife's reply startled me even more. I remember it only too well: she said, 'How did we get to *Paris* five hundred years ago?'

We stood marvelling at what we apparently *both* now saw, picking out individual items, pointing, questioning each other as to details, and so forth. Curiously, we found ourselves swaying back and forth, and began to feel very weak, so I called out to Fred, whose white shirt was fast disappearing ahead.

I don't remember what happened then but we tried to run towards him and, feeling dizzy, sat down on what we were *convinced* was a tall, rough curbstone. Fred came running back asking what was wrong but at first we did not know what to say. He was the 'keeper' of the cigarettes, of which we had about half a dozen left, and he sat down beside us and gave us each one. By the time the flame from his lighter had cleared from my eyes, so had fifteenth-century Paris, and there was nothing before me but the endless and damned thorn bushes and cactus and bare earth. My wife also 'came back' after looking into the flame. Fred had seen nothing, and was completely mystified by our subsequent babble, but he was not sceptical and insisted that we just sit and wait for the truck . . .

When eventually they arrived back home they were surprised to find that their servant woman had a hot meal waiting for them, and a large bowl of hot water, in which she insisted on washing Mrs Sanderson's feet; the head man had prepared hot baths for Sanderson and Fred Allsop. They would not explain how they knew that Sanderson and his companions would be back at dawn. But one of the young men in the village later said to Sanderson: 'You saw things, didn't you? You don't believe it, but you could *always* see things if you wanted to.'

Sanderson had obviously experienced a kind of 'time slip' into the past, and there are dozens – perhaps hundreds – of other recorded examples, the most famous undoubtedly being that of the two English ladies, Eleanor Jourdain and Charlotte Moberly, who in August 1901, walking in the gardens at Versailles, found themselves back in Versailles in 1789, just before the downfall of Louis XVI. Ten years later, their book describing their experience caused a sensation because it was so obvious that the two ladies – principals of an Oxford college – were of unquestioned integrity. Professor C.E.M.Joad, speaking about their 'adventure', used the phrase 'the undoubted queerness of time'. But he made no attempt to explain the mechanism of 'time slips'.

In my book *Mysteries* I record an equally remarkable example, taken directly from the person concerned, Mrs Jane O'Neill of Cambridge. In 1973 she was the first person to arrive at the scene of a serious accident, and helped injured passengers out of the wrecked bus. Later she began to suffer from insomnia, and the doctor told her this was due to shock. On holiday with a friend in Norfolk, she began experiencing 'visions' – sudden vivid pictures that lasted just a few seconds. After one of these she told her friend, 'I have just seen you in the galleys', and the friend replied: 'That's not surprising. My ancestors were Huguenots and were punished by being sent to the galleys.'

But the most remarkable event took place on a visit to Fotheringay church. She stood for some time in front of the picture of the Crucifixion behind the altar. Later, when she commented on it back in the hotel room, her friend asked: 'What picture?' A year later, when they revisited the church, the inside seemed quite different from the first visit, and there was no picture behind the altar. She wrote to Joan Forman, an expert on 'time slips', and through her contacted an antiquarian who was able to tell her that what she had seen had been the church as it *had* been before it had been pulled down in 1553.

Both Sanderson and Jane O'Neill were convinced that what they were looking at was real, not a hallucination, although the Sandersons felt dizzy when they tried to run. One of Jane O'Neill's 'visions' was of two figures walking beside a lake, 'and I knew, though I don't know why, that one of them was Margaret Roper', the daughter of Sir Thomas More. Sanderson and his wife 'knew' that they were looking at fifteenth-century Paris. So it seems clear that the vision was not some simple objective hallucination, like a mirage in the desert, but was due to some extent to their own minds. Sanderson and his wife presumably shared it because of some telepathic rapport of the kind that often develops between married couples. But this fails to explain why they saw Paris in Haiti. (Haiti was, of course, French, but not until the eighteenth century.)

In the mid-nineteenth century a theory of 'time slips' was developed by two American professors, Joseph Rodes Buchanan and William Denton. Through his experiments with his students,[1] Buchanan came to believe that human beings possess a faculty for 'reading' the history of objects; he called this 'psychometry' (see Chapter 27). Denton tested his own students with all kinds of geological specimens, and found that the 'sensitive' ones among them saw 'mental pictures' that were closely related to the object they were holding (and which Denton wrapped in thick brown paper, so they could have no idea of what it was). A piece of lava brought 'visions' of an exploding volcano; a fragment of meteor conjured up visions of outer space; a piece of dinosaur tooth brought visions of primeval forests. Denton was convinced that all human beings possess this faculty, which he described as 'a telescope into the past'.

But while the 'time slips' described by Sanderson and Jane O'Neill obviously have much in common with 'psychometric' visions, they were unquestionably far more than mental pictures or impressions. Yet this is not to say that they were not mental pictures. After her experience of the accident, Jane O'Neill kept on 'seeing' the injuries of the passengers; such visions are known as 'eidetic imagery'. The scientist Nicola Tesla possessed it to such an extent that he could construct a dynamo in his mind and actually watch it running. After experimenting all day with images of the sun, Isaac Newton found that he could produce a visual hallucination of the sun by simply imagining it. Like the strange abilities of calculating prodigies (see Chapter 15), this seems to be a faculty that all human beings possess, but that most of us never learn how to use. We may speculate that Jane O'Neill's traumatic experience activated this dormant faculty, and that it somehow continued to operate spasmodically in the succeeding months. If the image of the sixteenth-century church was some kind of 'eidetic image' floating in front

[1]Described in my book *The Psychic Detectives*.

of her eyes, there is no reason why she should have recognized it as a hallucination unless she tried to touch the picture above the altar; most of us accept the evidence of our senses without question. The same argument probably applies to the experience of Miss Moberly and Miss Jourdain at Versailles. They *saw* men and women dressed in the style of Louis XVI (and assumed it was a rehearsal for a costume drama) but naturally, they did not try to touch them, or even to speak to them. (Being English, they would have required an introduction!)

Another 'time slip' collected by Joan Forman offers us a further clue. Mrs Turrell-Clarke, of Wisley-cum-Pyrford in Surrey, was cycling along the modern road there on her way to evensong when the road suddenly became a field path, and *she seemed to be walking along it.* She was wearing a nun's robes, and she saw a man dressed in the peasant dress of the thirteenth century, who stood aside to allow her to pass. A month later, sitting in the village church, she suddenly saw the church change to its original state, with earth floor, stone altar, lancet windows, and brown-habited monks intoning the same plainsong chant that was at present being sung by the choir in the 'modern' church. At this moment Mrs Turrell-Clarke felt she was at the back of the church, watching the proceedings. So it seems clear that what happened was that her viewpoint changed, and she found herself *looking through someone else's eyes* – the eyes of a lady walking along the road and the eyes of a woman standing at the back of the church. When Jane O'Neill found herself looking at Sir Thomas More's daughter walking by a lake she wondered whether there might be some 'family' connection, since her own unmarried name was Moore. She may even have suspected that she had somehow slipped back into a previous incarnation. Again, it seems clear that she was seeing the scene through someone else's eyes – which explains how she knew that she was looking at Margaret Roper. And since the Sandersons knew they were looking at fifteenth-century Paris, we may assume that they were also looking through 'someone else's eyes'.

The late T.C.Lethbridge, a retired Cambridge don who devoted the last years of his life to studying the paranormal, came to the interesting conclusion that 'ghosts' are in fact a kind of 'tape recording': that powerful emotions can 'imprint' themselves on some sort of magnetic field, and that these 'recordings' can be 'picked up' by a person who is sensitive to them – for example, by a good dowser. (Dowsing involves sensitivity to the electromagnetic field of water.) Lethbridge himself, for example, experienced a strange feeling of foreboding and depression in a spot where the body of a suicide was concealed in a hollow tree. Joan Forman has also expressed her conviction that time slips 'have some connection with the human electromagnetic field'. She herself was standing in the courtyard of Haddon Hall in Derbyshire when she saw a group of four children playing on the steps and yelling with laughter. When she took a step forward the group vanished, but she later recognized one of the girls in an ancestral painting that hung on the walls. She also cites the experience of a Norwich teacher, Mrs Anne May, who was leaning against a monolith at the Clava Cairns, near Inverness, when she 'saw' a group of men in shaggy tunics and cross-gartered trousers, dragging one of the monoliths over the turf; when a group of tourists walked into the glade the figures vanished; apparently Mrs May had caught a glimpse of the original bronze-age builders of the monolithic circle. Joan Forman believes that the contact with the monolith was the 'trigger factor' that caused Mrs May to see her vision, and that in her own case it was the spot she was standing on.

Most students of the paranormal would admit another possibility: the notion that what is being 'contacted' is the mind of someone who lived in the distant past. In 1907 the architect Frederick Bligh Bond was appointed by the Church of England to take charge of the excavations at Glastonbury Abbey. What his employers did not know was that Bond was interested in spiritualism. Together with a friend named Bartlett, Bond attempted 'automatic writing', the aim being to learn where to start digging in the abbey grounds. When they asked about Glastonbury the pencil – which they were both holding – wrote: 'All knowledge is eternal and is available to mental sympathy.' And soon a communicator who signed himself Gulielmus Monachus – William the Monk – began giving extremely detailed instructions on where to excavate, and as a result Bond unearthed two chapels, each of precisely the dimensions given by William the Monk. Another 'communicator', Johannes, made the following interesting remark:

Why cling I to that which is not? It is I, and it is not I, butt parte of me which dwelleth in the past and is bound to that whych my carnal self loved and called 'home' these many years. Yet I, Johannes, amm of many partes, and ye better parte doeth other things .. only that part which remembereth clingeth like memory to what it seeth yet.

Bond's downfall came when he wrote a book describing how he had obtained the information that had made his excavations so successful; the Church of England dismissed him. But the book, *Gate of Remembrance*, remains an astonishing proof that a twentieth-century mind *can* apparently attain some kind of direct access to the past. 'All knowledge is eternal and is available to mental sympathy.' And the comments of Johannes seem to imply that a 'parte of me which dwelleth in the past . . . clingeth like memory to what it seeth yet'. It seems, therefore, remotely possible that some 'time slips' may involve contact with a mind 'which dwelleth in the past'.

Many writers describing time slips mention an odd sense of 'crossing a threshold'. When Miss Jourdain returned alone to Versailles a few months after her 'adventure' with Miss Moberly she suddenly felt 'as if I had crossed a line and was in a circle of influence', and saw oddly dressed labourers in bright tunics. A girl named Louisa Hand told Joan Forman how, when she was a child, she had entered her grandmother's cottage, and been puzzled to find herself in a place with older furniture. Thinking she had entered the wrong place, she went out to check, then went back in; still the room was different. But when she went in a third time things had returned to normal. She also mentioned the sensation of 'crossing a threshold', and of a feeling of silence associated with it.

It would seem, then, that the 'psychometric' theory of Buchanan and

Denton could account for the time-slip phenomenon. But this is far from the truth. It is also possible to 'slip' the other way, into the future. Joan Forman cites the case of a teacher from Holt, Norfolk, who while involved in a 'traffic contretemps' in the town noticed that a launderette that had been under construction was now finished and in use. He told his wife, who went there the next day with a bag of soiled laundry, and found that the place was still half-finished. The teacher had seen the shop as it *would* be in six weeks' time.

Most of the cases of 'future visions' cited in *The Mask of Time* are involved with dreams. In 1927 J. W. Dunne's book *An Experiment With Time*, with its study of 'precognitive dreams', caused a sensation. Dunne described a number of occasions on which he had dreamt of events that he would read about later in the newspapers. T. C. Lethbridge later had much the same experience; he carefully observed his dreams, and noticed how often he dreamt of some trivial event of the next day; for example, he woke up dreaming of the face of a man he did not know; the face seemed to be enclosed in a kind of frame, and the man was making movements with his hands in the area of his chin, as if soaping his face prior to shaving. The next day, driving along a country road, he saw the face of the man of his dream; he was behind the windscreen of an oncoming car – the 'frame' – and his hands were moving on the steering wheel, which was directly under his chin. Joan Forman cites many similar cases. All tend to have the same 'trivial' quality, as if the glimpse of the future is some kind of freak accident. One schoolteacher, lying in bed with a high temperature, had an odd hallucination involving hedgehogs walking round the bedroom floor, and building a high nest with sticks and straw. Three months later he was packing ceramic figures made by his pottery class to take them to the kiln; he packed them in a kind of layered nest, with straw between the layers. Several ceramic hedgehogs were on the floor around his feet. Suddenly he recognized his hallucination. Just before he began the packing operation, he experienced a feeling of 'a peculiar mechanical inevitability'.

An Oxford scientist, Michael Shallis, has written a book on the nature of time, [2] in the course of which he mentions two of his own odd experiences of 'prevision'. As a twelve-year-old boy he went into the house one day and called out to ask his mother what they were having for dinner. As he did so he experienced a feeling of *déja vu*, and knew that his mother would reply that they were having salad for dinner which she did.

This kind of 'prevision' is fairly common. Joan Forman quotes a letter she received from a man who often knew with absolute certainty that a cricketer would be bowled out before the ball left the bowler's hand; he comments that this often annoyed the batsman, who felt that he had somehow caused it. One explanation for such an ability might be some kind of unconscious 'computer' that swiftly assessed the whole situation – the stance of the batsman, the skill of the bowler – and 'saw' that the loss of the wicket was inevitable. But another experience cited by Shallis suggests that the problem is rather more complex than this.

[2]*On Time*, 1982.

A few years ago I was teaching a student physics in an upstairs lecture room .. I had reached the part of the tutorial where we were discussing radioactive half lives and I was again swamped with the deja-vu feeling. I knew I was going to suggest that I needed to show him some examples from a certain book in my office and then go and collect it. I resisted saying this to him, but the feeling it had all happened before was strong. I was determined to break the pattern of the event. I turned to my student and asked him if we had done this work before, believing that he might be sharing the experience. He looked puzzled and replied no. I struggled to avoid continuing the experience. I resolved not to go and fetch the book. Having made that resolution I turned again to the student and said: 'I think I had better show you some examples of these. I will just pop down to my room and get a book.' My awareness of the experience itself did not make it go away, even when I tried not to repeat its pre-set pattern.

There is an alarming implication in the words 'repeat its pre-set pattern'. *Is* it possible that we do what we 'have' to do, whether we want to or not, and that our sense of free will is a delusion? Shallis goes on to say:

There is an element of precognition itself in the experience, because the situation is so 'familiar' that one knows what will happen next. It is different from precognition, however, in that it is familiar; one is in a sense reliving a part of one's life, not predicting or sensing a remote event.

J.W.Dunne's explanation for such experiences involves what he calls 'serial time'. Basically, he is suggesting that there are several 'times'. When we say 'time flows', it means we are measuring it *against* something. That something must be another kind of time, 'time number two'. And this in turn could be measured against 'time number three'. We also have several 'selves'. Self number one is stuck in time number one; but we have another self which is not the physical body, which can rise above self number one and foresee the future.

In his book *Man and Time*, J.B.Priestley tells a story that seems to illustrate the difference between the two selves. A young mother dreamed that on a camping holiday she left her young son by the river while she went off to get the soap, and that when she came back he was drowned. On a camping holiday some time later she was about to go off and get the soap when she suddenly recognized the scene of her dream; so she tucked the baby under her arm before she went off to the tent. . . .

The implication here is important. We *do* possess a degree of free will, but it is hard to exercise in the material world of 'time number one'. It is like swimming against the current. Our human problem is not to remain stuck in 'time number one', the material world, with its repetitious futility, but to learn to spend as much time as possible in the mental world, the world of 'time number two'.

Priestley argues that Dunne is making things unnecessarily complicated in arguing for an infinite number of selves; according to Priestley, there are only three. Self number one is simply involved in living; it might say, for example: 'I feel depressed.' Self number two says: 'I know self number one is depressed.' Self three says: 'I know self two knows self one is depressed. But then, self one is a self-indulgent idiot.' Self one experiences; self two is conscious of experience; self three passes judgment on the experience. Priestley gives an example; in a plane accident, self one was hurled out of his seat; self two knew there was about to be an accident. Self three thought: 'Now I shall know what it's like to be fried alive.' It 'does not really care; it is as if it goes along with the other two just for the ride.'

This is perhaps one of the most interesting and important observations to arise from these speculations about the nature of time; the experience of what seems to be a 'higher self'. In his important book *A Drug-Taker's Notes*, R.H.Ward describes his experience under dental gas:

.. I passed, after the first few inhalations of the gas, directly into a state of consciousness already far more complete than the fullest degree of ordinary waking consciousness, and that I then passed progressively upwards .. into finer and finer degrees of heightened awareness. But although one must write of it in terms of time, time had no place in the experience. In one sense it lasted far longer than the short period between inhaling the gas and 'coming round', lasted indeed for an eternity, and in another sense it took no time at all.

Ward's observation here emphasizes that the nature of time is essentially *mental*. It might almost be said that the sense of time is produced by the stress between the physical world and the 'higher self', and that when this stress vanishes there is a sense of timelessness. The stress vanishes as a result of a withdrawal *inward*, as if towards another level of reality inside us, an inner world with its own reality. Ward says that when he later tried to recall the essence of his experience he found himself repeating 'Within and within and within . . .' like a recurring decimal.

He also quotes from the experience of a friend he calls A, who was on his way back from the station when he experienced mild indigestion. The thought occurred to him

It belongs only to my body and is real only to the physical not-self. There is no need for the self to feel it . . . Even as I thought this the pain disappeared; that is, it was in some way left behind . . . the sensation of 'rising up within' began . . . First there is the indescribable sensation in the spine, as of *something mounting up*, a sensation which is partly pleasure and partly pleasure and partly awe .. This is accompanied by an extraordinary feeling of *bodily lightness*, of well-being and effortlessness . . . Everything was becoming 'more', everything was *going up to another level*.

Here it sounds as if A's 'self number three' had decided to actively intervene, and the result was a sense of leaving the pain behind.

If there is any general conclusion to be drawn from these experiences of the 'undoubted queerness of time', it is this: that we are somehow mistaken in our natural and very understandable assumption that the physical world is the basic and perhaps the only reality. Experiences of 'time slips' and of precognition suggests that when the mind can slip into another 'gear' it escapes its normal enslavement to time, and achieves a state of serene detachment 'above' time.

The puzzling thing about such a notion is its implication that time is somehow unreal, or at least less real than we take it to be. Common sense and science are in agreement that the future cannot be predicted with any precision because it has not yet happened. Every 'cause' in the world of the present moment could have many different effects. When a gas is heated its molecules begin to move faster, and an increasing number of collisions will occur. Each of these collisions causes the molecules to change course, and so leads to a different set of collisions. So it would be virtually impossible to determine which molecules will be colliding with others in ten minutes' time; everything depends upon chance. In the same way, the four billion or so people in the world at the present moment will interact in unpredictable ways, and will determine what is happening in a week from now. In the case of the gas molecules, a sufficiently complex computer could in theory predict what will be happening a week from now; but no computer could make similar predictions about people.

Experiences of time slips and of precognition contradict this assertion. They clearly imply that in some sense the future *is* to some extent predetermined, as if it had already happened. This is, in fact, precisely what the materialist would assert. Free will is an illusion; therefore human beings obey mechanical laws. Yet apparently this cannot be entirely true, or Priestley's mother would not have been able to prevent her baby from drowning. In fact, the very existence of precognition means that the future cannot be entirely determined, for to know the future in advance is to be able, to some extent, to alter it. Even though Michael Shallis obeyed his compulsion to go to look for the book, he had nevertheless made an effort not to do so – thereby revealing that he was not completely 'determined'. (And, presumably, he would have been able to overcome the compulsion if he had felt strongly enough about it – for example, if his sense of *déja-vu* had warned him that he would meet with a serious accident on his way to his office.)

It is a disconcerting thought: that life is somehow basically 'scripted'. But what seems to be more important is the recognition that, with the right kind of effort, we can depart from the 'script'. Priestley takes issue with Professor Gilbert Ryle's view – in *The Concept of Mind* – that man is merely a living body, not a body controlled by a self or soul. Ryle calls this view 'the ghost in the machine'. Experiences of 'time in disarray' seems to support Priestley and contradict Ryle: in fact, to confirm the view that we have at least three 'selves' as distinct from the physical body, and that the third of these selves corresponds roughly to what Kant (and Husserl) meant by the 'transcendental ego', or 'the self that presides over consciousness'.

38 The Great Tunguska Explosion

On 30 June 1908 the inhabitants of Nizhne-Karelinsk, a small village in central Siberia, saw a bluish-white streak of fire cut vertically across the sky to the north-west. What began as a bright point of light lengthened over a period of ten minutes until it seemed to split the sky in two. When it reached the ground it shattered to form a monstrous cloud of black smoke. Seconds later there was a terrific roaring detonation that made the buildings tremble. Assuming that the Day of Judgment had arrived, many of the villagers fell on their knees. The reaction was not entirely absurd; in fact, they had witnessed the greatest natural disaster in the earth's recorded history. If the object that caused what is now known as 'the Great Siberian Explosion' had arrived a few hours earlier or later it might have landed in more heavily populated regions, and caused millions of deaths.

As it later turned out, the village of Nizhne-Karelinsk had been over 200 miles away from the 'impact point', and yet the explosion had been enough to shake debris from their roofs. A Trans-Siberian express train stopped because the driver was convinced that it was derailed, and seismographs in the town of Irkutsk indicated a crash of earthquake proportions. Both the train and the town were over 800 miles from the explosion.

Whatever it was that struck the Tunguska region of the Siberian forestland had exploded with a force never before imagined. Its shockwave travelled around the globe twice before it died out, and its general effect on the weather in the northern hemisphere was far-reaching. During the rest of June it was quite possible to read the small print in the London *Times* at midnight. There were photographs of Stockholm taken at one o'clock in the morning by natural light, and a photograph of the Russian town of Navrochat taken at midnight looks like a bright summer afternoon.

For some months the world was treated to spectacular dawns and sunsets, as impressive as those that had been seen after the great Krakatoa eruption in 1883. From this, as well as the various reports of unusual cloud formations over following months, it is fair to guess that the event had thrown a good deal of dust into the atmosphere, as happens with violent volcanic eruptions and, notably, atomic explosions.

Perhaps the strangest aspect of the Great Siberian Explosion was that no one paid much attention to it. Reports of the falling object were published in Siberian newspapers but did not spread any further. Meteorologists speculated about the strange weather, but no one came close to guessing its real cause.

It was not until the Great War had been fought, and the Russian

Revolution had overthrown the tsarist regime that the extraordinary events of that June day finally reached the general public. In 1921, as part of Lenin's general plan to place the USSR at the forefront of world science, the Soviet Academy of Sciences commissioned Leonid Kulik to investigate meteorite falls on Soviet territory. It was Kulik who stumbled upon the few brief reports in ten-year-old Siberian newspapers that finally led him to suspect that something extraordinary had happened in central Siberia in the summer of 1908.

Leonid found the reports confusing and contradictory. None of them seemed to agree quite where the object had exploded. Some even claimed that the 'meteor' had later been found. But when his researchers began to collect eyewitness reports of the event Kulik became convinced that whatever had exploded in the Tunguska forest was certainly not a normal meteorite.

These reports described how the ground had opened up to release a great pillar of fire and smoke which burned brighter than the sun. Distant huts were blown down and reindeer herds scattered. A man ploughing in an open field felt his shirt burning on his back, and others described being badly sunburnt on one side of the face but not the other. Many people claimed to have been made temporarily deaf by the noise, or to have suffered long-term effects of shock. Yet, almost unbelievably, not a single person had been killed or seriously injured. Whatever it was that produced the explosion had landed in one of the few places on earth where its catastrophic effect was minimized. A few hours later, and it could have obliterated St Petersburg, London or New York. Even if it had landed in the sea, tidal waves might have destroyed whole coastal regions. That day the human race had escaped the greatest disaster in its history, and had not even been aware of it.

Finally Kulik discovered that a local meteorologist had made an estimate of the point of impact, and in 1927 he was given the necessary backing by the Academy of Sciences to find the point where the 'great meteorite' had fallen.

The great Siberian forest is one of the least accessible places on earth. Even today it remains largely unexplored, and there are whole areas that have only ever been surveyed from the air. What settlements there are can be found along the banks of its mighty rivers, some of them miles in width. The winters are ferociously cold, and in the summer the ground becomes boggy, and the air is filled with the hum of mosquitoes. Kulik was faced with an almost impossible task: to travel by horse and raft with no idea of exactly where to look or what to look for.

In March 1927 he set off accompanied by two local guides who had witnessed the event, and after many setbacks arrived on the banks of the Mekirta river in April. The Mekirta is the closest river to the impact point, and in 1927 formed a boundary between untouched forest and almost total devastation.

On that first day Kulik stood on a low hill and surveyed the destruction caused by the Tunguska explosion. For as far as he could see to the north – perhaps a dozen miles – there was not one full-grown tree left standing. Every one had been flattened by the blast, and they lay like a slaughtered regiment, all pointing towards him. Yet it was obvious that what he was looking at was only a fraction of the devastation, since all the trees were facing in the same direction as far as the horizon. The blast must have been far greater than even the wildest reports had suggested.

Kulik wanted to explore the devastation; his two guides were terrified, and refused to go on. So Kulik was forced to return with them, and it was not until June that he managed to return with two new companions.

The expedition followed the line of broken trees for several days until they came to a natural amphitheatre in the hills, and pitched camp there. They spent the next few days surveying the surrounding area, and Kulik reached the conclusion that 'the cauldron' as he called it, was the centre of the blast. All around, the fallen trees faced away from it, and yet, incredibly, some trees actually remained standing although stripped and charred, at the very centre of the explosion.

The full extent of the desolation was now apparent; from the river to its central point was a distance of thirty-seven miles. So the blast had flattened more than four thousand square miles of forest.

Still working on the supposition that the explosion had been caused by a large meteorite, Kulik began searching the area for its remains. He thought he had achieved his object when he discovered a number of pits filled with water – he naturally assumed that they had been made by fragments of the exploding meteorite. Yet when the holes were drained they were found to be empty. One even had a tree-stump at the bottom, proving it had not been made by a blast.

Kulik was to make four expeditions to the area of the explosion, and until his death he remained convinced that it had been caused by an unusually large meteorite. Yet he never found the iron or rock fragments that would provide him with the evidence he needed. In fact, he never succeeded in proving that anything had even struck the ground. There was evidence of two blast waves – the original explosion and the ballistic wave – and even of brief flash fire; but there was no crater.

The new evidence only deepened the riddle. An aerial survey in 1938 showed that only 770 square miles of forest had been flattened, and that at the very point where the crater should have been the original trees were still standing. That suggested the vagaries of an exploding bomb, rather than that of the impact of a giant meteor – like the one that made the 600-foot-deep crater at Winslow, Arizona.

Even the way that the object fell to earth was disputed. Over seven hundred eyewitnesses claimed that it changed course as it fell, saying that it was originally moving towards Lake Baikal before it swerved. Falling heavenly bodies have never been known to do this, nor is it possible to explain how it could have happened in terms of physical dynamics.

Another curious puzzle about the explosion was its effect on the trees and insect life in the blast area. Trees that had survived the explosion had either stopped growing, or were shooting up at a greatly accelerated rate. Later studies revealed new species of ants and other insects which are peculiar to the Tunguska blast region.

It was not until some years after Kulik's death in a German prisoner-of-war camp that scientists began to see similarities between the Tunguska event and another even more catastrophic explosion: the destruction of Hiroshima and Nagasaki with thermonuclear devices.

Our knowledge of the atom bomb enables us to clear up many of the mysteries that baffled Kulik. The reason there was no crater was that the explosion confirmed this; at both Nagasaki and Hiroshima, buildings directly beneath the blast remained standing, because the blast spread sideways. Genetic mutations in the flora and fauna around the Japanese cities are like those witnessed in Siberia, while blisters found on dogs and reindeer in the Tunguska area can now be recognized as radiation burns.

Atomic explosions produce disturbances in the earth's magnetic field, and even today the area around the Tunguska explosion has been described as 'magnetic chaos'. It seems clear that an electro-magnetic 'hurricane' of incredible strength has ruptured the earth's magnetic field in this area.

Eye-witness accounts of the cloud produced by the explosion again support the view that it was some kind of atomic device; it had the typical shape of the atomic 'mushroom cloud'. Unfortunately, the one conclusive piece of evidence for the 'atom bomb' theory is lacking: by the time the area's radiation levels were tested, more than fifty years later, they were normal.

Later investigators also learned that Kulik had been mistaken in his theory about the water-filled holes; they were not caused by meteorite fragments but by winter ice forcing its way to the surface through expansion, then melting in summer. Kulik's immense labours to drain the holes had been a waste of time.

Unfortunately, none of the new evidence that has been uncovered by Russian – and even American – expeditions has thrown any light on the cause of the explosion. UFO enthusiasts favour the theory that the object was an alien space craft, powered by atomic motors, which went out of control as it struck the earth's atmosphere. It has even been suggested that such a space craft might have headed towards Lake Baikal because it was in need of fresh water to cool its nuclear reactors; before it could reach its objective the reactors superheated and exploded.

The scientific establishment is naturally inclined to discount this theory as pure fantasy. But some of its own hypotheses seem equally fantastic. A.A.Jackson and M.P.Ryan of the University of Texas have suggested that the explosion was caused by a miniature black hole – a kind of whirlpool in space caused by the total collapse of the particles inside the atom. They calculated that their black hole would have passed straight through the earth and come out on the other side, and the Russians were sufficiently impressed by the theory to research local newspapers in Iceland and Newfoundland for June 1980; but there was no sign of the Tunguska-like catastrophe that should have occurred if Jackson and Ryan were correct.

Other American scientists suggested that the explosion was caused by anti-matter, a hypothetical type of matter whose particles contain the opposite electric charge to those of normal matter. In contact with normal matter, anti-matter would explode and simply disappear. Only atomic radiation would be left behind. But there is even less evidence to support this theory than there is for the black-hole explanation.

Slightly more plausible – but still highly improbable – is the theory of the English scientist Frank Whipple that the earth had been struck by a comet. Astronomers still have no idea where comets originate, or how they are formed. The two chief objections to the comet theory are that it would be unlikely to produce a 'nuclear' explosion, and that it would have been observed by astronomers long before it reached the earth. Supporters of the comet theory have pointed out that a comet coming in from the direction of the sun might be very hard to detect, and that the explosion of a comet might produce an effect similar to that of solar flares, which produce radio-activity. But none of the 120 observatories questioned by the Russians have any record of a comet on the trajectory of the Tunguska object.

More recently, it has been pointed out that the Tunguska event took place on 30 June and that on that same day each year the earth's orbit crosses that of a meteor stream called Beta Taurids, producing a 'meteor shower'. If one of these meteors had been exceptionally large, it could have survived burning up in the earth's atmosphere, and as its super-heated exterior reacted against its frozen interior, it would have shattered like molten glass suddenly plunged into freezing water. If this theory is correct, then it seems that Kulik was right after all. But that only reminds us that Kulik was unable to find the slightest shred of evidence for his theory. Eight decades after it took place, it seems increasingly unlikely that the mystery of the Tunguska explosion will ever be solved.

39 Unidentified Flying Objects

'Flying Saucers' have undoubtedly been *the* great mystery of the era that followed the Second World War, and theories to explain them have ranged from the belief that they are superior beings from another planet (or another dimension) to the suggestion that they are some kind of supernatural occurrence, allied to ghosts. Among intellectuals the most popular theory is that of Jung, who suggested that UFOs (unidentified flying objects) are 'projections' of the unconscious mind, which is a polite, scientific way of saying that they have no more objective reality than the pink elephants of a dipsomaniac. But most of these Jungians choose to ignore – or are unaware of – Jung's later retraction of this view; he told his niece not long before his death that he had come to accept that UFOs *are* real objects.

The story of modern sightings began on 24 June 1947, when a businessman named Kenneth Arnold was flying his private plane near Mount Rainier in Washington State; against the background of the mountain, he saw nine shining discs travelling very fast – he estimated their speed at a thousand miles an hour, far beyond the speed of which any aircraft was capable at that time. Arnold said they were flying in formation, like geese, and that they wove in and out of the mountain peaks; he later compared their flight to a 'saucer skipped across the water'. So UFOs came to be referred to as 'flying saucers'.

Arnold's story was widely reported in the American Press, for he had a good reputation and was taken seriously – he had been out searching for the wreckage of a lost plane at the time he made the sighting, and obviously had no reason to invent such a story. Four days later, two pilots and two intelligence officers saw a bright light performing 'impossible manoeuvres' over Maxwell Air Force Base in Montgomery, Alabama, and in Nevada on the same day another pilot saw a formation of 'unidentified flying objects'. As these and other sightings were reported the Press began to give prominence to stories of flying saucers, and by the end of that year there had been hundreds of sightings – a number that soon grew into thousands.

In January of the following year, 1948, an 'unidentified object' was spotted in the sky above Godman Air Force Base in Kentucky. Three F-51 Mustangs were diverted from a training exercise to investigate, and one of these, flown by Captain Thomas Mantell, had soon outdistanced the other two. The radio tower received a call: 'I see something above and ahead of me – I'm still climbing.' 'What is it?' 'It looks metallic and is tremendous in size.' Then he announced: 'It's above me and I'm gaining on it. I'm going to twenty thousand feet.' But these were the last words Mantell spoke. Later that day the remains of his plane were found ninety miles away from the base.

The story was a sensation – 'airman destroyed by flying saucer'. The Air Force announced that what Mantell had mistaken for a flying saucer was actually the planet Venus – a story that seemed, to put it mildly, unlikely. But then, the Air Force had shown the same confidence ten days after Arnold's original sighting when it had announced that Arnold had been 'hallucinating'.

It was obvious that the newspaper publicity was causing a certain amount of hysteria, and that many people thought they had seen flying saucers when they had only seen weather balloons or aircraft tail-lights. But was it conceivable that thousands of people – in fact, millions – could all be mistaken? For by 1966, a Gallup Poll revealed that five million Americans had seen flying saucers. And some of these sightings were at close quarters. A few days after Arnold's original sighting, the SS *Llandovery Castle* sailed from Mombasa *en route* to Cape Town. At about eleven one evening a Mrs A.M.King, of Nairobi, was on deck with another woman when they saw what appeared to be a bright star approaching the ship. Then a searchlight switched on, illuminating the sea about fifty yards from the ship. They saw an object made of steel and 'shaped like a cigar cut at the rear end'. It was about four times as big as the ship, and was travelling in the same direction; soon it vanished at a great speed, flames issuing from the 'flattened' end.

Yet in spite of an increasing number of reports of this type, and thousands of 'sky sightings', the Air Force continued to insist that UFO sightings were hoaxes, mistakes or downright lies. An official investigation, known as 'Project Sign', began in September 1947, and later became known as 'Project Blue Book'. One of its advisers was the astronomer J.Allen Hynek, who began as a sceptic, but was soon convinced by the obvious truthfulness of witnesses that UFOs were a reality. But the Air Force remained adamantly sceptical. By the mid-1960s the belief that it was involved in a cover-up became so persistent that in 1965 the Air Force itself ordered that a new scientific panel should be set up; Edward U. Condon, a well-known physicist, was appointed head of this panel, and it was sponsored by the University of Colorado. But when the panel issued its report in 1969 it was obvious that the scientists of the University of Colorado had reached the same conclusion as the Air Force investigators – one newspaper headline summarized the findings of the 965-page report in the headline: 'Flying Saucers Do Not Exist – Official.'

One basic problem was that many of the sightings were too preposterous to be taken seriously; the whole field of investigation had become a happy hunting-ground for cranks. In a book called *Flying Saucers Have Landed* a Polish-American named George Adamski claimed that in 1952 he and a number of other saucer enthusiasts drove into the California desert – their route dictated by Adamski's 'hunches' – and saw a huge cigar-shaped object in the sky. With a camera, Adamski wandered off alone, and saw a flying saucer land half a mile away. He hurried to the spot, and found a flying saucer, and a small man with shoulder-length blond hair, who identified himself in sign language as an inhabitant of the planet Venuis. Then he flew off in his space craft. His friends had witnessed the encounter from a distance, and later signed notarized statements to this effect. In a second book, *Inside the Space Ships*, Adamski told how he had been taken for a trip in a flying saucer – called a 'scout ship' – with his Venusian acquaintance, plus a man from Mars and a man from Saturn. On this occasion they flew into space and went on board the mother ship. On another occasion Adamski was taken to the moon, where he saw rich vegetation, including trees, and four-legged furry animals. He was also shown live pictures of Venus on a television screen, and saw that it had cities, mountains, rivers and lakes. Adamski died in 1965, four years before the moon landings, but three years after a space probe – Mariner II – had swept past Venus and revealed that it has an atmosphere of sulphuric acid gas, and that the surface is too hot to support life. But such small setbacks left Adamski unmoved – he was always able to claim that a mere space probe was less reliable than real Venusians – and he spent the final years of his life happily lecturing to audiences of UFO enthusiasts all over the world.

Adamski's friend Dr George Hunt Williamson, who had been one of the witnesses of Adamski's original 'contact', achieved a similar celebrity. In a book called *The Saucers Speak*, he told of how he had originally made contact with the inhabitants of flying saucers by means of automatic writing, and how later, a radio operator (whom he calls Mr R.) was able to establish direct contact. The 'space men' were from the planet Mars, which they called Masar, and they explained that the earth was in grave danger of destroying itself. 'Good and evil forces are working now. Organisation is important for the salvation of your world.' These space intelligences had been observing the earth for seventy-five thousand years, and were now prepared to save the world by revealing all kinds of astonishing secrets about Life, God and the Creator's place in the Divine Scheme. In a book called *Secret Places of the Lion* Williamson revealed some of these secrets – he claimed he had found them in a great library in a lost city high in the mountains of Peru, where a Master teacher, a survivor of the Elders, still lives and works. (This Master is thousands of years old – he lived on earth in the days when giants still roamed the planet.) This library (the author thanks one of the monks for translating its ancient records) reveals that the Star People came to earth eighteen million years ago (long before man appeared), and ever since then have been helping man to evolve. Their records are held in tombs and secret chambers, and one of their space-ships is at present hidden in the base of the Great Pyramid, which was built 24,000 years ago (and not a mere 4,500, as Egyptologists believe). These Star People were continually reincarnated as the great leaders and prophets of mankind, so Tiyi, the wife of the pharaoh Amenhotep III, later became the Queen of Sheba, Nefertiti, Queen Guinevere (wife of King Arthur) and Joan of Arc, while the Egyptian crown prince Seti became Isaiah, Aristotle, the apostle John and Leonardo da Vinci. *The Secret Places of the Lion* is a history of earth according to the ancient records, and is admittedly excellent value as historical entertainment. But the reader could be forgiven for thinking that Williamson decided that if Adamski could get away with it, then so could he. . . .

In 1960 there appeared in France an extraordinary book called *Morning of the Magicians*, by Louis Pauwels and Jacques Bergier; it became an instant best-seller, and was translated into many languages. It discussed various 'mysteries' – alchemy, astrology, black magic, mysterious ancient artifacts and the Great Pyramid – but its main argument is that much 'lost knowledge' was brought to our planet by visitors from outer space. It discusses, for example, the so-called Piri Reis maps, dating to the sixteenth century, which show Antarctica (although it was not discovered until three centuries later), and also show a land bridge between Siberia and Alaska – a bridge that vanished thousands of years ago, giving way to the Bering Strait – and argues that such maps prove that the earth must have been surveyed from the air more than two thousand years ago. It is also full of inaccuracies – for example, describing Piri Reis (who was a Turkish pirate who was beheaded in 1554) as an American naval officer of the nineteenth century. But it caused widespread excitement, and seemed to justify the increasing number of 'ufologists' who believed that the 'saucers' had been appearing for centuries, and that they are even described in the Bible (as the fiery chariots of the prophet Ezekiel, for example).

But it was in 1967 that the 'ancient astronaut theory' finally reached a worldwide audience, in the form of a book called *Memories of the Future*, translated into English as *Chariots of the Gods?* (One newspaper serialized it under the headline 'Was God an Astronaut?') Its author, Erich von Däniken, borrowed liberally – and without acknowledgment – from predecessors like Williamson, Bergier and Pauwels, but presented his own 'evidence' with a certain individual panache. His argument consists basically of the assertion that various ancient monuments – the Great Pyramid (naturally), the Easter Island statues, the Mexican pyramids, the megaliths of Carnac and Stonehenge – must have been erected with the aid of space men, because their technology would have been beyond the skills of the builders to whom they are attributed. It is full of misinformation – for example, he manages to multiply the weight of the Great Pyramid by five, and cites 'legends' from the *Epic of Gilgamesh* which are simply not to be found in that work. Most of his major arguments proved to be faulty. He insists that the Easter Island statues were too big to be erected by natives; but the explorer Thor Heyerdahl persuaded modern Easter Islanders to carve and erect a similar statue in a few weeks. He asserts that the pyramids had to be built by ancient astronauts because the Egyptians had no rope – but pyramid texts show the use of rope. What Däniken claimed to be a picture of a man taking off in a space ship on the Palenque funerary tablet in Guatemala was shown by scholars to be a typical Mayan religious inscription, full of their basic symbols – birds, serpents and so on. He cites the mysterious Nazca lines on the plains of Peru as examples of structures that could only be understood when seen from the air, and suggests that they were giant runways for space craft – he even has a photograph of an aircraft 'parking bay'. But the lines are drawn on the pebbly surface of the desert, and would be instantly blown away if an aircraft tried to land on them. The 'parking bay' turned out to be a detail from the leg of a bird – its knee – and was hardly large enough to park a bicycle. Däniken insisted that this was a mistake made by an editor; but he has allowed it to stand in subsequent editions of his book.

The mistake about the desert surface seems typical of Däniken's cavalier attitude to facts. Another can be found in *Gold of the Gods*, where Däniken offers a photograph of a skeleton carved out of stone, and wants to know how ancient sculptors knew about skeletons in the days before x-rays – overlooking the fact that every graveyard was full of them. It is also in *Gold of the Gods* that Däniken claims to have been taken into an underground city where he examined a secret library with books made of metal leaves. His companion, he said, was an explorer named Juan Moricz. When Moricz flatly denied the whole story Däniken hastened to concede that he had invented the underground library, but insisted that in Germany authors of popular non-fiction works are permitted to use certain 'effects' – that is, to tell lies – provided they are merely incidental and do not touch the facts . . . And in spite of these embarrassments, Däniken continued to publish more books, each one of which, he claimed, helped to establish his astronaut theory beyond all possible doubt.

Understandably, then, the increasing flood of books by 'ufologists' aroused most serious investigators to fury or derision.

Yet there were notable exceptions. J. Allen Hynek, as we have already observed, was part of Project Blue Book, and the evidence he studied finally convinced him that, no matter how many cranks, simpletons and downright liars managed to obscure the facts, these facts unequivocally indicated the real existence of flying saucers, and even of 'space men'. It was Hynek who coined the phrase 'close encounters of the third kind' meaning encounters with grounded saucers and 'humanoids' and he begins his chapter on such encounters (in *The UFO Experience, A Scientific Enquiry*): 'We come now to the most bizarre and seemingly incredible aspect of the entire UFOs phenomenon. To be frank, I would gladly omit this part if I could without offense to scientific integrity ..' And he goes on to consider a number of cases which, although they sound preposterous, were too well-authenticated to be dismissed. One typical case will suffice.

On 11 August 1955 a flying saucer was seen to land in farming country near Kelly-Hopkinsville, Kentucky. An hour later members of the Sutton family were alerted by the barking of the dog to the presence of an intruder near their farmhouse, and saw 'a small "glowing" man with extremely large eyes, his arms extended over his head'. The two Sutton men fired at him with a rifle and shotgun, and there was a sound 'as if I'd shot into a bucket', and the 'space man' turned and hurried off. When another visitor appeared at the window the rifle was again fired and they ran outside to see if the creature had been hit. As one of them stopped under a low portion of the roof a claw-like hand reached down from it and touched his hair. More shots were fired at the creature on the roof, and although it was hit directly it floated down to the ground and hurried away. For the next three hours the eleven occupants of the house remained behind bolted doors, frequently seeing the 'space men' at the windows. Finally, they all bolted out of the house, piled into two cars, and drove to the nearest police station. Police could find no signs of the spacemen, but as soon as they were gone the creatures reappeared. The next day a police artist got witnesses to describe what they had seen; the pictures that emerged was of tiny creatures with round heads and saucer-like eyes, and arms twice as long as their legs.

The family was subjected to a great deal of harassment as a result of their story; but serious investigators who questioned them had no doubt whatever that they were telling the truth.

Perhaps the most famous case of a 'close encounter of the third kind' was that of Barney and Betty Hill. In September 1961 they were returning through New Hampshire from a holiday in Canada when they saw a flying saucer apparently in the process of landing. Two hours later they found themselves thirty-five miles from this spot, with no recollection of what had happened in the meantime. Eventually they consulted an expert in amnesia, Dr Benjamin Simon, who placed them under hypnosis; the Hills then described – independently – what had happened. They had been taken aboard the 'saucer' by a number of uniformed men who looked more or less human (Barney said they reminded him of red-haired, round-faced Irishmen), subjected to a number of medical tests or experiments – skin and nail shavings were taken, and Betty Hill had a needle inserted into her navel – then they were hypnotized and told to forget everything that had happened. Allen Hynek himself was later present when Barney Hill was placed under hypnosis, and was allowed to question him. He ended by being convinced of the genuineness of the experience.

What has been called the 'ultimate in contact stories' happened to Antonio Villas-Boas, a 23-year-old Brazilian farmer. On 15 October 1957, Villas-Boas claims that he was ploughing his fields when an egg-shaped UFO descended in front of his tractor. He tried to run away, but was grabbed by 'humanoids' in tight grey overalls and helmets, and carried into the saucer. The space men communicated with sounds like yelps or barks. Villas-Boas was stripped naked and washed, then a blood sample was taken. After this a beautiful naked woman – about 4 foot 6 inches tall – came into the room. She soon induced Villas-Boas to make love to her, although he says that she had an off-putting way of grunting at intervals that made him feel he was having intercourse with an animal.

Villas-Boas's story would be an obvious candidate for the 'hoax' category but for one thing. Dr Olavo T.Fontes examined him soon after the 'encounter', and found that Villas-Boas had been subjected to a very high dose of radiation. And at the point on his chin where he claimed the needle had been inserted for the blood sample the doctor found two small marks. Villas-Boas's story is documented with convincing details in *The Humanoids*, edited by Charles Bowen.

Like Hynek, the journalist John Keel was also mildly sceptical about flying saucers until he tried the unusual expedient of studying the subject instead of passing a priori judgements. In 1952 he prepared a radio documentary on things seen in the sky, and came to believe that – even then – there had been too many sightings of flying saucers to dismiss them as mistakes or lies. In 1953, in Egypt, he saw his first UFO, a metallic disc with a revolving rim, hovering over the Aswan dam in daylight. Yet even so, it was not until 1966 that he decided to undertake a careful study of the subject, and subscribed to a press-cutting bureau. What then staggered him was the sheer number of the sightings – he often received 150 clippings in a day. (In those days press clippings were only a few pence each; twenty years later, at about a pound each, the experiment would be beyond the resources of most journalists.) Moreover, it soon became clear that even these were only a small percentage of the total, and that thousands of sightings were going unrecorded. (This is in fact the chief disadvantage of an article like this one; it cannot even begin to convey the sheer volume of the sightings. Any sceptic should try the experience of reading, say, a hundred cases, one after theother, to realize that the 'delusion' theory fails to hold water.) What also fascinated Keel was that so many witnesses who had seen UFOs from their cars had later seen them over their homes; this suggested that the 'space men' were not merely alien scientists or explorers, engaged in routine surveying work.

In the following year, 1967, Keel was driving along the Long Island Expressway when he saw a sphere of light in the sky, pursuing a course parallel to his own. When he reached Huntington he found that cars were parked along the roads, and dozens of people were staring at four lights that were bobbing and weaving in the sky; the light that had followed Keel joined the other four. Keel was in fact on his way to interview a scientist, Phillip Burckhardt, who had seen a UFO hovering above some trees close to his home on the previous evening, and had examined it through binoculars; he had seen that it was a silvery disc illuminated by rectangular lights that blinked on and off. The nearby Suffolk Air Force Base seemed to know nothing about it.

Like Hynek, Keel was impressed by the witnesses he interviewed; most were ordinary people who had no obvious reason for inventing a story about UFOs. His study of the actual literature convinced him that it was 98 per cent nonsense; but most individual witnesses were obviously telling the truth. Keel had soon accumulated enough cases to fill a 2000-page typescript; this had to be severely truncated before it was published under the title *UFOs: Operation Trojan Horse.*

As his investigation progressed, Keel became increasingly convinced that UFOs had been around for thousands of years, and that many biblical accounts of fiery chariots or fireballs are probably descriptions of them. In 1883 a Mexican astronomer named Jose Bonilla photographed 143 circular objects that moved across the solar disc. In 1878 a Texas farmer named John Martin saw a large circular object flying overhead, and actually used the word 'saucer' in a newspaper interview about it. In 1897 people all over American began sighting huge airships – cigar-shaped craft. (This was before the man-made airship had been invented.) Dozens of other early 'UFO' sightings have been chronicled in newspaper reports or pamphlets; Chapter 26 of Charles Fort's *Book of the Damned* – written thirty years before the UFO craze – is devoted to strange objects and lights seen in the sky. One of the most convincing sightings was made by the Russian painter Nicholas Roerich (who designed Stravinsky's *Rite of Spring* ballet); in his book *Altai*

Himalaya (1930) he describes how, making his way from Mongolia to India in 1926, he – and the whole party – observed a big shiny disc moving swiftly across the sky. Like so many modern UFOs, this one suddenly changed direction above their camp. (In many UFO reports, the object seems to defy the laws of momentum by turning at right angles at great speed.) It vanished over the mountain peaks.

Keel was also interested by the parallels between reports of 'space men' and descriptions by people who claim to have had supernatural experiences. The 'angel' that instructed Joseph Smith – founder of the Mormons – to go and dig for engraved gold tablets sounds very like the kind of space visitor described by Adamski and so many others. During the First World War three children playing in meadows near Fatima, Portugal, saw a shining globe of light, and a woman's voice spoke from it. (Only two of the three heard it, although all saw it, suggesting that it was in their minds rather than in the objective world.) Crowds began to visit the spot every month where the 'Lady of the Rosary' (as she called herself) appeared to the three children – only the children were able to see and hear her. But on 13 October 1917, when the Lady had announced that she would provide a miracle to convince the world, the rainclouds parted, and a huge silver disc descended towards the crowd of seventy thousand people. It whirled and bobbed – exactly like the UFOs Keel had seen and changed colour through the whole spectrum; all watched it for ten minutes before it vanished into the clouds again. Many other people in the area saw it from their homes. The heat from the 'object' dried the wet clothes of the crowd. Keel cites this and other 'miracles' (such as one that occurred in Heede, Germany), and argues that they sound curiously similar to later UFO accounts.

There also seemed to be a more sinister aspect to the UFO affair; witnesses began to report that 'government officials' had called on them and warned them to be silent; these men were usually dressed in black, although sometimes they wore military uniforms. No government department had – apparently – ever heard of them. Albert K.Bender of Bridgeport, Connecticut, suddenly closed down his International Flying Saucer Bureau in 1953, and declared that three dark-skinned men with glowing eyes had pressured him into abandoning his researches. Most UFO enthusiasts blamed the government; but when Bender published his full account ten years later it was obvious that something much stranger was involved; the three men materialized and dematerialized in his apartment, and on one occasion had transported him to a UFO base in Antarctica. Jacques Vallee, another scientist who had become interested in the UFO phenomenon, noted the similarity between this story and medieval legends about fairies and 'elementals'.

When Keel began to investigate sightings in West Virginia of a huge winged man who seemed to be able to keep up with fast-moving cars, he himself began to encounter vaguely hostile entities. A photographer took his picture in an empty street, then ran away. Just after arranging to meet another UFO expert, Gray Barker, a friend revealed that she had been told about the meeting two days ago before Keel had even thought of it. 'Contactees' would ring him up and explain that they were with someone who wished to speak to him; then he would have conversations with men who spoke in strange voices. (He sometimes got the feeling he was speaking to someone in a trance.) Keel would be instructed to write letters to addresses which upon investigation proved to be non-existent; yet he would receive prompt replies, written in block letters. On one occasion, he stayed at a motel chosen at random, and found a message waiting for him at the desk. He says (in *The Mothman Prophecies*): 'Someone somewhere was just trying to prove that they knew every move I was making, listened to all my phone calls, and could even control my mail. And they were succeeding.' The entities also made many predictions of the assassination of Martin Luther King, of a planned attack on Robert Kennedy, of an attempt to stab the pope; but they frequently seemed to get the dates wrong. Keel concluded that 'our little planet seems to be experiencing the interpenetration of forces or entities from some other space-time continuum'.

The British expert on UFOs, Brinsley Le Poer Trench (the Earl of Clancarty), reached a similar kind of conclusion on the basis of his investigations. He expresses them (in *Operation Earth*) as follows:

.. there exist at least two diametrically opposed forces of entities interested in us. Firstly, those that are the real Sky People who have been around since time immemorial. Secondly, those that live in an area indigenous to this planet, though some of us believe they also live in the interior of the earth. There is obviously a 'War in the Heavens' between these two factions. However, it is not considered that battles are going on in the sense that humans usually envisage them. It is more of a mental affray for the domination of the minds of mankind.

Jacques Vallee, one of the most serious and intelligent writers on the subject, finally came to a similar conclusion. In earlier books like *Anatomy of a Phenomenon* and *Challenge to Science: The UFO Enigma*, he studied case reports with unusual thoroughness (and many statistical tables). In *Passport to Magonia* (1970) he pointed out that the picture we can form of the world of the UFO occupants is more like the mediaeval concept of Magonia, a land above the clouds, than some inhabited planet. By 1977 he had come to the strange conclusion that UFOs are basically 'psychic' in nature, a view he expressed in a book called *The Invisible College*. The invisible college is a group of scientists who are engaged in the study of UFO phenomena, and who decline to be intimidated by conservative scientific attitudes. Vallee, himself a computer expert, reached the conclusion that UFO phenomena are a 'control system' – that is, that they are designed to produce a certain specific effect on the human mind. He explains in *Messengers of Deception* (1979): that after a year researching the similarity between UFO phenomena and psychic phenomena 'I could no longer regard the "flying saucers" as simply some sort of spacecraft or machine, no matter how exotic its propulsion.' He went back to his computers, and concluded: 'The most clear result was that the phenomenon behaved like a conditioning process. The logic of conditioning uses absurdity and confusion to achieve its goal while hiding its mechanism. I began to see a similar structure in the UFO stories.'

Absurdity and confusion are certainly one of the most puzzling and irritating aspects of the UFO stories. Vallee devotes a chapter of *The Invisible College* to studying the case of Uri Geller. Geller, the Israeli psychic and 'metal-bender', was 'discovered' by the scientist Andrija Puharich. Geller's powers aroused such worldwide interest that it seemed inevitable that the first full-length book about him would become a bestseller. In fact Puharich's *Uri: A Journal of the Mystery of Uri Geller* (1974) came close to destroying Puharich's reputation as a serious investigator. It seems to be full of baffling confusions and preposterous and inexplicable happenings. Yet it also provides some vital clues to the mystery of 'space intelligences'. In 1952, long before he met Geller, Puharich was studying with a Hindu psychic named Dr Vinod when Vinod went into a trance and began to speak with an English voice; this trance-entity announced itself as a member of 'the Nine', superhuman intelligences who had been studying the human race for thousands of years, and whose purpose is to aid human evolution. Three years later, travelling in Mexico, Puharich met an American doctor who also passed on lengthy messages from 'space intelligences' – the odd thing being that they were a continuation of the messages that had come through Dr Vinod. When Puharich met Geller in 1971 the 'Nine' again entered the story; while Geller was in a trance a voice spoke out of the air above his head explaining that Geller had been programmed by 'space intelligences' from the age of three – the aim being to prevent the human race from plunging itself into catastrophe. Puharich goes on to describe UFO sightings, and an endless series of baffling events, with objects appearing and disappearing and recorded tapes being mysteriously 'wiped'. Puharich assured the present writer (CW) that he had left out some of the more startling items because they would be simply beyond belief.

After Puharich's break with Geller, the 'Nine' continued to manifest themselves through mediums. The story is told in *Prelude to a Landing on Planet Earth* by Stuart Holroyd, and it is even more confusing than Puharich's book. The 'Nine' finally sent Puharich and his companions on a kind of wild-goose chase around the Middle East and other remote places; the main purpose was apparently to pray for peace, and the 'intelligences' assured them that they had averted appalling international catastrophes.

In fact, the mention of mediums may provide a key to the mystery. Modern spiritualism began in the mid-nineteenth century, when 'spirits' began to express themselves through the mediumship of two teenage girls named Fox; soon thousands of 'mediums' were causing mysterious rapping noises (one knock for yes, two for no), making trumpets and other musical instruments float through the air and apparently play themselves, and producing spirit voices – and even spirit forms – by going into a trance. No one who has studied the phenomena in depth can believe that they were all fraudulent. Moreover, the theory that they were somehow produced by the unconscious minds of the participants must also be reluctantly dismissed, since in many cases 'spirits' were able to use different 'mediums' in order to reveal fragments of the same message – fragments which interlocked like a jigsaw puzzle.

But what soon becomes equally clear to any student of the subject is that the 'spirits' cannot be taken at their own valuation. As often as not, they told lies. Emanuel Swedenborg, the eighteenth-century visionary, warned that there are basically two varieties of spirit, a 'higher order' and a 'lower order'. A psychiatrist, Wilson Van Dusen, who studied hundreds of cases of hallucinations at the Mendocino State Hospital in California, noted that 'the patients felt as if they had contact with another world or order of beings. Most thought these other persons were living. All objected to the term "hallucination".' And he noted that the hallucinations seemed to fall into Swedenborg's two categories: 'helpful' spirits (about one-fifth of all cases), and distinctly unhelpful spirits whose aim seemed to be to cause the patients misery, irritation and anguish.

It is, of course, a major step for any normal, rational person to accept the real existence of disembodied spirits, or 'discarnates'. Yet anyone who is willing to study the evidence patiently and open-mindedly will undoubtedly arrive at that conclusion. In fact, anyone who has ever tried automatic writing or the ouija board or 'table turning' has probably reached the conclusion that there are 'intelligences' that are capable of manifesting through human beings. But the question of the precise nature of these entities is altogether more baffling. It seems clear that some can be taken seriously, others not. Many seem to behave like the traditional demons of the Middle Ages, telling whatever lie happens to enter their heads on the spur of the moment. Some of these 'intelligences' – known as poltergeists – can even manifest their presence by causing objects to fly around the room, or causing mysterious bangs and crashes. One interesting characteristic of the poltergeist is that it can cause an object travelling at high speed to change direction quite abruptly, in defiance of the Newtonian laws of motion. This also seems to be one of the characteristics of the flying saucer.

Jacques Vallee was intrigued by the number of cases in which UFOs behaved in a manner that contradicted the notion that they were simply the artifacts of some superior civilization; some have dissolved into thin air; some have vanished into the earth; some have expanded like balloons, then disappeared. Some 'spacemen' seem to have the power of reading thoughts and of predicting events which will occur in the future. Many of them like Puharich's 'Nine' insist that their purpose is to prepare the human race for some astonishing event, like a landing of UFOs on earth; but the landing never occurs.

Yet it may be simplistic to believe that UFOs are simply an up-dated version of medieval demons or nineteenth-century 'spirit communicators'. Vallee's belief is that the phenomenon is 'heuristic' that is, is designed to teach us something. Modern science and philosophy have accustomed us to materialistic theories of the universe, to the notion that living creatures are a billion-to-one accident, and that the human reality is simply the reality of our bodies and brains. In *Flying Saucers, A Modern Myth of Things Seen in the Skies,* Jung suggested that UFOs may be modern man's response to his craving for religious meanings, and Vallee seems to accept at least the basic implication of this theory. Like Jung, he also seems to believe that coincidences may be more than they seem. In *Messengers of Deception*, he describes his interest in a modern religious cult called the Order of Melchizedek, which believes that its basic doctrines have been received through extra-terrestrial intelligences. Then, as noted in Chapter 36, he began collecting all he could find about the biblical prophet Melchizedek. In February 1976 he asked a female taxi-driver in Los Angeles for a receipt; when he looked at the receipt it was signed 'M.Melchizedek'. He looked up Melchizedek in the Los Angeles phone directory; there was only one. . . .

This leads Vallee to an interesting speculation about the underlying reality of the world. He points out that we are confined to our space-time continuum, and all our concepts of knowledge are based on space and time. So in a library our 'information retrieval system' is based on alphabetical order. But modern computer scientists have developed another method; they 'sprinkle the records throughout storage as they arrive, and . . . construct an algorithm for retrieval based on some type ot keyword . . .' He concluded: 'The Melchizedek incident . . . suggested to me that the world may be organised more like a randomised data base than a sequential library.' In a computer 'library', the student enters a request for 'microwave' or 'headache' and finds twenty articles that he never even suspected had existed. Vallee had entered a request for Melchizedek, and some psychic computer had asked: 'How about this one?'

In *The Flying Saucer Vision* (1967), the English writer John Michell also takes his starting-point from Jung. Michell accepts Jung's view that the UFO phenomenon is somehow connected with the 'religious vacuum' in the soul of modern man. He associates UFOs with ancient legends about gods who descend in airships, and his conclusions are not dissimilar to those of von Däniken, although rather more convincingly argued. But Michell also has an original contribution to make to 'ufology'. In his researches he had stumbled upon Alfred Watkins's book *The Old Straight Track* (1925), in which Watkins argues that the countryside is intersected with ancient straight trackways which were prehistoric trade routes, and that these tracks connect 'sacred sites' such as churches, stone circles, barrows and tumuli. Watkins called these 'ley lines'. Michell argues that the ley lines are identical with lines that the Chinese call 'dragon paths' or *lung mei*. The Chinese science of *feng shui*, or geomancy, is basically a religious system concerned with the harmony between man and nature; it regards the earth as a living body. *Lung mei* are lines of force on the earth's surface, and one of the aims of *feng shui* is to preserve and concentrate this force, and prevent it from leaking away. Michell was mistaken to state that *lung mei* are straight lines, like Watkins' leys – in fact, the Chinese regard straight lines with suspicion; the essential quality of *lung meis* is that they are crooked. But Michell takes an important step beyond Watkins in regarding ley lines as lines of some earth force; he believes that ancient man selected spots in which there was a high concentration of this force as their sacred sites. Points where two or more ley lines cross have a special significance. Michell also points out that many sightings of flying saucers occur on ley lines, and particularly on their points of intersection – for example, Warminster, in Wiltshire, where a truly extraordinary number of sightings have been made. In a book called *The*

Undiscovered Country, Stephen Jenkins, another serious investigator of such matters, points out how often crossing-points of ley lines are associated with all kinds of 'supernatural' occurrences, from ghosts and poltergeists to strange visions of phantom armies. Once again we seem to have an interesting link between UFOs and the 'supernatural'.

Two more investigators deserve a mention in this context: T.C.Lethbridge and F.W.Holiday. Lethbridge was a retired Cambridge don who became fascinated by dowsing, and the power of the pendulum to detect various substances under the earth. (I have spoken of him at length in my book *Mysteries*.) Towards the end of his life (he died in 1971), Lethbridge became interested in flying saucers, and in a book called *Legend of the Sons of God* (1972) suggested that UFOs may be associated with ancient standing stones – in fact, that such stones may have been set up in the remote past as 'beacons' for ancient space craft. Lethbridge knew nothing of ley lines, but his own investigations led him to conclusions that are remarkably similar to Michell's.

F.W.Holiday was a naturalist and a fishing journalist who became fascinated by the mystery of the Loch Ness monster (*qv*) and wrote a book suggesting that it was a giant slug, or 'worm' (using this word in its medieval sense of 'dragon'). But after years of study of the phenomenon he found the Loch Ness monster and other lake monsters as elusive as ufologists have found flying saucers. He became increasingly convinced that both flying saucers and lake monsters belong to what he called 'the phantom menagerie' (see chapter 12 on The Grey Man of Ben MacDhui). This view was expressed in his book *The Dragon and the Disc*, and in his posthumous work *The Goblin Universe*. Like Vallee, Holiday finally became convinced that the answer to the UFO enigma lies in 'the psychic solution'. It must be acknowledged that there is a great deal of evidence that points in this direction. On the other hand, it would be premature to discount the possibility that they may be spacecraft from another planet or galaxy; this is a matter on which it would be foolish not to keep an open mind.

40 Velikovsky's Comet

When the bulky manuscript of *Worlds in Collision* landed on the desk of a New York editor in 1947 its tattered state left no doubt that it had been rejected many times. All the same, the editor was impressed. According to the author, Immanuel Velikovsky, the earth had been almost destroyed about three and a half thousand years ago by a near-collision with a comet; in the earthquakes and volcanic eruptions that followed, cities were wiped out and whole countries laid waste. It was a fascinating and erudite book, and its author – who was apparently a respectable psychiatrist – had the ability to write a clear and vigorous prose.

The editor cautiously recommended it. His superiors were worried; Macmillans was a reputable publisher with a large textbook list; they could not afford to be accused of encouraging the lunatic fringe. So they compromised, and offered Velikovsky a small advance and a contract that gave them the option to publish, but no guarantee that they would do so. A year later they finally decided to go ahead, and *Worlds in Collision* made its belated appearance on 3 April 1950. Within days it had climbed to the top of the best-seller list. When it appeared in England the following September its reputation had preceded it, so that it sold out its first impression even before publication. But by that time Macmillans' doubts had been justified; the denunciations of the book were so violent that they were forced into retreat, and *Worlds in Collision* had to be passed on to another publisher. By then Velikovsky had become one of the most famous and most vilified men in America.

Who was this controversial psychiatrist who also seemed to be an expert on astronomy, geology and world history? Immanuel Velikovsky was a Russian Jew, born in Vitebsk in June 1895, who had studied mathematics in Moscow. He went on to study medicine, qualifying in 1921, then studied psychiatry in Vienna with Freud's pupil Stekel. In 1924 he moved to Palestine to practise, and became increasingly interested in Biblical archaeology. The turning-point in his career was a reading of Freud's *Moses and Monotheism* (1937). In this book Freud proposes that Moses was not a Jew but an Egyptian, and that he was a follower of the monotheistic religion of the Pharaoh Akhnaton (see Chapter 7), the king who replaced the host of Egyptian gods with one single sun god. Freud proposed that Moses fled from Egypt after the death of Akhnaton (probably murdered) and imposed his religion on the Jews.

The obvious historical objection to this theory is that Moses is supposed to have lived about a century after the death of Akhnaton; but Freud contested this view, and moved fearlessly into the arena of historical research. Dazzled by his boldness, Velikovsky decided to do the same. His researches into Egyptian, Greek and Near Eastern history soon convinced him that much of the accepted dating is hopelessly wrong. But they led him to an even more unorthodox conclusion: that the pharaoh Akhnaton was none other than the legendary Oedipus of Greek myth, and that the story arose out of the fact that Akhnaton had murdered his father and married his mother.

Velikovsky went on to construct a theory beside which even Freud's heterodox views seemed conservative; that the various events that accompanied the plagues of Egypt – the crossing of the Red Sea, the destruction of the Egyptian armies by floods, the manna that fell from heaven – were the outcome of some great cosmic upheaval. And at this point Velikovsky came across exactly what he was looking for: a papyrus written by an Egyptian sage called Ipuwer, which contained an account of events that sounded strangely like the Bible story in Exodus.

In 1939 Velikovsky moved to the United States, and continued his researches in its libraries. What precisely *was* the 'great catastrophe'? The Austrian Hanns Hoerbiger had put forward the theory that the earth has had several moons (see Chapter 1), and that the collapse of one of these moons on the earth caused the great floods and upheavals recorded in the Bible and in other ancient documents. But Velikovsky came to reject the Hoerbiger theory. There was a far more exciting clue. Before the second millennium BC – and even later – the planet Venus was not grouped by ancient astronomers with the other planets. That might have been because it was so close to the sun that they mistook it for a star – in fact, it is called the morning star. But what if it was because Venus was not in its present position at that time? Velikovsky found tantalizing references in old documents to something that sounded like a near-collision of a comet with the earth. In legends from Greece to Mexico he found suggestions that this catastrophe was somehow linked with Venus. Only one thing puzzled him deeply: that other legends seemed to link the catastrophe with Zeus, the father of the gods, also known as Jupiter. He finally reconciled these stories by reaching the astonishing conclusion that Venus was 'born out of' Jupiter – forced out by a gigantic explosion. Venus began as a comet, and passed so close to Mars that it was dragged out of its orbit; then it came close to earth, causing the Biblical catastrophes; then it finally settled down near the sun as the planet Venus.

It sounds like pure lunacy; but Velikovsky argued it with formidable erudition. And, unlike the usual crank, he spent a great deal of time searching for scientific evidence. He needed, for example, a spectroscopic analysis of the atmospheres of Mars and Venus, and he decided to approach the eminent astronomer Harlow Shapley. Shapley had himself become a figure of controversy in 1919 when he announced his conclusion that our solar system is not – as had previously been believed – at the centre of the Milky Way, but somewhere much closer to its edge; perhaps it was the blow to human self-esteem that caused the opposition. At all events, Velikovsky seems to have reasoned that Shapley might be sympathetic to his own heterodox ideas. Shapley was polite, but said he was too busy to read *Worlds in Collision*; he asked a colleague, a sociologist named Horace Kallen, if he would read it first. Kallen did so, and was excited; he told Shapley that it seemed a serious and worthwhile book, and that even if it should prove to be nonsense, it was still a bold and fascinating thesis. The Macmillan editor agreed, and Velikovsky got his contract.

Three months before its publication, in January 1950, a preview of *Worlds in Collision* appeared in *Harper's* magazine, and aroused widespread interest. Shapley's reaction was curious. He wrote Macmillans a letter saying that he had heard that they had decided *not* to publish the book after all, and that he was greatly relieved; he had discussed it with various scientists, and they were all astonished that Macmillan should venture into 'the Black Arts'.

Macmillans replied defensively that the book was not supposed to be hard science, but was a controversial theory that scholars ought to know about. Shapley replied tartly that Velikovsky was 'complete nonsense', and that when he had introduced himself to Shapley in a New York hotel Shapley had looked around to see if he had his keeper with him. The book, he said, was 'quite possibly intellectually fraudulent', a legpull designed to make money, and if Macmillans insisted on publishing it, then they had better drop Shapley from their list.

Macmillans ignored this attempt at blackmail, and published the book in April. No doubt they were astonished to find that they had a best-seller on their hands. America has a vast audience of 'fundamentalists' – people who believe that every word of the Bible is literally true, and are delighted to read anything that seems to offer scientific support for this view. (The same audience made Werner Keller's *The Bible as History* a best-seller in 1956.) Now they rushed to buy this book that seemed to prove that the parting of the Red Sea and the destruction of the walls of Jericho had really taken place. So did thousands of ordinary intelligent readers who simply enjoyed an adventure in speculative thought.

Scientists did not share this open-mindedness. One exception was Gordon Atwater, chairman of the astronomy department at New York's Museum of Natural History; he published a review urging that scientists ought to be willing to consider the book without prejudice; the review resulted in his dismissal. James Putnam, the editor who accepted *Worlds in Collision*, was dismissed from Macmillan. Professors deluged Macmillan with letters threatening to boycott their textbooks unless *Worlds in Collision* was withdrawn. Macmillans failed to show the same courage that had led them to ignore similar veiled threats from Shapley; they passed on Velikovsky to the Doubleday corporation, who had no textbook department to worry about, and who were probably unable to believe their luck in being handed such a profitable piece of intellectual merchandise. Fred Whipple, Shapley's successor at Harvard, wrote to Doubleday[1] telling them that if they persisted in publishing Velikovsky, he wanted them to take his own book *Earth, Moon and Planets* off their list. (Twenty years later, he denied in print ever writing such a letter.)

[1] In fact, to the Doubleday subsidiary, Blakiston: see *Velikovsky Reconsidered*, p. 25.

Velikovsky himself was rather bewildered by the sheer violence of the reactions; it had taken him thirty years to develop his theory, and he had expected controversy; but this amounted to persecution. He was willing to admit that he could be wrong about the nature of the catastrophe; but the historical records showed that *something* had taken place. Why couldn't they admit that, and *then* criticize his theory, instead of treating him as a madman? The only thing to do was to go on collecting more evidence.

And more evidence was produced in intimidating quantities during the remaining twenty-nine years of Velikovsky's life; he died on 17 November 1979, at the age of eighty-four. In 1955 came *Earth in Upheaval*, in many ways his best book, presenting the scientific evidence for great catastrophes. But again it outraged scientists – this time biologists – by suggesting that there are serious inadequacies in Darwin's theory of 'gradual evolution', and arguing that a better explanation would be the effect of radiation due to 'catastrophes' on the genes. Then came four books in a series that Velikovsky chose to call *Ages in Chaos*, whose main thesis is that historians of the ancient world have made a basic mistake in their dating, and that a period of about six or seven centuries needs to be dropped from the chronological record. In Velikovsky's dating, Queen Hatshepsut, generally assumed to have lived about 1500 BC, becomes a contemporary of Solomon more than four centuries later (in fact, Velikovsky identifies her with the Queen of Sheba), while the pharaoh Rameses II – assumed to live around 1250 BC – becomes a contemporary of Nebuchadnezzar more than six centuries later. The great invasion of barbarians known as the Sea Peoples, usually dated about 1200 BC, is placed by Velikovsky in the middle of the fourth century BC, about the time of the death of Plato. The arguments contained in *Ages in Chaos* (1953), *Oedipus and Akhnaton* (1960), *Peoples of the Sea* (1977) and *Rameses II and his Time* (1978) are of interest to historians rather than to scientists, but, like the earlier works, are totally absorbing to read. Two other projected volumes, *The Dark Age in Greece* and *The Assyrian Conquest*, have not so far been published. But a third volume of the *Worlds in Collision* series, *Mankind in Amnesia*, appeared posthumously in 1982. It expands a short section in *Worlds in Collision* arguing that catastrophic events produce a kind of collective amnesia. It is his most Freudian book, but it reveals that he never lost that curious ability to produce a state of intellectual excitement in the reader, even when his arguments seem most outrageous.

How far does Velikovsky deserve to be taken seriously? Should he be regarded as another Freud, or merely as another Erich von Däniken? It must be admitted that the basic thesis of *Worlds in Collision* sounds preposterous: that various Biblical events, like the parting of the Red Sea and the fall of the walls of Jericho, can be explained in terms of an astronomical catastrophe. But it is possible to entertain doubts about this aspect of Velikovsky's thesis without dismissing the most important part of his theory: that Venus may be far younger than the rest of the solar system. Moreover, whether or not Velikovsky is correct about the origin of Venus, there can be no doubt whatever that many of his controversial insights have been confirmed. Astronomers object that Jupiter was not likely to be the source of a 'comet' because it is too cold and inactive. However, a standard textbook of astronomy – Skilling and Richardson (1947) states 'From the fact that Jupiter is 5.2 times as far from the source of heat as is the earth, it can be seen that it should receive only $1/5.2^2$, or $1/27$ as much heat as does the earth. The temperature that a planet should have as the result of this much heat is very low – in the neighbourhood of $-140°C$.' But space probes have since revealed that the surface temperature on Jupiter is around $-150°C$, and that its surface is extremely turbulent, with immense explosions. The same textbook of astronomy states that the temperature on the surface of Venus 'may be as high as boiling water'. Velikovsky argued that it should be much higher, since Venus is so 'young' in astronomical terms. Mariner 2 revealed that the temperature on the surface of Venus is about $900°C$. It also revealed the curious fact that Venus rotates backward as compared to all the other planets, an oddity that seems incomprehensible if it was formed at the same time and evolved through the same process.

Russian space probes also revealed that Venus has violent electrical storms. Velikovsky had argued that the planets have powerful magnetic fields, and that therefore a close brush between the earth and a 'comet' would produce quite definite effects. The discovery of the Van Allen belts around the earth supported Velikovsky's view. There also seem to be close links between the rotation of Venus and Earth – Venus turns the same face to earth at each inferior conjunction, which could have come about through an interlocking of their magnetic fields. In the 1950s Velikovsky's assertion about electromagnetic fields in space was treated with contempt – in *Fads and Fallacies in the Name of Science*, Martin Gardner remarked dismissively that Velikovsky had invented forces capable of doing whatever he wanted them to do. His electromagnetic theory also led Velikovsky to predict that Jupiter would be found to emit radio waves, and that the sun would have an extremely powerful magnetic field. One critic (D.Menzel) retorted that Velikovsky's model of the sun would require an impossible charge of 10^{19} volts. Since then, Jupiter *has* been found to emit radio waves, while the sun's electrical potential has been calculated at about 10^{19} volts. It could be said that many of Velikovsky's theories are now an accepted part of astrophysics except, of course, that no one acknowledges that Velikovsky was the first one to formulate them.

Another matter on which Velikovsky seems to have been proved correct is the question of the reversal of the earth's magnetic poles. When molten volcanic rocks cool, or when clay or brick is baked, the magnetic minerals in it are magnetized in the direction of the earth's magnetic field. At the turn of the century Giuseppe Folgerhaiter examined Etruscan vases, looking for minor magnetic variations, and was astonished to find that there seemed to have been a complete reversal of the magnetic field around the eighth century BC. Scientists explained his findings by declaring that the pots must have been fired upside down. But in 1906 Bernard Brunhes found the same complete reversal in certain volcanic rocks. Further research revealed that there had been at least nine such reversals in the past 3.6 million years. No one could make any plausible suggestion as to why this had happened. Velikovsky's suggestion was that it was due to the close approach of other celestial bodies, and that the earth's brush with Venus should have produced such a reversal. His critics replied that there have been no reversals in the past half-million years or so. But since then two more have been discovered – one 28,000 years ago, the other about 12500 BC, and one of Velikovsky's bitterest opponents, Harold Urey, has come to admit that the 'celestial body' theory is the likeliest explanation of pole-reversal. Yet so far the crucial piece of evidence – volcanic rock revealing a reversal about 1450 BC – has not been forthcoming.

Those who regard Velikovsky as an innovator comparable to Freud should also be prepared to admit that he had many of Freud's faults – particularly a tendency to jump to bold and unorthodox conclusions, and then to stick by them with a certain rigid dogmatism. Yet it must also be admitted that whether or not his Venus theory proves to be ultimately correct, his 'guesses' have often been amazingly accurate. Like Kepler, who came to all the right conclusions about the solar system for all the wrong reasons (including the belief that it is somehow modelled on the Holy Trinity), Velikovsky seems to possess the intuitive genius of all great innovators. Even one of his most dismissive critics, Carl Sagan, admits: 'I find the concatenation of legends which Velikovsky has accumulated stunning . . . If twenty per cent of the legendary concordances . . . are real, there is something important to be explained.'

41 Who Was Harry Whitecliffe?

According to a book published in France in 1978, one of England's most extraordinary mass murderers committed suicide in a Berlin gaol in the middle of the jazz era. His name was Harry Whitecliffe, and he murdered at least forty women. Then why is his name not more widely known – at least to students of crime? Because when he was arrested he was masquerading under the name Lovach Blume, and his suicide concealed his true identity from the authorities.

The full story can be found in a volume called *Nouvelles Histoires Magiques – New Tales of Magic –* by Louis Pauwels and Guy Breton, published by Editions J'ai Lu. In spite of the title – which sounds like fiction – it is in fact a series of studies in the paranormal and bizarre; there are chapters on Nostradamus, Rasputin and Eusapia Palladino, and accounts of such well-known mysteries as the devil's footprints in Devon (see my Chapter 8).

According to the chapter 'The Two Faces of Harry Whitecliffe', there appeared in London in the early twenties a collection of essays so promising that it sold out in a few days; it consisted of a series of marvellous pastiches of Oscar Wilde. But its author, Harry Whitecliffe, apparently preferred to shun publicity; he remained obstinately hidden. Would-be interviewers returned empty-handed. Then, just as people were beginning to suggest that Whitecliffe was a pseudonym for some well-known writer – Bernard Shaw, perhaps, or the young T.S.Eliot – Whitecliffe finally consented to appear. He was a handsome young man of twenty-three, likeable, eccentric and fond of sport. He was also generous; he was said to have ended one convivial evening by casually giving a pretty female beggar five hundred pounds. He professed to adore flowers, but only provided their stems were not more than twenty centimetres long. He was the kind of person the English love, and was soon a celebrity.

Meanwhile he continued to write: essays, poetry and plays. One of his comedies, *Similia*, had four hundred consecutive performances in London before touring England. It made him a fortune, which he quickly scattered among his friends. By the beginning of 1923 he was one of the 'kings of London society'.

Then, in September of that year, he vanished. He sold all his possessions, and gave his publisher carte blanche to handle his work. But before the end of the year he reappeared in Dresden. The theatre there presented *Similia* with enormous success, the author himself translating it from English into German. It went on to appear in many theatres along the Rhine. He founded a press for publishing modern poetry, and works on modern painting –

Dorian Verlag – whose editions are now worth a fortune.

But he was still something of a man of mystery. Every morning he galloped along the banks of the river Elbe until nine o'clock; at ten he went to his office, eating lunch there. At six in the evening, he went to art exhibitions or literary salons, and met friends. At nine, he returned home and no one knew what he did for the rest of the evening. And no one liked to ask him.

One reason for this regular life was that he was in love – the girl was called Wally von Hammerstein, daughter of aristocratic parents, who were favourably impressed with the young writer. Their engagement was to be announced on 4 October 1924.

But on the previous day Whitecliffe disappeared again. He failed to arrive at his office, and vanished from his flat. The frantic Wally searched Dresden, without success. The police were alerted – discreetly – and pursued diligent inquiries. Their theory was that he had committed suicide. Wally believed he had either met with an accident or been the victim of a crime – he often carried large sums of money. As the weeks dragged by her desperation turned to misery; she talked about entering a convent.

Then she received a letter. It had been found in the cell of a condemned man who had committed suicide in Berlin – he had succeeded in opening his veins with the buckle of his belt. The inscription on the envelope said: 'I beg you, monsieur le procureur of the Reich, to forward this letter to its destination without opening it.' It was signed: Lovach Blume.

Blume was apparently one of the most horrible of murderers, worse than Jack the Ripper or Peter Kürten, the Düsseldorf sadist. He had admitted to the court that tried him: 'Every ten days I have to kill. I am driven by an irresistable urge, so that until I have killed, I suffer atrociously. But as I disembowel my victims I feel an indescribable pleasure.' Asked about his past, he declared: 'I am a corpse. Why bother about the past of a corpse?'

Blume's victims were prostitutes and homeless girls picked up on the Berlin streets. He would take them to a hotel, and kill them as soon as they were undressed. Then, with a knife like a Malaysian 'kriss', with an ivory handle, he would perform horrible mutilations, so awful that even doctors found the sight unbearable. These murders continued over a period of six months, during which the slum quarters of Berlin lived in fear.

Blume was finally arrested by accident, in September 1924. The police thought he was engaged in drug trafficking, and knocked on the door of a hotel room minutes after Blume had entered with a prostitute. Blume had just committed his thirty-first murder in Berlin; he was standing naked by the window, and the woman's body lay at his feet.

He made no resistance, and admitted freely to his crimes – he could only recall twenty-seven. He declared that he had no fear of death – particularly the way executions were performed in Germany (by decapitation), which he greatly preferred to the English custom of hanging.

This was the man who had committed suicide in his prison cell, and who addressed a long letter to his fiancée, Wally von Hammerstein. He told her that he was certain the devil existed, because he had met him. He was, he explained, a kind of Jekyll and Hyde, an intelligent, talented man who suddenly became cruel and bloodthirsty. He thought of himself as being like victims of demoniacal possession. He had left London after committing nine murders, when he suspected that Scotland Yard was on his trail. His love for Wally was genuine, he told her, and had caused him to 'die a little'. He had hoped once that she might be able to save him from his demons, but it had proved a vain hope.

Wally fainted as she read the letter. And in 1925 she entered a nunnery and took the name Marie de Douleurs. There she prays for the salvation of a tortured soul. . . .

This is the story, as told by Louis Pauwels – a writer who became famous for his collaboration with Jacques Bergier on a book called *The Morning of the Magicians*. Critics pointed out that that book was full of factual errors, and a number of these can also be found in his article on Whitecliffe. For example, if the date of Blume's arrest is correct – 25 September 1924 – then it took place before Whitecliffe vanished from Dresden, on 3 October 1924 . . . But this, presumably, is a slip of the pen.

But who was Harry Whitecliffe? According to Pauwels, he told the Berlin court that his father was German, his mother Danish, and that he was brought up in Australia by an uncle who was a butcher. His uncle lived in Sydney. But in a 'conversation' between Pauwels and his fellow-author at the end of one chapter, Pauwels states that Whitecliffe was the son of a great English family. But apart from the three magistrates who opened the suicide letter – ignoring Blume's last wishes – only Wally and her parents knew Whitecliffe's true identity. The judges are dead, so are Wally's parents. Wally is a 75-year-old nun who until now has never told anyone of this drama of her youth. We are left to assume that she has now told the story to Pauwels.

This extraordinary tale aroused the curiosity of a well-known French authoress, Françoise d'Eaubonne, who felt that Whitecliffe deserved a book to himself. But her letters to the two authors – Pauwels and Breton – went unanswered. She therefore contacted the British Society of Theatre Research, and so entered into a correspondence with the theatre historian John Kennedy Melling. Melling had never heard of Whitecliffe, or of a play called *Similia*. He decided to begin his researches by contacting Scotland Yard, to ask whether they have any record of an unknown sex killer of the early 1920s. Their reply was negative; there was no series of Ripper-type murders of prostitutes in the early 1920s. He next applied to J.H.H.Gaute, the possessor of the largest crime library in the British Isles; Gaute could also find no trace of such a series of sex crimes in the 1920s. Theatrical reference books contained no mention of Harry Whitecliffe, or of his successful comedy *Similia*. It began to look – as incredible as it sounds – as if Pauwels had simply invented the whole story.

Thelma Holland, Oscar Wilde's daughter-in-law, could find no trace of a volume of parodies of Wilde among the comprehensive collection of her late husband, Vyvyan Holland. But she had a suggestion to make – to address inquiries to the Mitchell Library in Sydney. As an Australian, she felt it was probably Melling's best chance of tracking down Harry Whitecliffe.

Incredibly, this long shot brought positive results: not about Harry

Whitecliffe, but about a German murderer called Blume – not Lovach, but Wilhelm Blume. The *Argus* newspaper for 8 August 1922 contained a story headed 'Cultured Murderer', and sub-titled: 'Literary Man's Series of Crimes'. It was datelined Berlin, 7 August.

Wilhelm Blume, a man of wide culture and considerable literary gifts, whose translations of English plays have been produced in Dresden with great success, has confessed to a series of cold-blooded murders, one of which was perpetrated at the Hotel Adlon, the best known Berlin hotel.

The most significant item in the newspaper report is that Blume had founded a publishing house called Dorian Press (Verlag) in Dresden. This is obviously the same Blume who – according to Pauwels – committed suicide in Berlin.

But Wilhelm Blume was not a sex killer. His victims had been postmen, and the motive had been robbery. In Germany postal orders were paid to consignees in their own homes, so postmen often carried fairly large sums of money. Blume had sent himself postal orders, then killed the postmen and robbed them – the exact number is not stated in the *Argus* article. The first time he did this he was interrupted by his landlady while he was strangling the postman with a noose; and he cut her throat. Then he moved on to Dresden, where in due course he attempted to rob another postman. Armed with two revolvers, he waited for the postman in the porch of a house. But the tenant of the house arrived so promptly that he had to flee, shooting one of the policemen. Then his revolvers both misfired, and he was caught. Apparently he attempted to commit suicide in prison, but failed. He confessed – as the *Argus* states – to several murders, and was presumably executed later in 1922 (although the *Argus* carries no further record).

It seems plain, then, that the question 'Who was Harry Whitecliffe?' should be reworded 'Who was Wilhelm Blume?' For Blume and Whitecliffe were obviously the same person.

From the information we possess, we can make a tentative reconstruction of the story of Blume-Whitecliffe. He sounds like a typical example of a certain type of killer who is also a confidence man – other examples are Landru, Petiot, the 'acid bath murderer' Haigh, and the sex killer Neville Heath. It is an essential part of such a man's personality that he is a fantasist, and that he likes to pose as a success, and to talk casually about past triumphs. (Neville Heath called himself 'Group Captain Rupert Brooke'.) They usually start off as petty swindlers, then gradually become more ambitious, and graduate to murder. This is what Blume seems to have done. In the chaos of postwar Berlin he made a quick fortune by murdering and robbing postmen. Perhaps his last coup made him a fortune beyond his expectations, or perhaps the Berlin postal authorities were now on the alert for the killer. Blume decided it was time to make an attempt to live a respectable life, and to put his literary fantasies into operation. He moved to Dresden, called himself Harry Whitecliffe and set up Dorian Verlag. He became a successful translator of English plays, and may have helped to finance their production in Dresden and in theatres along the Rhine. Since he was posing as an upper-class Englishman, and must have occasionally run into other Englishmen in Dresden, we may assume that his English was perfect, and that his story of being brought up in Australia was probably true. Since he also spoke perfect German, it is also a fair assumption that he was, as he told the court, the son of a German father and a Danish mother.

He fell in love with an upper-class girl, and told her a romantic story that is typical of the inveterate daydreamer: that he was the son of a 'great English family', that he had become an overnight literary success in London as a result of his pastiches of Oscar Wilde, but had at first preferred to shun the limelight (this is the true Walter Mitty touch) until increasing success made this impossible. His wealth is the result of a successful play, *Similia*. (The similarity of the title to *Salome* is obvious, and we may infer that Blume was an ardent admirer of Wilde.) But in order to avoid too much publicity – after all, victims of previous swindles might expose him – he lives the quiet, regular life of a crook in hiding.

And just as all seems to be going so well – just as success, respectability, a happy marriage, seem so close – he once again runs out of money. There is only one solution: a brief return to a life of crime. One or two robberies of postmen can replenish his bank account and secure his future. . . . But this time it goes disastrously wrong. Harry Whitecliffe is exposed as the swindler and murderer Wilhelm Blume. He makes no attempt to deny it, and confesses to his previous murders; his world has now collapsed in ruins. He is sent back to Berlin, where the murders were committed, and he attempts suicide in his cell. Soon after, he dies by the guillotine. And in Dresden the true story of Wilhelm Blume is soon embroidered into a horrifying tale of a Jekyll-and-Hyde mass murderer, whose early career in London is confused with Jack the Ripper. . . .

Do any records of Wilhelm Blume still exist? It seems doubtful – the fire-bombing of Dresden destroyed most of the civic records, and the people who knew him more than sixty years ago must now all be dead. Yet Pauwels has obviously come across some garbled and wildly inaccurate account of Blume's career as Harry Whitecliffe. It would be interesting to know where he obtained his information; but neither Françoise d'Eaubonne nor John Kennedy Melling have been successful in persuading him to answer letters.

42 Patience Worth

Or the Ghost Who Wrote Novels

On an August day in 1912 two women sat in a house in St Louis, Missouri, and played with an ouija board. They were Emily Grant Hutchings and Pearl Curran, and both were married to successful businessmen – their husbands were in fact playing cards in the next room. It was Mrs Hutchings who was interested in trying to 'contact the spirits'; her friend Pearl Curran thought it was all a waste of time. And on that first August afternoon she proved to be right. The pointer of the ouija board spelt out a few recognizable words, but it was mostly nonsense.

But in spite of her friend's boredom, Emily Hutchings insisted on trying again. They tried repeatedly over the next ten months. And finally, on 22 June 1913, the board spelled out the word PAT several times, then went on to write:

Oh, why let sorrow steel thy heart?
Thy bosom is but its foster-mother,
The world its cradle and the loving home its grave.

This was not only intelligible, but intelligent – although a careful reading is required before it can be seen to make sense.

That same afternoon the board went on to utter a number of similar sentiments, most of which sound like the utterances of a sentimental lady novelist of the Victorian period:

'Rest, weary heart. Let only sunshine light the shrine within. A single ray shall filter through and warm thy frozen soul.'

There were several more aphoristic sentences of the same nature.

The next time the ladies met was on 2 July 1913, and once again the ouija board began spelling out words with bewildering speed. 'Dust rests beneath, and webs lie caught among the briars. A single jewel gleams as a mirrored vision of rising Venus in a mountain lake . . .' And after more poetic sentiments of the same kind, it declared: 'All those who so lately graced your board are here, and as the moon looks down, think ye of them and their abode as a spirit song, as spirit friends, and close communion held twixt thee and them. Tis but a journey, dost not see?' And when the ladies asked for some elucidation the board replied: 'Tis all so clear behind the veil ..' And when they asked its name it answered: 'Should one so near be confined to a name? The sun shines alike on the briar and the rose . . .' But at the next session, six days later, it finally condescended to reveal its identity. 'Many moons ago I lived. Again I come – Patience Worth my name.' But she seemed reluctant to disclose more details. 'About me you would know much. Yesterday is dead.' And she was inclined to express herself in aphorisms; at a later seance, when they asked her to hurry up, she replied: 'Beat the hound and lose the hare.' She had a sharp tongue and a ready wit, although the old-fashioned language often made it difficult to understand. She seems to have taken a dislike to a Mrs Pollard, Pearl Curran's mother, who was present at some of the sessions, and when asked by Emily Hutchings what she thought of Mrs Pollard, replied: 'The men should stock her.' Did she mean that Mrs Pollard should be put in the stocks? asked Mrs Hutchings. 'Aye, and leave a place for two' snapped Patience.

But shortly before Christmas Patience displayed an interesting ability to predict the future. Mrs Hutchings asked her what Pearl Curran intended to give her for Christmas; Patience replied: 'Fifteen pieces, and one cracked.' In fact Mrs Curran had ordered a set of kitchen jars for her friend, and when they were delivered the next day one of the fifteen proved to be cracked. Asked what Emily Hutchings intended to give Pearl Curran for Christmas, Patience answered: 'Table store, cross-stitched.' Again this was accurate – she had bought some cross-stitched table linen. Asked by Mrs Pollard for an inscription for a present to her daughter, Patience replied: 'A burning desire never to be snuffed; a waxing faith, ever to burn.' It was remarkably appropriate: Mrs Pollard had bought her daughter a candle and snuffer.

Eventually Patience offered a little more information about herself. She was a Quaker girl, born either in 1649 or 1694 (the board dictated 1649, then changed its mind and added 94) and had been born in Dorset. She had worked hard – apparently on a farm – until her family emigrated to America, and had shortly thereafter been killed by Indians. She was certainly a talkative lady – even the incomplete records of the sessions with her, cited in *The Case of Patience Worth* by Walter Franklin Prince, are exhausting to read. And she was inclined to dictate lengthy 'poems' which lack rhyme and show an uncertainty about metre. Her best-known utterance runs as follows:

Ah God, I have drunk unto the dregs,
And flung the cup at Thee!
The dust of crumbled righteousness
Hath dried and soaked unto itself
E'en the drop I spilled to Bacchus,
Whilst Thou, all-patient,
Sendest purple vintage for a later harvest.

This has most of the characteristics of Patience's literary utterances. On first reading, it seems meaningless; on a second or third reading, it yields up its meaning. But the reader may be left in some doubt as to whether it was worth saying in the first place.

In 1915 Patience became something of a celebrity when Caspar Yost, the editor of the Sunday supplement of the *St Louis Globe-Democrat*, wrote a series of articles about her, although he was careful not to identify the two ladies who had 'discovered' her. The articles caused a sensation, and Yost went on to write a book. Another St Louis journalist, William Marion Reedy, editor of *Reedy's Mirror* – and one of the best literary critics of his time also attended some of the séances, and to his own astonishment was much impressed by Patience. Yost and Reedy were responsible for making the name of Patience Worth known all over America.

By now Patience had embarked upon more ambitious literary composition. First came *Red Wing*, a six-act medieval play. Next there was a 60,000 word medieval novel, *Telka*. And here it must be admitted at once that Patience is a disappointing writer. If the works were literary masterpieces, or even highly competent hack-work, they would deserve to be kept permanently in print. In fact, they are so long-winded as to be almost unreadable. 'Historical' novels like *Telka* and *The Sorry Tale* (set in the time of Jesus) are written in an 'archaic' style that demands close attention and offers no adequate reward. This is from *The Sorry Tale*: 'And his beard hung low upon his breast, and he spoke unto the Rome's men: "The peace of Jehovah be upon you" And they spat upon his fruits and made loud words, saying: "Behold, Jerusalem hath been beset of locusts and desert fleas . . ." ' It reads like second-rate Biblical pastiche. A 'modern'novel, *Hope Trueblood*, begins: 'The glass had slipped thrice, and the sands stood midway through, and still the bird hopped within its wicker. I think the glass had slipped through a score of years, rightfully set at each turning, and the bird had sung through some of these and mourned through others. The hearth's arch yawned sleepily . . .' And after half a page of this the reader is also yawning sleepily.

Certainly Patience seems to have known little of the virtue of brevity. When a psychic named Arthur Delroy addressed a meeting in St Louis he remarked that the ouija board was of no more value than a doorknob, and that Patience's language was not archaic English but the kind of language learned at Sunday school. (He added unkindly that he would not be surprised to learn that Mrs Curran had spent a great deal of time at Sunday school.) When this was reported to Patience, she replied: 'Tis fools that smite the lute and set it awhir o' folly song, when sage's hand do be at loth to touch.' To this Delroy replied, in Patience's own style: 'Nay, thou puttest me among the nobles. I be not the wise man from the East who wouldst prithee never be the last word, but wouldsy patiently wait, yea, t'll'st the millionth Patient utterance . . .' Her reply, if she made one, is not recorded.

In November 1915 Mr and Mrs Curran decided to go to the east coast, where Patience was widely known, and to take the ouija board. Asked if she was willing to accompany them, Patience replied in her usual long-winded style: 'E'en as doth the breath o' thee to hug, so shall I, to follow thee. Think ye I'd build me a cup and leave it dry?' And when Patience was interviewed by the eminent psychologist Morton Prince in Boston he also found her wordiness rather trying. Asked if she objected to the investigation, she replied at inordinate length, beginning: 'Ye be at seek o' a measure o' smoke's put . . .' He repeated the question, and Patience explained lucidly: 'Ye turn up a stone, ayea, and aneath there be a toad, aye, and he blinketh him at the light. . . .' And when Prince in desperation repeated the question a third time, she explained: 'Here be a one who hath 'o a ball o' twine and be not asatisfied with the ball, but doth to awish that I do awind it out. List thee, brother, at thy poke aneath the stone! Tis well and alike unto me.' And hours of interrogation brought forth a great many more of these labyrinthine obscurities. Patience seems incapable of using one word where ten will do, bringing to mind Lincoln's remark: 'He can compress the most words into the smallest ideas of any man I ever met.' It was impossible to get her to answer even the simplest question with a direct reply. When Prince asked her how old she was when she came to America, she replied: 'A goodly dame', and when he repeated the question, advised him to look at a parable she had written about an ass. Patience herself ended the interview – the last – with an abrupt 'Good night.'

Prince's feeling was that they had been basically a waste of time. Whether or not Patience was genuine, she was certainly evasive. Mrs Curran flatly refused Prince's suggestion that she should be hypnotized, and the Currans gave to the newspapers an account of the interviews that struck Prince as inaccurate, leading to some bad-tempered exchanges.

After this unsatisfactory encounter, the Currans went on to New York, where Patience met her future publisher Henry Holt, and rambled on in her usual infuriatingly prolix manner. But Holt was impressed, and in the following February – 1916 – brought out Caspar Yost's book *Patience Worth – A Psychic Mystery*, which met, on the whole, with an excellent reception. Critics described Patience as a 'powerful, unique but impalpable personality' and her work as 'entertaining, humourous and beautiful'. But a dissenting note was sounded by Professor James Hyslop, of the American Society for Psychical Research, who deplored the total lack of scientifically convincing evidence, and dismissed Patience as a 'fraud and a delusion'.

In June 1917 Henry Holt published the vast pseudo-Biblical epic *The Sorry Tale*, more than a quarter of a million words long. Again, many papers were ecstatic; the *Boston Transcript* wrote: 'If, however, on account of its psychic claims, one approaches the story with unbelief or scoffing, one is instantly rebuffed by its quality', while *The Nation* said that it 'deserved to be weighed as a piece of creative fiction'. The modern reader will find these claims incomprehensible; the writing is atrocious, and often illiterate. 'Sheep, storm-lost, bleated, where, out upon the hills, they lost them.' 'The temples stood whited and the market place shewed emptied.' 'And the Rome's men bared their blades and the air rocked with cries of mock prayers from Rome's lips.' If Patience had been an ambitious shop girl the novel would have been dismissed as a bad joke.

On the other hand, the book seemed to indicate a knowledge of ancient Rome that Mrs Curran insisted she had never possessed. The distinguished psychical investigator G.N.M. Tyrrell, writing thirty years later, said: 'There is not here the greatness of genius, but . . . there is a fount of inspiration which might have provided the material for a work of genius had it been expressed through the conscious mind of, say, a Coleridge instead of . . . Mrs Curran', and he went on to quote Caspar Yost's view that the book revealed an intimate knowledge of the Rome of Augustus and Tiberius, and also of the topography of Jerusalem and the Holy Land. But then, of course, Yost was a somewhat biased witness, having been one of the original 'discoverers' of Patience Worth.

One of the most bizarre episodes in the entire story began in August 1916, while *The Sorry Tale* was still being dictated. In her usual circumlocutory way, Patience announced that her works would bring in a great deal of money ('a-time a later the purse shall fatten'), but that this money 'be not for him who hath'. The Currans were told 'ye shall seek a one, a wee bit, one who hath not', and added 'Aye, this be close, close.' And soon it became clear that what Patience meant – she seems to have been incapable of saying anything in plain words – was that the Currans, who were childless, should adopt a baby, and that this baby would be in some sense Patience's own daughter. By 'the merest accident', a pregnant widow was located – her husband had been killed in a mill accident – and she agreed to relinquish her unborn child to the Currans. Patience seemed quite certain it would be a daughter. And one evening, as she was dictating *The Sorry Tale*, Patience broke off abruptly with the comment 'This be "nuff".' An hour later the Currans heard that the baby had been born. It was indeed a girl, and had red hair and brown eyes – a description Patience had formerly given of herself. On Patience's instructions the child was called Patience Worth Wee Curran.

In that same year – 1916 – Emily Hutchings called upon the eminent literary critic William Marion Reedy, and showed him the first ten thousand words of a novel about Missouri politics and journalism. In recent years Emily had dropped out of the limelight, for it had become clear that her presence was not essential for Patience to manifest herself. Reedy was impressed by the novel, and congratulated her. A week later he probably felt like eating his words when Emily called again, and confessed that the novel had been 'dictated' by the spirit of Mark Twain – then proceeded to produce several pages with the help of the ouija board. The novel was accepted, and published under the title of *Jap Herron*, and was well received – although it was generally agreed that its quality was much inferior to the works Mark Twain had produced while he was alive. An effort by Mark Twain's publishers to suppress the novel was unsuccessful.

During this period Patience's fame continued to grow. The Victorian novel *Hope Trueblood* met with an enthusiastic reception from many respectable journals, although the reading public found that even Patience's 'modern' style was too wordy. In England the book was issued without any indication of its 'psychic' origin, and received mixed reviews; but at least most of the critics seemed to assume that it was the first novel of an English writer. The Currans also launched *Patience Worth's Magazine*, to make Patience's poems and lesser writings accessible to her admirers; it was edited by Caspar Yost, and ran to ten issues.

But by 1918 there were signs that Patience's vogue was coming to an end. In *The Atlantic Monthly* that August a writer named Agnes Repplier poured scorn on this latest fad for books written by spirits, and expressed dismay at the thought that Patience, being dead, might be on the literary scene for ever.

Of Patience's books, Miss Repplier said tartly that 'they were as silly as they were dull'. In retrospect, it seems surprising that no other reputable critic had already made this assessment.

The blast of ridicule was in effect the end of Patience Worth's period of literary celebrity; Agnes Repplier had stated that the emperor was naked, and now everybody realized that it had been obvious all along. A new book by Caspar Yost on Patience's religion and philosophy was turned down by Henry Holt; so was a volume of Patience's poems. Pearl Curran (who had always strenuously denied that she had any writing talent) herself wrote a short story about a Chicago salesgirl – who, significantly, is 'taken over' by a secondary personality – and it was accepted by the *Saturday Evening Post*; but Pearl's most recent biographer, Irving Litvag, admits (in *Singer in the Shadows*) that the story 'never rises above the level of bad soap opera'.

When William Marion Reedy died in 1920 Patience lost one of her most influential defenders. And another sign of Patience's sinking reputation was a hostile article by a critic called Mary Austin in the *Unpartizan Review*; what made it worse was that the magazine was published by Henry Holt.

John Curran's health began to fail, and he died in June 1922, after fourteen months of illness. Pearl, who was now thirty-nine years old, was pregnant with their first child; a girl was born six months later. Pearl had four people to support – herself, her mother, Patience Wee and her new daughter – on a dwindling income. Far from making them a fortune, Patience's literary works had cost them money; the novels had sold poorly, and the magazine was an expensive production. Pearl was forced to accept an offer to give several lectures in Chicago; she was reluctant to do this because she had always insisted that her position as Patience's mouthpiece brought her no profit; but there was no alternative. The death of her mother was another blow. But at this point a New York admirer, Herman Behr, came to the rescue; he not only made her an allowance of $400 a month but also paid for the publication of Patience's poems, which appeared under the title *Light From Beyond*. But it failed to revive the interest of the American reading public in the Patience Worth phenomenon. In the age of James Joyce and Ernest Hemingway and John Dos Passos, the rambling productions of Patience Worth seemed irrelevant.

Litvag comments: 'The next three years were lonely, rather despairing ones for Pearl Curran. No longer a celebrity, largely ignored by the public .. periodically in ill health, she was often depressed and morose.' In 1923 she allowed Patience Wee to go to California. In 1926 she married a retired doctor, Henry Rogers, many years her senior; but the marriage was unsuccessful, and ended in divorce. In 1930 Pearl moved to California, where in Los Angeles she once again acquired some degree of celebrity among a group of devoted admirers. In 1931 she married again – this time to a man to whom she had been briefly engaged when she was nineteen; she and her husband – Robert Wyman – moved to Culver City, and Patience began to dictate a new literary work, a play about Shakespeare. At séances she continued to be as garrulous and evasive as ever – the simplest question could be guaranteed to provoke a five-minute answer. In 1934 Patience Wee who was eighteen married, and Patience provided a lengthy blessing, signed 'Thy Mither'.

Then in November 1937 Pearl, who was fifty-four, suddenly announced to her old friend Dotsie Smith that 'Patience has just shown me the end of the road, and you will have to carry on as best you can.' She seemed to be in excellent health. But on Thanksgiving Day she caught a cold; on 3 December 1937 she died of pneumonia in a Los Angeles hospital. That was in effect the end of the Patience Worth phenomenon. Patience Wee, who by the age of twenty-seven had been twice married, died equally suddenly in 1943, after a mild heart ailment had been diagnosed; inevitably, there were those who felt that Patience had finally claimed her 'daughter'.

The last chapter of Irving Litvag's book on Patience is entitled 'Who was Patience Worth?', but he admits almost immediately that he has no idea. Writers on the case tend to be equally divided between the two obvious theories: that Patience was a 'secondary personality' of Pearl Curran, and that she was more or less what she claimed to be, a 'spirit'. Both Morton Prince and Walter Franklin Prince (they were unrelated) had produced classic studies of cases of multiple personality; Morton Prince's 'Sally Beauchamp' case (described in *The Dissociation of a Personality*) has achieved the status of a classic; Walter Franklin Prince's 'Doris Fischer' case deserves to be equally well known, but never achieved circulation beyond the pages of the *American Journal for Psychical Research* (1923) and *Contributions to Psychology*.[1] But anyone who reads the Patience Worth case after studying Sally Beauchamp and Doris Fischer is bound to feel that they have very little in common. Most 'multiple personalities' have a history of childhood abuse and misery; Pearl Curran seems to have had a normal childhood, and to have been a perfectly ordinary, unremarkable person until the coming of Patience Worth. Although it *is* conceivable that Pearl Curran was a case of dual personality, the clinical evidence for it is not particularly convincing.

For those who are willing to accept the possibility of life after death, the most convincing explanation is certainly that Patience was a 'spirit'. But that does not necessarily mean that she was really what she claimed to be. Anyone who has studied 'spirit communication' soon recognizes that 'spirits' are very seldom what they claim to be; G.K.Chesterton put it more bluntly and said that they are liars. If Patience *was* a seventeenth-century Quaker who was killed by Red Indians, it is difficult to understand why she was so evasive and why she failed to answer straightforward questions that might have enabled the Currans to prove that such a person really existed. Litvag's book leaves one with the conviction that if Patience was a spirit, then it was probably the spirit of a frustrated would-be writer with a strong tendency to mythomania.

[1] For an account of both cases, see my book *Mysteries*.

Index